The
Rockin'
'50s

The Rockin' '50s

Brock Helander

THE PEOPLE WHO
MADE THE MUSIC

SCHIRMER BOOKS
NEW YORK

Schirmer Books
1633 Broadway
New York, NY 10019

Library of Congress Catalog Card Number: 98-9610

Printed in the United States of America

Printing Number
1 2 3 4 5 6 7 8 9 10

Library of Congress Cataloging-in-Publication Data

Helander, Brock.
    The rockin' '50s : the people who made the music / Brock Helander.
        p.   cm.
    Includes bibliograhical references and index.
    ISBN 0-02-864872-2
    1. Rock music—To 1961—Discography.   I. Title
    ML 156.4.R6H45 1999
    871.66—dc21   98-9610
                                                                CIP
                                                                MN

CONTENTS

PREFACE

This volume is a critical and historical discography of rock 'n' roll music and its antecedents, encompassing major musical artists who have contributed significantly to the development of rock 'n' roll and contemporary popular music. In addition to musicians and singers, this volume includes disc jockey Alan Freed, Sun Records founder Sam Phillips, TV host Dick Clark, and several songwriting-production teams.

In this book, I include extensive discographies of music available on record albums, cassettes, and CDs that were regular releases in the United States. No foreign releases or so-called bootleg albums are listed. Recording artists are listed in alphabetical order, by group name for groups and by last name for individual artists. Albums are listed in recording order rather than release order, and anthology albums are often listed separately.

In the discussion of hit singles, the gradation from biggest to smallest success is indicated in the following order:

Top: Number 1 hit
Smash: Top 10
Major: Top 25
Moderate: Top 40
Minor: Top 100

These designations will give you an idea of the relative success of a single; chart numbers are not always reliable, particularly those from the '50s when record companies manipulated the charts regularly to produce "number 1 hits." Plus, with more than one chart source, a song could have scored a number 1 hit on one chart and only reached number 5 on another. Hit singles are discussed in the context of the three major chart categories: pop, R&B, and country-and-western.

I have tried to provide a comprehensive and definitive critical and historical discography of rock-and-roll and its antecedents.

Brock Helander
Sacramento, California

ACKNOWLEDGMENTS

First, I would like to thank my parents, Ed and Helen, and my brother, Bruce, for their support and encouragement with my book-writing projects over the years. I would also like to thank my faithful friends who have supported me throughout this project, particularly Mark Staneart, Gerry Helland, Tom Partington, and Carol Tozer. Others I gratefully acknowledge for their assistance over the years include Frank Kofsky, Joel Selvin, Jeff Hughson, and Ken Stuart. I am especially grateful to my current editor, Richard Carlin, for tracking me down in 1993 to update and revise *The Rock Who's Who*, originally published by Schirmer in 1982. Finally, I thank the following record companies and their representatives for providing current issues of their catalogs: Del-Fi, Flying Fish, One Way, Razor & Tie, Rhino, Rounder, and Sundazed.

The discographies in this book were compiled from the following sources:

Brock Helander. *Rock 'n' Roll to Rock: A Discography.* Privately published, 1978.
Brock Helander. *The Rock Who's Who.* New York: Schirmer Books, 1982.
Brock Helander. *The Rock Who's Who,* Second Edition. New York: Schirmer Books, 1996.

For the following discographies, I would like to acknowledge the assistance of the authors:

for the Alan Freed discography: John A. Jackson. *Big Beat Heat: Alan Freed and the Early Years of Rock 'n' Roll.* New York: Schirmer Books, 1991.
for the Ritchie Valens discography: Beverly Mendheim: *Ritchie Valens: The First Latino Rocker.* Tempe, AZ: Bilingual Press, 1987.

USE OF THE DISCOGRAPHIES

The organization of the discographies is illustrated by the examples below:

The "Chirping" Crickets	Brunswick	54038	'57	
	MCA	31182	'88	CD
	MCA	25170	'88	CS
reissued as Buddy Holly and the Crickets	Coral	57405	'62	
Buddy Holly: A Rock 'n' Roll Collection	Decca	(2)7207	'72	†
	MCA	(2)4009		†

From left to right, the five columns supply the following information:

1. The album title. Other information is included parenthetically following the album title. Such information includes movie sound track, original cast, television recording information, and recording date information.
2. The name of the record label on which the album was released. Albums are often reissued on a label different from the original.
3. The record label's catalog number for the album. Albums were originally issued in mono. Beginning in 1958, a separate stereo catalog number was sometimes assigned; when this is the case, only the mono number is given. Although for a while electronically rechanneled "stereo" versions (E) of original mono recordings were marketed either on LP, cassette, or CD, generally today the "original" mono source is reproduced as being the most authentic, so many CD reissues of '50s material are "mono" only. When an album is a multiple-record set, the number of LPs, cassettes, or compact discs is indicated parenthetically before the catalog number.
4. The release year. When no information is available, the column is left open. If two dates appear, the second is the year of release on compact disc.
5. The format in which the release is or was available. Formats are LP (vinyl), CS (cassette), and CD (compact disc). If no information appears in the column, then the release was an LP. A dagger (†) in this column indicates the release was unavailable at regular retail outlets as of the summer of 1997. These titles may be found at used record and CD stores.

INTRODUCTION

Popular music of the latter half of the twentieth century has been classified into three distinct genres: country-and-western (country), rhythm-and-blues (R&B), and pop. Country developed as a rural music of poor white people in the South, based on the folk ballads and string band tradition of England, Ireland, Scotland, and Wales. With Jimmie Rodgers and the Carter Family as the popular originators, country evolved from early string bands into cowboy music, Western swing, bluegrass, hillbilly boogie, and honky-tonk music.

R&B developed out of the blues as performed by black musicians and singers, initially centered in the South. With its roots in field hollers, church music, and minstrelsy from the nineteenth century and before, the blues became urbanized and expanded beyond the South in the early twentieth century. With W. C. Handy as the popular originator, the blues included both rural and urban blues, and evolved into jazz, boogie woogie, swing, and jump blues.

Popular music was the music of the white middle- and upper-class masses. From Irish tenors and parlor music to marching bands, show tunes, and big-band music, popular music was the most widespread and lucrative genre of music.

Pop music was the dominant form of music at the beginning of the '50s. Controlled by a half dozen "major" record companies, popular music consisted of three elements: songwriters working in the Tin Pan Alley tradition of professional, factory-style songwriting; the record company's artist-and-repertoire (A&R) representative, who matched the song with the musical artist and often commissioned the song's arrangement and musicians; and the musical artist, contracted to the record label, who had little or no input into decisions regarding song selection and arrangements.

Rock 'n' roll revolutionized the popular music industry. Singers often wrote their own songs, recorded for tiny, independent record labels not controlled by the majors, and made their living from performing live. In the '50s, rock 'n' roll could be described as having three subgenres: R&B, rockabilly, and doo-wop. R&B developed from urbanized blues, with boogie woogie, jump blues, and the "blues shouter" vocalist as its primary antecedents. Rockabilly developed from country-and-western, with Western swing, hillbilly boogie, and honky-tonk music as its roots, with the additional influence of up-tempo blues. Doo-wop developed out of the black vocal group tradition of the Mills Brothers and the Ink Spots, and could be created on the spot, without instrumental accompaniment.

In the following sections, I give an overview of the roots of rock, noting key performers, and providing discographies of their works, along with key anthology recordings, for those who want to trace the history of the rock 'n' roll style.

KEY TO ABBREVIATIONS

Abbreviations of instruments played and positions held by personnel are listed below.

bar	baritone
bjo	banjo
brs	brass
bs	bass
drm	drums
fly	flute
gtr	guitar
har	harmonica
kybd	keyboard
mdln	mandolin
org	organ
perc	percussion
pno	piano
rds	reeds
sax	saxophone
sop	soprano
ten	tenor
trmb	trombone
trpt	trumpet
synth	synthesizer
vln	violin
voc	vocals
wdwnd	woodwinds

BLUES WITH A RHYTHM

BOOGIE WOOGIE

Boogie woogie developed as a highly percussive, piano-based music in the late '20s, and was characterized by a constantly repeating rhythmic figure played by the pianist's left hand, freeing the right hand for melody and improvisation. Sometimes called "barrelhouse" piano, it helped popularize the "walking bass" form of accompaniment, still heard in the rock piano styles of pioneers like Jerry Lee Lewis. A danceable and joyful kind of music, boogie woogie included among its prime practitioners Jimmy Yancey, Meade Lux Lewis, Albert Ammons, and Pete Johnson. The latter three joined forces in the late '30s as the Boogie Woogie Boys, enjoying a four-year residency at the exclusive clubs, the Cafe Society Uptown and Downtown in New York, into the '40s. Pete Johnson also was often the accompanist of Big Joe Turner, a noted blues shouter. Thanks to the jazz critic John Hammond, who promoted these artists, the boogie style enjoyed a brief vogue of popularity from the mid '30s through World War II.

Jimmy Yancey

In the Beginning	Jazzology	51		LP
In the Beginning	Solo Art	1	'90	CD

Meade Lux Lewis

1927–1939	Classics	722	'93	CD
1939–1941	Classics	743	'93	CD
1939–1954	Story of Blues	3506	'91	CD
The Blues Piano Artistry of Meade Lux Lewis	Fantasy/OJC	1759		LP/CD

Albert Ammons and Meade Lux Lewis

The First Day (rec. 1939)	Blue Note	98450	'92	CD

Pete Johnson

1938–1939	Classics	656		CD
1939–1941	Classics	665	'92	CD
Central Avenue Boogie (rec. 1947)	Delmark	656	'92	CD
King of Boogie	Milan	35622	'92	CS/CD
Pete's Blues, House Rent Party	Savoy Jazz	0196	'93	CD

Boogie Woogie Compilations

Boogie Woogie Rarities (1927–1943)	Milestone	2009		LP
Masters of Boogie Woogie	Classics	(3)42	'93	CD
The Best of Boogie Woogie	EPM	15740	'91	CD
The Best of Boogie Woogie, Vol. 3	EPM	15848	'96	CD
The Boogie Woogie Giants	Jazz Hour	73533	'95	CD

BLUES SHOUTERS

Blues shouters developed their raucous style in order to be heard above the big bands of the '30s and '40s. Even in the country blues styles that preceded them, "shouting" was a way of expressing deep emotion, often heard in gospel styles as well. This raspy, strident vocal style matched in intensity the big-band style. Prime representatives of the shouter tradition include Jimmy Rushing, who performed with the Count Basie Orchestra, Big Joe Turner, and, later, Wynonie Harris and Roy Brown.

Vocalist-drummer Wynonie Harris, born in Nebraska, moved to Los Angeles in 1940 and sang with the Lucky Millinder band. First recording in 1944, Harris scored nearly a dozen smash R&B hits on King Records from 1948 to 1952, including Roy Brown's "Good Rockin' Tonight" (later covered by Elvis Presley), the top hit "All She Wants to Do Is Rock," and Hank Penny's "Bloodshot Eyes."

New Orleans-born vocalist-pianist Roy Brown moved to Los Angeles in 1942 and sang professionally from 1945. He achieved more than a dozen smash R&B hits for the Deluxe subsidiary of King Records between 1948 and 1951. These included his own "Good Rockin' Tonight" (a major pop and R&B hit), the top R&B hits "'Long About Midnight" and "Hard Luck Blues," plus the R&B smashes "Rockin' at Midnight" and "Boogie at Midnight." In 1957 he scored a smash R&B and major pop hit with "Let the Four Winds Blow," covered by Fats Domino in 1961.

Wynonie Harris

1944–1945	Classics	885	'96	CD
Women, Whiskey & Fish Tails	Ace	457	'93	CD
Bloodshot Eyes: The Best of Wynonie Harris	Rhino	71544	'94	CD

Roy Brown

Good Rockin' Tonight	Intermedia	5027		LP/CS
Mighty Mighty Man!	Ace	459	'93	CD
The Complete Imperial Recordings	Capito	131743	'95	CD

JUMP BLUES

Jump blues developed in the late '30s among the swing bands of Count Basie ("One O'Clock Jump," "Jumpin' at the Woodside"), Cab Calloway ("Jumpin' Jive"), Erskine Hawkins ("Do You Wanna Jump, Chillun'?"), Lionel Hampton, and Lucky Millinder. However, it was several smaller post-World War II combos that popularized the style. The prime purveyor of jump blues and its most successful practitioner, Louis Jordan, enjoyed enormous success, both in the R&B and pop fields, between 1942 and 1951 (see separate entry for his life and career).

By the second half of the '40s, jump blues had become the dominant form of black popular music. Among its successful practitioners were brothers Joe and Jimmy Liggins, Roy Milton and His Solid Senders with boogie woogie pianist Camille Howard, Amos Milburn, and in the '50s the Italian vocalist Louis Prima with Sam Butera and the Witnesses.

Joe and Jimmy Liggins were born in Oklahoma and moved to San Diego in 1932. Pianist Joe Liggins created a big-band sound with his small combo, the Honeydrippers. They achieved their greatest success between 1945 and 1951 on Exclusive and Specialty Records, with hits that included the top R&B and major pop hit "The Honeydripper," "Left a Good Deal in Mobile," "Blow Mr. Jackson," and "Pink Champagne." Vocalist-guitarist Jimmy Liggins and His Drops of Joy enjoyed their greatest success with "Tear Drop Blues" and "Don't Put Me Down" on Specialty Records in 1948–49.

Born in Tulsa, Oklahoma, vocalist-drummer Roy Milton moved to the West Coast in 1935 and formed the Solid Senders with vocalist/boogie-woogie pianist Camille Howard in the mid '40s. They scored a smash R&B hit on Juke Box Records with "Milton's Boogie" in 1946, and recorded nearly twenty more R&B hits for Specialty between 1947 and 1953, including "Hop, Skip and Jump," Paul Williams's "The Hucklebuck," "Information Blues," and "Best Wishes." Milton then toured and recorded with the Camille Howard Trio, beginning in 1948. They achieved their biggest hit that year with the instrumental "X-Temperaneous Boogie." In 1961 Milton scored two major R&B hits with "Red Light" and "Baby You Don't Know."

Vocalist-pianist Amos Milburn was born in Houston, Texas, and formed his first band there in 1945. He began recording for Aladdin Records in 1946 and achieved nearly twenty smash R&B hits for the label between 1948 and 1954. "Chicken Shack Boogie," "Bewildered," "Roomin' House Boogie," and "Bad Bad Whiskey" became top R&B hits. The smash hits included "In the Middle of the Night," "Let's Rock a While," and "Let Me Go Home Whiskey."

Joe Liggins and His Honeydrippers

Joe Liggins & the Honeydrippers	Specialty	7006	'90	LP/CS/CD
Dripper's Boogie, Vol. 2	Specialty	7025	'92	CD

Jimmy Liggins and His Drops of Joy

Jimmy Liggins and His Drops of Joy	Specialty	7005	'90	CS/CD
Rough Weather Blues, Vol. 2	Specialty	7026	'92	CD

Roy Milton and His Solid Senders

Roy Milton and His Solid Senders	Specialty	7004	'90	LP/CS/CD
Vol. 2: Groovy Blues	Specialty	7024	'93	CD
Vol. 3: Blowin' with Roy	Specialty	7060	'94	CD

Camille Howard

Vol. 1: Rock Me Daddy	Specialty	7046	'93	CD
Vol. 2: X-Temperaneous Boogie	Specialty	7062	'96	CD

Amos Milburn

Blues, Barrelhouse & Boogie: The Best of, 1946–1955	Capitol	(3)36879	'96	CD
The Complete Aladdin Recordings	Mosaic	(10)155/(7)155		LP/CD

Louis Prima

Swing with (rec. mid '50s)	Fat Boy	234	'96	CD
Capitol Collector's Series	Capitol	94072	'91	CS/CD

Jump Blues and Anthologies

Blues Masters: The Essential Blues Collection, Vol. 5: Jump Blues Classics	Rhino	71125	'92	CS/CD
Blues Masters: The Essential Blues Collection, Vol. 14: More Jump Blues Classics	Rhino	71133	'93	CS/CD
Specialty Legends of Jump Blues	Specialty	7058	'94	CD
Chicago Jump Bands: Early R&B, Vol. 1, 1945–53	RST	91577	'96	CD

BIBLIOGRAPHY

Berry, Jason, Jonathan Foose, and Ted Jones. *Up from the Cradle of Jazz: New Orleans Music since World War II*. Athens: University of Georgia Press, 1986.

Bronson, Fred, and Adam White. *The Billboard Book of Number One Rhythm and Blues Hits*. New York: Billboard Books, 1993.

Broven, John. *Rhythm and Blues in New Orleans.* Gretna, LA: Pelican, 1988.

Deffa, Chip. *Blue Rhythms: Six Lives in Rhythm and Blues.* Urbana: University of Illinois Press, 1996.

Dickerson, James. *Goin' Back to Memphis: A Century of Blues, Rock 'n' Roll, and Glorious Soul.* New York: Schirmer Books, 1996.

Erlewine, Michael, Chris Woodstra, Vladimir Bogdanov, and Cub Koda, eds. *All Music Guide to the Blues: The Experts' Guide to the Best Blues Recordings.* San Francisco: Miller Freeman, 1996.

Gillett, Charlie. *Making Tracks: Atlantic Records and the Growth of a Multi-Billion Dollar Industry.* New York: Dutton, 1974.

Gonzalez, Fernando L. *The Discographical Catalog of American Rock and Roll and Rhythm and Blues and Blues Vocal Harmony Vocal Groups.* Flushing, NY: Gonzalez, 1977.

Gregory, Hugh. *Soul Music A–Z.* London: Blandford; NY: distributed by Sterling, 1991.

Guralnick, Peter. *Sweet Soul Music: Rhythm and Blues and the Southern Dream of Freedom.* New York: Harper & Row, 1986.

Haralambos, Michael. *Right On: From Blues to Soul in Black America.* New York: Drake, 1975; New York: Da Capo, 1979.

Herzhaft, Gerard. *Encyclopedia of the Blues.* Fayetteville: University of Arkansas Press, 1992.

Hildebrand, Lee. *Stars of Soul and Rhythm and Blues.* New York: Billboard Books, 1994.

Hoare, Ian, ed. *The Soul Book.* New York: Dell, 1976.

Leadbitter, Mike, and Neil Slaven. *Blues Records: 1943–1966.* New York: Oak, 1968.

———. *Blues Records: 1943–1970.* London: Record Information Services, 1987.

Nelson, George. *The Death of Rhythm and Blues.* New York: Pantheon, 1988.

Osborne, Jerry. *Blues, Rhythm & Blues, Soul.* Phoenix: O'Sullivan Woodside, 1980.

Pascall, Jeremy, and Rob Burt. *The Stars and Superstars of Black Music.* Secaucus, NJ: Chartwell, 1977.

Pruter, Robert. *Chicago Soul.* Urbana: University of Illinois Press, 1991.

———, ed. *The Blackwell Guide to Soul Recordings.* Cambridge, MA: Blackwell, 1993.

Santelli, Robert. *The Big Book of Blues: A Biographical Encyclopedia.* New York: Penguin, 1993.

Scott, Frank. *The Down Home Guide to the Blues.* Pennington, NJ: A Cappella, 1991.

———, and Al Ennis. *The Roots & Rhythm Guide to Rock.* Pennington, NJ: A Cappella, 1993.

Shaw, Arnold. *The World of Soul: Black America's Contirbution to the Pop Music Scene.* New York: Cowles, 1970.

———. *Honkers and Shouters: The Golden Years of Rhythm and Blues.* New York: Macmillan, 1978.

———. *Black Popular Music in America.* New York: Schirmer Books, 1986; New York: Macmillan, 1990.

Tee, Ralph. *Soul Music: Who's Who.* Rocklin, CA: Prima, 1992.

———. *The Best of Soul: The Essential CD Guide.* San Francisco: Collins, 1993.

Tudor, Dean, and Nancy Tudor. *Black Music.* Littleton, CO: Libraries Unlimited, 1979.

Wexler, Jerry, and David Ritz. *Rhythm and the Blues: A Life in American Music.* New York: Knopf, 1993.

Whitburn, Joel. *Top R & B Singles 1942–1988.* Menomenee Falls, WI: Record Research, 1988.

COUNTRY STYLES

WESTERN SWING

Western swing developed out of the string band tradition in the Southwest, primarily in Texas, during the '30s. The prototypical Western swing band included the stringed instruments—such as fiddle and guitar—associated with old-time bands along with new instrumentation inspired by the popular dance bands of the era: banjo, brass instruments, piano, bass, drums. Perhaps the first Western swing band of note was the Wills Fiddle Band (later the Light Crust Doughboys when they gained the sponsorship of Burrus Mills, a local flour manufacturer). It was formed in 1930 by fiddler-vocalist Bob Wills and guitarist Herman Arnspiger, soon adding vocalist Milton Brown. Brown left in September 1932 to form his own band, the Musical Brownies, adding electric steel guitarist Bob Dunn (among the first musicians to play an electric instrument in country music) in late 1934. Playing blues, jazz, and swing in a string band context, Brown was on the verge of major success when he died in a car wreck in 1936.

Meanwhile, Wills continued to lead the original Doughboys. Electric steel guitarist Leon McAuliffe joined the group in 1935, but the band was soon without a sponsor, consequently moving to Tulsa, Oklahoma, and becoming the Texas Playboys. With fiddles, banjo, saxophones, piano, and drums, Bob Wills and the Texas Playboys produced an amazingly diverse sound, from string band to big band. First recording in 1935 for the American Recording Company (ARC, later purchased by Columbia), they produced classics such as "Steel Guitar Rag" and "That's What I Like 'Bout the South" in the '30s. The group's lead vocalist, Tommy Duncan, was a crooner in the Bing Crosby mold, and his pop stylings helped them build their popularity. Another major attraction was the personality of bandleader Wills, whose cheerful yodeling and announcing of band members from the stage (and on disc) helped give them a distinctive sound.

The group added electric guitarist Eldon Shamblin in 1938 and scored a major pop hit with "San Antonio Rose" in 1939. Achieving pop hits throughout the first half of the '40s, including "New San Antonio Rose" and "You're from Texas," Bob Wills expanded his audience and influence when he moved to California around 1943. During the latter half of the '40s, despite a decrease in the size of the band, they scored an amazing series of country hits, including the top hits "New Spanish Two Step" and "Sugar Moon," plus "Hang Your Head in Shame," "Stay a Little Longer," "Bubbles in My Beer," and "Ida Red Likes the Boogie." They recorded for Columbia Records until 1947 and subsequently recorded for MGM, Decca, and Liberty.

Wills's success inspired dozens of imitators, including his brother Johnnie Lee, who eventually scored a hit in 1950 with the classic "Rag Mop." Wills alumnus Leon McAuliffe formed the Cimarron Boys in 1946 and scored a smash country hit with his own "Panhandle Rag" in 1949. The original Musical Brownies also spawned successors after Milton Brown's death. Fiddler Cliff Bruner had joined the Brownies in 1934, and subsequently formed the Texas Wanderers around 1936. The band's members included pianist Moon

Mullican (later a successful honky-tonk artist on his own) and electric steel guitarist Bob Dunn. They scored their biggest hit with Floyd Tillman's "It Makes No Difference Now" in 1938.

Western swing was given an additional boost by the singing cowboy craze. Radio and film stars like Gene Autry and Roy Rogers were often accompanied by pop-flavored, swinging bands. In turn, many Western swing bands took on a "cowboy" image, including Wills, who appeared in a number of B-grade Westerns in the '40s. Texas guitarist Bill Boyd formed the Cowboy Ramblers in 1932, recorded a popular version of "Under the Double Eagle" in 1934, and eventually achieved a smash country hit with "New Steel Guitar Rag" in 1946. Alabama vocalist Hank Penny formed the Radio Cowboys around 1938 and scored smash country hits with the instrumental "Steel Guitar Stomp" and "Get Yourself a Red Head" in 1946, and the classic "Bloodshot Eyes" in 1950. Oklahoma fiddler Spade Cooley formed his orchestra in California with Illinois-born guitarist-vocalist Tex Williams in 1942, scoring smash country hits with "Shame on You" and "Detour" in 1945–46. Williams and most of the band left Cooley in 1946 to form the Western Caravan, best remembered for the 1947 top country hit "Smoke! Smoke! Smoke! (That Cigarette)" (written by Merle Travis) and 1948's smash "Talking Boogie."

The Western swing tradition was maintained into the '50s with Texan Hank Thompson and His Brazos Valley Boys, whose smash country hits included the classic "The Wild Side of Life," "Honky-Tonk Girl," "A Six Pack to Go," and "Hangover Tavern." Later practitioners of Western swing included Alvin Crow and the Pleasant Valley Boys, and, most recently, Asleep at the Wheel, a country-rock outfit that helped revitalize interest in the style in the '70s, and who are still active today.

Bob Wills

Bob Wills	Columbia Historic Edition	37468		CS/CD
The Golden Era	Columbia Historic Edition	(2)40149	'87	CS
The Essential	Columbia/Legacy	48958	'92	CS/CD
24 Greatest Hits	Polydor	827573		CS
Bob Wills and His Texas Playboys	MCA	526	'58	CS
Living Legend	MCA	546		CS
The Best of	MCA	153		CS
The Best of, Vol. 2	MCA	(2)4092		CS
The King of Western Swing	MCA	(2)38019		CS
The Best of	MCA	5917		CD
Greatest Hits	Curb/CEMA	77389	'90	CS/CD
Anthology (1935–1973)	Rhino	(2)70744	'91	CS/CD
Legacy	Collector's Edition	12	'96	CD
The Best of	RCA-Camden	3023		CS
21 Golden Hits	Hollywood/IMG	411		CS/CD
Bob Wills Fiddle	Country Music Foundation	010		LP/CS

Hank Penny and His Radio Cowboys

Hank Penny & His Radio Cowboys	Rambler	103		LP

Spade Cooley

Spadella!: The Essential (rec.1944–1946)	Columbia/Legacy	57392	'94	CD

Tex Williams and His Western Caravan

Vintage Collection	Capitol Nashville	36184	'95	CS/CD

Hank Thompson and His Brazos Valley Boys

Vintage Collection	Capitol	36901	'96	CD
Western Swing Anthologies				
Hillbilly Fever, Vol. 1: Legends of Western Swing	Rhino	71900	'95	CS/CD
Western Swing Legends	Special Music	5151	'95	CS/CD
Western Swing	Old Timey	105		LP
Western Swing, Vol. 3	Old Timey	117		LP
Western Swing, Vol. 4	Old Timey	119		LP
Western Swing, Vol. 5	Old Timey	120		LP
Western Swing, Vol. 6	Old Timey	121		LP
Western Swing, Vol. 7	Old Timey	122		LP
Western Swing, Vol. 8	Old Timey	123		LP

HONKY-TONK

Honky-tonk music developed during the '30s in the South and Southwest. Played in road-houses, taverns, and beer halls known as "honky-tonks," the music encompassed up-tempo dance songs about drinking, carousing, and fighting, and slow mournful songs about lost love and hard times. Featuring fiddle, guitar, and steel guitar, early honky-tonk recordings include Al Dexter's "Honky Tonk Blues" and Bob Dunn's "Stompin' at the Honky Tonk." The biggest and most influential star of honky-tonk music was Hank Williams (see separate entry).

The most important honky-tonk artist of the '40s was Texan Ernest Tubb. Signing with Decca Records in 1940, he came to realize that acoustic guitar could not be heard in noisy taverns, and thus recorded his own "Walkin' the Floor Over You" with electric guitar in 1941. The song became a huge hit and even penetrated the pop charts. Tubb became the first musician to use an electric guitar on the *Grand Ole Opry* in 1943 and scored a smash country hit with "Try Me One More Time" in 1944. In 1946 he began recording solely with his band, the Texas Troubadours, and became one of the first country artists to record in Nashville. An immensely popular country artist in the '40s, Tubb's string of smash country hits extended into '60s. Important hits included "Drivin' Nails in My Coffin," "Have You Ever Been Lonely (Have You Ever Been Blue)" backed with "Let's Say Goodbye Like We Said Hello," Floyd Till-man's "Slipping Around," Leon Payne's "I Love You Because," Stuart Hamblen's "(Remember Me) I'm the One Who Loves You," "Thanks a Lot," and "Waltz Across Texas." Tillman, Payne, and Hamblen all became successful honky-tonk artists in the late '40s.

Louisiana-born songwriter-guitarist Ted Daffan was another early honky-tonk artist, writing and performing his own songs, such as "Worried Mind," "Born to Lose," "Headin' Down the Wrong Highway," and "I'm a Fool to Care." Texan Al Dexter broke through in 1943 with the top pop and country hit "Pistol Packin' Mama" and maintained a string of smash country hits through 1948 with "Too Late to Worry, Too Blue to Cry," the instrumental "Guitar Polka," "Wine, Women and Song," and "Down at the Roadside Inn." Kentucky songwriter-guitarist Merle Travis was also popular in the second half of the '40s, scoring top country hits with "Divorce Me C.O.D." and "So Round, So Firm, So Fully Packed." Milwaukee-born Pee Wee King, leader of the Golden West Cowboys, bridged the gap between Western swing and honky-tonk. Between 1948 and 1954 he had several smash country hits, including three with his own compositions "Tennessee Waltz," "Changing Partners," and the top pop and country hit "Slow Poke."

Kentuckian Red Foley achieved his initial success on the *National Barn Dance* radio show on Chicago's WLS from 1930 to 1937. He signed with Decca Records in 1941 and, in 1945 became the first country artist to record in Nashville. One of the first country artists to record and perform with electric guitar and drums, Foley's earliest hits were covers of songs such as "Shame on You," "That's How Much I Love You," and "Freight Train Boogie." Although primarily a ballad singer, he scored a number of up-tempo hits between 1948 and 1952, including the top country hits "Tennessee Saturday Night," "Chattanoogie Shoe Shine Boy," "Birmingham Bounce," and "Mississippi." Other smash country hits for Foley were "Tennessee Border," "Hobo Boogie," "Alabama Jubilee," and "Milk Bucket Boogie" backed with "Salty Dog Rag." He recorded with Ernest Tubb in the early '50s and with Kitty Wells in the mid '50s, but subsequently concentrated on recording religious material.

The '50s saw a burst of new honky-tonk stars, following in Hank Williams's wake. Texan Lefty Frizzell, second to only Hank Williams in popularity in the first half of the '50s, achieved top country hits with "If You've Got the Money I've Got the Time" backed with "I Love You a Thousand Ways," "I Want to Be with You Always," "Always Late (with Your Kisses)," and "Give Me More, More, More (of Your Kisses)." He also scored smash country hits with "Look What Thoughts Will Do," "Don't Stay Away (Till Love Grows Cold)," "I'm an Old Old Man (Tryin' to Live While I Can)," and "The Long Black Veil."

Canadian Hank Snow first recorded in 1936 and moved to the United States in the mid '40s. His country hits began in 1950, culminating in three consecutive top hits, "I'm Movin' On," "The Golden Rocket," and "The Rhumba Boogie." Snow's country hits through 1955 included the top hits "I Don't Hurt Anymore" and "Let Me Go, Lover!," and the smashes "The Gold Rush Is Over" and "The Gal Who Invented Kissin'." Later country hits included the top hits "I've Been Everywhere" (1962) and "Hello Love" (1974) and the smash "Ninety Miles an Hour (Down a Dead End Street)" (1963).

Webb Pierce, from Louisiana, formed a band in the early '50s that included talented accompanists (and future stars) Faron Young, Floyd Cramer, Tillman Franks, and the Wilburn Brothers. Pierce began his series of smash country hits on Decca Records in 1952 with the top hit "Wondering." Other top country hits for Pierce through 1957 included "Back Street Affair," "There Stands the Glass," "More and More," Jimmie Rodgers's "In the Jailhouse Now," "I Don't Care," "Love, Love, Love," and "Honky Tonk Song." In 1956 Pierce scored a near-smash country hit with the rockabilly-styled "Teenage Boogie."

Texan Ray Price, favoring the sadder side of honky-tonk music, began recording in 1952. Top country hits through 1959 included "Crazy Arms," "My Shoes Keep Walking Back to You," "City Lights," and "The Same Old Me." Price's smash country hits of the '50s included Slim Willet's "Don't Let the Stars Get in Your Eyes," "If You Don't, Somebody Else Will," "I've Got a New Heartache," "Invitation to the Blues," and "Heartaches by the Number." Later hits included "Make the World Go Away" and Kris Kristofferson's "For the Good Times."

Faron Young, from Louisiana, initially favored the up-tempo, rough-edged side of honky-tonk, scoring his first country hit, a smash, with "Goin' Steady" in 1953. Subsequent hits through 1956 included "A Place for Girls Like You," "If You Ain't Lovin'," the top hit "Live Fast, Love Hard, Die Young," and "I've Got Five Dollars and It's Saturday Night." Later top country hits included "Alone with You," "Country Girl," Willie Nelson's "Hello Walls," and "It's Four in the Morning."

Texan George Jones, after an initial flirtation with rockabilly, achieved a smash country hit in late 1955 with "Why Baby Why." After 1959's "White Lightning" and "Who Shot Sam," Jones scored top country hits with "Tender Years" and "She Thinks I Still Care" in 1961–62. Later country hits for Jones included "The Race Is On" (1964), "Love Bug" (1965), "A Good Year for the Roses" (1970), the top hit "The Grand Tour" (1974), "Bartender's Blues" with James Taylor (1978), and the top hit classic "He Stopped Loving Her Today" (1980). George Jones continued to perform and record honky-tonk throughout his career, despite the rise of the "countrypolitan" sound in the '60s.

Johnny Horton, born in Los Angeles and raised in California and Texas, joined the *Louisiana Hayride* radio show in late 1951. Recording for Abbott and Mercury Records ("Tennessee Jive"), Horton joined Columbia in late 1955, scoring a near-smash country hit with "Honky-Tonk Man" in the spring of 1956. He soon hit with "I'm a One-Woman Man," and Columbia subsequently issued "I'm Coming Home," "The Woman I Need," "Lover's Rock," and "Honky Tonk Hardwood Floor." Horton enjoyed his greatest commercial success in the late '50s with so-called saga songs, contemporary songs written in the style of folk ballads, such as "The Battle of New Orleans," "Sink the Bismarck," and "North to Alaska," but his career was tragically ended when he was killed in an automobile accident on November 5, 1960.

The honky-tonk tradition was reinforced in the '60s by the arrival of California country stars Buck Owens and Merle Haggard, and the return of Jerry Lee Lewis. The country "outlaw" movement of the mid '70s, with Waylon Jennings and Willie Nelson, served once again to popularize both the celebratory and mournful style of honky-tonk music. Current country artists recording in the honky-tonk tradition include Marty Stuart, Dwight Yoakam, Joe Ely, Junior Brown, and Wayne Hancock.

Ernest Tubb

Greatest Hits	MCA	16	'68	CS
The Country Music Hall of Fame	MCA	10086	'91	CS/CD

Merle Travis

Best	Rhino	70993	'90	CS/CD
Saturday Night Shuffle: A Celebration of Merle Travis	Shanachie	6006	'93	CS/CD
The Merle Travis Story	CMH	(2)9018		LP
	CMH	9018		CS/CD

Red Foley

The Country Music Hall of Fame	MCA	10084	'91	CS/CD

Lefty Frizell

Greatest Hits	Columbia	09288	'66	CS
American Originals (rec. 1950–1965)	Columbia	45067	'90	CS/CD
Best	Rhino	71005	'91	CS/CD

Hank Snow

Collector's Series	RCA Nashville	52279	'90	CS/CD
All-Time Greatest Hits	RCA	9968		CS/CD

Webb Pierce

Greatest Hits	MCA	120		CS
King of Honky Tonk (rec. Nashville, 1951–1959)	Country Music Foundation	0019		CS/CD

Early Ray Price

Greatest Hits	Columbia	08866	'61	CS/CD
American Originals	Columbia	45068	'89	CS/CD
The Essential Ray Price 1951–1962	Columbia/Legacy	48532	'91	CS/CD

Faron Young

Live Fast, Love Hard: Original Capitol Recordings, 1952–1962	Country Music Foundation	020	'95	CD

Early George Jones

Sings His Greatest Hits	Starday	150		LP/CS
Honky Tonkin'	Polygram	836691		CS

The Best of George Jones, Vol. 1: Hardcore Honkytonk	Mercury Nashville	848978	'91	CS/CD
Cup of Loneliness: The Classic Mercury Years	Mercury Nashville	(2)522635	'94	CD
The Classic Years	Mercury	532341	'96	CS/CD
The Best of George Jones (1955–1967)	Rhino	70531	'91	CS/CD
Johnny Horton				
Honky Tonk Man: The Essential, 1956–1960	Columbia	(2)64761	'96	CD
Anthologies				
Country Honky Tonk Heroes	K-Tel	3380	'95	CS/CD
Hillbilly Fever, Vol. 2: Legends of Honky Tonk	Rhino	71901	'95	CS/CD

HILLBILLY BOOGIE

Hillbilly boogie was a variation of honky-tonk music that usually favored up-tempo songs. It married country topics with the upbeat, jazzy feeling of the jump bands of the late '40s. The Delmore Brothers, from Alabama, were one of the earliest purveyors of hillbilly boogie. Formed in the '20s, they first recorded in 1931, already showing a strong propensity for the blues. After the war, the brothers regrouped with a fuller backup band, and jazzed up their style even further, recording spirited songs such as "The Nashville Blues," "Boogie Woogie Baby," and "Used Car Blues." They scored a smash country hit with "Freight Train Boogie" in 1947, later topping the country charts in 1949 with "Blues Stay Away from Me," often regarded as one of the earliest examples of rockabilly. During the late '40s the Delmore Brothers worked with Grandpa Jones and Merle Travis, recording gospel music as the Brown's Ferry Four. In 1950 the Delmore Brothers scored a near-smash country hit with "Pan American Boogie."

Texas pianist Moon Mullican, considered a major influence on Jerry Lee Lewis, worked with the Blue Ridge Playboys and Cliff Bruner's Texas Wanderers in the early '40s, launching a solo career in 1946. He scored a smash country hit with a version of the classic Cajun song "New Jole Blon" in 1947, and later country successes included the top hit "I'll Sail My Ship Alone" (1950) and the smash "Cherokee Boogie (Eh-Oh-Aleena)" (1951), and 1961's major hit "Ragged But Right."

The Maddox Family, originally from Alabama, arrived in California in 1933. With vocalist Rose Maddox only eleven years old, the Maddox Brothers and Rose was formed in 1937 and became one of the most popular West Coast hillbilly bands. They combined the sultry sexiness of Rose with the comic antics of the brothers, who often clowned around on stage and during recordings, particularly on the group's up-tempo numbers. The group's career was interrupted by World War II, but they regrouped in 1946 and recorded for Four Star Records until 1951, including a reworking of the Jimmie Rodgers classic "New Muleskinner Blues," Woody Guthrie's ballad "Philadelphia Lawyer," and the more modern honky-tonk stylings of "Alimony" and "Mean and Wicked Boogie." The move to more modern styles continued after the band switched to Columbia Records in 1951, with songs such as "Hey Little Dreamboat," "Wild Wild Young Men," and "Ugly and Slouchy." They broke up in 1957, and Rose Maddox subsequently pursued her own career, scoring smash country hits with "Mental Cruelty" and "Loose Talk" in duet with Buck Owens in 1961, and "Sing a Little Song of Heartache" in 1963. Since recording a bluegrass album in 1962, Rose Maddox has been a favorite on the bluegrass circuit.

Other hillbilly boogie hits of the late '40s included Bob Wills's "Bob Wills Boogie," Jack Guthrie and His Oklahomans' "Oakie Boogie," Hawkshaw Hawkins's "Dog House Boogie,"

Tex Williams and His Western Caravan's "Talking Boogie," and Merle Travis's "Merle's Boogie Woogie" and "Crazy Boogie." Wayne Raney, who worked with the Delmore Brothers in the late '40s, scored major country hits with "Lost John Boogie" and "Jack and Jill Boogie" in 1948, and Arthur "Guitar Boogie" Smith had near-smash country hits with "Banjo Boogie" and "Guitar Boogie" in 1948–49. (In the mid '50s, he returned with the classic "Feudin' Banjos," in duet with Don Reno; this was revived in the '70s as the theme for the film *Deliverance,* and became a novelty hit on the pop charts.)

One of the key purveyors of boogie early in his career was "Tennessee" Ernie Ford, who launched his recording career with a cover of Red Foley's "Tennessee Border." Through 1952 Ford scored smash country hits with "Smokey Mountain Boogie," "Anticipation Blues," "The Cry of the Wild Goose," and "Blackberry Boogie." "Mule Train" became a top hit for Ford in 1950, as did "The Shot Gun Boogie" in 1951 and Merle Travis's "Sixteen Tons" in 1955–56. His affable style made him a favorite on television in the '50s, and he soon turned to more popular-oriented recordings. He later became one of the most successful country artists to record Christian music.

The Delmore Brothers

Sand Mountain Blues (rec. 1944–1949)	County	110	'87	CS/CD
Freight Train Boogie	Ace	455	'93	CD

Moon Mullican

Moonshine Jamboree	Ace	458	'93	CD
Sings His All-Time Hits	King	555		LP/CS/CD
The Old Texan	King	628		LP/CS
22 Greatest Hits	Deluxe	7813		CS
I'll Sail My Ship Alone	Richmond	2182		CS

The Maddox Brothers and Rose

Maddox Brothers & Rose	King	677		LP/CS
Maddox Brothers & Rose	Arhoolie	222		CS
America's Most Colorful Hillbilly Band	Arhoolie	391	'93	CD
America's Most Colorful Hillbilly Band, Vol. 2	Arhoolie	437	'95	CD

"Tennessee" Ernie Ford

Sixteen Tons of Country Boogie: The Best of	Rhino	70975	'90	CS/CD
Greatest Hits	Curb/Warner Brothers	77625	'93	CS/CD
Sixteen Tons	Capitol Nashville	33833	'95	CS/CD

Hillbilly Boogie

Rarest Rockabilly & Hillbilly Boogie	Ace	44		LP
Hillbilly Boogie	Columbia/Legacy	53940	'94	CD

BIBLIOGRAPHY

Allen, Bob, ed. *The Blackwell Guide to Recorded Country Music.* Cambridge, MA: Blackwell, 1994.

Bufwack, Mary A., and Robert K. Oermann. *Finding Her Voice: The Saga of Women in Country Music.* New York: Crown, 1993.

Carlin, Richard. *The Big Book of Country Music: A Biographical Encyclopedia.* New York: Penguin, 1995.

Carr, Joe, and Alan Munde. *Prairie Nights to Neon Lights: The Story of Country Music in West Texas.* Lubbock: Texas Tech University Press, 1995.

Country Music Foundation, comp. *Country: The Music and the Musicians: From the Beginning to the 90's.* New York: Abbeville, 1994.

Editors of *Country Music Magazine. The Comprehensive Country Music Encyclopedia.* New York: Times Books, 1994.

Dellar, Fred, Roy Thompson, and Douglas B. Green. *The Illustrated Encyclopedia of Country Music.* New York: Harmony, 1977.

————, Allan Cackett, Roy Thompson, and Douglas B. Green. *The Harmony Illustrated Encyclopedia of Country Music.* New York: Harmony, 1987.

Eichenlaub, Frank and Patricia. *All American Guide to Country Music.* Castine, ME: Country Roads, 1992.

Erlewine, Michael, Vladimir Bogdanov, Chris Woodstra, and Stephen Thomas Erlewine, eds. *All Music Guide to Country.* San Francisco: Miller Freeman, 1997.

Gentry, Linnell. *A History and Encyclopedia of Country, Western and Gospel Music.* Nashville: McQuiddy, 1961; Nashville: Clairmont Corp., 1969.

Ginell, Cary. *Milton Brown and the Founding of Western Swing.* Urbana: University of Illinois Press, 1994.

Green, Douglas B. *Country Roots: The Origins of Country Music.* New York: Hawthorn, 1976.

Gregory, Hugh. *Who's Who in Country Music.* London: Weidenfeld and Nicholson, 1993.

Haislop, Neil, Ted Lathrop, and Harry Sumrall. *Giants of Country Music.* New York: Billboard Music, 1995.

Heggeness, Fred. *Goldmine Country & Western Record & CD Price Guide.* Iola, WI: Krause, 1996.

Kingsbury, Paul. *Country on Compact Disc: The Essential Guide to the Music.* New York: Grove, 1993.

McCall, Michael, Dave Hoekstra, and Janet Williams. *Country Music Stars: The Legends and the New Breed.* Lincolnville, IL: Publications International, 1992.

McCloud, Barry. *Definitive Country: The Ultimate Encyclopedia of Country Music and Its Performers.* New York: A Perigee Book, Berkley, 1995.

Millard, Bob. *Country Music: 70 Years of America's Favorite Music.* New York: Harper Perennial, 1993.

Oermann, Robert K., with Douglas B. Green. *The Listener's Guide to Country Music.* New York: Facts on File, 1983.

————. *America's Music: The Roots of Country.* Atlanta: Turner, 1996.

Stambler, Irwin, and Grelun Landon. *Encyclopedia of Folk, Country and Western Music.* New York: St. Martin's, 1969, 1983.

Stambler, Irwin. *Country Music: The Encyclopedia.* New York: St. Martin's, 1997.

Tosches, Nick. *Country: The Biggest Music in America.* New York: Stein and Day, 1977.

Townsend, Charles R. *San Antonio Rose: The Life and Music of Bob Wills.* Urbana: University of Illinois Press, 1976.

Tudor, Dean and Nancy. *Grass Roots Music.* Littleton, CO: Libraries Unlimited, 1979.

Vaughan, Andrew. *Who's Who in New Country Music.* New York: St. Martin's, 1989.

Whitburn, Joel. *Top Country Singles 1944–1993.* Menomonee Falls, WI: Record Research, 1994.

ROCKABILLY

Rockabilly developed in the early to mid '50s. It usually featured frantic, uninhibited lead vocals, a wild stinging lead guitar, and thumping stand-up bass. Rockabilly found its first widespread expression thanks to Sun Records, a Memphis-based label that made the early rockabilly recordings of Carl Perkins, Elvis Presley, Johnny Cash, and Jerry Lee Lewis.

Many artists fostered the transition from honky-tonk and hillbilly boogie to rockabilly in the early '50s. Alabaman Arthur "Hardrock" Gunter wrote and recorded "Birmingham Bounce," which became a top country and major pop hit for Red Foley in 1950. Gunter signed with Decca in 1951 and later wrote and recorded "Baby Let's Play House" for the Nashville-based Excello label in 1954. The song proved a regional hit and became Elvis Presley's first national country hit in 1955. Gunter continued to record for Excello until 1961, with little success.

Autry Inman, also from Alabama, toured with Cowboy Copas in the late '40s and scored a smash country hit with bluesman Arthur "Big Boy" Crudup's "That's All Right" in 1953. Elvis Presley recorded the song at his first formal session at Sun Records on July 6, 1954; it is not known whether he learned it from Crudup's or Inman's recording. Virginia country boogie pianist Roy Hall recorded the original version of "Whole Lotta Shakin' Goin' On" and Bobby Charles's "See You Later, Alligator" for Decca in 1955, as well as "Rockin' the Blues" for Strate 8, and "One Monkey Don't Stop the Show" for Pierce.

Missourian Onie Wheeler performed regionally after World War II, making his first recording in 1948. Beginning in 1953 he recorded for OKeh and then its parent label, Columbia, until 1957, recording honky-tonk songs such as his own "Run 'Em Off" (a near-smash country hit for Lefty Frizzell in 1954), "Little Mama," "That's What I Like," and "Steppin' Out." He subsequently recorded rockabilly for Sun Records for two years.

Pianist Merrill Moore, from Iowa, moved to San Diego in the late '40s and played country boogie with his band at local clubs. They signed with Capitol Records, but none of their recordings, including Moore's own "House of Blue Lights" and "Rock Rockola," became hits. Moore moved to Los Angeles in 1955 and later backed Wanda Jackson on some of her Capitol recordings.

Bill Haley and the Comets were perhaps the earliest purveyors of rockabilly, combining Western swing and jump-blues in a small combo context. Haley, born in Michigan, had originally led a cowboy-flavored group called the Saddlemen. When the group began covering R&B hits, they changed their name to the Comets; by then Haley was much older than the typical teen idol. They scored major pop hits from 1953 to 1956 with songs such as "Crazy, Man, Crazy," "Dim, Dim the Lights," the classic "Rock Around the Clock" (a top pop and smash R&B hit in 1955), "Burn That Candle," and "See You Later, Alligator." However, when Haley appeared on film and teens could see that their idol was an older, not particularly hip looking man, his career fizzled.

Rockabilly found its widest-spread dissemination from the Memphis-based Sun Records label. Elvis Presley signed with Sun in 1954, recording Arthur Crudup's "That's All Right" and Roy Brown's "Good Rockin' Tonight" that year. In 1955 he scored major country hits with Arthur Gunter's "Baby Let's Play House" and Junior Parker's "Mystery Train." Elvis's backup band consisted of a single guitarist—Scotty Moore—and bassist Bill Black; Elvis himself played rhythm. Black's powerful bass rhythms and Moore's sharp electric guitar leads and distinctive rhythm playing set the model for all of the rockabilly groups to come. Presley capitalized on rockabilly's early success by signing with RCA Records in late 1955, initiating a string of three-way crossover hits with "Heartbreak Hotel" that endured through 1957's simultaneous top pop, country, and R&B hit "Jailhouse Rock."

However, Carl Perkins is probably most closely associated with the style. He launched rockabilly with early 1956's top country-and-western and smash pop and R&B classic "Blue Suede Shoes," "Honey Don't," and a cover of Blind Lemon Jefferson's classic "Matchbox [Blues]." Perkins switched to more teen-oriented material after he left Sun in 1958, but was unable to maintain the momentum of his original hits. Johnny Cash recorded rockabilly country hits for Sun such as "Cry, Cry, Cry," and "Get Rhythm" before moving to Columbia in 1958 and switching to a country/folk orientation. Roy Orbison scored the early rockabilly hit "Ooby Dooby " for Sun in 1956, before switching in the early '60s to the symphonic pop style that made him famous. Jerry Lee Lewis began his career in 1957 with the top country-and-western and R&B and smash pop hit "Whole Lotta Shakin' Goin' On" that sustained through 1958's three-way crossover hit "High School Confidential." Lewis's career, of course, collapsed with his infamous marriage to his thirteen-year-old cousin and the subsequent press uproar.

Other Sun artists recorded excellent rockabilly, yet failed to achieve any major hits. Arkansan Sonny Burgess, one of the wildest rockabilly artists, recorded for Sun from 1956 to 1959. With his band, the Pacers, Burgess recorded powerful rockabilly songs such as "We Wanna Boogie," "Red Headed Woman," and Hank Williams's "My Bucket's Got a Hole in It." In the late '80s, Burgess was "rediscovered" and began recording again, still performing his old repertoire in its original style.

Arkansan Billy Riley, also known as Billy Lee Riley, first worked at Sun as a session musician, playing guitar, bass, drums, and harmonica. He subsequently formed his own band, the Little Green Men, with guitarist Roland Janes and drummer Jimmy Van Eaton. They recorded "Flying Saucers Rock 'n' Roll" and "Rock with Me Baby," with the addition of Jerry Lee Lewis on piano, both of which have become cult classics. Riley also recorded "Baby Don't Leave Me" and the classic "Red Hot" for Sun. He left the label in 1960 and eventually achieved a minor pop hit with "I Got a Thing About You" in 1972.

Mississippian Warren Smith was discovered by Carl Perkins and occasionally recorded at Sun with guitarist Roland Janes, bassist Billy Riley, and drummer Jimmy Van Eaton. Equally adept at rockabilly and country ballads, Smith's rockabilly repertoire included "Rock 'n' Roll Ruby," "Miss Froggie," "Ubangi Stomp," "Red Cadillac and a Black Moustache," and "Uranium Rock"; many of these have become favorites among rockabilly revivalists. He managed one minor pop hit with "So Long I'm Gone," written by Roy Orbison, in 1957. After leaving Sun in 1959, he scored smash country hits with "I Don't Believe I'll Fall in Love Today" and "Odds and Ends (Bits and Pieces)" on Liberty Records in 1960–61. He left music for a decade after a 1965 automobile accident and died of a heart attack on January 30, 1980, at the age of forty-six.

Arkansan Ed Bruce signed with Sun in 1957, and recorded rockabilly tunes such as "Rock Boppin' Baby" and "Sweet Woman." He moved to Nashville in 1964 and achieved a number of country hits between 1967 and 1986. Between 1981 and 1986 he scored the country smashes "You're the Best Break This Old Heart Ever Had," "My First Taste of Texas," and "After All" on MCA, and "You Turn Me On (Like a Radio)" and "Nights" on RCA. He also worked as an actor, but achieved his greatest recognition as a songwriter, composing "The Man That Turned My Mama On" (a smash country hit for Tanya Tucker in

1974) and "Mammas, Don't Let Your Babies Grow Up to Be Cowboys" (a top country hit for Waylon Jennings and Willie Nelson in 1978). Since 1986, Ed Bruce has concentrated on his acting career.

Arkansan Charlie Rich became a regular Sun sessions pianist in 1958, recording with Jerry Lee Lewis, Johnny Cash, Warren Smith, and Billy Lee Riley, among others. He also wrote "Breakup" for Jerry Lee Lewis and "The Ways of a Woman in Love" for Johnny Cash. Rich made solo recordings for Sun in 1959, eventually achieving a major pop hit, "Lonely Weekends," on its subsidiary label, Phillips International, in 1960. Subsequent singles failed to become hits and Rich left Sun in 1964. He later scored a major pop hit with "Mohair Sam" on Smash Records in 1965 and broke through as a country crooner on Epic Records with the top country and major pop hit "Behind Closed Doors," followed by the top pop and country hit "The Most Beautiful Girl." Smash country hits continued through 1979, including the top hits "She Called Me Baby" (1974) and "Rollin' with the Flow" (1977), but Charlie Rich never made the country charts after 1981.

Some of Sun Records' tamest rockabilly came from Ray Smith and Carl Mann. In 1960, Smith achieved a major pop hit with "Rockin' Little Angel" on Judd, and Mann managed a major pop hit with "Mona Lisa" on Phillips International.

With the exception of Decca's Bill Haley and the Comets, Columbia Records was the first major label to record rockabilly. Marty Robbins, signed to Columbia in 1951, recorded early versions of "That's All Right" and Chuck Berry's "Maybellene" (near-smash country hits in early and late 1955, respectively), as well as "Pretty Mama," "Tennessee Toddy," and "Respectfully Miss Brooks." He soon scored pop and country hits with "Singing the Blues" and "A White Sport Coat (and a Pink Carnation)," before recording the western hits "El Paso" and "Big Iron" and enjoying an enormously successful career in country-and-western music.

Although they never enjoyed national success, two of Columbia's mid-'50s acts, Sid King and the Five Strings and the Collins Kids, recorded some of the fiercest rockabilly ever released by a major label. Sid King and the Five Strings signed with Starday Records in 1954, soon graduating to Columbia. There they recorded rockabilly classics such as "Drinkin' Wine Spo-Dee-Ooo-Dee," "Sag, Drag and Fall," and "Good Rockin' Baby" through 1959. Oklahomans Larry and Lorrie Collins moved to California in the early '50s and became regulars on the *Town Hall Party* television show. Signed to Columbia Records as the Collins Kids in 1955 at the ages of eleven and thirteen, respectively, the brother-sister act recorded white hot rockabilly, often accompanied by guitar wizard Joe Maphis. Never achieving a national hit, their rockabilly classics included "Just Because," "Hoy Hoy," "Whistle Bait," "Mercy," "Party," and Larry's instrumental duet with Maphis, "Hurricane," all contained on their sole 1958 album. The act broke up in 1959 when Lorrie got married; Larry later cowrote the smash country hits "Delta Dawn" (Tanya Tucker, 1972) and "You're the Reason God Made Oklahoma" (David Frizzell and Shelly West, 1981). During the '70s, the Collinses performed as a lounge act, retiring in 1987, but returning to rockabilly in 1992.

Other important rockabilly recordings on Columbia included Bobby Lord's "Everybody's Rockin' But Me," Werly Fairburn's "Everybody's Rockin'," and Ronnie Self's unrestrained "Bop-a-Lena" (a minor 1958 pop hit written by Mel Tillis and Webb Pierce). Missourian Ronnie Self, who had earlier recorded for ABC ("Pretty Bad Blues") and later recorded for Decca and Kapp, also wrote a number of pop hits for Brenda Lee, including the smashes ""Sweet Nothins" and "Everybody Loves Me But You," and the top hit "I'm Sorry."

RCA, after winning the bidding contest for Elvis Presley, recorded rockabilly by Janis Martin and Ric Cartey. Born in Virginia, Janis Martin toured with Hank Snow and performed on television and the *Grand Ole Opry*. Billed as "the female Elvis," Martin came closest to scoring a national hit with 1956's "Will You, Willyum." Her recordings for RCA through 1958 included "Drugstore Rock and Roll," Roy Orbison's "Ooby Dooby," "My Boy Elvis," "Love Me to Pieces," and "Bang Bang." However, she soon dropped out of music and, after an attempted comeback on Palette Records in 1960 failed, she retired. Ric Cartey, from Georgia, scored his biggest success as coauthor of Sonny James's top pop and country and smash R&B hit "Young Love." His releases on RCA in 1957–58 included the raunchy "Heart Throb," "Born to Love One Woman," and "Mellow Down Easy," but he never achieved a national hit.

Many other labels had their country acts record a rockabilly song or two. Many stars who became country legends—such as Conway Twitty—began their careers by riding the rockabilly wagon. There were also dozens of "one-hit wonders," who made a single seminal recording that has become prized by collectors before dropping off into obscurity.

Several independent labels were important in the development of rockabilly, including King, Roulette, Starday, Imperial, and Liberty. King Records' principal rockabilly artists were Mac Curtis and Charlie Feathers. Texan Mac Curtis recorded rockabilly favorites such as "If I Had Me a Woman," "Grandaddy's Rockin'," "Say So," and "Little Miss Linda" in the mid '50s. He was in the military service from 1957 to 1960 and later worked as a disc jockey, scoring a moderate country hit with Carl Perkins's "Honey Don't" in 1970.

Mississippian Charlie Feathers first recorded for Sun in 1955 ("Defrost Your Heart") and cowrote Elvis Presley's first top country-and-western hit, "I Forgot to Remember to Forget." He also recorded for Memphis labels such as Meteor ("Tongue Tied Jill") and Memphis ("Wild Wild Party"), but achieved his greatest recognition with King. His classic recordings for King included "Everybody's Loving My Baby," "One Hand Loose," and "I Can't Hardly Stand It." Benefiting from the rockabilly revival of the early '80s, Feathers recorded his first major label album in 1991, and continues to be popular as a live act, primarily in Europe.

Guitarist Buddy Knox (from Texas) and bassist Jimmy Bowen (from New Mexico) formed the Rhythm Orchids at West Texas State University in 1956, recording "I'm Stickin' with You" and "Party Doll" (the first attributed to Bowen, the second to Knox) at Norman Petty's Clovis, New Mexico, studio. Initially released on Triple-D Records, the songs were released nationally by Roulette Records. In early 1957, both became hits. Through 1958, Bowen managed several more minor pop hits, while Knox scored major hits with "Rock Your Little Baby to Sleep," "Hula Love," and "Somebody Touched Me," originally recorded by Ruth Brown in 1954. On his own, Knox achieved a major pop hit with the Clovers' "Lovey Dovey" in late 1960. Bowen later turned to studio work, producing Frank Sinatra, Sammy Davis Jr., and Dean Martin at Reprise. He formed his own Amos label in 1969 and moved to Nashville in 1977. There he served as general manager of MCA Records' Nashville unit until moving to Elektra/Asylum in 1979, signing Hank Williams Jr. and Conway Twitty. In 1984 Jimmy Bowen became the president of MCA Records in Nashville. Other noteworthy rockabilly artists to record for Roulette included Jimmy Lloyd ("Got a Rocket in My Pocket"), Jimmy Isle ("Goin' Wild"), Johnny Strickland ("She's Mine"), and the Rock-a-Teens (the major pop hit "Woo-Hoo" and "Doggone It Baby").

Starday Records made the early recordings of Sid King and the Five Strings, Sleepy La Beef, Rudy Grayzell ("Duck Tail"), and guitarist Link "Lucky" Wray. Starday's most prolific rockabilly artists were Sonny Fisher ("Rockin' Daddy," "Rockin' and a-Rollin' ") and Cajun Link Davis ("16 Chicks," "Don't Big Shot Me").

Ricky Nelson, after a brief stint with Verve Records, recorded rockabilly for Imperial Records early in his career, most notably Johnny and Dorsey Burnette's "Waitin' in School" and "Believe What You Say," Dorsey Burnette's "It's Late," and Johnny Burnette's "Just a Little Too Much." The Burnette Brothers ("Warm Love") and Dorsey Burnette ("Way in the Middle of the Night") also recorded for Imperial. Imperial's other principal rockabilly artist was Texan Bob Luman. In 1957 he recorded "Red Cadillac and a Black Mustache," "All Night Long," and "Red Hot." Luman's biggest success came in 1960 on Warner Brothers with the satirical near-smash pop and country hit "Let's Think About Living," written by Boudleaux Bryant. In 1972 Luman scored a smash country hit with "Lonely Women Make Good Lovers" on Epic Records. Other Imperial rockabilly artists included Lew Williams ("Cat Talk," "Bop Bop Ba Doo Bop," and "Gone Ape Man"), Dennis Herrold ("Hip Hip Baby"), Laura Lee Perkins ("Kiss Me Baby"), and Bill Allen ("Please Give Me Something"). Liberty Records recorded Eddie Cochran and the early '60s hits of Johnny Burnette (see separate entries).

Other independent labels were less involved in the recording of rockabilly. Chess Records recorded Dale Hawkins from 1956 to 1961. He scored a smash R&B and major pop hit with "Susie-Q," featuring guitarist James Burton, in the summer of 1957. Chess also recorded Bobby Sisco ("Go Go Go"), Billy Barrix ("Cool Off Baby"), and Rusty York ("Sugaree," a minor pop hit in 1959). Its Argo subsidiary recorded Mel Robbins ("Save It") and distributed Eddie Fontaine's minor pop hit from 1958, "Nothin' Shakin'." Dot Records recorded John Ashley ("Born to Rock") and Nervous Norvus (1956's near-smash pop novelty hit "Transfusion"), and distributed Sanford Clark's near-smash 1956 pop hit "The Fool" and Robin Luke's smash 1958 pop hit "Susie Darlin'." Era recorded Glen Glenn ("Everybody's Movin'") and the '60s pop hits of Dorsey Burnette. Fraternity recorded Dale Wright ("She's Neat," a moderate pop hit in 1958)) and Sparkle Moore ("Rock-a-Bop"), while Rockin' Records recorded Ronnie Dawson ("Rockin' Bones"). Dawson reemerged in the mid '80s, recording in England in the late '80s and touring again in the mid '90s.

Several rockabilly artists recorded for a number of different labels. Philadelphian Charlie Gracie first recorded for Cadillac Records ("Boogie Woogie Blues" and "Rockin' and Rollin'") and was a regular on television's *American Bandstand* from 1952 to 1958. He recorded the original version of "Butterfly," a top pop and near-smash R&B hit on Cameo Records in 1957 that was instantly covered by pop crooner Andy Williams. Gracie toured Great Britain in 1957, 1979, and 1993. Arkansan Bobby Lee Trammell recorded for Fabor ("Shirley Lee" and "You Mostest Girl"), Atlanta ("Come On"), and Hot ("Betty Jean").

Sleepy La Beef, born in Arkansas, first recorded for Starday around 1957 ("I'm Through") and subsequently recorded for Mercury ("I'm Through") and Crescent ("Turn Me Loose"). He moved to Nashville in 1964 and eventually scored a minor country hit with "Every Day" on Columbia in 1968. He switched to Plantation in 1969, managing a minor country hit for the label with "Blackland Farmer" in 1971. He recorded for the revived Sun Records label in the '70s and signed with Rounder Records in 1980. He continues to tour to this day.

Texan Ray Campi recorded rockabilly in the late '50s for TNT, Dot, D, and Domino Records. He moved to southern California in the mid '60s and dropped out of the music business to teach junior high school. In the '70s he returned to rockabilly, forming Ray Campi and the Rockabilly Rebels and recording a number of albums for the Rollin' Rock label. He has since recorded for Rounder, Flying Fish, and Mouth Piece Records.

Although rockabilly was dominated by young white males, several black artists and a number of women also recorded rockabilly. Important black contributors to rockabilly included Billy "The Kid" Emerson, G. L. Crockett, and Al Downing. Emerson recorded for Sun, VeeJay, and Chess, and wrote the oft-covered rockabilly classic "Red Hot." Crockett recorded the rockabilly favorite "Look Out Mabel" in 1958. Pianist Big Al Downing recorded a number of dynamic rock-and-roll songs in the '50s and backed a number of the recordings of Wanda Jackson.

Female rockabilly performers included Wanda Jackson, Janis Martin, and Lorrie Collins, with her brother Larry. Brenda Lee and Patsy Cline recorded rockabilly early in their careers. Other women rockabilly artists included Jo Ann Campbell ("Rock and Roll Love"), Jean Chapel ("I Won't Be Rockin' Tonight"), Sparkle Moore ("Rock-a-Bop"), Martha Carson ("Now Stop"), Alvadean Coker ("We're Gonna Bop"), and Jackie Dee (née

DeShannon) ("Buddy"). Many of these artists abandoned the rockabilly style after it was past its prime, and recorded in either a pop or country vein with greater or lesser success.

Although rockabilly's popularity had faded by the end of the '50s, the music enjoyed a remarkable renewal of interest on several occasions. Shakin' Stevens recorded rockabilly in England in the '70s and '80s, and Robert Gordon recorded with Link Wray in the late '70s. Dave Edmunds promoted rockabilly in the early '80s, producing the Stray Cats, who scored smash pop hits with "Rock This Town," "Stray Cat Strut," and "(She's) Sexy + 17" in 1982–83. Contemporary rockabilly acts include Big Sandy and His Fly-Rite Boys and Rosie Flores; recent groups that show the influence of rockabilly include the Blasters, the Fabulous Thunderbirds, the Georgia Satellites, the Beat Farmers, Jason and the Scorchers, Los Lobos, Omar and the Howlers, the Cigar Store Indians, and the Dave and Deke Combo.

SUN ROCKABILLY ACTS

Roy Orbison

The Sun Years	Rhino	70916	'89	CS/CD

The Sun Rhythm Section

Old Time Rock 'n Roll	Flying Fish	90445	'87	CS

Sonny Burgess

We Wanna Boogie	Rounder	36	'90	CS/CD
Tennessee Border	Hightone	8039	'92	CS/CD
Sonny Burgess Has Still Got It	Rounder	3144	'96	CD

Billy Lee Riley

Blue Collar Blues	Hightone	8040	'92	CS/CD

Charlie Rich

The Sun Sessions	Varese Sarabande	5695	'96	CD

Sun Records

Sun's Gold Records	Sun	1250	'61	LP
Sun Rockabilly, Vol. 1	Sun	1010		LP
The Sun Story	Rhino	(2)71103	'86	CS
	Rhino	75884	'86	CD
The Sun Records Collection	Rhino	(3)71780	'94	CD
Sun's Greatest Hits	RCA	66059	'92	CS/CD
Sun Rockabilly: The Classic Recordings	Rounder	37	'90	LP/CS/CD

OTHER ROCKABILLY STARS

Marty Robbins

The Essential 1951–1982	Columbia/Legacy	(2)48537	'91	CS/CD
The Story of My Life: The Best of, 1952–1965	Columbia/Legacy	64763	'96	CS/CD

Sid King and His Five Strings

Rockin' on the Radio	Schoolkids'	1549	'96	CD

Mac Curtis

Rockabilly Uprising: The Best of Mac Curtis	Rollin' Rock	6601	'97	CD

Charlie Feathers

Charlie Feathers	Elektra/Nonesuch	61147	'91	CD

Buddy Knox and Jimmy Bowen

The Rhythm Orchids: The Complete Roulette Recordings	Sequel	(2)278		CD

Dale Hawkins

Oh! Susie Q: The Best of Dale Hawkins	Chess	9356	'95	CD

Glen Glenn

The Glen Glenn Story/ Everybody's Movin' Again	Ace	403	'92	CD

Dale Wright

She's Neat — The Fraternity Sides	Ace	402		CD

Ronnie Dawson

Rockinitis (rec. in England in 1989)	Crystal Clear Sound	9619	'96	CD
Just Rockin' & Rollin'	Upstart	032	'96	CD

Charlie Gracie

Live at the Stockton Globe	Schoolkids'	1547	'96	CD

Sleepy LaBeef

It Ain't What You Eat . . . It's the Way How You Chew It	Rounder	3052	'80	CS
Electricity	Rounder	3070	'82	CS
Nothin' But the Truth	Rounder	3072	'87	CS/CD
Strange Things Happen	Rounder	3129	'94	CS/CD
I'll Never Lay My Guitar Down	Rounder	3142	'96	CD

Ray Campi

Gone, Gone, Gone	Rounder	3047	'80	CS
Ray Campi with Friends in Texas	Flying Fish	70518	'91	CS/CD
Train Rhythm Blue	Mouth Piece	6018	'98	CD

COMPILATIONS

Rockabilly Stars, Vol. 1	Sony	75064	'92	CS/CD
	K-Tel	75064	'95	CS/CD
Rockabilly Stars, Vol. 2	Sony	75065	'92	CS/CD
	K-Tel	75065	'95	CS/CD
Rockabilly Stars, Vol. 3	Sony	37984	'92	CS/CD
	K-Tel	37984	'95	CS/CD
Get Hot or Go Home: Vintage RCA Rockabilly '56–'59	Country Music Foundation	014	'89	CS/CD
Rockabilly Classics (1956–1961)	MCA	5935	'87	CD
Wild, Wild Young Women	Rounder	1031	'87	LP/CS
Let's Have a Party: The Rockabilly Influence	Capitol	12455	'81	LP/CS
Rarest Rockabilly & Hillbilly Boogie	Ace	44		LP
The Best of Ace Rockabilly	Ace	45		LP
Rockabilly Shakeout, No. 1!	Ace	191	'87	CD
Memphis Rockabilly	Ace	197		LP
The '50s: Rockabilly Fever	Ace	218	'87	LP/CD
All-American Rock 'n Roll From Fraternity Records	Ace	316		CD
El Primativo: American Rock 'n' Roll & Rockabilly	Ace	473	'93	CD

Get With the Beat: The Mar-Vel Masters (originally released 1952–1966)	Rykodisc	20126	'89	CS/CD
Rock This Town: Rockabilly Hits, Vol. 1	Rhino	70741	'91	CS/CD
Rock This Town: Rockabilly Hits, Vol. 2	Rhino	70742	'91	CS/CD
Rockin' in the Farmhouse: Original Rockabilly and Chicken Bop	Hollowbody	12001		CD
Rockin' in the Farmhouse: Original Rockabilly and Chicken Bop, Vol. 2	Hollowbody	12002	'92	CD
Rockin' in the Farmhouse: Original Rockabilly and Chicken Bop: Wail Man Wail!	Hollowbody	12003		CD
Rockabilly Memories	Intersound	5005	'92	CD
Memphis Rocks: Rockabilly in Memphis 1954–1968	Smithsonian	051	'92	CD
Rockabilly Riot	K-Tel	3436	'95	CS/CD
Twenty Great Rockabilly Hits of the 50s	Cascade	1003		LP
Twenty Great Rockabilly Hits of the 50s, Vol. 2	Cascade	1009		LP
Rockabilly Psychosis & the Garage Disease	Big Beat	18		LP

That'll Flat Get It Series

Vol. 1: Rockabilly from the Vaults of RCA Records	Bear Family	(2)15622		CD
Vol. 2: Rockabilly from the Vaults of US Decca Records	Bear Family	15623	'92	CD
Vol. 3: Rockabilly from the Vaults of Capitol Records	Bear Family	15624	'92	CD
Vol. 4: Rockabilly from the Vaults of Festival Records	Bear Family	15630	'94	CD
Vol. 6: Rockabilly from the Vaults of US Decca Records	Bear Family	15733	'94	CD
Vol. 7: Rockabilly from the Vaults of M-G-M Records	Bear Family	15789	'96	CD
Vol. 8: Rockabilly from the Vaults of Abbott, Fabor, Radio Records	Bear Family	15936	'96	CD

ROCKABILLY REVIVALISTS

The Stray Cats

Rock This Town: The Best of	EMI	94975	'90	CS/CD

Big Sandy and His Fly-Rite Boys

Jumping from 6 to 6	Hightone	8053	'94	CS/CD
Swingin' West	Hightone	8064	'95	CS/CD
Feelin' Kinda Lucky	Hightone	8083	'97	CD

Rosie Flores

Rockabilly Filly	Hightone	8067	'95	CS/CD

BIBLIOGRAPHY

Bridgerman, Chuck. *Record Collector's Fact Book: Handbook of Rock & Roll, Rhythm & Blues, and Rockabilly Originals and Reproductions,* Vol. 1. 45 RPM 1952–1965. Westminster, MD: Dis Publishers, distributed by Liberty, 1982.

McNutt, Randy. *We Wanna Boogie: An Illustrated History of the American Rockabilly Movement.* Hamilton, OH: HHP, 1988.

Cooper, B. Lee. *Rockabilly: A Bibliographic Resource Guide.* Metuchen, NJ: Scarecrow, 1990.

Escott, Colin. *Good Rockin' Tonight: Sun Records and the Birth of Rock 'n' Roll.* New York: St. Martin's, 1991.

Morrison, Craig. *Go Cat Go!: Rockabilly Music and Its Makers.* Urbana: University of Illinois Press, 1996.

DOO-WOP

The roots of doo-wop music can be found in the music of the Mills Brothers and the Ink Spots, black vocal groups that enjoyed popularity with both black and white audiences beginning in the '30s and '40s, respectively. Doo-wop was primarily though not exclusively black vocal group music, characterized by group harmony, the use of discrete vocal parts (lead and supporting voices, including tenor, baritone, bass, and falsetto), and the use of nonsense syllables in the supporting vocal parts. The harmonies of doo-wop differed from those of the Mills Brothers and the Ink Spots in that while the earlier groups' harmonies were predominantly hummed, doo-wop harmonies were produced by blowing air out of the mouth, thus the term "blow harmonies." Doo-wop could be performed with subdued musical accompaniment or without musical accompaniment (a cappella). Many of the doo-wop groups began performing literally on street corners, at local social clubs, or in the basements of homes, and this homemade quality added to the charm of the groups—and to their success.

Doo-wop emerged in the late '40s around the time the big bands were dissolving. The earliest successful doo-wop groups were the Ravens and the Orioles. The Ravens, with high tenor Maithe Marshall and bass vocalist Jimmy Ricks, began in New York City in 1945 and first recorded in 1946. Between 1948 and 1950 they scored a series of smash R&B hits such as "Write Me a Letter" (a major pop hit) and "Send for Me If You Need Me," primarily on National Records. They also achieved an R&B smash with "Rock Me All Night Long" on Mercury Records in 1952. The Orioles, with lead vocalist Sonny Til, were formed in Baltimore in 1947, and scored top R&B hits in 1948–49 with "It's Too Soon to Know" (a major pop hit) and "Tell Me So" on Jubilee. They also achieved a top R&B and major pop hit with the classic "Crying in the Chapel" in 1953 on Jubilee.

Doo-wop groups began proliferating in the early '50s, with the most prominent and successful being the Clovers, Billy Ward's Dominoes, and Hank Ballard and the Royals (see separate entries). Lead vocalists for the Dominoes, whose 1951 top R&B and major pop hit "Sixty-Minute Man" is often considered the first rock-and-roll song, were Clyde McPhatter (1950–53) and Jackie Wilson (1953–57), who later enjoyed successful solo careers (see individual entries). A number of other doo-wop groups enjoyed success in the early '50s. The Cardinals were formed in Baltimore in 1946 and scored smash R&B hits on Atlantic Records in 1951, 1952, and, most successfully, 1955, with "The Door Is Still Open." The Five Keys were formed in Virginia in the late '40s and recorded for Aladdin, Capitol, and King Records during the '50s, scoring a top R&B hit with "The Glory of Love" on Aladdin in 1951 and the R&B smash and major pop hit "Ling Ting Tong" on Capitol in 1955. The "5" Royales, from North Carolina, first recorded in 1951, and scored top R&B hits with "Baby, Don't Do It" and "Help Me Somebody" in 1953 on Apollo Records. One of the group's principals, Lowman Pauling, wrote "Dedicated to the One I Love," a smash R&B and pop hit for the Shirelles in 1961. The Spaniels, with lead vocalist James "Pookie" Hudson, were formed in Indiana in 1952, and scored a number of major R&B hits in the early '50s, including the smash R&B and major pop hit classic "Goodnite Sweetheart Goodnite" on Vee-Jay Records in 1954.

Many other early '50s doo-wop groups are remembered as "one-hit wonders." The Harptones, with lead tenor Willie Winfield, began in Harlem in 1953 and recorded for Bruce, Paradise, and Rama Records in the '50s. Although they achieved only one national hit (1961's minor pop hit "What Will I Tell My Heart"), their '50s recordings included "Sunday Kind of Love," "My Memories of You," "Life Is But a Dream," and "That's the Way It Goes." The Chords were formed in the Bronx, New York, in 1954, and scored a smash R&B and pop hit with the classic "Sh-Boom," later covered by the Crew Cuts. The Crows were formed in Harlem in the early '50s and achieved a smash R&B and major pop hit with "Gee" in 1954.

The second generation of doo-wop groups, at least in terms of hit making, included a number of legendary groups. The Penguins, with lead vocalist Cleveland Duncan, were formed in Los Angeles in 1954 and scored a top R&B and near-smash pop hit on Dootone Records with "Earth Angel," cowritten by Jesse Belvin, at year's end. They moved to Mercury Records with the Platters in 1955, and achieved a major R&B hit with "Pledge of Love" on Atlantic in 1957. In 1963 Frank Zappa wrote and produced their cult classic "Memories of El Monte." Otis Williams and the Charms were formed in Cincinnati in 1953, and achieved a series of smash R&B and major pop hits between late 1954 and 1957 on the Deluxe subsidiary of King Records, including the oft-covered "Hearts of Stone," "Ling Ting Tong," and "Ivory Tower."

Lee Andrews and the Hearts began around 1953 in Philadelphia and recorded for Rainbow and Gotham Records before achieving crossover hits on Chess with "Long Lonely Nights" and "Teardrops" in 1957–58. The Flamingos were formed in Chicago in 1952 and recorded for Chance Records in 1953–54. The group scored smash R&B and major pop hits with "I'll Be Home" on Checker Records in 1956 and "I Only Have Eyes for You" on End Records in 1961. Nate Nelson, a member since 1954, joined the Platters in 1966, and the Flamingos continued to record well into the '70s.

The Cadillacs were formed in Harlem in 1953 and were one of the first vocal groups to feature extensive use of choreography on stage. Recording one of the many versions of "Gloria" in 1954, the Cadillacs scored a smash R&B and major pop hit with "Speedo" in 1956, hitting in both fields with "Peek-a-Boo" in 1958–59. Lead vocalist Earl "Speedo" Carroll later joined the Coasters.

The years 1955–59 are considered the classic years of doo-wop. Among the groups active during this period were the Moonglows, the Platters, Frankie Lymon and the Teenagers, the Coasters, the Del Vikings, and Little Anthony and the Imperials (see separate entries). Among other popular groups were the Jacks and the Cadets, originally formed as a gospel group in Los Angeles in 1947 performing as the Santa Monica Soul Seekers. In 1954 they began recording as the Cadets (with lead vocals by Aaron Collins or Will "Dub" Jones) for Modern Records and as the Jacks (with lead vocals by Willie Davis) for its subsidiary label RPM. The Jacks scored a smash R&B hit with "Why Don't You Write Me" in 1955, and the Cadets achieved a smash R&B and major pop hit with the novelty song "Stranded in the Jungle" in 1956. Collins and Davis later manned the Flares, who managed a major pop and R&B hit with "Foot Stompin'" in 1961. Jones was a member of the Coasters from 1958 to 1968.

The Jayhawks began in Los Angeles in 1956 and scored a near-smash R&B and major pop hit with their version of "Stranded in the Jungle" only days after the Cadets' original was released. They changed their name to the Vibrations in 1960 and scored major pop and R&B hits with "The Watusi" in 1961 and "My Girl Sloopy" in 1964. They also recorded as the Marathons in 1961, achieving a major pop and R&B hit with "Peanut Butter."

The Heartbeats were formed in 1954 in Queens, New York, and scored a smash R&B hit with "A Thousand Miles Away" on Rama Records in late 1956. The group disbanded in 1960, and vocalist James "Shep" Sheppard subsequently formed Shep and the Limelites, achieving a smash pop and R&B hit with "Daddy's Home" on Hull Records in 1961.

The Nutmegs and the Five Satins were from Connecticut. The Nutmegs were formed in 1954 and scored a smash R&B hit with "Story Untold" and a major R&B hit with "Ship of Love" on Herald Records in 1955. The Five Satins scored smash R&B and major pop hits with lead singer Fred Parris's classic "In the Still of the Nite" in 1956 and "To the Aisle" (with Bill Baker on lead vocals) in 1957.

Later black doo-wop groups included the El Dorados, the Cleftones, the Hollywood Flames, the Olympics, the Falcons, and the Crests. The El Dorados, formed in Chicago in 1952, scored a top R&B and major pop hit with "At My Front Door" in 1955 and a near-smash R&B hit with "I'll Be Forever Loving You" in 1956. The Cleftones, formed in Queens, New York, in 1955, scored near-smash R&B hits on Gee Records with "Little Girl of Mine" in 1956 and "Heart and Soul" in 1961.

The Hollywood Flames, formed in Los Angeles by Bobby Day, achieved a smash R&B and major pop hit with "Buzz-Buzz-Buzz" in 1957. As Bobby Day and the Satellites, the group recorded the original version of Day's "Little Bitty Pretty One," a smash pop and R&B hit for Thurston Harris in 1957. Day alone scored a top R&B and smash pop hit with "Rock-in Robin" in 1958. The Olympics, formed in Compton, California, in 1954, had a near-smash pop and R&B hit with "Western Movies" in 1958. They later scored a R&B near-smash with "Big Boy Pete" in 1960, and major R&B hits with "The Bounce" in 1963 and "Baby, Do the Philly Dog" in 1966.

The Falcons were formed in Detroit in 1955 with Eddie Floyd and Joe Stubbs, the brother of the Four Tops' Levi Stubbs. With Stubbs on lead vocals, the group scored a smash R&B and major pop hit with "You're So Fine" in 1959. Wilson Pickett joined the group in 1960 and performed lead vocals on the 1962 R&B smash "I Found a Love." Both Eddie Floyd and Wilson Pickett enjoyed success as soul artists in the '60s, Floyd on Stax Records and Pickett on Atlantic Records.

The Crests started out in Manhattan as a black vocal quartet, but added white, Brooklyn-born lead singer Johnny Maestro in 1956. They scored a smash pop and R&B hit with "16 Candles" in 1958–59 and major pop and R&B hits with "Six Nights a Week" and "The Angels Listened In" in 1959. The following year, they had major pop hits with "Step by Step" and "Trouble in Paradise." Johnny Maestro, born John Mastrangelo, left the group in 1960 for a solo career, achieving a major pop hit with "Model Girl" in 1961. Maestro also lead the vocal quartet the Del Satins, who backed Dion DiMucci in his early solo career. In 1967 the Del Satins joined the band the Rhythm Method to form the Brooklyn Bridge, who scored a smash pop hit with "The Worst That Could Happen" at the end of 1968.

Just as in the early '50s, there were scores of groups who scored only one hit before disappearing from the charts. The most curious were the Dells, formed in Illinois in the early '50s. They first recorded for Chess Records as the El-Rays in 1953 and switched to VeeJay Records in 1955, where they scored a smash R&B hit with the classic "Oh What a Night" in 1956. Except for one personnel change in 1960, the group remained intact into the '80s, achieving their biggest success in the late '60s and early '70s on Cadet Records with such hits as "Stay in My Corner," "Always Together," a remake of "Oh What a Night," and "Give Your Baby a Standing Ovation."

Among the black doo-wop groups that managed only one national hit were a number of groups from the New York area. These included the Charts (1957's "Deserie"), the Rays (1957's classic "Silhouettes"), Little Joe and the Thrillers (1957's "Peanuts"), the Monotones (1958's classic "Book of Love"), the Danleers (1958's "One Summer Night"), and the Fiestas (1959's "So Fine"). The Dubs scored the biggest of their three hits with "Could This Be Magic" in late 1957, and the integrated group the Impalas (lead vocalist Joe "Speedo" Frazier was black) achieved a smash pop and major R&B hit with "Sorry (I Ran All the Way Home)" in 1959. Other "one-hit wonders" included Philadelphia's Turbans (1955's "When You Dance") and Silhouettes (1958's classic "Get a Job"), Louisiana's Bobby Mitchell and the Toppers (1956's "Try Rock and Roll"), Los Angeles's Shields (1958's "You Cheated") and Eugene Church and the Fellows (1959's "Pretty Girls Everywhere"), and the Pastels (1958's "Been So Long").

Still other significant black doo-wop groups never achieved a national hit. These included Vernon Green and the Medallions ("Buick '59"), the racially integrated group Don Julian and the Meadowlarks ("Heaven and Paradise"), Earl Lewis and the Channels ("The Closer You Are"), the Laddins, and the Solitaires.

Women were little represented in the ranks of doo-wop groups; the few exceptions included Shirley Gunter and the Queens, the Bobbettes, and the Poni-Tails. The most prominent female doo-wop group of the '50s, the Chantels, is covered separately in this book.

Shirley Gunter and the Queens were formed in Los Angeles and scored a near-smash R&B hit with "Oop Shoop" in 1954. Shirley's brother was Cornelius Gunter, later with the Coasters, and the Queens included Zola Taylor, later with the Platters. The school-aged Bobbettes were initially formed in New York City as the Harlem Queens. They achieved a top R&B and smash pop hit with "Mr. Lee" in 1956, supposedly inspired by their school teacher of the same name, later managing a minor pop hit with the follow-up "I Shot Mr. Lee" in 1960. The Poni-Tails, a white female trio formed in Ohio, scored a near smash pop and R&B hit with "Born Too Late" in 1958.

A number of doo-wop groups contained male and female members. These included the Sensations, the Six Teens, the Tuneweavers, the Quintones, the Fleetwoods, and, in the '60s, the Essex and the Ad Libs. The Sensations, with colead vocalists Yvonne Baker and Tommy Wicks, achieved a major R&B hit with "Please Mr. Disc Jockey" in 1956. Reformed in 1961 with Baker and one other original member, the Sensations scored a smash pop and R&B hit with "Let Me In" in 1962. The Six Teens (three men and three women) were formed in Los Angeles in 1956, soon scoring a near-smash R&B and major pop hit with "A Casual Look." The Tuneweavers (two men and two women), with lead vocalist Margo Sylvia, began in Massachusetts in 1956 and achieved a smash pop and R&B hit with "Happy, Happy Birthday Baby" in 1957. The Quintones (four women and two men, including lead singer Roberta Haymon and pianist Ronnie Scott) were formed in Pennsylvania and scored a smash R&B and major pop hit with "Down the Aisle of Love" in 1958.

The white trio the Fleetwoods (one man and two women) were formed in Olympia, Washington, in 1958. They scored a series of hits between 1959 and 1962, including the top pop and smash R&B hits "Come Softly to Me" and "Mr. Blue." Subsequent pop-only hits included "Runaround," "Tragedy," and "(He's) the Great Impostor." The Essex were formed by four black Marines at Camp LeJeune, North Carolina, in 1962, soon adding white female lead vocalist Anita Humes. In 1963 they scored a top pop and R&B hit with "Easier Said Than Done" and a major pop and R&B hit with "A Walkin' Miracle." The Ad Libs (four men plus lead singer Mary Ann Thomas) achieved a smash R&B and major pop hit with "The Boy from New York City" in 1965.

In the latter half of the '50s, a number of Italian-American groups, primarily based in the New York area, began recording doo-wop. The most popular of these, Dion and the Belmonts, are covered in this volume. Other important doo-wop groups formed by Italians included the Elegants, formed on Staten Island in 1957. Comprising veterans of other groups, the Elegants scored a top pop and R&B hit with "Little Star" in 1958. The Bell-Notes were formed on Long Island, achieving a smash pop and major R&B hit with "I've

Had It" in 1959. The Duprees, formed in Jersey City, New Jersey, had major pop-only hits with "You Belong to Me," "My Own True Love," and "Have You Heard" in 1962–63.

Lesser-known Italian-American groups included the Mystics, the Passions, and the Classics, all formed in Brooklyn. In 1959 the Mystics had a major pop-only hit with "Hushabye," and the Passions had a minor pop-only hit with "Just to Be with You." The Classics had a major pop-only hit with "Till Then" in 1963. The Capris and Randy and the Rainbows were formed in Queens, New York. The Capris, originally formed in 1958, reunited in 1961 when their previously released "There's a Moon Out Tonight" became a smash pop and major R&B hit. Randy and the Rainbows scored a major pop and R&B hit with "Denise" in 1963. The Earls and the Regents were formed in the Bronx in 1957 and 1958, respectively. The Regents scored a major pop and near-smash R&B hit with "Barbara-Ann" in 1961. The Earls achieved a major pop and R&B hit with "Remember Then" in 1963.

The most successful and popular Italian doo-wop group of the '60s was originally formed in Newark, New Jersey, as the Four Lovers in 1955. They managed a minor pop-only hit with "You're the Apple of My Eye" in 1956. Adding Bob Gaudio of the Royal Teens in 1959, the group changed its name to the Four Seasons in 1961 and began an incredible string of hits in 1962 with the top pop and R&B hits "Sherry" and "Walk Like a Man."

Other white groups recorded in the doo-wop style in the late '50s, including two Canadian groups, the Crew Cuts and the Diamonds, formed in Toronto in 1952 and 1953, respectively. They both served as a cover groups for Mercury Records, making white versions of black hits that the label could then market to the mainstream, pop listener. Beginning in 1954, the Crew Cuts covered "Sh-Boom" (the Chords), "Oop Shoop" (Shirley Gunter and the Queens), "Earth Angel" (the Penguins), "Ko Ko Mo" (Gene and Eunice), "A Story Untold" (the Nutmegs), and "Gum Drop" (the Charms). They disbanded in 1963. Beginning in 1955, the Diamonds covered "Why Do Fools Fall in Love" (Frankie Lymon and the Teenagers), "Church Bells May Ring" (the Willows), "Love, Love, Love" (the Clovers), their biggest hit, "Little Darlin'" (the Gladiolas), "Silhouettes" (the Rays), their second biggest hit, "The Stroll" (cowritten by Clyde Otis, Brook Benton's songwriting partner), and "One Summer Night" (the Danleers). The Diamonds continue to perform today.

White doo-wop groups of the late '50s who performed their own material, rather than just covering black acts, included Danny and the Juniors, the Mello-Kings, and the Fireflies. Danny and the Juniors were formed in Philadelphia in 1955 and scored a top pop and R&B hit with "At the Hop" in 1957 and a major pop and R&B hit with "Rock and Roll Is Here to Stay" in 1958. The Mello-Kings, from upstate New York, managed a minor pop hit with "Tonite, Tonite" in 1957. The Fireflies produced a major pop hit with "You Were Mine" in 1959.

Two other white vocal groups included members that went on to later success. The Royal Teens scored a smash pop and R&B hit in 1958 with the novelty song "Short Shorts." Member Bob Gaudio left in 1959 to join the group that would become the Four Seasons, and was replaced for a short time by Al Kooper, later a noted session musician and founder of Blood, Sweat and Tears. In 1958 the Los Angeles trio the Teddy Bears scored a top pop and major R&B hit with "To Know Him Is to Love Him." The group included Phil Spector, who later formed Philles Records and achieved enormous success in the first half of the '60s as a producer.

The turn of the decade saw a few more white doo-wop groups hit the charts. In 1959 the Pittsburgh quintet the Skyliners, with Jimmy Beaumont on lead vocals, achieved a smash R&B and major pop hit with "Since I Don't Have You" and a major pop and R&B hit with "This I Swear." The Tokens were originally formed in Brooklyn in 1955 with Hank Medress and Neil Sedaka (later a noted songwriter and performer in the '60s). Medress reformed the group with new members in 1960 and in 1961 they scored a major pop hit with "Tonight I Fell in Love" and a top pop and near-smash R&B hit with "The Lion Sleeps Tonight" (based on the Weavers' early '50s folk hit "Wimoweh"), used years later in the animated movie *The Lion King*. The Dovells were formed in Philadelphia with Len Barry as one of its members. They achieved smash pop and near-smash R&B hits with "Bristol Stomp" and "You Can't Sit Down" in 1961 and 1963, respectively, and managed major pop-only hits with "Bristol Twistin' Annie" and "Hully Gully Baby" in 1962. Len Barry left in late 1963 and scored a smash pop and major R&B hit with "1-2-3" in 1965.

By 1960 the most popular era of doo-wop had ended. Nonetheless, the tradition was maintained into the '60s with such groups as Maurice Williams and the Zodiacs, the Marcels, the Jive Five, and the Rivingtons. As the Gladiolas, Maurice Williams and the Zodiacs had achieved a major R&B hit with "Little Darlin'" in 1957. Changing their name in 1959, the group scored a top pop and smash R&B hit with the classic "Stay" in 1960. The racially integrated Marcels achieved hits with doo-wop versions of two standards in 1961: "Blue Moon" became a top pop and R&B hit and "Heartaches" was a near-smash pop and major R&B hit. The Jive Five scored a top R&B and smash pop hit with "My True Story" in 1961, and the Rivington's achieved minor pop hits in 1962–63 with the outrageous "Papa-Oom-Mow-Mow" and "The Bird Is the Word."

Many doo-wop groups of the early '60s managed only one hit. The Blue Notes achieved a major R&B hit with "My Hero" on Val-ue Records in 1960. Originally formed in 1954 in Philadelphia, the Blue Notes persevered through the '60s, adding Teddy Pendergrass in 1970. They enjoyed considerable success as Harold Melvin and the Bluenotes on Philadelphia International Records through 1977.

Further one-hit wonders included the Paradons, who had a major pop and R&B hit in 1960 with "Diamonds and Pearls," and the Shells, who scored a major pop hit with "Baby Oh Baby." The Jarmels achieved a near-smash pop and R&B hit with "A Little Bit of Soap" in 1961. The Halos scored a major pop hit with "Nag," and backed Curtis Lee on his near-smash pop hit "Pretty Little Angel Eyes." Other major pop doo-wop hits in 1961 included the Velvets' "Tonight (Could Be the Night)," the Dreamlovers' "When We Get Married," the Echoes' "Baby Blue," and Little Caesar and the Romans' "Those Oldies But Goodies." The Edsels belatedly scored a major pop hit with "Rama Lama Ding Dong" and backed songwriter-producer Barry Mann's near-smash pop novelty hit, "Who Put the Bomp (in the Bomp, Bomp, Bomp)." In 1961 the Blue Jays managed a moderate pop hit with "Lover's Island," and the Paragons and the Showmen achieved minor pop hits with "If" and "It Will Stand," respectively.

The Castells managed major pop hits with "Sacred" and "So This Is Love" in 1961–62. With the Dukays, Gene Chandler scored a top pop and R&B hit with "Duke of Earl" in 1962. He soon left for a solo career that produced R&B smashes with "Nothing Can Stop Me" (1965), "I Fooled You This Time" (late 1966), and "Groovy Situation" (1970), also major pop hits.

Major pop doo-wop hits of 1962 included the Volumes' "I Love You," the Corsairs' "Smoky Places," and the Majors' "A Wonderful Dream." The Philadelphia-based Orlons scored smash pop and R&B hits with "The Wah Watusi," "Don't Hang Up," and "South Street," and a two-way near-smash with "Not Me" in 1962–63. In 1963 Johnny Cymbal achieved a major pop hit with the novelty song "Mr. Bass Man." The Raindrops, actually songwriters Jeff Barry and Ellie Greenwich, managed a minor pop hit with "What a Guy" and a major pop hit with "The Kind of Boy You Can't Forget" in 1963. In the early '60s, Barry and Greenwich also provided hit compositions to "girl groups" such as the Crystals, the Ronettes, and the Dixie Cups.

The sound and style of doo-wop music were enormously influential on the "girl groups" of the '60s, and virtually all the group recordings for Motown Records in the '60s. The a cappella tradition has been maintained by groups from the Persuasions to the Nylons and the Bobs.

The Ravens

Old Man River	Savoy Jazz	0260	'95	CD
Rarities	Savoy Jazz	0261	'95	CD
The Greatest Group of Them All	Savoy Jazz	0270	'95	CD

Sonny Til and the Orioles

Greatest Hits	Collectables	5014		LP/CS/CD

The Five Keys

Rhythm & Blues Hits Past and Present	King	692		LP/CS/CD

The "5" Royales

Dedicated to You	King	580	'57	LP/CS/CD
The "5" Royales Sing for You	King	616	'59	LP/CS/CD
The "5" Royales	King	678	'60	LP/CS/CD
Monkey Hips & Rice: The "5" Royales Anthology	Rhino	(2)71546	'94	CD

The Spaniels

Golden Hits	Juke Box Treasures	6023	'96	CD

The Harptones

The Harptones, Featuring Willie Winfield, Vol. 1	Relic	5001		LP
Vol. 2	Relic	5003		LP

The Penguins

Golden Classics	Collectables	5045		LP/CS/CD
Earth Angel	Ace	249		CD
The Best of: The Mercury Years	Mercury/Chronicles	532735	'96	CS/CD

Otis Willaims and the Charms

Otis Williams and the Charms	King	570		LP/CS/CD

Lee Andrews and the Hearts

Gotham Recording Sessions	Collectables	5003		LP/CS/CD
Biggest Hits	Collectables	5028		LP/CS/CD

The Flamingos

Doo Bop She Bop: The Best of	Rhino	70967	'90	CS/CD
I Only Have Eyes for You	Remember	75036	'96	CD

The Flamingos and the Moonglows

The Flamingos Meet the Moonglows on the Dusty Road of Hits	VeeJay	706	'93	CS

The Cadillacs

The Best of	Rhino	70955	'90	CS/CD

The Jacks

Greatest Hits (1955–1956)	Relic	5023		LP
Jacks Are Wild	Rounder	9016	'88	CS

The Cadets

Greatest Hits (1955–1957)	Relic	5025		LP

The Heartbeats and Shep and the Limelights

The Best of the Heartbeats	Rhino	70952	'90	CS/CD
(includes tracks from Shep and the Limelites)				
Daddy's Home	Remember	75044	'96	CD

The Nutmegs

The Nutmegs Featuring Larry Griffin	Relic	5002		LP

The Five Satins

Greatest Hits, Vol. 1	Relic	5008		LP
Greatest Hits, Vol. 2	Relic	5013		LP
Greatest Hits, Vol. 3	Relic	5024		LP
The Five Satins Sing Their Greatest Hits	Collectables	5017		LP/CS

The Cleftones

The Best of the Cleftones	Rhino	70951	'90	CS/CD

The Hollywood Flames

The Hollywood Flames	Specialty	7021	'92	CD

The Olympics

Do the Hully Gully/Dance by the Light of the Moon/Party Time	Ace	324		CD

The Olympics and the Marathons

The Olympics Meet the Marathons	Collectables	5081		LP/CS/CD

The Falcons

The Falcons' Story, Part One: 1956–1959	Relic	8005		LP
The Falcons' Story, Part Two: 1960–1964	Relic	8006		LP

The Crests

Greatest Hits	Collectables	5009		LP/CS/CD
Best of (featuring Johnny Maestro)	Ace	297		LP/CD
Best of	Rhino	70948		CS/CD

The Charts

Greatest Hits	Collectables	5029		LP/CS/CD

The Danleers

The Best of: The Mercury Years	Mercury/ Chronicles	532732	'96	CS/CD

The Turbans

Greatest Hits (1955–1957)	Relic	5006		LP

Bobby Mitchell and the Toppers

I'm Gonna Be a Wheel Someday	Night Train	7079		CD

Vernon Green and the Medallions

Golden Classics	Collectables	5047		LP/CS/CD

Don Julian and the Meadowlarks

Golden Classics	Collectables	5046		LP/CS/CD
Heaven and Paradise (rec. 1955–1958)	Ace	552	'95	CD

Earl Lewis and the Channels

New York's Finest: The Best of	Collectables	5012		LP/CS/CD

The Laddins

Greatest Hits (1957–1963)	Relic	5018		LP

The Solitaires

Walking Along with	Ace	383		CD

The Fleetwoods

The Best of the Fleetwoods	Rhino	70980	'90	CS/CD
Come Softly to Me: The Very Best of	Dolton	98830	'93	CD

The Duprees

The Best of	Rhino	71004	'90	CS/CD
The Best of	Collectables	5008		LP/CS/CD

The Mystics

16 Golden Classics	Collectables	5043		LP/CS/CD

The Mystics and the Passions

The Mystics and the Passions	Laurie	4010		CS

The Capris

Gotham Recording Stars	Collectables	5000		LP/CS/CD
There's a Moon Out Tonight	Collectables	5016		LP/CS

Randy and the Rainbows

Remember	Rounder	601	'85	LP/CS

The Earls

Remember Then—The Best of	Ace	366		CD

The Mello-Kings

Greatest Hits	Relic	5035		LP
Greatest Hits	Collectables	5020		LP/CS

The Royal Teens

Short Shorts: Golden Classics	Collectables	5078		LP/CS/CD

The Skyliners

Greatest Hits	Original Sound	8873		LP/CS/CD
Since I Don't Have You	Ace	78		CD
Pre-Flight (recorded late '50s-early '60s)	Relic	5053		LP
Encore of Golden Hits-Live	Juke Box Treasures	410	'96	CD

The Tokens

Wimoweh!: The Best of	RCA	66474	'94	CS/CD
The Lion Sleeps Tonight	RCA	66510	'94	CS/CD

Maurice Williams and the Zodiacs

Best	Relic	5017		LP
Best	Collectables	5021		LP/CS
Songs of Love	Laurie	6013		CS/CD

The Marcels

The Best of	Rhino	70953	'90	CS/CD

The Jive Five

Way Back	Rounder	801	'85	LP/CS
Greatest Hits (1961–1963)	Relic	5020		LP
Greatest Hits	Collectables	5022		LP/CS/CD
Our True Story	Ace	76		LP/CD

The Shells

Golden Classics	Collectables	5077		LP/CS/CD

The Blue Notes

The Early Years	Collectables	5006		LP/CS

The Jarmels

Golden Classics	Collectables	5044		LP/CS/CD

The Dreamlovers

When We Get Married	Original Sound	8879		CS
Best of	Collectables	5004		LP/CS/CD
Best, Vol. 2	Collectables	5005		LP/CS/CD

Leon Peels and the Bluejays

Lover's Island	Relic	5054		LP

The Paragons

The Best of the Paragons	Collectables	5035		LP/CS/CD

The Showmen

Golden Classics	Collectables	5162		LP/CS/CD

The Castells

Best of the Castells	ERA	5019	'94	CS/CD
The Sweet Sound of	Collectables	5002		LP/CS/CD

The Volumes

I Love You: Golden Classics	Collectables	5032		LP/CS/CD
The Volumes	Relic	5062		LP

Various Artists' Doo-Wop

Doo Wop Ballads (1954–1961)	Rhino	70181	'87	CS
Doo Wop Uptempo (1955–1963)	Rhino	70183	'87	CS
Doo Wop Ballads (1954–1961), Vol. 2	Rhino	70904	'89	CS
Doo Wop Uptempo (1955–1963), Vol. 2	Rhino	70905	'89	CS
The Doo Wop Box	Rhino	(4)71463	'94	CS/CD
Doo Wop Memories, Vol. 1	Rhino	72156	'95	CS/CD
Doo Wop Memories, Vol. 2	Rhino	72157	'95	CS/CD
The Best of Doo Wop Ballads	Rhino	75763		CD
The Best of Doo Wop Uptempo	Rhino	75764		CD
West Coast Doo-Wop	Ace	87		LP
The '50s: R&B Vocal Groups	Ace	212	'87	CD
Old Town Doo Wop, Vol. 1				
Old Town Doo Wop, Vol. 2	Ace	470	'93	CD
Old Town Doo Wop, Vol. 3	Ace	471	'93	CD
Dootone Doo Wop Vol. 1	Ace	579	'95	CD
The Best of Chess Vocal Groups, Vol. 1	Chess	9282(B)	'88	CD
The Best of Chess Vocal Groups, Vol. 2	Chess	9283(B)	'88	CD
Doo Wop	Specialty	2114		LP/CS
Doo Wop from Dolphins' of Hollywood, Vol. 1	Specialty	2173	'92	CS/CD
Doo Wop from Dolphins' of Hollywood, Vol. 2	Specialty	2174	'92	CS/CD
Hardcore Doo-Wop: In the Hallway-Under the Street Lamp	Specialty	7049	'93	CD
Jubilee & Josie R&B Vocal Groups, Vol. 3	Sequel	756	'96	CD
Jubilee & Josie R&B Vocal Groups, Vol. 4	Sequel	757	'96	CD
More Rockin' Doowop	Sequel	767		CD
Echoes Down the Hall: 16 Original Doo-Wop Classics	Arista	8605	'89	CS/CD
Original Doo-Wop Classics: The '50s: R&B Vocal Groups	Flair	86305	'92	CD
The Best of a Cappella, Vol. 1	Relic	101		LP
The Best of a Cappella, Vol. 4	Relic	104		LP
The Best of a Cappella, Vol. 5	Relic	105		LP
The Best of a Cappella, Vol. 6	Relic	108		LP
A Taste of Doo Wop, Vol. 1	VeeJay	709		CD
A Taste of Doo Wop, Vol. 2	VeeJay	715		CD

13 of the Best Doo Wop Love Songs	Original Sound	8905	CS/CD
13 of the Best Doo Wop Love Songs, Vol. 2	Original Sound	9328	CS/CD
The Doo-Wop Era Harlem N.Y.: 40 Hits	Collectables	(2)7001	LP/CS/CD
Doo-Wop Gold, Vol. 1	Laurie	4014	CS
Philadelphia's Doo-Wop Sound: Swan Masters, Vol. 1	Dee jay	55038	CD
Swing Time Doo Wop	Night Train	7019	CD
Twenty Great Doo Wop Recordings	Cascade	1008	CS/CD

The Golden Group Series

Vol. 1: The Best of Onyx Records, Part 1 (1956–1958)	Relic	5005	LP
Vol. 2: The Best of Vita Records (1955–1957)	Relic	5007	LP
Vol. 3: The Best of Angletone and Atlas Records, Part 1 (1953–1959)	Relic	5012	LP
Vol. 4: The Best of Celeste Records (1956–1957)	Relic	5014	LP
Vol. 5: The Best of Herald Records, Part 1 (1954–1962)	Relic	5015	LP
Vol. 6: The Best of Ember Records, Part 1 (1953–1964)	Relic	5016	LP
Vol. 7: The Best of Winley Records (1956–1960)	Relic	5019	LP
Vol. 8: The Best of Red Top Records (1957–1961)	Relic	5021	LP
Vol. 9: The Best of Club Records (1956–1965)	Relic	5022	LP
Vol. 10: The Best of Tip Top Records (1954–1962)	Relic	5026	LP
Vol. 11: The Best of Relic Records, Part 1 (1962–1963)	Relic	5027	LP
Vol. 12: The Best of Beltone Records (1961–1963)	Relic	5028	LP
Vol. 13: The Best of X-tra Records (1957–1960)	Relic	5029	LP
Vol. 14: The Best of Johnson Records (1957–1960)	Relic	5031	LP
Vol. 15: The Best of Times Square Records (1961–1964)	Relic	5032	LP
Vol. 16: The Best of Rainbow Records (1950–1956)	Relic	5034	LP
Vol. 17: The Best of Relic Records, Part 2 (mid-'60s)	Relic	5036	LP
Vol. 18: The Best of Premium Records (1955–1957)	Relic	5037	LP
Vol. 19: The Best of Jay-Dee Records (1953–1959)	Relic	5038	LP
Vol. 20: The Best of Valmor Records (1960–1962)	Relic	5042	LP
Vol. 21: The Best of Lu-Pine Records (1957–1962)	Relic	5043	LP
Vol. 22: The Best of Klik Records (1956–1958)	Relic	5044	LP
Vol. 23: The Best of Showtime Records (1954–1959)	Relic	5045	LP
Vol. 24: The Best of Bruce Records (1954–1958)	Relic	5046	LP
Vol. 25: The Best of Herald Records, Part 2 (1953–1962)	Relic	5047	LP
Vol. 26: The Best of Ember Records, Part 2 (1956–1964)	Relic	5048	LP
Vol. 27: The Best of Flash Records (1955–1959)	Relic	5049	LP
Vol. 28: The Best of Onyx Records, Part 2 (1956–1958)	Relic	5050	LP
Vol. 29: The Best of Angletone and Atlas Records, Part 2 (1954–1960)	Relic	5051	LP
Vol. 30: The Best of Dig Records (1955–1957)	Relic	5052	LP
Vol. 31: The Best of Specialty Records (1953–1958)	Relic	5054	LP
Vol. 32: The Best of Class Records, Part 1 (1956–1962)	Relic	5055	LP
Vol. 33: The Los Angeles Groups (late '50s)	Relic	5056	LP
Vol. 34: The Best of Class Records, Part 2 (1956–1962)	Relic	5057	LP
Vol. 35: The Best of Club 51 Records (1951–1957)	Relic	5059	LP
Vol. 36: The Best of Swingin' Records (1959–1964)	Relic	5060	LP
Vol. 37: The Best of Milestone Records (1960–1961)	Relic	5061	LP
Vol. 38: The Best of Chex Records (1961–1963)	Relic	5063	LP
Vol. 39: The Best of Nu-Kat Records (1957–1959)	Relic	5065	LP
Vol. 40: The Best of Len Records (1958–1960)	Relic	5066	LP
Vol. 41: The Best of V-Tone Records (1959–1962)	Relic	5067	LP

Contemporary Doo-Wop

Modern A Cappella	Rhino	71083	'92	CS/CD

BIBLIOGRAPHY

Gribin, Anthony Joel, and Matthew M. Schoff. *Doo-Wop: The Forgotten Third of Rock 'n Roll.* Iola, WI: Krause, 1992.

Groia, Philip. *They All Song on the Street Corner: New York City's Rhythm and Blues Vocal Groups of the 1950's.* Setauket, NY: Edmond, 1974.

————. *They All Sang on the Corner: A Second Look at New York City's Rhythm and Blues Vocal Groups.* West Hempstead, NY: P. Dee, 1983.

Gonzalez, Fernando L. *Disco-File: The Discographical Catalog of American Rock and Roll and Rhythm and Blues Vocal Harmony Groups.* Flushing, NY: Gonzalez, 1977.

Warner, Jay. *Billboard Book of American Singing Groups: A History, 1940–1990.* New York: Billboard Books, 1992.

INDEPENDENT RECORD LABELS

Rock 'n' roll, in all its forms, would never have achieved popularity without independent record labels. The major record companies—Columbia, RCA-Victor, Decca, Capitol, Mercury, MGM, and later ABC-Paramount—dominated record sales and geared their product to the mass white audience. They were closely associated with the American Society of Composers, Authors, and Publishers (ASCAP), formed in 1914 to administer and control the publishing and performing rights to songs registered with their organization. For years, the majors and ASCAP ignored "minority" music such as country-and-western and R&B. Radio stations had long resented the high fees that ASCAP charged for the performance of its copyrighted music, and during a tussle with the organization in the '40s, were forced to play only "public domain" works, such as classical tunes or older songs like Stephen Foster's "Oh! Susannah." In self-defense, they pushed for the formation of another music licensing agency, which became Broadcast Music, Inc. (BMI) in 1940. Because ASCAP controlled most mainstream popular music, BMI began aggressively signing minority and country songwriters. This in turn opened the door for the recording of these musical styles.

The most important independent record labels in the dissemination of rock 'n' roll were Atlantic, Chess, and Sun. Atlantic Records was formed in New York City in 1947 by Herb Abramson and Ahmet Ertegun. Initially favoring jazz releases, Atlantic became the most important R&B label of the '50s. The company's acts included groups such as the Clovers, the Drifters, and the Coasters and individuals such as Ray Charles, Ruth Brown, Big Joe Turner, Lavern Baker, and Clyde McPhatter. Jerry Wexler joined as producer-talent scout in 1953 and Neshui Ertegun (Ahmet's brother) joined in 1956. Atlantic Records signed Jerry Leiber and Mike Stoller as the first independent songwriting-production team in 1956. Subsidiary labels Cat and Atco were set up in the mid '50s. In the '60s Atlantic Records distributed the Memphis-based Stax label, and recorded soul acts such as Otis Redding, Sam and Dave, and Solomon Burke. Later in the decade Atlantic signed a variety of white acts such as the Buffalo Springfield, the (Young) Rascals, Led Zeppelin, and Crosby, Stills and Nash. With the takeover of Atlantic by Warner Communications as part of the Warner-Elektra-Atlantic conglomeration in 1968, Atlantic became a major label.

Chess Records was initially formed as Aristocrat Records in 1947 in Chicago by brothers Leonard and Phil Chess. The label became Chess in 1949 and was among the most prominent labels in the promotion of the blues during the '50s. The company's acts included Muddy Waters, Howlin' Wolf, John Lee Hooker, and Elmore James. Willie Dixon became the company's principal songwriter-producer in 1952, and the Checker subsidiary was set up in 1953 to record Little Walter, Lowell Fulson, and Sonny Boy Williamson. Doo-wop acts included the Moonglows on Chess and the Flamingos on Checker. Prominent rock 'n' roll acts included Chuck Berry on Chess and Bo Diddley on Checker. The Argo subsidiary (which later became Cadet) was set up in 1956 to record jazz acts as well as Clarence "Frogman" Henry, the Dells, and Etta James. After the death of Leonard Chess in

1969, the company was sold to GRT and went out of business in 1975, eventually coming under the control of MCA Records.

Sun Records was established in Memphis in 1953 by Sam Phillips. The company recorded a number of blues acts such as Little Junior Parker and Rufus Thomas before concentrating on white acts. The label made the initial recordings of Elvis Presley and established itself as the primary purveyor of rockabilly with Carl Perkins's smash 1956 crossover hit "Blue Suede Shoes." Other artists to start their careers in rockabilly at Sun Records were Johnny Cash, Roy Orbison, and Jerry Lee Lewis, as well as Billy Lee Riley, Sonny Burgess, and Warren Smith. The Phillips International label was established in 1957, achieving hits with Bill Justis, Charlie Rich, and Carl Mann. All of Sun's major acts had left for major labels by 1963, and Phillips sold the remaining Sun masters to Shelby Singleton in 1968.

Important independent record companies in the development of R&B included Apollo Records, based in New York City, and Savoy Records, based in Newark, New Jersey. Apollo Records was formed around 1942 by Ike and Bess Berman. The label recorded gospel acts such as Mahalia Jackson and the Dixie Hummingbirds and R&B acts such as Wynonie Harris and the Five Royales. Savoy Records was formed by Herman Lubinsky around 1942. The label recorded R&B acts such as Johnny Otis, Little Esther, and Nappy Brown.

Three independent Los Angeles labels formed in 1945 were important in the promotion of R&B. Aladdin Records was formed by Eddie and Leo Mesner, and the label's roster included Amos Milburn and Charles Brown. Formed by Jules and Saul Bihari, Modern Records recorded Pee Wee Crayton, John Lee Hooker, Etta James, and the Cadets. Its RPM subsidiary, formed in 1950, recorded the Jacks and the Teen Queens, and recorded B. B. King from 1950 to 1957. Specialty Records, formed by Art Rupe, recorded Joe and Jimmy Liggins, Roy Milton, Percy Mayfield, and, later, Lloyd Price, Little Richard, Larry Williams, and Don and Dewey.

King Records, formed in Cincinnati in 1945 by Sydney Nathan, recorded both R&B and country performers. Prominent R&B acts included Wynonie Harris during his most popular period, Bullmoose Jackson, and Jimmy Witherspoon, as well as the instrumental acts of Bill Doggett and Earl Bostic. Nathan acquired the DeLuxe catalog in 1949, enjoying the label's biggest success with Roy Brown and Otis Williams and the Charms. King Records also made the early recordings of the Platters and recorded Little Willie John for virtually his entire career. The subsidiary label Federal included on its roster a number of early doo-wop groups, including the Dominoes and the Royals/Midnighters (later known as Hank Ballard and the Midnighters), as well as James Brown. King Records also recorded country acts such as the Delmore Brothers, Hank Penny, and Moon Mullican, and rockabilly artists such as Mac Curtis and Charlie Feathers. King Records merged with Starday Records in 1967, and Syd Nathan died in 1968.

Many of the most important independent record companies in the popularization of doo-wop were based in New York City. Jubilee Records, formed in 1948 by Jerry Blaine, recorded the Orioles, while the subsidiary label Josie, formed in 1954, recorded the Cadillacs. Herald/Ember Records was formed around 1952 by Al Silver, and was active for a decade. The Nutmegs, the Turbans, and the Mello-Kings recorded for Herald, while the Five Satins and the Silhouettes recorded for Ember. Laurie Records was formed in 1958 by Gene Schwarz. The label recorded Dion and the Belmonts (and Dion solo), the Mystics, the Jarmels, and the Chiffons. Other significant New York-based doo-wop labels included Whirlin' Disc (Earl Lewis and Channels), Fury (Lewis Lymon and the Teenchords), Everlast (the Charts), Old Town (the Solitaires and the Fiestas), and Winley (the Jesters and the Paragons).

George Goldner was principal in a number of New York record labels, including Rama (1953), Gee (1956), and Gone/End (1957). Rama recorded the Crows and the Harptones, while Gee recorded Frankie Lymon and the Teenagers and the Cleftones. The Dubs recorded for Gone, while the Chantels, the Flamingos, and Little Anthony and the Imperials recorded for End. In 1956 Goldner formed Roulette Records with notorious industry insider Morris Levy. Issuing the early recordings of rockabilly artists Buddy Knox and Jimmy Bowen, the label also recorded Jimmie Rodgers, the Royal Teens, Ronnie Hawkins, and Joey Dee and the Starliters. Roulette also distributed Coed Records (the Crests and the Duprees) and the Hull Records (Shep and the Limelites.)

Three other labels were important in the popularization of doo-wop music, VeeJay, Dootone, and Cameo. VeeJay Records was formed in Chicago in 1953 by Vivian Carter and James Bracken, and was among the first black-owned and operated labels. As well as recording blues artist Jimmy Reed, VeeJay recorded the doo-wop vocal groups the Spaniels, the El Dorados, and the Dells, and solo artists Gene Allison, Dee Clark, and Gene Chandler. Dootone Records, formed in Los Angeles in 1954 by Dootsie Williams, recorded the Penguins, Don Julian and the Meadowlarks, and Vernon Green and the Medallions. Cameo Records, formed in Philadelphia in 1956 by Bernie Lowe and Kal Mann, recorded the Rays and the Orlons, while the subsidiary label Parkway recorded the Dovells. Additionally, Bobby Rydell recorded for Cameo and Chubby Checker recorded for Parkway.

Although the majors dominated the field of rockabilly, a number of independent labels helped advance the music, most notably Sun and King. Other independent labels promoting rockabilly included Starday, Roulette, Imperial, and Liberty. Starday, formed in Texas in 1953, made the early rockabilly recordings of Sid King and the Five Strings and George Jones, and later recorded Sonny Fisher and Link Davis. Roulette released the rockabilly recordings of Jimmy Bowen and Buddy Knox, along with Jimmy Lloyd, Jimmy Isle, and the Rock-a-Teens. Imperial Records, formed in Los Angeles in 1947 by Lew Chudd, enjoyed its greatest success with Fats Domino, the second biggest selling artist of the '50s, and Ricky Nelson. The label also recorded the rockabilly of Bob Luman, Lew Williams, and Bill Allen. Liberty Records, formed in Los Angeles in 1955 by Al Bennett, recorded Eddie Cochran.

Other important independent labels in the promotion of rock 'n' roll were Cadence, Keen, and Jamie. Cadence Records, formed in New York in 1953 by Archie Bleyer, recorded the Everly Brothers from 1957 to 1960. Keen Records, formed in Los Angeles in 1957 by Bob Keene, recorded Sam Cooke from 1957 to 1960. Its subsidiary label Del-Fi recorded Ritchie Valens. Jamie Records, founded in 1958 in Philadelphia by Harold Lipsius and others, recorded Duane Eddy.

AFTERWORD

COVER RECORDS, TEEN IDOLS, AND CORPORATE RAIDING

The major record labels were caught unaware by the enormous popularity of rock 'n' roll with the youthful white audience. Although they quickly moved into the rockabilly market, a field dominated by young white male artists, the majors largely ignored doo-wop and R&B in the '50s. In an effort to gain control over rock 'n' roll, the majors embarked on a three-pronged attack on the music. First, particularly in the case of Mercury Records, they "covered" doo-wop and R&B hits with their own white artists. Second, they promoted a number of young, good-looking white males as "teen idols." And third, when they finally realized that rock 'n' roll wasn't the short-lived fad they had earlier assumed, they signed a number of artists away from their independent labels. In the '60s, many independents failed financially and the majors bought some of them out.

Mercury and Dot Records were the most active labels in the practice of covering R&B and doo-wop hits. Already discussed is how they used the white doo-wop groups the Crew Cuts and the Diamonds successfully to cover R&B hits. Mercury used female chanteuse Georgia Gibbs to bring black blues numbers to the white market. In early 1955 Gibbs scored a top pop hit with Lavern Baker's "Tweedle Dee" and a smash pop hit with Etta James's "Dance with Me Henry (The Wallflower)."

The independent Dot Records label, formed by Randy Wood in Gallatin, Tennessee, in 1951, exploited covers as vigorously as any major label. The Fontane Sisters, who backed recordings by Perry Como between 1949 and 1952, scored a top pop hit with the Charms' "Hearts of Stone" in late 1954. Subsequent covers through 1956 included rockabilly Boyd Bennett's "Seventeen," the Drifters' "Adorable," and the Teen Queens' "Eddie My Love."

Dot's most successful cover act was Pat Boone. Between 1955 and 1958 Boone scored more than a dozen major hits for Dot, including top pop hit versions of Fats Domino's "Ain't That a Shame" and Ivory Joe Hunter's "I Almost Lost My Mind." Smash pop hit covers by Boone included the El Dorados' "At My Front Door (Crazy Little Mama)," The Flamingos' "I'll Be Home," Little Richard's "Long Tall Sally," and the Orioles' "It's Too Soon to Know." Major pop hit covers included the Charms' "Two Hearts," the Five Keys' "Gee Whittakers," Little Richard's "Tutti Frutti," and Joe Turner's "Chains of Love." Other hits recorded by Pat Boone were the top pop hits "Don't Forbid Me," "Love Letters in the Sand," "April Love," and "Moody River," and the near-smashes "Remember You're Mine" and "Speedy Gonzales."

Decca also enjoyed success with cover songs in the '50s. Bill Haley covered Big Joe Turner's "Shake, Rattle and Roll" in a bowdlerized version, and the McGuire Sisters scored a near-smash pop hit with the Spaniels' "Goodnight, Sweetheart, Goodnight" in 1954 and a top pop hit with the Moonglows' "Sincerely" in 1955 on the subsidiary label, Coral.

Perhaps the most egregious instance of a cover song outdistancing the original version was "The Twist." A near-smash R&B and major pop hit for its author, Hank Ballard, on King Records in July 1960, the song became a top pop and smash R&B hit for Chubby Checker (real name Ernest Evans) on Philadelphia's Parkway Records only days later and again in late 1961. Checker's version of the song, a virtual note-for-note copy of the original, launched the international dance craze. To this day, "The Twist" is identified with Chubby Checker, and not Hank Ballard, its originator.

In the wake of Elvis Presley's success, a number of good-looking white male artists including Ricky Nelson, Paul Anka, Neil Sedaka, Dion, and Bobby Darin (see individual entries) were promoted by their record labels. Ricky Nelson recorded some early rockabilly and continued as a pop star on the Los Angeles independent label Imperial. Paul Anka, on ABC-Paramount, and Neil Sedaka, on RCA, were able to sustain their careers on the strength of their songwriting. Bobby Darin pursued a multifaceted career as one of the few white artists signed to the independent New York-based Atlantic family of labels (Atco), and Dion and the Belmonts were the most successful white doo-wop group of the '50s.

Two of the earliest teen idols were actors Tab Hunter and Tommy Sands. Hunter scored a top pop hit with Sonny James's "Young Love" and a major pop hit with "Ninety-Nine Ways" on Dot Records in 1957. Sands achieved a smash pop hit with "Teen-Age Crush," introduced on television in 1957, and managed major hits with "Goin' Steady" and "Sing Boy Sing" into 1958.

Most of the teen idols were recorded by Philadelphia labels and promoted on Dick Clark's popular TV show *American Bandstand,* which originated from that city. Frankie Avalon, Fabian, and Bobby Rydell were all from Philadelphia. Born Francis Avallone, Frankie worked in bands and on radio and television, scoring a near-smash pop hit with "Dede Dinah" on Chancellor Records at the beginning of 1958. Later successes on Chancellor included the top pop hits "Venus" and "Why" and the near-smashes "Ginger Bread" and "Bobby Sox to Stockings."

Fabian, born Fabian Forte, had near-smash pop hits with "Turn Me Loose" and "Hound Dog Man," provided by songwriters Doc Pomus and Mort Shuman, and a smash pop hit with "Tiger" in 1959, also on Chancellor Records. Bobby Rydell, born Robert Ridarelli, appeared on Paul Whiteman's television show in the early '50s and scored his first major hit on Cameo Record in 1959 with "Kissin' Time." Later smash pop hits for Rydell on Cameo included "We Got Love," "Wild One," and "Swinging School," all written by Karl Mann, Bernie Lowe, and Dave Appell. Subsequent pop hits through 1963 included "Volare," "The Cha-Cha-Cha," and "Forget Him."

Two of the more dynamic teen idols were Jimmy Clanton and Freddy Cannon. Born in Baton Rouge, Louisiana, Jimmy Clanton recorded for the Ace label, based in Jackson, Mississippi. Recording with New Orleans sessions musicians such as Huey "Piano" Smith, Earl King, and Lee Allen, Clanton scored smash pop hits with "Just a Dream," "Go, Jimmy, Go," and "Venus in Blue Jeans," written by Neil Sedaka, between 1959 and 1962. Freddy Cannon, born Frederick Picariello in Massachusetts, achieved smash pop hits on Philadelphia's Swan Records with "Tallahassee Lassie," "Way Down Yonder in New Orleans," and "Palisades Park." Later major pop hits included "Abigail Beecher" and "Action," the theme to Dick Clark's television show *Where the Action Is.*

Although very few doo-wop, blues, or R&B acts graduated to major labels, many white acts were signed by majors after their initial success on independents. RCA bought Elvis Presley's contract from Sun Records in November 1955, and in 1958 Sun alumni Johnny Cash and Carl Perkins signed with Columbia Records. In 1963 Jerry Lee Lewis switched from Sun to the Smash subsidiary of Mercury Records. In the early '60s, Duane Eddy switched from Jamie to RCA, Dion moved from Laurie to Columbia, and Rick Nelson switched from Imperial to Decca Records.

The few black acts to move to major labels were major hit makers. The Platters switched from King to Mercury in 1956 and were promoted as a pop vocal group, rather than as an R&B one. Ray Charles (Atlantic) moved to ABC in 1959, as did B. B. King in 1962, and Fats Domino (Imperial) in 1963. Sam Cooke switched from Keen to RCA in 1960.

Many independent labels experienced change during the '60s. Atlantic Records, along with latter-day independents Warner Brothers and Elektra, essentially became a major when the Kinney Corporation set up WEA (Warner-Elektra-Atlantic) in 1969. The masters from Chess, Sun, and King were sold. Other independent labels also endured hard times. By 1957, only the Crown and Kent divisions of Modern Records continued operations, as Modern, RPM, and Flair were phased out. Herald/Ember Records went out of business in 1962. Cameo Records was sold in 1963 and went out of business in 1968. VeeJay Records went out of business in 1966. Specialty Records ceased operations in the '60s and ended up the property of Fantasy Records in 1990. Cameo-Parkway was sold in 1968. Dot Records was eventually absorbed by ABC. The Savoy catalog was purchased by Arista in 1975. Aladdin Records was purchased by Imperial around 1961; Imperial was bought out by Liberty in 1963. Liberty later joined United Artists and was absorbed by EMI (Capitol) in the late '70s.

With the deaths of Buddy Holly and Eddie Cochran, and the travails of Little Richard, Chuck Berry, and Jerry Lee Lewis, rock 'n' roll had lost much of its impetus by the end of the '50s. The popularity of rockabilly faded after 1958, as did that of doo-wop after 1959. Elvis Presley was drafted and disappeared from the scene for two years; on his return, he took refuge in Hollywood. Meanwhile, the major labels promoted manufactured acts of little consequence. Songwriter-producers such as Leiber and Stoller and Pomus and Shuman (and later Phil Spector) were in the ascendancy. Independent labels declined in importance as some went out of business and others were bought out.

Rock 'n' roll would have to wait for a new wave of independent labels and the development of girl groups, surf music, and soul music to regain its popularity. And . . . the British were coming!

FOLK AND BLUES: SEE YA LATER, ALLIGATOR

Folk and blues music had little direct impact on rock 'n' roll during the '50s. Folk music was tainted by the specter of communism. Although he wrote and performed some of America's finest songs, Woody Guthrie had been associated with the political left wing since the late '30s. Guthrie, Lee Hays, and Pete Seeger formed the Almanac Singers at the beginning of the '40s, but the group was forced to disband in 1943 as a result of blacklisting. The Weavers, with Hays, Seeger, Ronnie Gilbert, and Fred Hellerman, were formed in 1949 and popularized folk music, scoring smash pop hits with "Tzena, Tzena, Tzena" backed with Leadbelly's "Goodnight, Irene," Guthrie's "So Long (It's Been Good to Know Ya)," and "On Top of Old Smoky" in 1950–51. The Weavers' recording career was also cut short by blacklisting and the group disbanded until 1955, when their successful reunion concert at Carnegie Hall led to concert tours and renewed interest in folk music.

In popular terms, this revival enjoyed its greatest commercial success in 1956–57 with folk songs from the Caribbean, such as Harry Belafonte's "Jamaica Farewell," the Tarriers' "Banana Boat Song" (covered by Belafonte), and Terry Gilkyson and the Easy Riders' "Marianne" (covered by the Hilltoppers). As a consequence of folk music's newfound popularity, a number of college-educated acoustic musicians began performing and recording folk music in the late '50s, most notably the Kingston Trio (see separate entry). Folk music's real impact on rock 'n' roll and popular music came in the early '60s with the emergence of Peter, Paul and Mary, Bob Dylan, Joan Baez, and Judy Collins, and in the mid '60s when Dylan and the Byrds began playing folk-rock.

Similarly, the blues artists of the '50s, except perhaps for Jimmy Reed and B. B. King, enjoyed limited success at best during the decade. Their popularity was primarily with the black audience, and their first recognition by the mass white audience did not come until the folk movement of the early '60s, particularly through blues festivals. Although the roots of R&B were the blues, the music did not make a significant impact on rock 'n' roll and popular music until the development of blues-rock by white practitioners such as Eric Clapton and Mike Bloomfield in the late '60s.

ROCK ARTISTS OF THE FIFTIES

PAUL ANKA
Born July 30, 1941, in Ottawa, Ontario, Canada.

PAUL ANKA, 1956. PHOTO BY POPSIE RANDOLPH

One of the more sophisticated performers and songwriters to come out of the '50s, Paul Anka scored a number of hits with his own compositions while still a teenager, beginning with 1957's "Diana." He ultimately sold more than 100 million records and, like a number of teen idols, quickly switched his attention to the nightclub and cabaret circuit. He subsequently pursued a career as a songwriter, composing over 400 songs, including the English lyrics to "My Way," adopted by Frank Sinatra as his theme song, and "The Tonight Show Theme." During the mid '70s, Anka relocated to Las Vegas and enjoyed renewed popularity with several huge pop and easy-listening hits.

Raised in Canada, Paul Anka first performed in public at the age of twelve. Traveling to Hollywood in 1956, he recorded his first—albeit unsuccessful—single, "I Confess," for Modern/RPM Records. In the spring of 1957, at the age of fifteen, Anka auditioned a song for Don Costa of ABC-Paramount Records in New York that would become one of the biggest selling singles of the '50s, "Diana." Signed to the label, he hit the pop charts consistently over the next three years with compositions that often reflected the simple, even naive, but nonetheless poignant concerns of teenagers. His best-remembered smash hits of the period include "You Are My Destiny," "Lonely Boy" (also a smash R&B hit), "Put Your Head on My Shoulder," "Puppy Love," and "My Home Town."

Paul Anka first performed in Las Vegas in 1959 and became the youngest performer to star at New York's Copacabana nightclub in 1960. He also appeared in several movies, most notably 1962's *The Longest Day* (for which he also wrote the theme song), and had switched to RCA Records by the beginning of 1962. No longer making the charts after 1963, Anka continued to perform on the nightclub circuit, including lucrative engagements in Las Vegas. Having written songs for others beginning in 1958 with "It Doesn't Matter Anymore" for Buddy Holly, Anka concentrated on his songwriting. Subsequently, his "Tonight Show Theme" became one of his most profitable compositions; yet his English lyrics to the French ballad "Comme d'Habitude"— under the new name "My Way"—in 1969 became perhaps his best-known song and Frank Sinatra's theme song. Anka's "She's a Lady" became a smash hit for Tom Jones in 1971.

Paul Anka reestablished himself as a recording artist in 1974–75 on United Artists Records beginning with the top hit "(You're) Having My Baby," recorded with Odia Coates, with whom he toured for several years. Other near-smash hits of the era included "One Man Woman/One Woman Man" (with Coates), "I Don't Like to Sleep Alone," and "Times of Your Life," a top easy-listening hit. Following this brief flourish, Anka continued to write, record, tour, and appear in the occasional television show or movie.

DISCOGRAPHY

Paul Anka	ABC-Paramount	240	'58	LP†
My Heart Sings	ABC-Paramount	296	'59	LP†
Swings for Young Lovers	ABC-Paramount	347	'60	LP†
At the Copa	ABC-Paramount	353	'60	LP†
It's Christmas Everywhere	ABC-Paramount	360	'60	LP†
Instrumental Hits	ABC-Paramount	371	'61	LP†
Diana	ABC-Paramount	420	'62	LP†
Young, Alive and in Love	RCA	2502	'62	LP†
Let's Sit This One Out	RCA	2575	'62	LP†
Our Man Around the World	RCA	2614	'63	LP†
Italiano	RCA-Italian	10130	'63	LP†
Songs I Wish I'd Written	RCA	2744	'63	LP†
		2482	'77	
Excitement on Park Avenue	RCA	2966	'64	LP†
Strictly Nashville	RCA	3580	'66	LP†
Live!	RCA	3875	'67	LP†
Goodnight My Love	RCA	4142	'69	LP†
Sincerely	RCA	4203	'69	LP†
Life Goes On	RCA	4250	'69	LP†
Paul Anka in the 70s	RCA	4309	'70	LP†
		66203	'93	CS/CD†
Paul Anka	Buddah	5093	'71	LP†
Jubilation	Buddah	5114	'72	LP†
Anka	United Artists	314	'74	LP†
Feelings	United Artists	367	'75	LP†
	Liberty	10149	'82	
Times of Your Lives	United Artists	569	'75	LP†
Live	Barnaby	6013	'75	LP†
The Painter	United Artists	653	'76	LP†
The Music Man	United Artists	746	'77	LP†
Listen to Your Heart	RCA	2892	'78	LP†

Headlines	RCA	3382	'79	LP†
Both Sides of Love	RCA	3926	'81	LP†
Walk a Fine Line	Columbia	38442	'83	LP†
Live	Columbia	39323	'84	LP†

Anthologies and Compilations

Sings His Big 15	ABC-Paramount	323	'60	LP†
Sings His Big 15, Vol. 2	ABC-Paramount	390	'61	LP†
Sings His Big 15, Vol. 3	ABC-Paramount	409	'62	LP†
21 Golden Hits (rerecordings)	RCA	2691	'63	LP†
	RCA	3808	'67/'84	CS/CD
Remember Diana	RCA	0896	'75	LP†
	RCA-Camden	2713		CS/CD
She's a Lady	RCA	1054	'75	LP†
	RCA	1098	'75	LP†
	Accord	7117	'81	LP†
	Richmond	2353		CS/CD
Sings His Favorites	RCA	1584	'76	LP†
Diana and Other Hits	RCA	2086	'90	CS
My Way	Camden	0616	'76	LP†
This Is Paul Anka	Buddah	5622	'75	LP†
The Essential Paul Anka	Buddah	(2)5667	'76	LP†
His Best	United Artists	922	'78	†
	Liberty	10000		LP/CS†
	EMI-Manhattan	46739	'88	CS/CD
The Best of the United Artists Years (1973–1977)	EMI	36993	'96	CD
Songs I Wrote and Sing (rec. 1974–1978)	Pair	(2)1129	'86	CS†
Best of Paul Anka	Pair	1204		CD
Gold–28 Original Hit Recordings	Sire	(2)3704	'74	LP†
Vintage Years (1957–1961)	Sire	6043	'77	LP†
Puppy Love	Pickwick	3508	'76	LP†
Lonely Boy	Pickwick	3523	'76	LP†
Paul Anka	Pickwick	(2)2087	'76	LP†
Very Best	Ranwood	8203	'81	LP/CS
Black Tie	Piccadilly	3403	'82	LP†
Teach Me Tonight	Richmond	2349		CS
Best (14 Original Hits, 1957–1961)	Rhino	70220	'86	LP†
30th Anniversary Anthology (1950–1980)	Rhino	(2)71489	'89	CS/CD
Five Decades of Hits	Curb/Warner Bros.	77467	'91	CS/CD
Sings His Big 10, Vol. 1	Curb/Warner Bros.	77557	'91	CS/CD
Sings His Big 10, Vol. 2	Curb/Warner Bros.	77558	'91	CS/CD
Classic Hits	Curb/Warner Bros.	77566	'92	CS/CD
Live	GNP Crescendo	2175		LP/CS

LAVERN BAKER

Born Dolores Williams on November 11, 1929, in Chicago, Illinois; died March 10, 1997, in New York City.

A major R&B artist of the '50s, Lavern Baker scored some of the earliest crossover hits onto the pop charts, including "Tweedle Dee" and "Jim Dandy." However, the recording of cover versions of several of her hits, primarily by white artist Georgia Gibbs, kept Baker from achieving as large a sales success as she might have. Performing in early rock 'n' roll movies and tours, Baker's career went into eclipse in the mid '60s with the rise of soul music. She eventually reemerged in the '90s, performing on the cabaret and nightclub circuit, as well as in blues and rock-revival festivals, until her death in 1997.

Dolores Williams began singing in church at the age of twelve, and started performing professionally at Chicago's Club DeLisa in 1946, billed as "Little Miss Sharecropper." Spotted by bandleader Fletcher Henderson, she initially recorded for the OKeh subsidiary of Columbia Records in 1948, subsequently recording for RCA-Victor in 1949. Adopting the name Lavern Baker, she performed and recorded for King Records with Todd Rhodes's band in 1952–53, and signed with Atlantic Records in 1953 upon her return from a solo European tour. Her third release, Winfield Scott's novelty song "Tweedle Dee," became a smash R&B/major pop hit in early 1955. However, white artist Georgia Gibbs quickly covered the song for Mercury and scored an even bigger pop hit. Through 1956 Baker scored smash R&B hits with "Bop-Ting-a-Ling"/"That's All I Need" and the ballads "Play It Fair" and "Still" (covered by the Commodores in 1979), backed with "I Can't Love You Enough," a major pop hit. In 1957 "Jim Dandy" became a top R&B/major pop hit and was succeeded by the inevitable follow-up "Jim Dandy Got Married." She toured with deejay/promoter Alan Freed's rock 'n' roll stage shows, and performed in two of his movies, *Rock, Rock, Rock* and *Mister Rock and Roll,* both in 1957.

In 1958 Lavern Baker achieved her biggest hit with the soulful ballad "I Cried a Tear," featuring saxophonist King Curtis. She also recorded her acclaimed *Sings Bessie Smith* album, on which she paid homage to the famous blues queen, an unusual move for a pop songstress. Subsequent hits included "I Waited Too Long," written by Neil Sedaka, the rousing "Saved," written and produced by Jerry Leiber and Mike Stoller, and blues legend Ma Rainey's "See See Rider." By 1964 Baker had left Atlantic, managing her final, albeit minor, hit with "Think Twice," recorded with Jackie Wilson, on Brunswick Records in 1966. While touring Asia in 1969 she became seriously ill and moved to the Philippines, where she managed and occasionally performed at a Marine NCO club on Subic Bay for over twenty years. She briefly returned to the United States for Atlantic's fortieth anniversary celebration at Madison Square Garden in 1988, and later came back to take Ruth Brown's place in the musical *Black and Blue* during the second half of 1990. Baker was awarded the Rhythm and Blues Foundation's Career Achievement Award in 1990 and inducted into the Rock and Roll Hall of Fame in 1991. She resumed touring and recording, including "Slow Rollin' Mama" for the sound track to the film *Dick Tracy,* but suffered two strokes, as well as diabetes. She died at a New York hospital on March 10, 1997.

BIBLIOGRAPHY

Garvey, Dennis. "Lavern Baker: The 'Tweedle-Dee' Girl Is Back" (Discography by Neal Umphred). *Goldmine* 17, no. 14 (July 17, 1991): 11–15, 18, 19, 151.

DISCOGRAPHY

Lavern	Atlantic	8002	'56	LP†
Lavern Baker	Atlantic	8007	'57	LP†
Sings Bessie Smith	Atlantic	1281	'58	LP†
	Atlantic	90980	'88	CD
Blues Ballads	Atlantic	8030	'59	LP†
Precious Memories	Atlantic	8036	'59	LP†
Saved	Atlantic	8050	'61	LP†

See See Rider	Atlantic	8071	'63	LP†
Best	Atlantic	8078	'63	LP†
Soul on Fire: The Best of Lavern Baker	Atlantic	82311	'91	CS/CD
Her Greatest Recordings	Atco	33–372	'71	LP†
Let Me Belong to You	Brunswick	754160	'70	LP†
Live in Hollywood '91	Rhino	70565	'91	CS/CD
Woke Up This Morning	Swing	8433	'92	CS/CD

HANK BALLARD

Born on November 18, 1936, in Detroit, Michigan.

HANK BALLARD AND THE MIDNIGHTERS, 1950s

As lead singer and songwriter with the Royals/the Midnighters, Hank Ballard helped bring the open sexuality of R&B into early rock 'n' roll with the 1954 smash "Work with Me Annie." Enduring the song's banishment from radio airplay, Ballard wrote and recorded the dance classic "The Twist" in 1959, which became one of the all-time best-selling singles and launched the international dance craze of the '60s when recorded by Chubby Checker.

The Detroit-based Royals were originally formed in 1950, with members Jackie Wilson and Levi Stubbs (later of the Four Tops). The group's membership eventually stabilized with Henry Booth and Charles Sutton (leads and tenors), Lawson Smith (baritone), and Sonny Woods (bass), with Alonzo Tucker on guitar. Spotted by R&B talent scout Johnny Otis in early 1952 at the Paradise Club in Detroit, the Royals signed with Cincinnati's Federal label on Otis's recommendation and achieved early success with the Otis ballad "Every Beat of My Heart." Hank Ballard joined in 1953 when Lawson Smith was drafted into the army, and the Royals soon registered an R&B smash with "Get It." Changing their name to the Midnighters in April 1954, the group scored a top R&B hit with Ballard's blatantly sexual "Work with Me Annie." Although banned from radio station airplay, the song sold over a million copies. Through 1955, the Midnighters achieved major R&B

hits with "Sexy Ways," the inevitable follow-ups—"Annie Had a Baby" and "Annie's Aunt Fannie"—and "It's Love Baby (24 Hours a Day)." Etta James recorded the "answer" to the Annie songs entitled "The Wallflower" (subtitled "Roll with Me Henry"), with songwriting credit going to James, Ballard, and Otis. White cover artist Georgia Gibbs quickly coopted the song for a major pop hit.

In the second half of the '50s, the Midnighters underwent a number of personnel changes, including the departures of Charles Sutton and Sonny Woods, the return of Lawson Smith, and the addition of guitarist Cal Green and vocalist Norman Thrasher. They switched to King Records for singles releases, and became Hank Ballard and the Midnighters in 1959. Their 1959 smash R&B hit "Teardrops on Your Letter" was backed by Ballard's "The Twist," which initially drew little attention. Rereleased after another dance-novelty number, "Finger Poppin' Time," became a smash pop/R&B hit for the group in 1960, "The Twist" became an R&B smash. However, it took Chubby Checker's cover version—a blatant copy of Ballard's record—to capitalize on the song, scoring top pop hits with it in both 1960 and 1961, and thus launching the international dance craze.

Despite losing out on the Twist craze, Hank Ballard and the Midnighters continued to enjoy popularity on the R&B and pop charts. They scored their biggest popular success with the late 1960s' "Let's Go, Let's Go, Let's Go," a smash pop/top R&B hit. Other major pop hits through 1961 included "The Hoochi Coochi Coo" and "The Switcheroo," but after 1962 neither the Midnighters nor Ballard solo achieved another major hit. The group disbanded in the mid '60s, and Ballard left the King label in 1969. He subsequently joined the James Brown Revue in the late '60s and early '70s, dropping out of the music scene from 1974 to 1982. Hank Ballard resumed touring in the '80s, eventually recording for After Hours Records in the '90s. Ballard was inducted into the Rock and Roll Hall of Fame in 1990.

DISCOGRAPHY

Hank Ballard and the Midnighters

Sing Their Greatest Juke Box Hits	King	541	'56'/89	LP/CS/CD
Hank Ballard and the Midnighters	King	581	'56/89	LP/CS/CD
Singin' and Swingin'	King	618	'59/89	LP/CS/CD
The One and Only	King	674	'60/89	LP/CS/CD
Mr. Rhythm and Blues	King	700	'60/89	LP/CS/CD
reissued as Finger Poppin' Time	Power Pak	276		LP†
	Richmond	2216		CS
Spotlight on Hank Ballard	King	740	'61/89	LP/CS/CD
Let's Go Again	King	748	'61	LP†
Dance Along	King	759	'61/89	LP/CS/CD
The Twistin' Fools	King	781	'62	LP†
Jumpin' Hank Ballard	King	793	'63	LP†
The 1963 Sound	King	815	'63	LP†
Greatest Hits	King	867	'64	LP†
A Star in Your Eyes	King	896	'64	LP†
Those Lazy, Lazy Days	King	913	'65	LP†
Glad Songs, Sad Songs	King	927	'66	LP†
24 Hit Tunes	King	950	'66	LP/CS/CD
Hank Ballard Sings 24 Great Songs	King	981	'68	LP†
20 Hits (1953–1962)	King	5003	'77	LP†
20 Original Greatest Hits	Deluxe	7836		CS
Work with Me Annie: The Best of Hank Ballard and the Midnighters	Rhino	71512	'93	CD

Solo

You Can't Keep a Good Man Down	King	1052	'69	LP†
Naked in the Rain	After Hours	4137	'92	CS/CD

With the King All Stars (Hank Ballard, Fred Wesley, Bootsy Collins, Bill Doggett, Alfred "Pee Wee" Ellis, and Bobby Byrd)

The King All Stars	After Hours	4116	'91	LP/CS/CD

BROOK BENTON

Born Benjamin Peay on September 9 (or 19), 1931, in Camden, South Carolina; died April 9, 1988, in New York City.

One of the few artists of the rock 'n' roll era to write his own material, Brook Benton was one of the first soul artists, employing his gospel-trained, mellifluous baritone voice over pop-style arrangements featuring string accompaniment on well-crafted ballads. Scoring his last major hit for years in 1962, Benton reemerged with the 1970 smash "Rainy Night in Georgia" and subsequently continued on the club circuit until his death in 1988.

In the late '40s and early '50s, Brook Benton toured the gospel circuit with the Camden Jubilee Singers, the Bill Landford Spiritual Singers, and the Golden Gate Quartet. Signed as solo artist to Epic Records in 1953, Benton also recorded for the RCA subsidiary Vik before meeting songwriter Clyde Otis around 1957. Benton, Otis, and arranger Belford Hendricks subsequently formed a songwriting partnership. Recording hundreds of demonstration records with Otis, the pair cowrote Nat "King" Cole's "Looking Back," and Benton cowrote Clyde McPhatter's "A Lover's Question" and the Diamonds' "The Stroll," all smash hits from 1958. In 1959 Otis persuaded Mercury Records to sign Benton. Over the next four years the team provided Benton with a number of hit recordings on Mercury, including the top R&B/smash pop hit "It's Just a Matter of Time," "Endlessly," "Thank You Pretty Baby," "Kiddio," and "The Boll Weevil Song." Other hits recorded by Benton included "So Many Ways" (a top R&B/smash pop hit) and the pop/R&B smash "Hotel Happiness." "So Close," "Think Twice," and "Lie to Me" became R&B smashes.

In late 1959 Brook Benton recorded *The Two of Us* with Dinah Washington, and the album yielded two huge hits with "Baby (You've Got What It Takes)" and "A Rockin' Good Way." He continued to record for Mercury with modest commercial success, switching to RCA in 1965 and Reprise in 1967. He eventually scored his final smash hit on Cotillion with Tony Joe White's "Rainy Night in Georgia" in 1970. He later recorded for MGM and All Platinum and maintained his career on the club circuit. On April 9, 1988, Brook Benton died in New York at the age of fifty-six of complications from spinal meningitis.

Brook Benton and Jesse Belvin

Brook Benton and Jesse Belvin	Crown	350		LP†

Brook Benton and Dinah Washington

The Two of Us	Mercury	60244	'60	LP†
	Mercury	824823	'85	CS†
	Mercury	526467		CD

Brook Benton

At His Best	RCA	3573	'59	†
Brook Benton	Camden	564	'60	†
It's Just a Matter of Time	Mercury	60077	'59	†
Endlessly	Mercury	60146	'59	†
So Many Ways I Love You	Mercury	60225	'60	†

Songs I Love to Sing	Mercury	60602	'60	†
If You Believe	Mercury	60619	'61	†
The Boll Weevil Song	Mercury	60641	'61	†
There Goes That Song Again	Mercury	60673	'62	†
Lie to Me	Mercury	60740	'62	†
	Polygram	836687		CS
Best Ballads of Broadway	Mercury	60830	'63	†
Born to Sing the Blues	Mercury	60886	'64	†
On the Country Side	Mercury	60918	'64	†
This Bitter Earth	Mercury	60934	'64	†
Mother Earth	Mercury	16314	'66	†
Mother Nature, Father Time	RCA	3526	'65	†
That Old Feeling	RCA	3514	'66	†
My Country	RCA	3590	'66	†
Sings a Love Song	RCA	1044	'75	†
Laura, What's He Got That I Ain't Got	Reprise	6268	'67	†
Do Your Thing	Cotillion	9002	'69	†
Today	Cotillion	9018	'70	†
Home Style	Cotillion	9028	'70	†
Gospel Truth	Cotillion	058	'71	†
Story Teller	Cotillion	9050	'72	†
Something for Everyone	MGM	4874	'73	†
This Is Brook Benton	All Platinum	3015	'76	†

Anthologies

Golden Hits	Mercury	60607	'61	†
Golden Hits, Vol. 2	Mercury	60774	'63	†
It's Just a Matter of Time: His Greatest Hits	Mercury	822321		CS
Best	Mercury	830772	'87	CD
40 Greatest Hits	Mercury	836755	'89	CD†
The Dynamic Brook Benton Sings	Strand	1121		†
Soul	Harmony	7346	'65	†
I Wanna Be with You	Camden	2431	'70	†
As Long as She Needs Me	Pickwick	3217		†
Greatest Hits	Pickwick	8005		†
This Is Brook Benton	RCA	9597	'89	CS/CD
The Brook Benton Anthology (1959–1970)	Rhino	(2)71497	'86	CS
Greatest Hits	Curb/Warner Bros.	77445	'91	CS/CD
Greatest Songs	Curb/Atlantic	77741	'95	CS/CD
At His Best	Pair	1289		CS/CD
All His Best	Special Music	4825		CS/CD
Best	Dominion	7203		CD†
20 Golden Hits	Deluxe	7861		CS/CD
Best of Easy Listening	Richmond	2123		CS

CHUCK BERRY

Born October 18, 1926, in St. Louis, Missouri (although a number of sources give San Jose,
California).

Certainly the single most influential black artist in the history of rock 'n' roll, Chuck
Berry is arguably the most important figure, regardless of race, in rock history. As the first

CHUCK BERRY, 1956

major rock artist to compose virtually all of his own material, Berry provided songs that were aggressive, exuberant, and wry, and reflected the romance between rock 'n' roll and the male youth culture and its concerns (school, cars, girls, and dancing). He is often cited as rock's first folk poet. With his engaging lyrics, enticing music, and uncommonly clear diction, Berry became the first black artist to achieve mass popularity with the young white audience. Moreover, his innovative use of boogie-woogie and shuffle rhythms, his alternating chord changes on rhythm guitar, and his distinctive off-time double-note lead guitar playing set the early standard for rock guitar and helped popularize the electric guitar. Despite his personal penchant for the blues, Chuck Berry's primary influence came through his up-tempo rock songs. The Beatles, the Rolling Stones, and most other British groups recorded his songs during their early careers, and the Beach Boys' "Surfin' U.S.A." is an obvious reworking of "Sweet Little Sixteen." Bob Dylan's first rock hit, "Subterranean Homesick Blues," bears a remarkable resemblance to Berry's "Too Much Monkey Business." Virtually every rock group performing today has at least one Chuck Berry song in its repertoire.

Charles "Chuck" Berry began singing in a St. Louis church at age six, later taking up guitar while in high school. After serving time for armed robbery from 1944 to 1947, he formed his first group with pianist Johnnie Johnson in St. Louis in 1952. The group became the area's top club band, and in May 1955 Berry traveled to Chicago where he met blues great Muddy Waters, who introduced him to Leonard Chess of Chess Records. Signed immediately, Berry recorded at Chess with pianist Johnnie Johnson and house bassist Willie Dixon. Berry's first single, "Maybellene," ostensibly cowritten with disc jockey Alan Freed, became a huge hit, one of rock 'n' roll's first. Excelling on stage, his now-signature "duck walk" was fortuitously introduced into his act in New York in 1956, and the following year he appeared in the film *Rock, Rock, Rock*. Success continued through 1959 with the smash R&B/major pop hit "Roll Over, Beethoven" and the crossover smashes "School Days," "Rock and Roll Music," "Sweet Little Sixteen," and the autobiographical "Johnny B. Goode." Other hit recordings of the era included "Too Much Monkey Business"/"Brown-Eyed Handsome Man," "Carol," " Sweet Little Rock and Roll," "Almost Grown," and "Back in the U.S.A." Berry also appeared in the films *Mister Rock and Roll* (1957), *Go, Johnny, Go* (1959), and *Jazz on a Summer's Day* (1959), filmed and recorded at the 1958 Newport Jazz Festival.

In July 1959, Chuck Berry was arrested for violation of the Mann Act. Convicted at a second trial, he served time at the federal penitentiary in Terre Haute, Indiana, from February 1962 to October 1963. Upon his release, he came back with the major pop hits "Nadine," "No Particular Place to Go," and "You Never Can Tell." His minor hit from 1964, "Promised Land," was recorded by a wealth of artists, including Elvis Presley. In 1964 he toured Great Britain for the first time and recorded an album with guitarist Bo Diddley, *Two Great Guitars.* He also opened the amusement park Berry Park, near Wentzville, Missouri, in the early '60s. In 1966 Berry switched to Mercury Records, and Chess reissued all of his earlier albums. His Mercury albums, including *Live at the Fillmore,* recorded with the Steve Miller Blues Band, failed to sell, and in 1970 Berry returned to Chess Records. The Chess albums *Back Home, San Francisco Dues,* and *Bio* are considered among his finest. His first and only top pop hit came in 1972 with the childishly risque "My Ding-a-Ling," from *The London Chuck Berry Sessions,* recorded in part with members of the British group the Faces.

Chuck Berry appeared in the 1973 film *Let the Good Times Roll,* compiled from Richard Nader's rock 'n' roll revival shows, and the 1978 film *American Hot Wax,* a fictionalized "week in the life of rock 'n' roll," with disc jockey Alan Freed as its central character. Berry also toured regularly and appeared on numerous television shows during the decade but was imprisoned for four months in 1979 for income tax evasion. He reemerged with a new round of touring and his first album of new material in years, *Rockit.* Chuck Berry was inducted into the Blues Foundation's Hall of Fame in 1985 and the Rock and Roll Hall of Fame in its inaugural year, 1986. In 1987 Harmony Books published his totally self-written autobiography and the following year the movie *Hail! Hail! Rock' n' Roll,* filmed and recorded at a 1986 concert in St. Louis organized by Keith Richards to celebrate Berry's sixtieth birthday and featuring Richards and Eric Clapton, was released. In 1993 Berry performed at President Bill Clinton's inaugural.

Pianist Johnnie Johnson, the backbone of Chuck Berry's recorded sound since the mid '50s, began recording for himself in the '90s, recording *Johnnie B. Bad* with Keith Richards and Eric Clapton, and *That'll Work* with the Kentucky Headhunters. After several additional albums, Johnson joined Bob Weir's Ratdog in 1996.

BIBLIOGRAPHY

Berry, Chuck. *Chuck Berry: The Autobiography.* New York: Harmony, 1987.

De Witt, Howard A. *Chuck Berry: Rock 'N' Roll Music.* Fremont, CA: Horizon, 1981; Ann Arbor, MI: Pierian, 1985.

Koda, Cub. "Chuck Berry: And the Joint Was Rockin' " (Discography by Neal Umphred). *Goldmine* 17, no. 25 (December 13, 1991): 8–16, 18, 20, 22, 24, 124, 126, 128, 129.

Reese, Krista. *Chuck Berry: Mr. Rock n' Roll.* London, New York: Proteus, 1982.

Chuck Berry

After School Sessions	Chess	1426	'57	†
	Chess	9284		CD†
	MCA	20873	'95	CS/CD
One Dozen Berrys	Chess	1432	'58	†
Chuck Berry Is on Top	Chess	1435	'59	†
	Chess	9256	'87	CS
	Chess	31260	'87	CD
Rockin' at the Hops	Chess	1448	'60	†
	Chess	9259	'87	CS/CD
New Juke Box Hits	Chess	1456	'60	†
	Chess	9171		CS/CD

Chuck Berry Twist	Chess	1465	'62	†
reissued as More Chuck Berry	Chess	1465	'63	†
Chuck Berry on Stage	Chess	1480	'63	†
St. Louis to Liverpool	Chess	1488	'64	†
	Chess	31261		CD†
Chuck Berry in London	Chess	1495	'65	†
Fresh Berrys	Chess	1498	'65	†
In Memphis	Mercury	61123	'67	†
	Polydor	836071		CD†
Live at the Fillmore	Mercury	61138	'67	†
	Polydor	836072		CD†
From St. Louie to Frisco	Mercury	61176	'68	†
	Polydor	836073		CD†
Concerto in B. Goode	Mercury	61223		†
	Polydor	836074		CD†
St. Louie to Frisco to Memphis	Mercury	(2)6501	'72	†
Back Home	Chess	1550	'70	†
San Francisco Dues	Chess	50008	'71	†
The London Chuck Berry Sessions	Chess	50001	'72	†
	Chess	60020	'72	†
	Chess	9295	'89	CS/CD
Bio	Chess	50043	'73	†
Chuck Berry	Chess	60032	'75	†
Rockit	Atco	38–118	'79	†
Live on Stage (recorded 1983 in the United Kingdom)	Magnum Archives	16	'95	CD
Hail! Hail! Rock 'n' Roll (music from sound track)	MCA	6217	'88	CS/CD

Chuck Berry and Bo Diddley

Two Great Guitars	Checker	2991	'64	†
	Chess	9170	'92	CD

Anthologies

Greatest Hits	Chess	1485	'64	†
Golden Decade	Chess	(2)1514	'67	†
Golden Decade, Vol. 2	Chess	(2)60023	'73	†
Golden Decade, Vol. 3	Chess	(2)60028	'74	†
The Great 28	Chess	(2)8201	'82	†
	Chess	(2)92500		CS
	Chess	92500		CD
Rock 'n' Roll Rarities (recorded 1957–1965)	Chess	92521	'86	CS/CD
More Rock n' Roll Rarities From The Golden Era of Chess Records	Chess	9190	'86	LP/CS/CD†
The Chess Box	Chess	(6)80001	'88	LP
	Chess	(3)80001	'88	CS/CD
Missing Berries: Rarities, Vol. 3	Chess	9318	'90	LP/CD
His Best, Vol. 1	MCA/Chess	9371	'97	CD
Golden Hits	Mercury	61103	'67	†
	Mercury	826256		CS/CD
Johnny B. Goode	Pickwick	3327	'72	†
Sweet Little Rock and Roller	Pickwick	3345	'73	†
Flashback	Pickwick	(2)2061	'74	†
Wild Berrys	Pickwick	3392	'74	†

Greatest Hits	Archive of Folk and	321	'76	†
	Jazz Music/Everest			†
Best	Gusto	0004	'78	†
16 Greatest Hits	Trip	1655	'78	†
Live in Concert	Magnum	(2)703	'78	†
All-Time Hits	Up Front	199	'79	†
Best	Vogue	600033	'86	CD†
Roll Over Beethoven	Allegiance	72912	'88	CD†
On the Blues Side	Ace	397	'93	CD
The Incredible Chuck Berry	RCA-Camden	5010		CS
Best of the Best of Chuck Berry	Hollywood/IMG	100		CS/CD
21 Greatest Hits	Zeta	520		CD†
Live Hits	Quicksilver	1017		LP/CD
Johnnie Johnson				
Johnnie B. Bad	Elektra/Nonesuch	61149	'91	CS/CD
That'll Work	Elektra/Nonesuch	61476	'93	CS/CD
Blue Hand Johnnie	Evidence	26017	'93	CD
Blues, Ballads and Jumpin' Jazz	Fantasy/OBC	570	'94	CD
Stompin' at the Penny	Columbia/Legacy	57829	'94	CS/CD†
Johnnie Johnson Band				
Johnnie Be Back	MusicMasters	65131	'95	CS/CD

RUTH BROWN

Born Ruth Weston on January 30, 1928, in Portsmouth, Virginia.

The most prolific black female vocalist of the '50s, rivaling Dinah Washington for a time, Ruth Brown helped establish Atlantic Records as a major purveyor of R&B music. Atlantic's top-selling artist of the '50s, surpassing even Ray Charles, Ruth Brown helped form the link between R&B and rock 'n' roll through her appearances on Alan Freed's pioneering shows. Out of music for fifteen years, Brown reemerged in the mid '70s to record, perform in films, musicals, and television, and establish the Rhythm and Blues Foundation.

Ruth Weston sang in her father's church choir before beginning her professional singing career in 1946, adopting the name Ruth Brown. She sang briefly with the Lucky Millinder Band and moved to Washington, D.C., where she performed at Blanche Calloway's Crystal Cavern nightclub. Brought to the attention of Herb Abramson of the newly formed Atlantic Records label by Calloway, Brown signed with the label in 1948, only to be hospitalized before her first recording session for nine months as the result of an automobile accident. Her eventual debut release, "So Long," became a smash R&B hit and the first of a series of hits that lasted through 1960. Between 1950 and 1954 she scored five top R&B hit with "Teardrops from My Eyes," "5–10–15 Hours," "(Mama) He Treats Your Daughter Mean," "Oh What a Dream," and "Mambo Baby." "(Mama) He Treats Your Daughter Mean" also became a major pop hit. Other R&B hits through 1956 included "Daddy Daddy," "Wild Wild Young Men," and "As Long as I'm Moving."

In 1956 Ruth Brown began performing on Alan Freed's rock 'n' roll shows. Later R&B hits such as 1957's "Lucky Lips" (written by Leiber and Stoller) and 1958's "This Little Girl's Gone Rockin' " (written by Bobby Darin) became major pop hits, establishing her as a rock 'n' roll artist. Subsequent successes in both fields included "I Don't Know" and "Don't Deceive Me," but by 1962 she had left Atlantic for Phillips, only to soon retire. She eventually reemerged in the '70s with new recordings and appeared in several television situation comedies, including *Hello Larry* from 1979 to 1981. Brown also fought to recover royalties from her early Atlantic recordings and was eventually awarded $2,000,000, which allowed her to establish the nonprofit Rhythm and Blues Foundation. In the '80s she appeared in a number of Off-Broadway musicals, including *Staggerlee*. She also appeared in the 1988 film *Hairspray,* won a Tony for her performance in the Broadway musical *Black and Blue,* and began recording jazz-style albums for the Fantasy label. Ruth Brown was inducted into the Rock and Roll Hall of Fame in 1993.

BIBLIOGRAPHY

Brown, Ruth, with Andrew Yule. *Miss Rhythm: The Autobiography of Ruth Brown, Rhythm and Blues Legend.* New York: Donald I. Fine, 1996.

Ruth Brown

Ruth Brown	Atlantic	8004	'57	†
Late Date with Ruth Brown	Atlantic	1308	'59	†
Miss Rhythm	Atlantic	8026	'59	†
Best	Atlantic	8080	'63	†
Miss Rhythm (Greatest Hits and More)	Atlantic	(2)82061	'89	CD
Along Comes Ruth	Phillips	600028	'62	†
Ruth Brown '65	Mainstream	6044	'64	†
reissued as Help a Good Girl Go Bad	DCC Jazz	602		CS/CD
Softly	Mainstream	369		†
Fine Brown Frame (recorded 1968)	Capitol Jazz	81200		†
	Blue Note	81200	'93	CD
Black Is Brown and Brown Is Beautiful (recorded 1969)	DCC Jazz	620		†
Black and Blue (original cast)	DRG	19001	'89	CS/CD
Have a Good Time	Fantasy	9661	'88	CS/CD
Blues on Broadway	Fantasy	9662	'89	CS/CD
Fine and Mellow	Fantasy	9663	'91	CS/CD
The Songs of My Life	Fantasy	9665	'93	CS/ CD
Live in London	Ronnie Scott's Jazz House	46	'95	CD
Best	Rhino	72450	'96	CD

Ruth Brown and the Millstone Singers

Gospel Time	Phillips	600055	'62	†
	Lection	839315	'89	CS/CD

JOHNNY AND DORSEY BURNETTE

Johnny Burnette (born March 25, 1934, in Memphis, Tennessee; died August 1, 1964, in Clear Lake, California), gtr, voc; Dorsey Burnette (born December 28, 1932, in Memphis; died August 19, 1979, in Canoga Park, California), bs, voc. The Rock 'n Roll Trio's lead guitarist, Paul Burlison, was born February 4, 1929, in Brownsville, Tennessee.

With electric lead guitarist Paul Burlison and brother Dorsey Burnette, Johnny Burnette founded the pioneering but largely overlooked rockabilly group the Johnny Burnette Rock 'n Roll Trio in the early '50s. Although they never enjoyed national acclaim, the group provided some of the wildest rockabilly of the era. Disbanding the group in 1957, the brothers moved to California, where they wrote hits for Ricky Nelson and launched their own solo careers.

Johnny and Dorsey Burnette began playing in bands with electric lead guitarist Paul Burlison while still in high school. In 1952 all three worked as electricians for Crown Electric Company, which later employed a truck driver named Elvis Presley. Officially formed in 1953, the Johnny Burnette Rock 'n Roll Trio auditioned for Sam Phillips's Sun Records following the local success of Presley's "That's All Right." Although they were not signed, they persevered, traveling to New York in late 1955, where they won *The Ted Mack Amateur Hour* television competition three times in a row. Soon signed to Coral Records, the group recorded its first single in New York City in May 1956. The wild rockabilly classic "Tear It Up" became a regional hit in Boston and Baltimore, but failed to make the national charts. The group toured nationally and finished its first album in Nashville at the Barn under producer Owen Bradley. They returned to the Nashville studio in July, recording "The Train Kept A-Rollin'." Years later the Yardbirds would rerecord the song, recreating it virtually note-for-note. The group toured with Carl Perkins and Gene Vincent and appeared in the 1957 film *Rock, Rock, Rock*. The group went into the studio for the third and final time in March 1957, but Dorsey Burnette soon departed, to be replaced by Bill Black's brother Johnny. The Johnny Burnette Rock 'n Roll Trio officially disbanded in the fall of 1957.

Dorsey and Johnny Burnette moved to California in 1958, where they concentrated on songwriting and recording demonstration records. They provided Ricky Nelson with two of his most boisterous hits, "Waitin' in School" and "Believe What You Say." Dorsey supplied Nelson with "It's Late" while Johnny furnished him with "Just a Little Too Much." Johnny Burnette recorded for Freedom and Liberty, while Dorsey recorded for Era and later Dot. The most interesting of these recordings were "Way in the Middle of the Night," "Sweet Baby Doll," and "Cincinnati Fireball." In 1960 Dorsey scored hits with "Tall Oak Tree" and "Hey Little One" on Era, while Johnny hit with "Dreamin'" and the classic "You're Sixteen" on Liberty. The following year Johnny had success with "Little Boy Sad," the forlorn "Big Big World," and "God, Country and My Baby," but on August 1, 1964, he died in a boating accident on Clear Lake in California. Dorsey switched to country music in the '60s and achieved a number of moderate country-and-western hits between 1972 and his August 19, 1979, death of a heart attack in Canoga Park, California.

Dorsey Burnette's son Billy (born May 8, 1953, in Memphis) played in his father's band in the '70s and had modest recording success in the country field in the early '80s. He was a member of Fleetwood Mac from 1987 to 1993, returning for their 1994 tour. Johnny Burnette's son Rocky (born Jonathan Burnette on June 12, 1953, in Memphis) had a smash pop hit in 1980 with "Tired of Toein' the Line." Each recorded an album in the '90s.

Johnny Burnette and the Rock 'n Roll Trio

Johnny Burnette and the Rock 'n Roll Trio	Coral	57080	'56	†
	Solid Smoke	8001	'78	†
Listen to Johnny Burnette and the Rock 'n Roll Trio	MCA	1513	'82	†
The Johnny Burnette Trio, Vol. 2	MCA	1561		†

Johnny and Dorsey Burnette

Together Again	Solid Smoke	8005	'80	†

Johnny Burnette

Dreamin'	Liberty	7179	'60	†
Johnny Burnette	Liberty	7183	'61	†
Johnny Burnette Sings	Liberty	7190	'61	†
Roses Are Red	Liberty	7255	'62	†
Hits and Other Favorites	Liberty	7206	'63	†
	Liberty	10144		†
The Johnny Burnette Story	Liberty	7389		†
Dreamin'	Sunset	5179	'67	†

Very Best	United Artists	432	'75	†
You're Sixteen: The Best of Johnny Burnette	Liberty	99997	'92	CS/CD
Dorsey Burnette				
Tall Oak Tree	Era	102	'60	†
Greatest Hits	Era	800	'69	†
Best: The Era Years	Era	5021	'94	CS/CD
Dorsey Burnette Sings	Dot	25456	'63	†
Here and Now	Capitol	11094	'72	†
Dorsey Burnette	Capitol	11219	'73	†
Rock & Roll	Richmond	2134		CS
Billy Burnette				
Billy Burnette	Entrance	31228	'72	†
Billy Burnette	Polydor	6187	'79	†
Between Friends	Polydor	6242	'79	†
Billy Burnette	Columbia	36792	'80	†
Gimme You	Columbia	37460	'81	†
Coming Home	Capricorn	42007	'93	CS/CD†
Rocky Burnette				
The Son of Rock and Roll	EMI America	17033	'80	†
Tear It Up	Core	9465	'96	CD

JOHNNY CASH

Born February 26, 1932, in Kingsland, Arkansas.

Although his greatest significance came in the late '60s when he popularized country-and-western music with the mainstream audience and became the first international country star, Johnny Cash was one of the first rockabilly stars of the '50s, along with Sun Records stablemates Carl Perkins, Jerry Lee Lewis, and Elvis Presley. Switching to the major label Columbia in 1958, Cash later recorded folk-oriented material in the mid '60s and brought an unprecedented level of social consciousness to country music with 1964's "Ballad of Ira Hayes" from *Bitter Tears,* his monumental tribute to the American Indian. His ABC television series, *The Johnny Cash Show* (1969–71), was instrumental in widening the audience for country music and helped introduce Bob Dylan and Kris Kristofferson to broader public acceptance. In the '80s and '90s Johnny Cash enjoyed success with Kris Kristofferson, Willie Nelson, and Waylon Jennings in the Highwaymen, and in 1994 he achieved his first album chart entry in eighteen years with *American Recordings.*

Johnny Cash grew up in Dyess, Arkansas, where he had moved at the age of three. Writing his first song at the age of twelve, Cash joined the U.S. Air Force after high school graduation. Stationed in West Germany, he learned guitar and formed his first group. Upon his discharge in July 1954, he traveled to Memphis, where he met guitarist Luther Perkins and bassist Marshall Grant. With Cash playing guitar and singing in a deep baritone voice of exceptionally low and narrow range, the three practiced together, eventually auditioning for Sam Phillips of Sun Records in March 1955. Signed to Sun as Johnny Cash and the Tennessee Two, their first single, "Cry, Cry, Cry," became a moderate country hit. After the two-sided country smash "So Doggone Lonesome"/"Folsom Prison Blues," the group scored their first major pop hit/top country hit with Cash's own "I Walk the Line" (backed by "Get Rhythm") in 1956. The group appeared on the *Louisiana Hayride* in December 1955, becoming regulars, graduating to *Grand Ole Opry* in July 1956. They subsequently achieved major pop/top country hits on Sun with "Ballad of a Teenage Queen" and "Guess

JOHNNY CASH

Things Happen That Way" in 1958. That year the group became Johnny Cash and the Tennessee Three with the addition of W. S. Holland, one of country music's first drummers.

In August 1958 Johnny Cash and the Tennessee Three switched to Columbia Records, soon managing a moderate pop/top country hit with "Don't Take Your Guns to Town." Leaving the *Grand Ole Opry* and moving to California, Cash started working with June Carter, of the legendary Carter Family, in 1961. He began feeling the strain of constant touring, and the collapse of his first marriage and the death of friend Johnny Horton were serious personal blows. As a consequence Cash started taking amphetamines and tranquilizers to cope with his hectic life. In 1963 he scored his first major pop/top country hit on Columbia with "Ring of Fire," written by Merle Kilgore and June Carter.

Johnny Cash was soon frequenting the Greenwich Village folk music scene, and his next moderate pop hit (also a top country hit), "Understand Your Man," had a distinctive folk feel to it. In 1964 he appeared with Bob Dylan at the Newport Folk Festival and recorded *Bitter Tears,* his tribute to the plight of the American Indian. It yielded a smash country hit with Peter LaFarge's "Ballad of Ira Hayes," and soon Cash and June Carter scored a smash country hit with Dylan's "It Ain't Me, Babe." Cash's 1965 album *Orange Blossom Special* yielded a smash country/minor pop hit with the title song and included three Dylan songs.

Despite increasing popular success, Johnny Cash's life seemed to deteriorate. In October 1965 he was arrested at El Paso International Airport in possession of hundreds of stimulants and tranquilizers. After being found near death in a small Georgia town in 1967, Cash decided to reform. With June Carter providing moral support, he cleaned up his act. The couple scored a smash country hit with "Jackson" in 1967 and married in March 1968. In early 1970 they had a smash country/moderate pop hit with Tim Hardin's "If I Were a Carpenter."

Although Luther Perkins died accidentally in 1968, Johnny Cash persevered, replacing him with Bob Wooten. The 1968 album *Johnny Cash at Folsom Prison* revitalized his career and made him an international country star. The album yielded a moderate pop/top country hit with "Folsom Prison Blues" (it was a live version of Cash's 1956 country hit). Carl Perkins was a member of Cash's touring troupe from 1965 to 1975, and in late 1968 Cash scored a top country/moderate pop hit with Perkins's "Daddy Sang Bass." Cash's penchant for novelty songs, as evidenced by 1959's "I Got Stripes" and 1966's "The One on the Right Is on the Left," culminated in the top country/smash pop hit, "A Boy Named Sue," from *Johnny Cash at San Quentin,* another best-seller.

The June 1969 debut show for Johnny Cash's ABC network television series featured a film of Cash and Bob Dylan recording "Girl from the North Country." The song later appeared on Dylan's first country album, *Nashville Skyline.* Later shows featured artists such as Gordon Lightfoot, Kris Kristofferson, Waylon Jennings, and Joni Mitchell. During the 1969 Newport Folk Festival, Johnny Cash introduced Kris Kristofferson, later recording his "Sunday Morning Coming Down" (a top country hit for Cash). Johnny Cash also demonstrated his social consciousness in the early '70s with "What Is Truth" (a major pop/ smash country hit) and "Man in Black" (a smash country hit). He also narrated and coproduced the sound track to the Christian epic *Gospel Road* and assisted in the production of *The Trail of Tears,* a dramatization of the tragedy of the Cherokee Indians, broadcast on public television (PBS).

Johnny Cash scored a top country/major pop hit (his last) with the novelty song "One Piece at a Time" in 1976 and a smash country hit in 1978 with "There Ain't No Good Chain Gangs," recorded with Waylon Jennings. In 1980 Cash returned to his early style of music, recording *Rockabilly Blues* with Nick Lowe and Dave Edmunds of Rockpile. The album included songs by Lowe, Billy Joe Shaver, Kris Kristofferson, Steve Goodman, and John Prine. His last major country hit came with "The Baron" in 1981, the year he recorded *The Survivors* in West Germany with Carl Perkins and Jerry Lee Lewis. During the '70s daughter Rosanne Cash and step-daughter Carlene Carter worked with the Johnny Cash Road Show, and future country star Marty Stuart was a member of Cash's band from 1979 to 1985.

In 1985 Johnny Cash joined Waylon Jennings, Willie Nelson, and Kris Kristofferson to tour and record as the Highwaymen. They achieved a top country hit with Jimmy Webb's "The Highwayman" and a major country hit with Guy Clark's "Desperados Waiting for a Train." Cash later scored a moderate country hit with Waylon Jennings with "Even Cowgirls Get the Blues" and a major country hit with Hank Williams Jr. with "That Old Wheel." In 1986 Cash reunited with old Sun Records alumni Carl Perkins, Jerry Lee Lewis, and Roy Orbison for *Class of '55,* contributing "I Will Rock & Roll with You."

Also in 1986 Johnny Cash was dropped from the Columbia Records roster after twenty-eight years with the label. He subsequently signed with Mercury Records, switching to American Records in 1993. In 1990 he rejoined Jennings, Nelson, and Kristofferson as the Highwaymen for another album and a round of touring. Johnny Cash was inducted into the Roll and Roll Hall of Fame in 1992. In 1993 he sang "The Wanderer" with U2, included on their *Zooropa* album, and later recorded the moody, acoustic *American Recordings* album, produced by Rick Rubin, best known for his work with Run-D.M.C., Public Enemy, and the Red Hot Chili Peppers. The album included songs by Leonard Cohen, Tom Waits, and Nick Lowe. In 1995 Cash once again joined the Highwaymen, to tour and record for Liberty Records *The Road Goes on Forever,* which included Steve Earle's "The Devil's Right Hand," Stephen Bruton's "It Is What It Is," Billy Joe and Eddie Shaver's "Live Forever," and Robert Earl Keen's title song. Cash's 1996 album *Unchained* was recorded with Tom Petty and the Heartbreakers and featured several Cash originals as well as songs by contemporary artists such as Petty, Beck, and Chris Cornell of Soundgarden.

Over the years Johnny Cash has appeared in dramatic roles in films (1970's *A Gunfight* with Kirk Douglas) and television (1986's *Stagecoach* with the other Highwaymen, and 1988's *Davy Crockett*), and even written a novel (1986's *Man in White*). Despite health problems (he had a double-bypass heart operation in 1988), Johnny Cash continued to tour with his wife, June, and son John Carter Cash.

BIBLIOGRAPHY

Govoni, Albert. *A Boy Named Cash.* New York: Lancer, 1970.

Wren, Christopher. *Winners Got Scars, Too: The Life and Legends of Johnny Cash.* New York: Dial, 1971.

Coon, Charles P. *The New Johnny Cash.* New York: Family Library; Old Tappan, NJ: Revell, 1973.

Cash, Johnny. *Man in Black.* Grand Rapids, MI: Zondervan, 1975.

_____. *Man in White: A Novel.* San Francisco: Harper & Row, 1986.

Smith, John L., comp. *The Johnny Cash Discography 1954–1984.* Westport, CT: Greenwood, 1985.

_____. *The Johnny Cash Discography 1984–1993.* Westport, CT: Greenwood, 1994.

_____. *The Johnny Cash Record Catalog.* Westport, CT: Greenwood, 1994.

Sun Recordings

Johnny Cash with His Hot and Blue Guitar	Sun	1220	'56	†
Sings the Songs That Made Him Famous	Sun	1235	'58	†
Greatest!	Sun	1240	'59	†
Sings Hank Williams	Sun	1245	'60	†
Now Here's Johnny Cash	Sun	1255	'61	†
All Aboard the Blue Train	Sun	1270	'63	†
Original Sun Sound	Sun	1275	'65	†
Original Golden Hits, Vol. 1	Sun	100	'69	†
Original Golden Hits, Vol. 2	Sun	101	'69	†
Story Songs of Trains and Rivers	Sun	104	'69	†
Get Rhythm	Sun	105	'69	†
Showtime	Sun	106	'69	†
The Singing Storyteller	Sun	115	'70	†
Living Legend	Sun	118	'70	†
Rough Cut King of Country Music	Sun	122	'70	†
The Man, The World, His Music	Sun	126	'71	†
Original Golden Hits, Vol. 3	Sun	127	'72	†
I Walk the Line	Sun	139		†
Folsom Prison Blues	Sun	140		†
Blue Train	Sun	141		†
Greatest Hits	Sun	142		†
Superbilly (1955–1958)	Sun	1002	'78	†
The Original	Sun	1006		†
Sun Story, Vol. 1	Sunnyvale	901	'77	†
The Sun Years	Rhino	70950	'90	CS/CD

Johnny Cash and Jerry Lee Lewis

Sunday Down South	Sun	119		†
Sing Hank Williams	Sun	125		†

Columbia Recordings

The Fabulous Johnny Cash	Columbia	8122	'58	†
	K-Tel	75024	'95	CS/CD
Hymns by Johnny Cash	Columbia	8125	'59	†
Songs of Our Soil	Columbia	8148	'59	†
Now, There Was a Song!	Columbia	8254	'60	†
	Columbia/Legacy	66506	'94	CD
Ride This Train	Columbia	8255	'60	†
	K-Tel	75026	'95	CS/CD
Hymns From the Heart	Columbia	8522	'62	†
The Sound of Johnny Cash	Columbia	8602	'62	†
Blood, Sweat and Tears	Columbia	8730	'63	†
	Columbia/Legacy	66508	'94	CD

Ring of Fire—The Best of Johnny Cash	Columbia	8853	'63	†
Christmas Spirit	Columbia	8917	'63	†
I Walk the Line	Columbia	8990	'64	†
Bitter Tears	Columbia	9048	'64	†
	Columbia/Legacy	66507	'94	CD
3-Pak: Ring of Fire/Blood, Sweat & Tears/	Columbia	64812	'95	CD†
Johnny Cash Sings the Ballads of the American Indian: Bitter Tears				
Orange Blossom Special	Columbia	9109	'65	†
Ballads of the True West	Columbia	(2)838	'65	†
Mean as Hell	Columbia	9246	'66	†
Everybody Loves a Nut	Columbia	9292	'66	†
That's What You Get for Lovin' Me	Columbia	9337	'66	†
From Sea to Shining Sea	Columbia	9447	'67	†
Greatest Hits	Columbia	9478	'67	CS/CD
	Columbia	00264		CS
At Folsom Prison	Columbia	9639	'68	†
The Holy Land	Columbia	9726	'69	†
At San Quentin	Columbia	9827	'69	CS
At Folsom Prison and San Quentin	Columbia	(2) 33639	'75	†
	Columbia/Legacy	33639	'75	CS/CD
Hello, I'm Johnny Cash	Columbia	9943	'70	†
The World of Johnny Cash	Columbia	(2)29	'70	†
The Johnny Cash Show	Columbia	30100	'70	†
I Walk the Line (sound track)	Columbia	30397	'70	†
Man in Black	Columbia	30550	'71	†
Greatest Hits, Vol.2	Columbia	30887		CS
A Thing Called Love	Columbia	31332	'72	†
America: A 200-Year Salute in Story and Song	Columbia	31645	'72	†
Any Old Wind That Blows	Columbia	32091	'73	†
Gospel Road (sound track)	Columbia	(2)32253	'73	†
	Priority	(2)32253	'82	†
That Ragged Old Flag	Columbia	32917	'74	†
Five Feet High and Rising	Columbia	32951	'74	†
The Junkie and the Juicehead Minus Me	Columbia	33086	'74	†
Sings Precious Memories	Columbia	33087	'75	CS
	Priority	33087	'84	†
John R. Cash	Columbia	33370	'75	†
Look at Them Beans	Columbia	33814	'75	†
Strawberry Cake	Columbia	34088	'76	†
One Piece at a Time	Columbia	34193	'76	†
Last Gunfighter Ballad	Columbia	34314	'77	†
The Rambler	Columbia	34833	'77	†
I Would Like to See You Again	Columbia	35313	'78	†
Greatest Hits, Vol. 3	Columbia	35637	'78	†
Gone Girl	Columbia	35646	'78	†
Silver	Columbia	36086	'79	†
A Believer Sings the Truth	Cachet	9001	'79	†
	Priority	38074	'82	†
	Columbia	38074		CS†
Rockabilly Blues	Columbia	36779	'80	†
Classic Christmas	Columbia	36866	'80	†

The Baron	Columbia	37179	'81	†
Encore	Columbia	37355	'81	†
The Adventures of Johnny Cash	Columbia	38094		†
Biggest Hits	Columbia	38317	'82	CS/CD
Johnny 99	Columbia	38696	'83	†
Columbia Records 1958–1986	Columbia	40637	'87	CS/CD†
Patriot (recorded 1964–1976)	Columbia	45384	'90	CS/CD
The Essential Johnny Cash (1955–1983)	Columbia	(3)47991	'92	CS/CD
The Gospel Collection	Columbia/Legacy	48952	'92	CS/CD
Personal Christmas Collection	Columbia/Legacy	64154	'94	CS/CD

Budget Releases

Johnny Cash	Harmony	11342	'69	†
Walls of a Prison	Harmony	30138	'70	†
Johnny Cash Songbook	Harmony	31602	'72	†
Ballad of the American Indians	Harmony	32388	'73	†
I Walk the Line/Rock Island Line	Pickwick	(2)2045		†
Johnny Cash	Pickwick	(2)2052		†
I Walk the Line	Pickwick	6097		†
Rock Island Line	Pickwick	6101		†
Folsom Prison Blues	Hilltop	6116	'72	†
	Pickwick	6114		†
Big River	Pickwick	6118		†
Country Gold	Power Pak	246		†
Johnny Cash	Archive of Folk and Jazz Music	278		†
Classic Cash	Pair	(2)1107	'86	†
This Is Johnny Cash	RCA-Camden	3014		CS

Johnny Cash and June Carter

Carryin' On	Columbia	9528	'67	†
Johnny Cash and His Woman	Columbia	32443	'73	†
The Johnny Cash Family	Columbia	31754	'72	†
Super Hits	Columbia	66773	'94	CS/CD
Give My Love to Rose	Harmony	31256	'72	†

The Tennessee Three

The Sound Behind Johnny Cash	Columbia	30220	'71	†

Recent Releases

Believe in Him	Word	8333	'86	†
Johnny Cash Is Coming to Town	Mercury	832031	'87	LP/CS/CD†
Classic Cash (rerecordings)	Mercury	834526	'88	CS/CD
Water From the Wells of Home	Mercury	834778	'88	LP/CS/CD†
Boom Chick a Boom	Mercury	842155	'90	CS/CD†
The Mystery of Life	Mercury	848051	'91	CS/CD†
Wanted Man (1986–91)	Mercury	522709	'94	CS/CD
Greatest Hits	CSI	40105	'91	CD†
Best	Curb/Warner Bros.	77494	'91	CS/CD
American Recordings	American	45520	'94	CS/CD
Live Recording	Fat Boy	235	'96	CD
Unchained	American	43097	'97	CD

Johnny Cash, Jerry Lee Lewis, and Carl Perkins

The Survivors	Columbia	37961	'82	LP/CS†
	Razor & Tie	2077	'95	CS/CD

Johnny Cash and Waylon Jennings

Heroes	Columbia	40347	'86	LP/CS†
	Razor & Tie	2078	'95	CS/CD

Johnny Cash, Jerry Lee Lewis, Roy Orbison, and Carl Perkins

Class of '55	America/Smash	830002	'86	LP/CS/CD†
	Mercury	830002	'94	CS/CD

Johnny Cash, Willie Nelson, Waylon Jennings, and Kris Kristofferson (The Highwaymen)

The Highwayman	Columbia	40056	'85	CS/CD†
Highwayman II	Columbia	45240	'90	CS/CD
The Road Goes on Forever	Liberty	28091	'95	CS/CD

THE CHANTELS

Arlene Smith, lead voc (born October 5, 1941, in New York); Lois Harris, 1st ten (born 1940 in New York); Sonia Goring, 2d ten (born 1940 in New York); Jackie Landry, 2d alto (born 1940 in New York); Rene Minus, alto and bs (born 1943 in New York).

One of the first "girl groups" and the first female R&B vocal group to enjoy widespread popularity, the Chantels' sound was based on the soaring, plaintive voice of lead vocalist Arlene Smith, who wrote many of the group's songs. Nonetheless, the group was unable to sustain the enormous success of 1958's "Maybe," and by 1960 Smith had left the group and been replaced by Annette Smith, lead vocalist on 1961's "Look in My Eyes."

The future members of the Chantels began singing together in 1950 at their parochial school, Saint Anthony of Padua School in the Bronx, New York. Arlene Smith was classically trained and performed solo as a classical singer at Carnegie Hall at the age of twelve. By 1957 the group had begun appearing in local talents shows and had drawn the attention of singer-producer Richard Barrett, an associate of record entrepreneur George Goldner. Auditioning for Barrett, the Chantels signed with Goldner's newly formed End label in the summer of 1957. With Barrett producing, their first single, Arlene's "He's Gone," became a minor pop hit. The group gave their first live performance at the Apollo Theater, in the fall of 1957 and in early 1958 they scored a smash R&B and major pop hit with "Maybe," variously credited to Smith, Barrett, and Smith and Barrett. Subsequent major R&B and moderate pop hits for the Chantels included "Every Night (I Pray)" and "I Love You So."

However, End dropped the Chantels in the spring of 1959, and Lois Harris and Arlene Smith left the group. In 1961 Smith covered the Clovers' "Love, Love, Love," with apprentice Phil Spector producing, before getting out of the music business. Richard Barrett brought on Annette Smith of the Veneers to replace Arlene, and the Chantels moved to Carlton Records, where they managed a smash R&B/major pop hit with "Look in My Eyes" in 1961. Subsequently recording for Luther Dixon's Ludix label, the group later recorded for several other labels before disbanding in 1970. A later Richard Barrett group, the Three Degrees, scored hits with "Look in My Eyes" and "Maybe" in 1966 and 1970, respectively. In 1973 Arlene Smith reformed the Chantels with new members for oldies revival shows. She continued to sing with her own group of Chantels into the '80s.

We're the Chantels	End	301	'58	†
There's Our Song Again	End	312	'62	†

On Tour	Carlton	144	'61	†
Sing Their Favorites	Forum	9104		†
Arlene Smith and the Chantels	Roulette	59032	'87	†
reissued as "The Chantels"	Collectables	5423		†
Best of the Chantels	Rhino	70954	'90	CS/CD

RAY CHARLES

Born Ray Charles Robinson on September 23, 1930, in Albany, Georgia.

RAY CHARLES, C. 1954

A multitalented blind black musician, Ray Charles pioneered soul music, which became enormously popular among both black and white audiences beginning in the late '50s. In secularizing certain aspects of gospel music (chord changes, song structures, call-and-response techniques, and vocal screams, wails, and moans) and adding blues-based lyrics, he essentially invented a new genre of popular music. Along with musicians such as Horace Silver, Charles was instrumental in leading many jazz musicians away from the abstracted and relatively inaccessible music of bebop as practiced by Charlie Parker, John Coltrane, Dizzy Gillespie, and others, back to the roots of soul and funk musics.

Ray Charles's gospel-based vocal style influenced virtually all the soul singers of the '60s, as well as many of the white English singers that emerged in the '60s (Mick Jagger, Eric Burdon, Joe Cocker, Rod Stewart, and others). In using the electric piano on his first major pop hit, "What'd I Say," Charles introduced the instrument to jazz and rock music. Moreover, the vocal work of his female backup group, the Raeletts, set the standard for black vocal groups that was so successfully exploited by Motown Records in the '60s. Additionally, in applying his gospel-oriented style to country-and-western material in the early '60s, Ray Charles became the first black artist to score hits in the country field and the first male black singer to make a major impact on the white adult market.

Ray Charles grew up in Greenville, Florida, and was blinded by glaucoma at the age of seven. From 1937 to 1945 he attended the St. Augustine (Florida) School for the Deaf and Blind, where he learned piano and, later, clarinet and alto saxophone, as well as composing and arranging. Orphaned at fifteen, Charles struck out on his own, performing in bands around Florida. In 1948 he moved to Seattle and formed the Maxim Trio (also known as the McSon Trio and the Maxine Trio), a group grounded in the style of Nat "King" Cole and Charles Brown. As the Maxine Trio, they scored a major R&B hit in 1949 with "Confession Blues" on the Downbeat label. Charles toured with blues artist Lowell Fulson in the early '50s, scoring R&B hits with "Baby Let Me Hold Your Hand" and "Kiss Me Baby" on the small, Los Angeles-based Swingtime label.

In 1952 the New York-based Atlantic label bought Ray Charles's recording contract, and shedding his Nat "King" Cole stylization and adapting gospel music techniques to blues lyrics, he soon hit with "It Should Have Been Me." In 1954 he arranged and played piano on Guitar Slim's top R&B hit "Things That I Used to Do" for Specialty and formed his own band. In early 1955, Charles hit in both the popular and R&B fields with his own composition, "I've Got a Woman." Using top-flight studio musicians such as saxophonist David "Fathead" Newman, Charles scored consistently on the R&B charts through the late '50s with songs such as "A Fool for You," "Drown in My Own Tears," "Hallelujah I Love Her So," and "Lonely Avenue," the recording debut of his backup female vocal group, the Raeletts. He also became popular with jazz fans, recording two highly acclaimed records with Modern Jazz Quartet vibraphonist Milt Jackson and performing a startling set at the 1958 Newport Jazz Festival. Finally, in 1959, Charles established himself as a popular recording artist and pioneer of soul music with the release of his own top R&B/smash pop hit composition "What'd I Say." The song was later covered by a variety of artists, including Jerry Lee Lewis, Bobby Darin, and Elvis Presley.

Sensing that Atlantic was still basically an R&B organization, Ray Charles switched to ABC-Paramount Records in late 1959. Through 1961 he scored with the top pop hits "Georgia on My Mind" and "Hit the Road Jack" (a top R&B hit) and the major pop hits "Ruby" and "Unchain My Heart" (another top R&B hit). He also recorded *Genius + Soul = Jazz* for Impulse (ABC's jazz subsidiary label), with arrangements by Quincy Jones played by the Count Basie Orchestra. Yielding a near-smash pop/top R&B hit with the instrumental "One Mint Julep," this album and one recorded with Betty Carter for ABC-Paramount brought him an increasing measure of popularity with jazz fans, black and white.

In 1962 Ray Charles formed Ray Charles Enterprises, comprised of Tangerine Records, Tangerine Music, and Racer Music Company, opening studios and offices in Los Angeles in 1963. By then he was utilizing forty-piece orchestras and large vocal choruses for his recordings. With this full, commercial sound, his *Modern Sounds in Country and Western* became phenomenally popular, producing the crossover smash hits "I Can't Stop Loving You" backed with "Born to Lose," and "You Don't Know Me." Within a year, volume 2 of country-and-western material was released with the crossover smash hits "You Are My Sunshine" backed with "Your Cheating Heart," and "Take These Chains from My Heart." On ABC Charles scored major pop hits with "Busted," "That Lucky Old Sun," "Crying Time," and "Together Again." Major hits on ABC/Tangerine included "Let's Go Get Stoned" (a top R&B hit), "Here We Go Again," and the Beatles' "Yesterday" and "Eleanor Rigby."

During the '60s Ray Charles also became involved with film work, appearing in the 1962 film *Swingin' Along* (AKA *Double Trouble*) and the 1966 British film *Ballad in Blue* (AKA *Blues for Lovers*), and recording the sound tracks for the films *The Cincinnati Kid* (1965) and *In the Heat of the Night* (1967). By 1967 he had begun performing on the nightclub circuit, touring with his own package revue from 1969 into the '70s.

In 1973 Ray Charles left ABC Records, retaining the rights to his ABC material and transferring his Tangerine operation to the new label Crossover. During 1976 he recorded *Porgy and Bess* with English songstress Cleo Laine for RCA Records. He returned to Atlantic in 1977, moving to Columbia in the '80s and Warner Brothers in the '90s. In 1978 Dial Press published Ray Charles's autobiography, written with David Ritz, and in 1980 Charles appeared in *The Blues Brothers* movie and scored a minor country hit for his duet with Clint

Eastwood, "Beers to You," from the film *Any Which Way You Can*. Charles achieved a major country hit with "Born to Love Me" in 1982 and later recorded duets with country stars on *Friendship*. The album yielded five major country hits, including "We Didn't See a Thing" (with George Jones), "Seven Spanish Angels" (with Willie Nelson), and "Two Old Cats Like Us" (with Hank Williams Jr.). Charles also played a major role in the recording of USA for Africa's "We Are the World" single in 1985.

Inducted into the Blues Foundation's Hall of Fame in 1982, Ray Charles was inducted into the Rock and Roll Hall of Fame in its inaugural year, 1986. In late 1989 Charles had his first major pop hit in over twenty years with the Quincy Jones recording "I'll Be Good to You," featuring himself and Chaka Khan. During the '90s Ray Charles appeared in a series of stylish commercials for Pepsi and was the subject of a PBS documentary.

In the '90s Ray Charles continues to work about eight months a year, touring with a large orchestra. He lives in Los Angeles, where he is involved with RPM International, a corporation that includes Crossover Records, the music publishing companies Tangerine and Racer Music, and RPM Studios, where he records. In 1990 Ray Charles began recording for Warner Brothers Records, recording 1993's *My World* with Eric Clapton, Billy Preston, Mavis Staples and June Pointer.

BIBLIOGRAPHY

Charles, Ray, and David Ritz. *Brother Ray: Ray Charles' Own Story.* New York: Dial, 1978; New York: Da Capo, 1992.

Ritz, David. *Ray Charles: Voice of Soul.* New York: Chelsea House, 1994.

Early Recordings

Birth of a Legend (recorded 1949–1952)	Ebony	(2)8001/2	'92	CD
Original Ray Charles	Hollywood	504	'62	†
Fabulous Ray Charles	Hollywood	505	'63	†
Great Ray Charles	Premier	2004	'62	†
Fabulous Ray Charles	Premier	2005	'62	
Ray Charles	Design	145	'62	†
Ray Charles with Arbee Stidham, Lil Son Jackson and James Wayne	Mainstream	310	'71	†
Ray Charles	Archive of Folk and Jazz Music/Everest	244	'70	†
Ray Charles, Vol. 2	Archive of Folk and Jazz Music/Everest	292	'74	†
14 Hits: The Early Years	King	5011	'77	†
14 Original Great Hits	Deluxe	7844		CS
Sings 28 Great Songs	Deluxe	7859		CS
The Early Years (1947–1951)	Zeta	707	'89	CD†
	EPM	15707	'89	CD†
The Early Years	Tomato	(2)71656	'94	CD

Atlantic Recordings of the '50s and '60s

Hallelujah I Love Her So	Atlantic	8006	'57	†
The Great Ray Charles	Atlantic	1259	'57	CS
Ray Charles at Newport	Atlantic	1289	'58	†
Yes Indeed!	Atlantic	8025	'58	†
What'd I Say	Atlantic	8029	'59	†
The Real Ray Charles (compilation of above 2)	Pair	1139	'86	CS

The Genius of Ray Charles	Atlantic	1312	'59	CS/CD
The Great Ray Charles (includes The Great Ray Charles and 6 cuts from The Genius of Ray Charles)	Atlantic	81731		CD
Ray Charles in Person	Atlantic	8039	'60	†
Live (reissue of At Newport and In Person)	Atlantic	(2)503	'73	†
	Atlantic	503		CS
The Genius After Hours	Atlantic	1369	'61	†
	Atlantic	90464	'86	CS†
The Genius Sings the Blues	Atlantic	8052	'61	†
The Greatest Ray Charles/Do the Twist with Ray Charles!	Atlantic	8054	'61	CS
The Ray Charles Story, Vol. 1	Atlantic	8063	'62	†
The Ray Charles Story, Vol. 2	Atlantic	8064	'62	†
The Ray Charles Story, Vol.s. 1 and 2	Atlantic	(2)900	'62	†
The Ray Charles Story, Vol. 3	Atlantic	8083	'63	†
The Ray Charles Story, Vol. 4	Atlantic	8094	'64	†
Great Hits Recorded on 8-Track Stereo	Atlantic	7101	'64	†
Best	Atlantic	1543		CS/CD
Memories of a Middle-Aged Fan	Atco	33–263	'68	†
A Life in Music	Atlantic	(5)3700	'82	LP/CS†
Ray Charles Live	Atlantic	81732		CD
The Birth of Soul–The Complete Atlantic Rhythm & Blues Recordings, 1952–1959	Atlantic	(3)82310	'91	CS/CD

Ray Charles and Milt Jackson

Soul Brothers	Atlantic	1279	'58	CS
Soul Meeting	Atlantic	1360	'62	CS
Soul Brothers/Soul Meeting	Atlantic	(2)81951	'89	CD

The Ray Charles Sextette (with David "Fathead" Newman)

Ray Charles Sextet	Atlantic	1304	'59	†

ABC Recordings

The Genius Hits the Road	ABC	335	'60	†
Dedicated to You	ABC	355	'61	†
Genius + Soul = Jazz	Impulse	2	'61	†
	DCC	038	'88	CS/CD†
	Sandstone	33073	'92	CD†
Modern Sounds in Country and Western	ABC	410	'62	†
	Rhino	70099	'88	CS/CD
Greatest Hits	ABC	415	'62	†
Modern Sounds in Country and Western, Vol. 2	ABC	435	'62	†
Ingredients in a Recipe for Soul	ABC	465		†
	DCC	047		CS/CD†
	DCC	1027		CD†
	Sandstone	33074	'92	CD†
Sweet and Sour Tears	ABC	480	'64	†
Have a Smile with Me	ABC	495	'64	†
Live in Concert	ABC	500	'65	†
Together Again/Country and Western Meets Rhythm and Blues	ABC	520	'65	†
Crying Time	ABC	544	'66	†
Ray's Moods	ABC	550	'66	†
A Man and His Soul	ABC	(2)590	'67	†
25th Anniversary Salute	ABC	(3)731	'71	†

All-Time Greats	ABC	(2)781/2	'73	†
Invites You to Listen	ABC/Tangerine	595	'67	†
A Portrait of Ray	ABC/Tangerine	625	'68	†
I'm All Yours, Baby	ABC/Tangerine	675	'69	†
Doing His Thing	ABC/Tangerine	695	'69	†
Love Country Style	ABC/Tangerine	707	'70	†
Volcanic Action of My Soul	ABC/Tangerine	726	'71	†
Cryin' Time	ABC/Tangerine	744	'71	†
A Message for the People	ABC/Tangerine	755	'72	†
Through the Eyes of Love	ABC/Tangerine	765	'72	†

Other Sixties Recordings

Rock + Soul = Genius (recorded 1961)	Jazz Music Yesterday	1009	'91	CD
Berlin, 1962 March 6, 1962	Pablo	5301	'96	CD
Ray Charles	Time Volumes	(2)2/4	'63	†
Incomparable Ray Charles	Strand	1086	'63	†
The Cincinnati Kid (sound track)	MGM	4313	'65	†
In the Heat of the Night (sound track)	United Artists	5160	'67	†

Ray Charles and Betty Carter

Ray Charles and Betty Carter	ABC	385	'61	†
	DCC	039	'88	CS/CD
	DCC	2005	'95	LP

The Ray Charles Orchestra

My Kind of Jazz	Tangerine/ABC	1512	'70	†
Jazz Number II	Tangerine/ABC	1516	'73	†
My Kind of Jazz, Part 3	Crossover	9007	'75	†

The Raelettes

Ray Charles Presents the Raeletts, Yesterday . . . Today . . . Tomorrow	Tangerine	1515	'72	†

Ray Charles and Cleo Laine

Porgy and Bess	RCA	(2)1831	'76	CS/CD

Later Recordings

Come Live with Me	Crossover	9000	'74	†
Renaissance	Crossover	9005	'75	†
True to Life	Atlantic	19142	'77	†
Love and Peace	Atlantic	19199	'78	†
Ain't It So	Atlantic	19251	'79	†
Brother Ray Is at It Again	Atlantic	19281	'80	†
Wish You Were Here Tonight	Columbia	38293	'83	†
Do I Ever Cross Your Mind	Columbia	38990	'84	†
Friendship	Columbia	39415	'84	CD†
The Spirit of Christmas	Columbia	40125	'85	LP/CS/CD
From the Pages of My Mind	Columbia	40338	'86	CS†
Just Between Us	Columbia	40703	'88	CS/CD†
Seven Spanish Angels and Other Hits (1982–1986)	Columbia	45062	'89	CS/CD†
Would You Believe?	Warner Brothers	26343	'90	LP/CS/CD
My World	Warner Brothers	26735	'93	CS/CD
Strong Love Affair	Qwest/ Warner Brothers	46107	'95	CS/CD

Anthologies

20 Golden Pieces of Ray Charles	Bulldog	2012	'79	LP/CS
Anthology	Rhino	75759	'88	CD
Greatest Hits, Vol. 1	Rhino	70097	'88	CS
Greatest Hits, Vol. 2	Rhino	70098	'88	CS
Blues + Jazz (1950–59)	Rhino	(2)71607	'94	CD
Classics	Rhino	71874	'95	CS/CD
Greatest Hits, Vol. 1	DCC	036	'88	CD†
Greatest Hits, Vol. 2	DCC	037	'88	CD†
Greatest Hits, Vols. 1 and 2	DCC	(2)36/37		CD†
Greatest Country and Western Hits	DCC	040	'88	CS/CD†
	DCC	2012	'95	LP
	DCC	1086	'95	CD
Ray Charles	Bella Musica	89904	'90	CD†
Greatest Hits	CSI	40141	'91	CD†
His Greatest Hits	Sandstone	(2)33079	'92	CD†
The Session, Vol. 2	Royal Collection	83154	'92	CD
C. C. Rider	Drive	3233	'95	CD
See See Rider	Musketeer	9011	'95	CD
Walkin and Talkin	Fat Boy	325	'96	CD
Going Down Slow	CMA	8020	'96	CD
The Great Ray Charles	Goldies	63117	'96	CD
Best of Easy Listening	Richmond	2154		CS
Goin' Down Slow	Intermedia	5013		LP/CS

DICK CLARK

Born November 30, 1929, in Mount Vernon, New York.

As host of the first network television series devoted to rock 'n' roll and the longest-running musical show in television history, *American Bandstand,* Dick Clark made rock music palatable to the mainstream American public and helped promote the careers of many of the rock 'n' roll artists of the '50s, both the talents and no-talents. Presenting a sanitized, even emasculated form of rock 'n' roll, the show nonetheless influenced the dance and fashion trends of the day and opened the door for other music ventures on television, from *Soul Train* to MTV. Escaping most of the ill effects of the "payola" scandal of 1959, despite his heavy involvement with record labels and music publishing companies, Dick Clark prospered after the furor, whereas others (most notably Alan Freed) were totally ruined by the investigation.

Dick Clark majored in business administration at Syracuse University, where he served as a disc jockey on the campus radio station. After graduation in 1951, he worked as a news anchor on WKTV in Utica before moving to Philadelphia in 1952 to become a radio announcer at WFIL. By July 1956, WFIL-TV's dance-and-music show *Bandstand* (originally created by disc jockey Bob Horn in 1952) had become the city's top-rated daytime show.

Dick Clark took over as host of *Bandstand* and subsequently persuaded officials of ABC-TV to broadcast the show over the entire network as *American Bandstand* on weekday afternoons. The format generally included one or two guest stars synchronizing their lip movements to their recorded songs, teenagers dancing to records, and small talk and record ratings by members of the audience. Debuting on ABC on August 5, 1957, *American Bandstand* became enormously popular and a number of Philadelphia teenagers who regu-

DICK CLARK, 1965

larly appeared as dancers became household celebrities. The show provided the first national exposure of Chuck Berry, Jerry Lee Lewis, Buddy Holly, and Chubby Checker, among others. The success of the show also encouraged the proliferation of local labels such as Cameo-Parkway, Swan, Jamie, and Chancellor. Clark was financially involved in Swan and Jamie, and acts for these labels (locals Frankie Avalon, Fabian, Chubby Checker, and Bobby Rydell, plus Duane Eddy and Freddy Cannon) seemed to prosper more than most as a result of exposure on *American Bandstand.*

Called before the Senate investigating committee probing so-called payola (pay-for-play) activities among disc jockeys, Clark admitted to accepting a fur stole and expensive jewelry from a record company president. He was admonished for only this single transgression, despite the fact that songs and artists in which he had a considerable interest were frequently featured on *American Bandstand.* Clark had apparently divested himself of his music business holdings at a crucial time before appearing to testify.

In 1964 Dick Clark moved *American Bandstand* to Los Angeles, where he hosted the television program *Where the Action Is,* with house band Paul Revere and the Raiders, in the late '60s. During the '70s he expanded his media exploits through his Burbank-based Dick Clark Productions, producing television shows and specials. He has produced and hosted the *New Year's Rockin' Eve* since 1972, the game show *$25,000 Pyramid* since 1973, the *American Music Awards* since 1974, the *Academy of Country Music Awards* since 1978, and (with Ed McMahon) *TV's Bloopers and Practical Jokes* since 1984. He also hosts the syndicated radio shows *Rock, Roll and Remember* and *Countdown America* and is the founder and director of the Unistar Radio Network, which supplies programs to more than 1,800 radio stations. Furthermore, his company has produced the film *Remo Williams* (1985) and the made-for-TV movies *Elvis, The Birth of the Beatles* and *Promised a Miracle. American Bandstand* left ABC for syndication in 1987, and, in 1989 Clark stepped down as the show's host. It lasted only six months on the USA cable network with a new host. In 1993 Dick Clark was inducted into the Rock and Roll Hall of Fame and began hosting the game show *Scattergories.* In 1996 cable network VH-1 began rerunning episodes of *American Bandstand* that originally aired between 1975 and 1985.

BIBLIOGRAPHY

Jackson, John A. *American Bandstand: Dick Clark and the Making of a Rock & Roll Empire.* New York: Oxford University Press, 1997.

Uslan, Michael, and Bruce Solomon. *Dick Clark's The First 25 Years of Rock & Roll.* New York: Delacorte, 1981.

Shore, Michael, with Dick Clark. *The History of American Bandstand: It's Got a Great Beat and You Can Dance to It.* New York: Ballantine, 1985.

Clark, Dick, and Richard Robinson. *Rock, Roll & Remember.* New York: Crowell, 1976; New York: Popular Library, 1978.

———— with Bill Libby. *Looking Great, Staying Young.* Indianapolis: Bobbs-Merrill, 1980.

———— with Paul Francis. *Murder on Tour: A Rock 'n' Roll Mystery.* New York: Mysterious Press, 1989.

Dance with Dick Clark, Vol. 1	ABC-Paramount	258		†
Dance with Dick Clark, Vol. 2	ABC-Paramount	288	'59	†
20 Years of Rock 'n' Roll	Buddah	(2)5133	'73	†
Dick Clark's 21 All-Time Hits, Vol. 1	Original Sound	8891		CS/CD
Vol. 2	Original Sound	8892		CS/CD
Vol. 3	Original Sound	8894		CS/CD
Vol. 4	Original Sound	8895		CS/CD
Dick Clark's 21 All-Time Hits, Double Pack, Vols. 1–2	Original Sound	(2)9319		CD
Dick Clark's 21 All-Time Hits, Double Pack, Vols. 3–4	Original Sound	(2)9320		CD
Dick Clark's 21 All-Time Hits	Original Sound	(4)1234		CS/CD

THE CLOVERS

Lead ten John "Buddy" Bailey (born ca. 1930, Washington, D.C.); 2d ten Matthew Mc-Quater, bar Harold "Hal" Lucas (born ca. 1923, died January 6, 1994); bs voc Harold Winley; gtr Bill Harris (born April 14, 1925, in Nashville, Tennessee; died December 10, 1988). Other members included Charles White (born ca. 1930, Washington, D.C.) and Billy Mitchell.

The most popular R&B vocal group of the first half of the '50s, the Clovers were one of the first such groups to be acknowledged as rock 'n' roll artists, playing in Alan Freed's shows in 1954. Recording the classics "Blue Velvet," "Devil or Angel," and "Your Cash Ain't Nothin' But Trash," the Clovers featured the accompaniment of some of the finest saxophone players in New York and utilized twin lead tenors beginning in 1954, years before the Temptations adopted the practice.

Formed in 1946 in Washington, D.C., by Harold "Hal" Lucas," the group called themselves the Four Clovers after John "Buddy" Bailey joined the group. When Bill Harris joined in 1949, they officially became the Clovers. Signed to Atlantic Records after one single for Rainbow, the Clovers scored a string of top and smash R&B hits beginning in 1951 with "Don't You Know I Love You." Featuring the occasional ballad and saxophone accompaniment on up-tempo blues-based songs, they scored smash R&B hits with "Fool, Fool, Fool," "One Mint Julep" (covered by Ray Charles in 1961) backed with "Middle of the Night," "Ting-a-Ling" backed with "Wonder Where My Baby's Gone," "Hey Miss Fannie" (considered by some to be the first rock 'n' roll record) backed with "I Played the Fool," and "Crawlin'." In 1952 Charlie White became the new lead while Bailey served a stint in the Army. White was featured on the hits "Good Lovin'," "Comin' On," and "Lovey Dovey" (covered by Buddy Knox in 1961) backed with "Little Mama."

In early 1954 the Clovers performed on Alan Freed's first rock 'n' roll show. By April, White had left, to be replaced by Billy Mitchell. When Bailey returned in the fall of 1954 the group began featuring twin lead tenors Bailey and Lucas. Subsequent R&B hits included "I've Got My Eyes on You" backed with the classic "Your Cash Ain't Nothin' But Trash" (covered by Steve Miller in 1974), "Blue Velvet" (covered by Bobby Vinton in 1963), "Nip Sip," and "Devil or Angel" (covered by Bobby Vee in 1960) backed with "Hey, Baby Doll." The Clovers scored their first major pop hit in 1956 with "Love, Love, Love," but their Atlantic contract expired in July 1957. Subsequently recording for Poplar Records, they managed one final hit with "Love Potion No. 9" in late 1959 on United Artists. The group broke up in 1961, and Buddy Bailey and Harold Winley formed a new group of Clovers in 1961. Hal Lucas formed a second set of Clovers in 1962. Bill Harris died of pancreatic cancer on December 10, 1988; Hal Lucas died of cancer on January 6, 1994.

BIBLIOGRAPHY

Grendysa, Peter. "The Clovers: More Rhythm in Their Blues" (Discography by Neal Umphred). *Goldmine* 17, no. 3 (February 8, 1991): 7–10, 32, 36.

The Clovers	Atlantic	1248	'56	†
	Atlantic	8009	'57	†
Dance Party	Atlantic	8034	'59	†
Down in the Alley—The Best of the Clovers	Atlantic	82312	'91	CS/CD
Their Greatest Recordings	Atco	33–374	'71	†
In Clover	Poplar	1001	'58	†
	United Artists	3033	'59	†
Love Potion Number Nine	United Artists	6099	'59	†
The Original Love Potion Number Nine	Grand Prix	428	'64	†
The Best of the Clovers: Love Potion No. 9	EMI	96336	'91	CS/CD

THE COASTERS

Carl Gardner (born April 29, 1928, in Tyler, Texas), lead voc; Bobby Nunn (born 1925 in Birmingham, Alabama; died November 5, 1986, in Los Angeles), bs voc; Leon Hughes, ten (born ca. 1938); Billy Guy (born June 20, 1936, in Attasca, Texas), lead and bar voc; Adolph Jacobs, gtr. Later members included Young Jessie, Cornelius "Cornell" Gunter (born November 14, 1936, in Los Angeles; died February 26, 1990, in Las Vegas, Nevada); Will "Dub" Jones (born ca. 1939 in Los Angeles); Earl "Speedo" Carroll (born November 2, 1937, in New York City); and Ronnie Bright (born October 18, 1938).

Rock 'n' roll's first consistently successful comedy-vocal group, the Coasters provided a number of wry and satirical songs of adolescent pathos under the direction of the premier '50s songwriting-production team, Jerry Leiber and Mike Stoller. One of the first R&B vocal groups to achieve widespread popularity with white youth, the Coasters later featured the lusty saxophone playing of King Curtis, who helped establish the instrument as the third most important in rock 'n' roll, behind guitar and piano.

The Coasters evolved out of the Robins, an R&B vocal group formed in Los Angeles in 1949. In early 1950 the group scored an R&B hit with "If It's So, Baby," with the Johnny Otis Band, and backed Esther Phillips on her top R&B hit "Double Crossing Blues." Songwriters Jerry Leiber and Mike Stoller began recording the group after they formed Spark Records in late 1953. The Robins enjoyed regional success with the classic "Riot in Cell Block Number 9" and had their first national hit with "Smokey Joe's Cafe," when reissued on Atco in late 1955.

In 1955 Leiber and Stoller signed what was likely the first independent production deal with the Atco subsidiary of the New York-based Atlantic label. Atlantic acquired the Spark

THE COASTERS, 1956. PHOTO BY POPSIE RANDOLPH

catalog and the producers attempted to coax the Robins into joining them at the new label. Not all were willing, so Leiber and Stoller convinced Bobby Nunn and Carl Gardner to form a new group, the Coasters, with Leon Hughes, Billy Guy, and Adolph Jacobs. Their first single, "Down in Mexico," became a major R&B hit, and their third single, "Youngblood"/"Searchin'," became a smash pop/R&B hit for the group and their songwriter-producers.

In 1957 Young Jessie replaced Leon Hughes in the Coasters. Moving to New York with Leiber and Stoller by 1958, the group replaced Jessie with Cornelius Gunter and the retiring Bobby Nunn with Will "Dub" Jones of the Cadets ("Stranded in the Jungle"). Beginning with the smash hit "Yakety Yak," the Coasters were accompanied by the ribald saxophone playing of King Curtis. Through 1959 the group scored smash pop and R&B hits with "Charlie Brown," "Along Came Jones" (backed with "That Is Rock 'n' Roll"), and "Poison Ivy" (backed by the lewd "I'm a Hog for You"). "Run Red Run"/"What About Us" and "Wake Me, Shake Me" proved only moderate successes, and the funky "Shoppin' for Clothes," featuring an unusually lewd saxophone break by King Curtis, fared even less well. The Coasters achieved their last major hit with "Little Egypt" in 1961, the year Earl "Speedo" Carroll of the Cadillacs (1956's "Speedo") replaced Cornell Gunter. In 1963 Leiber and Stoller and the Coasters parted company, and by 1965 the group was comprised of Gardner, Guy, Carroll, and bass vocalist Ronnie Bright. They left Atco in 1966, subsequently recording for the Date subsidiary of Columbia.

The Coasters performed on various shows during the rock 'n' roll revival of the early '70s. Several editions of the Coasters toured during the '70s and '80s. The various leaders were Cornelius Gunter, Bobby Nunn, Will Jones and Billy Guy, Leon Hughes, and Carl Gardner and Ronnie Bright. Bobby Nunn died on November 5, 1986, of a heart attack in Los Angeles. Inducted into the Rock and Roll Hall of Fame in 1987, the Coasters (Gardner, Guy, Jones, and Gunter, with Tom Palmer) performed at Atlantic Records' fortieth Anniversary Birthday Concert in May 1988. Cornelius Gunter was found shot dead in his car in Las Vegas on February 26, 1990, at the age of fifty-three.

The Robins

Rock 'N' Roll With the Robins	Whippet	703	'58	†
Best	GNP Crescendo	9034	'75	†

The Coasters

The Coasters	Atco	33–101	'58	†
Greatest Hits	Atco	33–111	'59	†
	Atco	33111		CS/CD†
One by One	Atco	33–123	'60	†
Coast Along with the Coasters	Atco	33–135	'62	†
Greatest Recordings/The Early Years	Atco	33–371	'71	†
	Atco	33371		CS†
That's Rock and Roll	Clarion	605	'64	†
It Ain't Sanitary	Trip	8028	'72	†
On Broadway	King	1146	'73	†
Greatest Hits	Power Pak	310	'78	†
Greatest Hits	Pair	1306	'91	CS/CD
50 Coastin' Hits	Rhino	(2)71090	'92	CS/CD
Very Best	Rhino	71597	'94	CS/CD
The Ultimate Coasters	Warner	27604		CD
20 Greatest Hits	Deluxe	7786		CS/CD
Greatest Hits	Hollywood/IMG	282		CS/CD

EDDIE COCHRAN

Born October 3, 1938, in Oklahoma City, Oklahoma; died April 17, 1960, in Chippenham,
Wiltshire, England.

One of rock 'n' roll's first "legends" due to early accidental death, Eddie Cochran was an
early performer of rockabilly music and one of its most exciting and dynamic guitar players. He wrote many of his own songs and helped pioneer the studio technique of overdubbing, as evidenced by his oft-covered classic 1958 smash "Summertime Blues." Although his
popularity was short-lived in the United States, he remained remarkably popular in Great
Britain, even after his death in 1960, and his sound influenced British groups such as the
Who, the Sex Pistols, the Clash, and the Stray Cats.

With his family, Eddie Cochran moved to Albert Lea, Minnesota, as an infant, and then
to Bell Gardens, California, in 1949. He began playing guitar at twelve and joined country
singer Hank Cochran (no relation) as backup guitarist in 1954. They toured and recorded
as the Cochran Brothers until 1956. Switching to rock 'n' roll after seeing Elvis Presley in
Dallas in late 1955, Eddie Cochran demonstrated his skill as a rockabilly guitarist on a
number of sessions in Los Angeles. In the fall of 1956 he met songwriter Jerry Capehart,
who secured him a contract with Liberty Records. His first Liberty single, the tame "Sittin'
in the Balcony," became a major hit in early 1957. During the year, he appeared in two
films, *The Girl Can't Help It,* with Gene Vincent and Little Richard, performing the classic
"Twenty Flight Rock," and *Untamed Youth,* with Mamie Van Doren. However, his next hit
didn't come until the summer of 1958, when the classic "Summertime Blues" became a
near-smash. For the recording, Cochran overdubbed his voice (some say) or his voice and
all instruments (according to others). He toured tirelessly, yet his next single, the raucous
"C'mon Everybody," proved only a moderate hit.

In 1959 Eddie Cochran appeared in the film *Go, Johnny, Go* with Chuck Berry, Ritchie
Valens, and Jackie Wilson. Like Gene Vincent, Cochran was far more popular in England,

and in early 1960 he embarked on his only European tour. Upon completing the tour, while on his way to the airport in London, Eddie Cochran was killed in an auto crash near Chippenham, Wiltshire, on April 17, 1960. Seriously injured in the crash were his songwriting girlfriend, Sharon Sheeley (author of Rick Nelson's "Poor Little Fool" and coauthor of Cochran's "Somethin' Else"), and Gene Vincent. Cochran continued to have posthumous hits in Great Britain (although not in the United States) in the '60s and exerted a strong influence on the development of British rock 'n' roll. Eddie Cochran was inducted into the Rock and Roll Hall of Fame in 1987.

The Early Years	Ace	237	'88	LP/CD
Singin' to My Baby	Liberty	3061	'57	†
	Liberty	10137	'81	†
Eddie Cochran Memorial Album	Liberty	3172	'60	†
Never to Be Forgotten	Liberty	3220	'63	†
Singin' to My Baby/Never to Be Forgotten	EMI	80240	'93	CD
Best	EMI America	46580	'87	CD†
Great Hits	Liberty	10204		CS†
Summertime Blues	Sunset	1123	'58	†
Eddie Cochran	Sunset	5123	'69	†
Legendary Masters, Vol. 4	United Artists	(2)9959	'71	†
reissued as Eddie Cochran	EMI	92809		CS/CD†
On the Air	EMI	17245	'87	†
Very Best (15th Anniversary Album)	United Artists	428	'75	†
Singles Album	United Artists		'79	†
Greatest Hits	Curb/Warner Bros.	77371	'90	CS/CD

SAM COOKE

Born January 2 or 22, 1931, in Clarksdale, Mississippi (although some claim January 2 or 22, 1935, in Chicago); died December 11, 1964, in Los Angeles.

One of the most popular and influential black singers to emerge in the late '50s, Sam Cooke was one of the first black recording artists successfully to synthesize a popular blend of gospel music styling and secular themes. Eschewing the harsher shouting style of Ray Charles and emphasizing his high, clear, sensual tenor voice, Cooke, along with Charles, helped pioneer the sound that would become known as soul music, influencing black singers from Smokey Robinson to Al Green and Otis Redding to Aretha Franklin, and white British singers such as Mick Jagger and Rod Stewart. Along with James Brown, Sam Cooke was one of the first black artists to write his own songs and gain control over his recording career (he even founded two record labels). He also demonstrated a growing sense of social consciousness with the moving "A Change Is Gonna Come," a posthumous hit.

Raised in Chicago as the son of the Reverend Charles Cooke, Sam Cooke was a member of a family gospel quartet known as the Singing Children by age nine. Performing in the gospel group the Highway Q.C.s while still in high school, Cooke joined the Soul Stirrers, one of the most popular and influential gospel quartets of the '40s, as lead vocalist around 1950. He remained with the Soul Stirrers until 1956 (to be replaced by Johnny Taylor, who later enjoyed his own secular career, topped by 1968's "Who's Making Love"). Cooke also briefly manned the Pilgrim Travelers with Lou Rawls.

In 1956 Sam Cooke began recording pop material for Specialty Records, initially as Dale Cook. In late 1957 he scored a top R&B/pop hit on Keen Records with "You Send Me," written by his brother Charles "L. C." Cooke. Subsequent smash R&B and major pop hits through 1960 included "I'll Come Running Back to You" on Specialty and "You Were Made for Me," "Win Your Love for Me," "Everybody Loves to Cha Cha Cha," the classic "Only Sixteen," and "Wonderful World" on Keen.

In 1960 Sam Cooke accepted a lucrative offer to join RCA Records. Recorded with cloying pop arrangements featuring strings and horns under producers Hugo (Peretti) and Luigi (Creatore), Cooke scored a series of hits between 1960 and 1964. These included the pop and R&B smashes "Chain Gang," "Twistin' the Night Away," and "Another Saturday Night"; the smash R&B and major pop hits "Cupid," "Bring It on Home to Me" backed with "Having a Party," "Nothing Can Change This Love," "Send Me Some Lovin'," "Frankie and Johnny," and "Little Red Rooster." "(Ain't That) Good News" and "Good Times" became major R&B and pop hits.

In 1961 Sam Cooke launched Sar Records, followed by Derby Records in 1963. R&B/pop hits on Sar included "Lookin' for a Love" (1962) and "It's All Over Now" (1964) by the Valentinos (later covered by the J. Geils Band and the Rolling Stones, respectively), "Soothe Me" by the Sims Twins (1961), and "Meet Me at the Twistin' Place" by Johnnie Morisette (1962). "When a Boy Falls in Love" became a moderate pop/R&B hit for Mel Carter on Derby in 1963.

In early 1964 Sam Cooke announced that he was going to cut back on his touring to concentrate on running his record labels. Later that year the live set *At the Copa* was issued, but a far more representative set, *Feel It! Live at the Harlem Square Club, 1963,* recorded with saxophonist King Curtis, was eventually released in 1985.

Sam Cooke's career was secure by 1964, with enormous promise for the future, but on December 11, 1964, he was shot to death in Los Angeles. Posthumously, his "Shake" (covered by Otis Redding in 1967) became a near-smash hit in 1965, followed by his most enduring composition, "A Change Is Gonna Come," only a few days later. Sam Cooke was inducted into the Rock and Roll Hall of Fame in its inaugural year, 1986, and the Soul Stirrers were inducted into the Hall as Early Influences in 1990. In 1994 Abkco issued gospel and soul recordings made in the early '60s for Cooke's Sar Records, and in 1995 William Morrow published Daniel Wolff's Cooke biography, *You Send Me.*

BIBLIOGRAPHY

McEuen, Joe. *Sam Cooke: A Biography in Words and Pictures.* New York: Sire, dis. Chappell Music Co., 1977.

Wolff, Daniel, with S. R. Crain, Clifton White, and G. David Tenenbaun. *You Send Me: The Life and Times of Sam Cooke.* New York: Morrow, 1995.

Sam Cooke and the Soul Stirrers

In the Beginning	Ace	280	'89	CD
Sam Cooke and the Soul Stirrers	Specialty	2106(E)	'59	LP/CS
The Gospel Soul of Sam Cooke, Vol.1	Specialty	2116	'70	LP/CS
The Gospel Soul of Sam Cooke, Vol. 2	Specialty	2128	'71	LP/CS
The Original Soul Stirrers	Specialty	2137	'71	LP/CS
That's Heaven to Me	Specialty	2146	'72	LP/CS
Sam Cooke and the Soul Stirrers	Specialty	7009	'91	CD
Jesus Gave Me Water	Specialty	7031	'92	CD
Heaven Is My Home	Specialty	7040	'93	CD
The Last Mile of the Way	Specialty	7052	'93	CD

Sam Cooke

Two Sides of Sam Cooke	Specialty	2119	'57	LP/CS/CD

Ain't That Good News	Specialty	2115	'64	†
Forever Sam Cooke	Specialty	2164		†
Sam Cooke Sings	Keen	2001	'58	†
Encore	Keen	2003	'58	†
Tribute to the Lady	Keen	2004	'59	†
Encore, Vol. 2	Keen	2008		†
Hit Kit	Keen	86101	'60	†
I Thank God	Keen	86103	'60	†
Wonderful World	Keen	86106	'60	†
Sam's Songs	Famous	502	'61	†
Only Sixteen	Famous	505	'61	†
So Wonderful	Famous	508	'61	†
You Send Me	Famous	509	'62	†
Cha Cha Cha	Famous	512		†
Cooke's Tour	RCA	2221	'60	†
Hits of the 50s	RCA	2236	'60	†
One and Only	RCA	2264	'60	†
Sam Cooke–Swing Low	RCA	2293	'61	†
My Kind of Blues	RCA	2392	'61	†
Twistin' the Night Away	RCA	2555	'62	†
Best	RCA	2625	'62	†
	RCA	3863		LP/CS/CD
Mister Soul	RCA	2673	'63	†
Night Beat	RCA	2709	'63	†
	Abkco	1124	'95	LP/CS/CD
Feel It! Live at the Harlem Square Club, 1963	RCA	5181	'85	CS/CD
Ain't That Good News	RCA	2899	'64	†
At the Copa	RCA	2970	'64	†
	RCA	2658	'78	†
	Abkco	2970	'87	LP/CS/CD
Shake	RCA	3367	'65	†
Best, Vol. 2	RCA	3373	'65	†
Try a Little Love	RCA	3435	'65	†
The Unforgettable Sam Cooke	RCA	3517	'66	†
The Man Who Invented Soul	RCA	3991	'68	†
This Is Sam Cooke	RCA	(2)6027	'70	†
Interprets Billie Holiday	RCA	0899	'75	†
The Man and His Music	RCA	(2)7127	'86	LP/CS
	RCA	7127	'86	CD
The Rhythm and the Blues	RCA	66760	'95	CS/CD
One and Only	Camden	2264	'68	CS
Sam Cooke	Camden	2433	'70	†
The Unforgettable Sam Cooke	Camden	2610	'73	CS
You Send Me	Camden	0445	'75	†
Right On	Cherie	1001	'71	†
16 Greatest Hits	Trip	152	'72	†
Golden Sound	Trip	(2)8030	'73	†
Sings the Billie Holiday Story	Up Front	160	'73	†
You Send Me	Pair	1006	'86	CD
An Original	Pair	1186		CD

Sar Records

Sam Cooke's Sar Records Story	Abkco	(2)2231	'94	CD

BOBBY DARIN

Born Walden Robert Cassotto on May 14, 1936, in the Bronx, New York; died December 20, 1973, in Los Angeles.

Bobby Darin

One of the most popular rock 'n' roll teen idols of the late '50s, Bobby Darin moved into the pop mainstream and nightclub circuit with the definitive version of "Mack the Knife" in 1959. Embarking on a film career in the '60s, Darin later explored both country and folk music and formed his own record label, Direction, before ending his career at Motown Records. A childhood victim of rheumatic fever, Darin was not expected to live beyond twenty-five, yet he persevered until 1973, when he died at the age of thirty-seven.

Robert Cassotto contracted rheumatic fever at the age of eight and suffered health problems throughout his life. He learned to play drums, piano, and guitar as a child and studied drama for a time at Hunter College in New York. Changing his name to enter show business, Darin recorded unsuccessfully for Decca Records in 1956, switching to the Atco subsidiary of Atlantic Records in 1957. His first three singles for Atco failed to sell, and convinced the company was about to release him, he recorded his own composition, "Early in the Morning," for Brunswick, which released the song under the name the Ding Dongs to conceal his identity. Subsequently securing the rights to the song, Atco released it under the name Rinky Dinks, and the recording proved a major pop hit and was soon successfully covered by Buddy Holly. Darin finally broke through in mid 1958 with his own novelty song, "Splish Splash," a top R&B/smash pop/major country hit, quickly followed by the smash pop/R&B hit "Queen of the Hop."

Bobby Darin moved decisively into the popular mainstream with his album *That's All,* which produced a top pop hit with "Mack the Knife," based on Kurt Weill's 1928 "Moritat," from *The Threepenny Opera,* and a smash pop hit with "Beyond the Sea." His shift was completed with a live album recorded at the Copacabana and *Two of a Kind,* recorded with singer-lyricist Johnny Mercer. Subsequent pop hits included "Artificial Flowers," "Irresistible You" backed with "Multiplication," and the smash "Things," which he wrote. Darin also initiated an acting career in the '60s, garnering an Academy Award nomination as best supporting actor for his role in 1963's *Captain Newman, M.D.* He was married to actress Sandra Dee from 1960 to 1967.

In 1962 Bobby Darin signed with Capitol Records, scoring a smash pop/R&B hit with the country-styled "You're the Reason I'm Living" and a smash pop hit with "18 Yellow Roses" in 1963. Subsequent Capitol releases proved relative failures and Darin returned to Atlantic in 1965, where he rebounded with a near-smash hit version of Tim Hardin's "If I Were a Carpenter" the following year. He formed Direction Records in 1968, recording two albums for the label before moving to Motown Records in 1970. He managed his last minor hit in 1973 with "Happy," the love theme from the movie *Lady Sings the Blues.* On December 20, 1973, Bobby Darin died in Los Angeles of heart failure while undergoing an operation. He was inducted into the Rock and Roll Hall of Fame in 1990.

BIBLIOGRAPHY

DiOrio, Al. *Borrowed Time: The 37 Years of Bobby Darin.* Philadelphia: Running Press, 1981.

Darin, Dodd. *Dream Lovers: The Magnificent Shattered Lives of Bobby Darin and Sandra Dee.* New York: Warner, 1994.

Roeser, Steve. "Bobby Darin: Beyond the Sea Beyond the Music." *Goldmine* 21, no. 22 (October 27, 1995): 18–22, 24, 26, 28, 30, 32, 34, 38, 42, 44, 46, 48.

Bobby Darin	Atco	33–102	'58	†
	Atlantic	82626	'94	CS/CD
That's All	Atco	33–104	'59	†
	Atlantic	82627	'94	CS/CD
This Is Darin	Atco	33–115	'60	†
At the Copa	Atco	33–122	'60	†
	Bainbridge	6220		LP/CS
For Teenagers Only	Atco	1001	'60	†
It's You or No One (recorded 1960)	Atco	33–124	'63	†
The 25th Day of December	Atco	33–125	'60	†
	Atco	91772	'91	CS/CD
Two of a Kind (with Johnny Mercer)	Atco	33–126	'61	†
	Atco	90484	'85	CS/CD
The Bobby Darin Story	Atco	33–131	'61	†
	Atco	33131		CS/CD
Love Swings	Atco	33–134	'61	†
Twist with Bobby Darin	Atco	33–138	'61	†
Sings Ray Charles	Atco	33–140	'62	†
Things and Other Things	Atco	33–146	'62	†
Winners	Atco	33–167	'64	†
Splish Splash–The Best of Bobby Darin, Vol. 1	Atco	91794	'91	CS/CD
Mack the Knife–The Best of Bobby Darin, Vol. 2	Atco	91795	'91	CS/CD
Clementine	Clarion	603	'64	†
The Legendary Bobby Darin	Candlelite	(2)1959	'74	†
Oh! Look at Me Now	Capitol	1791	'62	†
Earthy	Capitol	1826	'63	†
You're the Reason I'm Living	Capitol	1866	'63	†
18 Yellow Roses	Capitol	1942	'63	†
Golden Folk Hits	Capitol	2007	'63	†
From Hello Dolly to Goodbye Charlie	Capitol	2194	'64	†
Venice Blue	Capitol	2322	'65	†
Best	Capitol	2571	'66	†

Bobby Darin	Capitol	91625	'89	CS/CD
Spotlight on Bobby Darin	Capitol	28512	'94	CS/CD
Sings the Shadow of Your Smile	Atlantic	8121	'66	†
In a Broadway Bag	Atlantic	8126	'66	†
If I Were a Carpenter	Atlantic	8135	'66	†
Inside Out	Atlantic	8142	'67	†
Sings Doctor Doolittle	Atlantic	8154	'67	†
Born Walden Robert Cassotto	Direction	1936	'68	†
Commitment	Direction	1937	'69	†
Bobby Darin	Motown	753	'72	†
1936–1973	Motown	813	'74	†
	Motown	5185	'89	CS/CD
Live at the Desert Inn	Motown	9070	'87	CD†
Best	Curb/Warner Bros.	77325	'90	CS/CD
As Long as I'm Singing: The Bobby Darin Collection	Rhino	(4)72206	'95	CD
The Ultimate Bobby Darin	Warner	27606		CD
As Long as I'm Singin'	Jass	9		LP/CS
	Jass	4		CD
As Long as I'm Singin': Rare'n Darin # 1	r 'n' d	1301		LP/CS/CD

THE DEL VIKINGS

Lead and ten Corinthian "Kripp" Johnson (born ca. 1933 in Cambridge, Maryland; died June 22, 1990, in Pontiac, Michigan); lead and ten Norman Wright (born October 21, 1937, in Philadelphia, Pennsylvania); 2d ten Dave Lerchey (born ca. 1946 in New Albany, Indiana); bar Don Jackson; bs singer Clarence Quick (born ca. 1944 in Brooklyn, New York). Later members included Donald "Gus" Backus (born ca. 1942 in Southampton, Long Island, New York); William Blakely; Chuck Jackson (born July 22, 1937, in Winston-Salem, North Carolina).

Rock 'n' roll's first successful racially integrated vocal group, the Del Vikings scored a smash hit with the doo-wop classic "Come Go with Me" in 1957. However, their impact became diluted when a second group began recording as Del Vikings. The second group included Chuck Jackson, who scored later scored a number of solo hits, including "Any Day Now (My Beautiful Bird)" in 1962.

Clarence Quick and four other black singers, including "Kripp" Johnson" and Don Jackson, began singing informally at Pittsburgh (Pennsylvania) Air Force base in 1955. Performing locally as the Del Vikings, the group replaced two departing members with Norman Wright and Dave Lerchey, the group's first white member. In 1956 the Del Vikings recorded at the behest of disc jockey Barry Kaye and producer Joe Averback, who at first leased the songs to Luniverse Records and later formed his own Fee Bee label. Quick's "Come Go with Me," leased nationally to Dot Records, quickly became a smash R&B/pop hit. In 1957 a second white singer, "Gus" Backus, replaced Jackson for their second round of recordings, which yielded a smash pop/R&B hit with "Whispering Bells" on Dot, with lead vocals by Johnson.

However, the group's new manager took four of the members—Quick, Wright, Lerchey, and Backus—to Mercury Records, adding William Blakely. Kripp Johnson remained at Fee Bee/Dot, forming an all-black Del Vikings with Chuck Jackson and a returned Don Jackson. The Mercury Del Vikings scored a near-smash pop/R&B hit with "Cool Shake," only weeks before the success of "Whispering Bells," and Mercury gained legal control of the Del Vikings name. With the expiration of his Fee Bee contract, Johnson rejoined the Del Vikings at Mercury.

Chuck Jackson pursued a solo career, scoring R&B smashes with "I Don't Want to Cry," "Any Day Now (My Wild Beautiful Bird)" (a major pop hit), and "Something You Got" through 1965 on Wand Records. The Del Vikings moved to ABC-Paramount in 1961, disbanding by the mid '60s. Johnson, Lerchey, Blakely, Wright, and Quick reunited in the '70s, and by the end of the decade two groups again were performing as the Del Vikings, one with Johnson and Lerchey, the other with Quick and Blakely. Kripp Johnson died of prostate cancer on June 22, 1990, at the age of fifty-seven.

BIBLIOGRAPHY

Grendysa, Peter. "The Coming and Going of the Del Vikings." *Goldmine* 18, no. 4 (February 21, 1992): 34, 40, 106.

The Del Vikings

1956 Audition Tapes	Collectables	5001	'87	†
Come Go with the Del Vikings	Luniverse	1000	'57	†
They Sing–They Swing	Mercury	20314	'57	†
A Swinging, Singing Record Session	Mercury	20353	'58	†
The Best of the Del Vikings: The Mercury Years	Mercury/ Chronicles	532733	'96	CS/CD
Newies & Oldies	Fee Bee	205		†
Best	Dot	1003		†
Come Go with Me	Dot	25695	'66	†
The Best of the Del Vikings	Collectables	5010	'87	LP/CS/CD

The Del Vikings/The Sonnets

The Del Vikings and the Sonnets	Crown	5368	'63	†

BO DIDDLEY

Born Ellas Bates on December 30, 1928, in McComb, Mississippi; adopted by the McDaniel family.

Best remembered for his percussive "shave-and-a-haircut" guitar-playing style that influenced the Yardbirds and the Rolling Stones, Bo Diddley was one of rock 'n' roll's first electric guitarist-singers. Combining crude energy, compulsive rhythms, and an open sense of sexuality, Diddley composed and recorded the oft-covered classics "I'm a Man," "Who Do You Love," and "Mona."

Ellas McDaniel moved to Chicago with his adopted family in 1934. Nicknamed Bo Diddley as a child, he began twelve years of violin studies on arrival and took up guitar as a teenager. He manned a washboard trio to play the streets and rent parties from 1946 to 1951, when he debuted at the 708 Club. Diddley began playing with maraca player Jerome Green, and eventually signed with Chess Records in 1955, recording on the sister label, Checker. His first single, "Bo Diddley"/"I'm a Man," became a top R&B hit, and Muddy Waters soon recorded his own smash hit version of "I'm a Man" as "Manish Boy." Subsequent R&B Diddley hits included "Diddley Daddy" and "Pretty Thing," but classics such as "Who Do You Love" and "Mona" failed to chart. He broke through into the pop field in 1959 with "Say Man," on which he traded insults with Green. In the early '60s he also hit with "Road Runner" and "You Can't Judge a Book by the Cover." Diddley toured throughout the '60s with Green and his half-sister guitarist-vocalist, simply known as "The Duchess."

BO DIDDLEY

Bo Diddley first toured Great Britain in 1963. His influence on '60s British groups became apparent when the Yardbirds hit with "I'm a Man" and the Rolling Stones recorded "Mona." During the '60s Diddley teamed with Chuck Berry for *Two Great Guitars,* Muddy Waters and Little Walter for *Super Blues,* and Muddy Waters and Howlin' Wolf for *Super, Super Blues Band.* Diddley worked the rock 'n' roll revival circuit from 1969–74, appearing in the 1973 film *Let the Good Times Roll.* After leaving Chess in 1974, he recorded an album for RCA. In 1979 he opened for the Clash on their debut tour of the United States.

Inducted into the Rock and Roll Hall of Fame in 1987, Bo Diddley toured with Ron Wood in 1988 and returned to recording with *Breaking Through the B.S.* on Triple X Records in 1989. In 1992 Rhino Records issued the tribute set *Bo Diddley Beats,* assembling recordings by Buddy Holly, Dee Clark, the Miracles, and others. In the mid '90s Bo Diddley recorded for MCA and Atlantic Records.

Bo Diddley

Bo Diddley	Checker	1431	'58	†
reissued as Boss Man	Checker	3007	'68	†
	Chess	9194	'87	CS
Go Bo Diddley	Checker	1436	'59	†
	Checker	3006	'68	†
Bo Diddley/Go Bo Diddley (recorded 1955–1958)	Chess	5904		CD
Have Guitar, Will Travel	Checker	2974	'60	†
In the Spotlight	Checker	2976	'60	†
	Chess	9264	'87	CS/CD
Bo Diddley Is a Gunslinger	Checker	2977	'60	†
	Chess	9285	'89	CS/CD
Bo Diddley Is a Lover	Checker	2980	'61	†
Bo Diddley's a Twister	Checker	2982	'62	†
reissued as Roadrunner	Checker	2982	'68	†
Bo Diddley	Checker	2984	'62	†
Bo Diddley and Company	Checker	2985	'63	†
Surfin' with Bo Diddley	Checker	2987	'63	†
Bo Diddley's Beach Party	Checker	2988	'63	†
16 All-Time Greatest Hits	Checker	2989	'64	†
Hey Good Lookin'	Checker	2992	'65	†
500 % More Man	Checker	2996	'66	†

The Originator	Checker	3001	'67	†
Black Gladiator	Checker	3013	'69	†
Another Dimension	Chess	50001	'71	†
Where It All Began	Chess	50016	'72	†
The London Bo Diddley Sessions	Chess	50029	'73	†
	Chess	9296	'89	CS/CD
Got My Own Bag of Tricks	Chess	(2)60005(E)	'72	†
Big Bad Bo	Chess	50047	'74	†
His Greatest Sides, Vol. 1	Chess	9106		LP/CS
The Chess Box	Chess	(3)19502	'90	CS
	Chess	(2)19502	'90	CD
Rare and Well Done	Chess	9331	'91	CS/CD
His Best	MCA/Chess	9373	'97	CD
20th Anniversary of Rock 'N' Roll	RCA	1229	'76	†
Toronto Rock and Roll Revival, Vol. 5	Accord	7812	'82	†
Give Me a Break	Check Mate	1960	'88	†
Breaking Through the B.S.	Triple X	51017	'89	†
Bo's Blues	Ace	396	'93	CD
Bo Knows Bo	MCA	20872	'95	CS/CD†
A Man Amongst Men	Atlantic	82896	'96	CS/CD
Mona	Drive	3247	'96	CD
Bo Diddley and Chuck Berry				
Two Great Guitars	Checker	2991	'64	†
	Chess	9170		CD
Bo Diddley, Muddy Waters, and Little Walter				
Super Blues	Checker	3008	'67	†
	Chess	9168		CS/CD
Bo Diddley, Muddy Waters, and Howlin' Wolf				
The Super Super Blues Band	Checker	3010	'68	†
	Chess	9169		CS/CD
Tribute Album				
Bo Diddley Beats	Rhino	70291	'92	CS/CD

DION (DIMUCCI) AND THE BELMONTS

Dion DiMucci (born July 18, 1939, in the Bronx, New York), lead voc; Angelo D'Aleo (born
February 3, 1940, in the Bronx), 1st ten; Fred Milano (born August 22, 1939, in the Bronx),
2d ten; Carlo Mastrangelo (born October 5, 1938, in the Bronx), bs voc.

The most successful white doo-wop vocal group, emerging from the New York a cappella
street corner scene of the '50s, Dion and the Belmonts were the first white group to work
Harlem's Apollo Theater. Their success paved the way for the Four Seasons and influenced a
generation of rock singers, from Paul Simon to Lou Reed. Dion launched a solo career in
1960, hitting with gutsy, conflict-ridden, even antagonistic and arrogant songs that bore sharp
contrast to the pop fluff of the early '60s. Reuniting with the Belmonts in 1967 and 1972,
Dion played the coffeehouse circuit after scoring a smash hit with the classic tribute song
"Abraham, Martin and John" in 1968. He later recorded a British-only album under Phil Spector in 1974 and recorded Christian music in the '80s, reemerging in 1989 with *Yo Frankie*.

Dion DiMucci started singing at the age of five and began making public appearances
playing acoustic guitar around the age of eleven. In 1957 he joined the Timberlanes to

record "The Chosen Few" for Mohawk Records, forming Dion and the Belmonts in 1958. Signing with the newly formed Laurie Records label, the group soon hit with "I Wonder Why" and "No One Knows." D'Aleo served in the Navy in 1959 while the group scored smash hits with Doc Pomus and Mort Shuman's "A Teenager in Love" and the Rodgers and Hart's classic "Where or When."

Dion left the group to pursue a solo career in the fall of 1960. He quickly hit with "Lonely Teenager," followed in 1961 by the top pop/smash R&B hit "Runaround Sue," backed by the Del Satins and cowritten with Ernie Maresca. (Maresca later scored a smash pop/major R&B hit with "Shout! Shout! Knock Yourself Out" in 1962.) Dion also appeared in the 1961 film *Teenage Millionaire*. In the meantime, Angelo D'Aleo rejoined the Belmonts, Carlo Mastrangelo switched to lead, and the group recorded for their own Sabina label. They achieved moderate hits with "Tell Me Why" and "Come On, Little Angel," but Mastrangelo left in 1962, to be replaced by Frank Lyndon. The Belmonts moved to United Artists in 1964, reuniting with Dion for 1967's *Together Again* on ABC and the live Warner Brothers set *Reunion,* recorded June 2, 1972, at Madison Square Garden. The Belmonts later recorded for Dot, Buddah, and Strawberry, eventually scoring a minor hit in 1981 with "Let's Put the Fun Back in Rock n Roll," recorded with Freddy Cannon.

Continuing to be backed by the Del Satins, Dion scored smash hits on Laurie with "The Wanderer" (written by Maresca), "Lovers Who Wander" (cowritten with Maresca), and his own "Little Diane," as well as the major hits "Love Came to Me" and "Sandy." Moving to Columbia and retaining the Del Satins, Dion scored smash pop hits with "Ruby Baby" (a smash R&B hit) and "Drip Drop," both previously recorded by the Drifters, and "Donna the Prima Donna" (cowritten with Maresca). In the mid '60s Dion began exploring blues material, with little commercial success.

In 1968 Dion moved to Florida, kicked a heroin habit that dated back to his early teens, and returned to Laurie Records. *Dion,* regarded as his most fully realized album, contained songs by contemporary artists such as Bob Dylan, Leonard Cohen, Fred Neil, and Joni Mitchell, and yielded a smash pop hit with Dick Holler's ode to assassinated leaders, "Abraham, Martin and John." Dion subsequently toured the college-and-coffeehouse circuit playing acoustic guitar, switching to Warner Brothers Records in 1970, with little success. He recorded *Born to Be with You* under producer extraordinaire Phil Spector in 1974; however, the album was released in England only.

For much of the '80s Dion recorded modern Christian music. He returned to rock 'n' roll in June 1987 with a series of sold-out concerts at Radio City Music Hall. He published his autobiography, *The Wanderer,* in 1988 and was inducted into the Rock and Roll Hall of Fame in 1989. Also that year, with the assistance of Paul Simon, Lou Reed, and k.d. lang, Dion recorded *Yo Frankie* under producer Dave Edmunds, managing a minor hit with "And the Night Stood Still." In 1990 Dion toured with Edmunds, Graham Parker, and Kim Wilson of the Fabulous Thunderbirds. By the mid '90s Dion had moved back to New York and formed the group Little Kings with guitarist Scott Kempner of the Dictators and the Del Lords, bassist Mike Mesaros of the Smithereens, and drummer Frank Funaro of the Del Lords for engagements on the East Coast.

BIBLIOGRAPHY

Dion, with Davin Seay. *The Wanderer: Dion's Story.* New York: Beech Tree, 1988.

Dion and the Belmonts

Presenting	Laurie	2002	'59	†
	Laurie	1002	'60	†

When You Wish Upon a Star	Laurie	2006	'60	†
	Collectables	5026	'84	LP/CS
By Special Request: Together on Record	Laurie	2016	'66	†
Everything You Always Wanted to Hear by Dion and the Belmonts	Laurie	4002		CS
60 Greatest Hits of Dion and the Belmonts	Laurie	(3)6000		LP
Together Again	Laurie	(2)6000		†
	ABC	599	'67	CS
Reunion: Live at Madison Square Garden, 1972	Warner Brothers	2664	'73	†
	Rhino	70228	'87	CS/CD
Doo-Wop	Pickwick	3521	'76	†
Best	Pai	1142	'86	CS
20 Golden Classics	Collectables	5041		LP/CS
The Wanderer	3C Recor	105		CD
The Fabulous Dion and the Belmonts	Ace	022		CS/CD

The Belmonts

Carnival of Hits	Sabina	5001(M)	'62	†
Summer Love	Dot	25949	'69	†
Cigars, Accapella, Candy	Buddah	5123	'73	†
Cheek to Cheek	Strawberry	6001	'78	†
The Laurie, Sabina and United Artists Sides, Vol. 1	Ace	580	'95	CD
Acapella Christmas	Performance	394		CS/CD

Dion (DiMucci)

Alone with Dion	Laurie	2004	'60	†
	Ace	115		†
Runaround Sue	Laurie	2009	'61	†
	Ace	148		†
	Collectables	5027		LP/CS
	The Right Stuff	27304	'93	CS/CD
Lovers Who Wander	Laurie	2012	'62	†
	Ace	163		†
	The Right Stuff	27305	'93	CS/CD
Love Came to Me	Laurie	2015		†
15 Million Sellers	Laurie	2019		†
More Greatest Hits	Laurie	2022		†
Dion Sings the Hits of the 50s and 60s	Laurie	4013		CS
Hits	Ace	176		LP/CD
Runaround Sue: The Best of The Rest	Ace	915		CD
The Fabulous Dion	Ace	008		CS/CD

Dion/Dion and the Belmonts

Sings His Greatest Hits	Laurie	2013	'62	†
Dion Sings to Sandy	Laurie	2017	'63	†
Greatest Hits	Columbia	31942	'73/'87	CS†
Presenting Dion and the Belmonts/Runaround Sue	Collectables	5025	'84	LP/CS
	Ace	966		CD
When You Wish Upon a Star/Alone with Dion	Ace	945		CD
Lovers Who Wander/So Why Didn't You Do That the First Time	Ace	943		CD

Later Dion

| Ruby Baby | Columbia | 8810 | '63 | † |
| | Columbia | 35577 | '79 | † |

Donna, the Prima Donna	Columbia	8907	'63	†
	Columbia	35995	'79	†
Bronx Blues: The Columbia Recordings (recorded 1962–1965)	Columbia/Legacy	46972	'91	CD
Wonder Where I'm Bound	Columbia	9773	'65	†
Greatest Hits	Columbia	31942	'73/'87	CS†
Dion	Laurie	2047	'68	†
	The Right Stuff	29667	'94	CS/CD
reissued as Abraham, Martin and John	Ace	204	'87	†
Sit Down Old Friend	Warner Brothers	1826	'70	†
You're Not Alone	Warner Brothers	1872	'71	†
Sanctuary	Warner Brothers	1945	'71	†
Suite for Late Summer	Warner Brothers	2642	'72	†
Streetheart	Warner Brothers	2954	'76	†
The Return of the Wanderer	Lifesong	35356	'78	†
	DCC	049		CS/CD†
24 Original Classics	Arista	(2)8206	'84	†
Yo Frankie	Arista	8549	'89	CS/CD
Dion at His Best: Classic Old and Gold, Vol. 3	3C Records	102		CD
Dion at His Best: Classic Old and Gold, Vol. 4	3C Records	103		CD
A Rock and Roll Christmas	The Right Stuff	66718	'93	CS/CD
Christian Music				
Inside Job	DaySpring	4022	'80	†
I Put Away My Idols	DaySpring	4109	'83	†
	DaySpring	8111	'85	†
Seasons	DaySpring	8112	'85	†
Kingdom in the Streets	Word	8285	'85	†
Velvet and Steel	Word	8372	'87	†
	Word/Epic	47798	'91	CS/CD

WILLIE DIXON

Born July 1, 1915, in Vicksburg, Mississippi; died January 29, 1992, in Burbank, California.

Perhaps the most critical link between the blues and rock 'n' roll through his songwriting and sessions work for Chuck Berry and Bo Diddley, Willie Dixon was essentially the architect of Chicago blues at Chess Records in the '50s, functioning as composer, producer, arranger, and sessions bassist. Advancing the careers of Muddy Waters, Howlin' Wolf, Little Walter, and others while remaining largely in the background, Dixon composed more than 500 songs, including literally dozens of blues classics later covered by '60s groups such as the Rolling Stones, the Doors, Cream, and Led Zeppelin. Achieving few hits during his own recording career and promoting the cause of the blues in the early '60s through organizational and performing efforts in the United States and Europe, Dixon eventually gained substantial recognition in the '70s and '80s.

Raised in Vicksburg, Mississippi, Willie Dixon began writing songs as a teenager and later joined the Union Jubilee Singers, who performed locally during the first half of the '30s. In 1936 he moved to Chicago, winning the Illinois State Golden Glove Heavyweight Boxing Championship in 1937. He soon turned to music, learning string bass and performing on street corners with singer Leonard "Baby Doo" Caston. With Caston on piano, the two formed the Five Breezes, recording for Bluebird in 1940 and playing engagements around Chicago until 1942. He formed the Four Jumps of Jive in 1945, recording for Mercury Records. In early 1946 he joined Caston and guitarist Bernardo Dennis (later replaced by Ollie Crawford) in the formation of the Big Three Trio. Recording for Columbia Records, the group scored a near-smash R&B hit with "You Sure Look Good to Me" in 1948. Dixon began playing sessions at Aristocrat Records (later Chess Records) in 1948 and went to work full-time at the Chess studio when the Big Three Trio broke up in 1952.

At Chess Records Willie Dixon played bass, wrote and arranged songs, and occasionally recorded his own material. His first recognition as a songwriter came with Muddy Waters's smash R&B hit recording of Dixon's "I'm Your Hoochie Coochie Man" in 1954. He became the label's principal songwriter, providing Muddy Waters with "I'm Ready" (a smash R&B hit), "I Just Want to Make Love to You," "I Love the Life I Live," and "You Need Me"; and Howlin' Wolf with "Back Door Man," "Evil," "I Ain't Superstitious," "Little Red Rooster," "Spoonful," and "Wang Dang Doodle." In 1955 Little Walter scored a top R&B hit with Dixon's "My Babe," and Dixon managed his only solo hit (a major R&B hit) with "Walking the Blues." Willie Dixon also produced a number of recording sessions while playing on virtually all of Chuck Berry's sessions through 1959. He provided Bo Diddley with the smash R&B hit "Pretty Thing" and played on the Bo Diddley sessions that produced "Diddy Wah Diddy," "Hey Bo Diddley," "Mona," and "You Can't Judge a Book by the Cover," another Dixon song.

Willie Dixon left Chess Records in 1956 in disputes over contracts and royalties, yet continued to play sessions for the label, most notably those of Chuck Berry. In the late '50s he worked for local labels such as Cobra and Abco, achieving his biggest success in 1956 with Otis Rush's recording of his "I Can't Quit You Baby" on Cobra. He returned to Chess in 1960, but with the popularization of the electric bass, he worked primarily as a producer and songwriter until 1971. During the late '50s and early '60s folk revival, Dixon toured and recorded with Memphis Slim. Dixon also played on the European concert series American Folk-Blues Festival in 1963 and 1964 and subsequently organized the music for the shows through 1971. During the '60s, Dixon's songs became hits for Sonny Boy Williamson ("Help Me," 1963); Sam Cooke ("Little Red Rooster," 1963); Johnny Rivers ("The Seventh Son," 1965); and Koko Taylor ("Wang Dang Doodle," 1966). During the latter half of the '60s, a wide variety of white bands, among them the Rolling Stones, the Doors, Cream, and Led Zeppelin, recorded his material.

In 1969 Dixon recorded *I Am the Blues* for Columbia Records with guitarist Johnny Shines, harmonica player Walter "Shakey" Horton, and pianists Sunnyland Slim and Lafayette Leake. In the late '60s and early '70s, Dixon operated his own Spoonful and Yambo labels, recording with the Chicago Blues All-Stars, a touring band he formed in 1969 with Horton and Leake. They performed at concerts in Europe in 1972 and 1973. Leake was principal pianist for *Maestro Willie Dixon and His Chicago Blues Band,* recorded with vocalists Larry Johnson and Victoria Spivey. Dixon continued to tour regularly until 1977, when he was hospitalized for diabetes.

In 1972 Led Zeppelin settled with Arc Music, the publishing wing of Chess Records, regarding the unauthorized recording of two songs, one of which, Dixon's "Bring It on Home," was credited to the group's members. In 1985 Dixon sued Led Zeppelin over the similarity of "Whole Lotta Love" to his "You Need Love." He eventually settled out of court in 1987. Made acutely aware of unpaid royalties due black blues songwriters, Dixon established the nonprofit Blues Heaven Foundation to secure rights to their songs, while assisting indigent blues musicians, funding musical scholarships, and promoting blues music.

In 1980 Willie Dixon was inducted into the Blues Foundation's Hall of Fame. He moved his family to southern California in 1983, and recorded for Pausa Records and later the album *Hidden Charms* in Los Angeles with Lafayette Leake, Earl Palmer, and T-Bone Burnett, the record's producer. He also wrote his autobiography, *I Am the Blues,* and worked on movie sound tracks, including *The Color of Money, La Bamba,* and *Ginger Ale Afternoon.* Dixon performed with Koko Taylor at President George Bush's inaugural ball in 1989. In fragile health for some time (he had lost a leg to diabetes), Willie Dixon died of heart failure at St. Joseph Medical Center in Burbank, California, on January 29, 1992, at the age of seventy-six. In 1994 he was inducted into the Rock and Roll Hall of Fame as an Early Influence.

BIBLIOGRAPHY

Dixon, Willie, with Don Snowden. *I Am the Blues: The Willie Dixon Story.* New York: Da Capo, 1989.

The Big Three Trio

The Big Three Trio	Columbia/Legacy	46216	'90	CS/CD

Chess Recordings

The Chess Box (recorded 1951– 1958)	Chess	(3)16500	'88	LP
	Chess	(2)16500	'88	CS/CD
The Original Wang Dang Doodle (recorded 1954, 1981, 1990)	Chess	9353	'95	CS/CD

Willie Dixon and Memphis Slim

Willie's Blues	Prestige/Bluesville	1003	'59	†
	Ace	349		CD
	Fantasy/OBC	501	'84	LP/CD
Memphis Slim and Willie Dixon	Folkways	2385	'59	†
At the Village Gate	Folkways	2386	'60	
The Blues Every Which Way	Verve	3007	'60	†
Live at the Trois Mailletz	Polydor	658148	'62	†
	Verve	519729	'92	CD
In Paris	Battle	6122	'63	†
In Paris: Baby Please Come Home (recorded November 1962)	Fantasy/OBC	582	'96	CD

Willie Dixon

I Am the Blues	Columbia	9987	'70	CS
	Mobile Fidelity	00872		CD†
With Chicago Blues All Stars	Yambo	77715	'71	†
Maestro Willie Dixon and His Chicago Blues Band	Spivey	1016	'73	†
Catalyst	Ovation	1433	'73	†
What's Happened to My Blues?	Ovation	1705	'76	†
Mighty Earthquake and Hurricane	Pausa	7157	'84	†
	Mighty Tiger	6002	'91	LP/CS/CD†
Backstage Access	Pausa	7183	'85	†
Hidden Charms	Capitol	90595	'88	CS/CD†
Ginger Ale Afternoon (sound track)	Varese Sarabande	5234	'89	CD

FATS DOMINO

Born Antoine Domino on February 26, 1928, in New Orleans.

The second (to Elvis) most commercially successful of the '50s rock 'n' rollers, selling more than sixty-five million records, Fats Domino made the transition from R&B to rock 'n' roll with his pleasant, upbeat songs and gentle, engaging piano style. An established R&B artist when he broke through into the pop field with "Ain't That a Shame" in 1955, Fats Domino would become the most famous musician from New Orleans since Louis

Armstrong. Far less frantic and threatening than many of his contemporaries, Domino cowrote virtually all of his hits with bandleader Dave Bartholomew, who, along with tenor saxophonists Herb Hardesty and Alvin "Red" Tyler and drummer Earl Palmer, helped produce his characteristic sound. Fats Domino helped focus attention on the music of New Orleans and inspired other Southern black singers such as Little Richard and Lloyd Price.

"Fats" Domino learned piano as a child, debuting professionally around the age of ten. By fourteen he had dropped out of school to perform in local nightclubs, including the Hideaway Club, where he was discovered by bandleader David Bartholomew in 1949. Joining Bartholomew's band, Domino signed with Lew Chudd's Imperial label. He had a string of ten years of smash hits recorded with cowriter-arranger-producer Bartholomew and tenor saxophonist Herb Hardesty beginning in 1950 with "The Fat Man." Domino formed his own touring band in the early '50s and produced smash R&B hits with "Every Night About This Time," "Goin' Home," "Goin' to the River," "Please Don't Leave Me," "Something's Wrong," and "Don't You Know."

Fats Domino broke through into the pop market in the spring of 1955 with "Ain't That a Shame." He appeared in the early rock 'n' roll movies *Shake, Rattle and Roll* and *The Girl Can't Help It* from 1956 and *Jamboree* and *The Big Beat* from 1957. In addition to the standard "Blueberry Hill" and Bobby Charles's "Walking to New Orleans," Domino scored smash pop and R&B hits with "I'm in Love Again," "Blue Monday," "I'm Walkin'," "It's You I Love," "Whole Lotta Loving," "I Want to Walk You Home," and "Be My Guest" through 1960. Major pop hits of the era included the standard "My Blue Heaven," "Valley of Tears," "I'm Ready," "I'm Gonna Be a Wheel Someday," and "My Girl Josephine," an early example of reggae rhythm.

In 1961 Fats Domino began performing frequently in Las Vegas, managing major hits on Imperial with "What a Price," "It Keeps Rainin'," "Let the Four Winds Blow," and "What a Party," and the Hank Williams classics "Jambalaya" and "You Win Again," through 1962. In 1963 he signed with ABC-Paramount Records, recording in Nashville, and subsequently switched to Mercury in 1965. He toured Great Britain in 1967 and moved to Reprise Records for his final pop hit with the Beatles' "Lady Madonna" in 1968. Domino appeared in the rock 'n' roll revival film *Let the Good Times Roll* in 1973 and toured six months out of every year until the mid '70s, after which he performed primarily in Las Vegas. He achieved a modest country hit with "Whiskey Heaven" from the movie *Any Which Way You Can* in 1980 and was inducted into the Rock and Roll Hall of Fame in its inaugural year, 1986. In 1993, Fats Domino recorded his first new album in over twenty years, *Christmas Is a Special Day,* and in 1996 EMI issued the tribute album *That's Fats,* which featured covers of Domino's songs by Ricky Nelson, the Band, Dr. John, Cheap Trick, and others.

Imperial Recordings

Rock and Rollin' with Fats Domino	Imperial	9004	'56	†
Rock and Rollin'	Imperial	9009	'56	†
This Is Fats Domino!	Imperial	9028	'57	†
Here Stands Fats Domino	Imperial	9038	'57	†
This Is Fats	Imperial	9040	'57	†
The Fabulous Mr. D	Imperial	9055	'58	†
	Liberty	10136	'81	†
Fats Domino Swings/12,000,000 Records	Imperial	9062	'59	†
Let's Play Fats Domino	Imperial	9065	'59	†
Sings Million Record Hits	Imperial	9103	'60	†
A Lot of Dominos	Imperial	12066	'61	†
I Miss You So	Imperial	12398	'61	†
Let the Four Winds Blow	Imperial	12073	'61	†
What a Party	Imperial	9164	'61	†
Twistin' the Stomp	Imperial	9170	'62	†
Million Sellers by Fats	Imperial	9195	'62	†
	Imperial	12195	'64	†
	United Artists	1027	'80	†
Just Domino	Imperial	9208	'62	†
Walking to New Orleans	Imperial	9227	'63	†
Let's Dance with Domino	Imperial	9239	'63	†
Here He Comes Again	Imperial	9248	'63	†
The Fat Man: 25 Classic Performances	Imperial	52326	'96	CD
Legendary Masters	United Artists	(2)9958	'72	†
Superpak-Cookin' with Fats	United Artists	(2)122	'73	†
Very Best	United Artists	233	'74	†
Play It Again, Fats—The Very Best	United Artists	380	'75	†
Best	EMI America	46851	'87	†
My Blue Heaven: The Best of Fats Domino	EMI	92808	'90	CS/CD
They Call Me the Fat Man: The Legendary Imperial Recordings	EMI	(4)96784	'91	CD

Later Recordings

Here Comes Fats Domino	ABC-Paramount	455	'63	†
Fats on Fire	ABC-Paramount	479	'64	†
Getaway with Fats Domino	ABC-Paramount	510	'65	†
'65	Mercury	61029	'65	†
Fats Is Back	Reprise	6304	'68	†
Fats	Reprise	6439	'71	†
Live in Montreux (recorded 1973)	Atlantic	81751	'74/'87	CS
	Atlantic	81751	'96	CS/CD
Sleeping on the Job	Polydor	3215	'79	†
Christmas Is a Special Day	The Right Stuff	27753	'93	CS/CD

Compilations

Fats Domino	Sunset	5103	'66	†
Stompin' Fats Domino	Sunset	5158	'67	†

Trouble in Mind	Sunset	5200	'69	†
Ain't That a Shame	Sunset	5299	'71	†
Fats Domino	Grand Award	267	'68	†
Fats Domino	Pickwick	2031		†
Blueberry Hill	Pickwick	3111	'69	†
My Blue Heaven	Pickwick	3295	'72	†
Fats' Hits	Pickwick	5005		†
When I'm Walking	Harmony	11343	'69	†
Fats Domino	Archive of Folk and Jazz Music/Everest	280	'74	†
Fats Domino, Vol. 2	Archive of Folk and Jazz Music/Everest	330	'77	†
When I'm Walking	Columbia	35996	'79/'87	CD†
Getaway with Fats	Ace	90		†
Boogie Woogie Baby	Ace	140		†
His Greatest Hits	Silver Eagle	6170	'88	CS/CD†
Whole Lotta Rock 'n' Roll	Pair	1123		CD†
The Best of Fats	Pair	1268	'90	CD
20 Hits	Fest	4400	'91	CS/CD
18 Hits	Fest	4402		CS/CD
All-Time Greatest Hits	Curb/Warner Bros.	77378	'91	CS/CD
Best of Fats Domino, Live, Vol. 1	Curb/Warner Bros.	77538	'91	CS/CD
Best of Fats Domino, Live, Vol. 2	Curb/Warner Bros.	77539	'91	CS/CD
Antoine "Fats" Domino	Tomato	(2)70391	'92	CS/CD
The Fat Man	SMS	2	'95	CD
Best of Fats Domino, Live!	Laserlight	12752	'96	CD
You Can Call Me Fats	Boomerang	1576	'97	CD
Greatest Hits	Special Music	4817		CS/CD
Live in Concert	K-Tel	619		CD†
16 Great Hits	Zeta	518		CD†
Live Hits	Quicksilver	1016		LP/CS
So Long	Polygram	838642		CS

Tribute Album

That's Fats: A Tribute to Fats Domino	EMI	37356	'96	CD

DUANE EDDY

Born April 26, 1938, in Corning, New York.

Rock 'n' roll's best-selling instrumentalist, Duane Eddy scored a series of pop hits between 1958 and 1963 that featured a deep "twangy" sound produced by playing the guitar's bass strings. As with many early rock 'n' rollers, Eddy retained his popularity much longer in England, and influenced a number of British guitarists, including Eric Clapton, George Harrison, and Mark Knopfler.

Duane Eddy started playing guitar at age five and moved with his family to the Phoenix, Arizona, area at thirteen. At sixteen he left high school and obtained a Chet Atkins-model Gretsch guitar, performing locally and meeting multi-instrumentalist Al Casey in 1955. While performing with Casey's group, Eddy devised the technique of playing lead on his guitar's bass strings to produce a low, reverberant "twangy" sound. In 1957 he met disc jockey Lee Hazlewood, who also wrote songs, published music, produced records, and ran a recording studio. Eddy recorded "Movin' and Groovin," a song cowritten with Hazlewood, with studio musicians dubbed the Rebels. Forwarded to Dick Clark, the song won Eddy a recording contract with Jamie Records.

The smash instrumental hit "Rebel Rouser," written by Eddy and Hazlewood, launched Duane Eddy's popular recording career. Recording with studio aces such as Al Casey, pianist Larry Knechtel, and saxophonists Plas Johnson, Jim Horn, and Steve Douglas, he scored a series of major pop instrumental hits on Jamie with "Ramrod," "Cannonball," "The Lonely One," the classic "Forty Miles of Bad Road," and "Peter Gunn." In 1960 Eddy toured Great Britain and made a cameo appearance in the film *Because They're Young,* scoring a smash hit with the title song, which featured one of the first uses of horns and strings on an instrumental rock single.

By 1962 Duane Eddy had left Lee Hazlewood and switched to RCA Records, where he achieved a moderate hit with an instrumental version of "The Ballad of Paladin," the theme for the CBS-television western *Have Gun Will Travel,* in which he appeared. He also managed hits with two songs recorded with the intrusive female chorus dubbed the Rebelettes (actually Darlene Love and the Blossoms), "(Dance with the) Guitar Man," and "Boss Guitar." Eddy continued to record for RCA, Colpix, and Reprise through the '60s with little success. He appeared in a straight dramatic role in the 1968 motorcycle movie *The Savage Seven* and later moved to California. He backed B. J. Thomas's 1972 hit "Rock and Roll Lullaby" and produced Phil Everly's 1973 album *Star Spangled Springer.* He moved to Lake Tahoe in 1976 and scored a British-only hit with "Play Me Like You Play Your Guitar" in 1975 and a country-only hit in 1977 with "You Are My Sunshine," backed by Waylon Jennings and Willie Nelson.

Duane Eddy returned to live performance in 1983, backed by Ry Cooder and Steve Douglas. He moved to Nashville in 1985 and the following year managed a moderate hit with "Peter Gunn," recorded with the British band the Art of Noise. During 1987 he recorded *Duane Eddy* for Capitol with George Harrison, Paul McCartney, John Fogerty, Jeff Lynne, and sessions guitarists Steve Cropper, David Lindley, James Burton, and Ry Cooder. Duane Eddy was inducted into the Roll and Roll Hall of Fame in 1994.

Duane Eddy and the Rebels

Have Twangy Guitar, Will Travel	Jamie	3000	'58	†
	Motown	5431	'89	CS/CD†
Especially for You	Jamie	3006	'59	†
The Twang's the Thang	Jamie	3009	'60	†
Plays Songs of Our Heritage	Jamie	3011	'60	†
$1,000,000 Worth of Twang	Jamie	3014	'60	†
	Motown	5424	'89	CS/CD†
Have Twangy Guitar, Will Travel/$1,000,000 Worth of Twang	Motown	9068		CD†
Girls! Girls! Girls!	Jamie	3019	'61	†
$1,000,000 Worth of Twang- Vol. 2	Jamie	3021	'62	†
Twisting with Duane Eddy	Jamie	3022	'62	†
Surfin' with Duane Eddy	Jamie	3024	'63	†
Duane Eddy with the Rebels–In Person	Jamie	3025	'63	†
16 Greatest Hits	Jamie	3026	'64	†

Duane Eddy and the Rebelettes

Twangy Guitar–Silky Strings	RCA	2576	'62	†
Dance With the Guitar Man	RCA	2648	'63	†
Duane Eddy Guitar Man	GTO	002	'75	†

Duane Eddy

Twistin' 'n' Twangin'	RCA	2525	'62	†

Twangs a Country Song	RCA	2681	'63		†
Twangin' Up a Storm	RCA	2700	'63		†
Lonely Guitar	RCA	2798	'64		†
Water Skiing	RCA	2918	'64		†
A-Go-Go	Colpix	490	'65		†
Goes Bob Dylan	Colpix	494	'65		†
The Biggest Twang of All	Reprise	6218	'66		†
The Roaring Twangies	Reprise	6240	'67		†
Duane Eddy	Capitol	12567	'87	LP/CS†
	Capitol	46897	'87	CD†

Compilations and Reissues

Twangin' the Golden Hits	RCA	2993	'65		†
Twangsville	RCA	3432	'65		†
Best	RCA	3477	'66		†
reissued as "Pure Gold"	RCA	2671	'78		†
Legend of Rock	Deram	5033/4	'75		†
The Vintage Years	Sire	(2)3707	'75		†
Compact Command Performance	Motown	9068	'87	CD†
Twang Thang	Rhino	71223	'93	CS/CD
Great Guitar Hits	Curb/Atlantic	77801	'96	CS/CD

EVERLY BROTHERS

Don Everly (born February 1, 1937, in Brownie, Kentucky) and Phil Everly (born January 19, 1939, in Brownie, Kentucky, although some say Chicago).

The most popular vocal duo from the rock 'n' roll '50s, the Everly Brothers introduced country harmonies into rock music, with Don usually singing tenor lead and Phil supplying high harmony. Their precise, assured harmonies influenced a whole generation of rock singers, from the Beatles to the Hollies, the Beach Boys to the Byrds, from Simon and Garfunkel to the Eagles. Aided immeasurably by the songwriting team of Felice and Boudleaux Bryant and the guitar playing and production of Chet Atkins, the Everly Brothers recorded songs on topics of concern to teenagers such as parents, school, and young love. Yet their appeal was so widespread that "Bye Bye Love," "Bird Dog," "Devoted to You," and "('Til) I Kissed You" became three-way crossover hits, hitting in the pop, country-and-western, and R&B fields. "Wake Up Little Susie" and "All I Have to Do Is Dream" topped all three charts. Without the assistance of the Bryants and Atkins, the Everly Brothers continued their hit-making ways from 1960 to 1962 at Warner Brothers. They continued to tour until 1973, when they broke up acrimoniously, eventually settling their differences and reuniting in 1983.

Don and Phil Everly were taught the guitar at an early age. Their parents, Ike and Margaret, were touring musicians and began hosting a weekly radio show on KMA in Shenandoah, Iowa, in 1945. The brothers began appearing on *The Everly Family Show* when Don was eight and Phil six. During summers they toured the country circuit with their parents. In 1954, with the help of family friend Chet Atkins, Don was signed to a songwriting contract with Acuff-Rose Publishing, providing Kitty Wells with the major country hit "Thou Shalt Not Steal." A year later the brothers moved to Nashville, recording briefly for Columbia Records in late 1955. Early the following year, Wesley Rose became their manager, introducing them to the songwriting team of Felice and Boudleaux Bryant in 1957.

THE EVERLY BROTHERS

Signed to Cadence Records, the Everly Brothers scored their first hit in 1957 with "Bye Bye Love," written by the Bryants. The song, like many that followed, became a three-way hit, making the pop, R&B, and country-and-western charts. "Wake Up Little Susie," written by the Bryants, topped all three charts, as did Boudleaux's "All I Have to Do Is Dream." The Bryants' "Problems" was a smash pop/major country hit, and Boudleaux's "Bird Dog" was a top pop/top country/smash R&B hit. The Everlys debuted at the *Grande Ole Opry* in May 1957 and appeared on CBS television's *Ed Sullivan Show* in August 1957. Major pop and country hits through 1958 included Ray Charles's "This Little Girl of Mine" and Roy Orbison's "Claudette," and Boudleaux's "Devoted to You" became a smash R&B/near-smash pop/near-smash country hit. The Everly Brothers briefly visited Great Britain in early 1959 and continued their string of pop hits with "Take a Message to Mary" backed with "Poor Jenny" (both by the Bryants). Don's "('Til) I Kissed You," recorded with the Crickets, was a smash pop/near-smash country/major R&B hit. The tender ballad "Let It Be Me" (their first recording with strings) and Phil's "When Will I Be Loved" became near-smash pop-only hits.

In 1960 the Everly Brothers were the first artists signed to the newly formed Warner Brothers label, for a reported $1,000,000. They toured Great Britain in the spring of 1960 and moved to Hollywood in early 1961. Without the services of producer Atkins, they scored a top pop/top R&B hit with their own "Cathy's Clown," ultimately their biggest selling record. "So Sad" was a near-smash pop/near-smash R&B hit, "Walk Right Back" (by Sonny Curtis) a near-smash pop hit, and "Ebony Eyes" (by John D. Loudermilk) a near-smash pop/major country/major R&B hit. Parting company with Wesley Rose in the summer of 1961, the brothers' last major pop hits (near-smashes) came in 1962 with "Crying in the Rain" (written by Carole King and Howie Greenfield) and "That's Old Fashioned." The brothers joined the Marine Corps Reserve in late 1961, serving six months' active duty. They reunited with the Bryants for *Gone, Gone, Gone,* which yielded a moderate hit with their own title song, and recorded *Two Yanks in England* in London with the assistance of Jimmy Page and Graham Nash, Allan Clarke, and Tony Hicks of the Hollies. The brothers scored a British smash with "The Price of Love" in 1965, and a moderate American pop hit with "Bowling Green" in 1967.

The Everly Brothers' 1968 *Roots* was acclaimed as one of the finest early country-rock albums, and in 1970 they hosted *The Everly Brothers Show,* a summer replacement for *The Johnny Cash Show,* on ABC-TV. By the early '70s they had switched to RCA Records, touring and recording the excellent 1972 set *Stories We Could Tell* with guitarist-keyboardist Warren Zevon and guitarist Waddy Wachtel. However, despite the inclusion of John Sebastian's title song, Rod Stewart's "Mandolin Wind," Jesse Winchester's "Brand New Tennessee Waltz," and Don's ironic "I'm Tired of Singing My Songs in Las Vegas," the album failed to sell, as did *Pass the Chicken and Listen,* recorded in Nashville with producer Chet Atkins.

On July 14, 1973, Phil Everly smashed his guitar and stormed off stage at Knotts Berry Farm in Buena Park, California, effectively ending the brothers' twenty-eight-year career. Both pursued solo careers and recorded solo albums. Don recorded *Sunset Towers* with British guitarist Albert Lee and scored his biggest solo hit in the country field with "Yesterday Just Passed My Way Again" in 1976. Phil performed on albums by John Sebastian, Dion, Warren Zevon (his debut), and J. D. Souther during the '70s. In 1978 Phil made a cameo appearance in the Clint Eastwood film *Every Which Way But Loose,* performing "Don't Say You Don't Love Me No More" with costar Sandra Locke. In 1983 Phil managed a moderate country hit with "Who's Gonna Keep Me Warm" and a major British hit with "She Means Nothing to Me," recorded with Cliff Richard.

Don and Phil Everly ended their bitter separation in September 1983 with concerts at London's Royal Albert Hall. The following year they recorded *EB '84* with producer Dave Edmunds, guitarist Albert Lee, and keyboardist Pete Wingfield (1975's "Eighteen with a Bullet"). The album produced a country/pop hit with Paul McCartney's "On the Wings of a Nightingale." They toured with Lee and Wingfield in 1984 and 1986 and recorded *Born Yesterday* under Edmunds. The Everly Brothers were inducted into the Rock and Roll Hall of Fame in its inaugural year, 1986, and recorded *Some Hearts* with Brian and Dennis Wilson of the Beach Boys in 1988. Don's youngest daughter, Erin, was briefly married to Axl Rose of Guns N' Roses in 1990. In 1992 Don's only son, Edan, recorded *Dead Flowers* with his band, Edan, for Hollywood Records. Despite a distinguished career, the Everly Brothers were without a record label by the mid '90s.

BIBLIOGRAPHY

Karpp, Phyllis. *Ike's Boys: The Story of the Everly Brothers.* Ann Arbor, MI: Pierian, 1988.

Dodge, Consuelo. *The Everly Brothers: Ladies Love Outlaws.* Starke, FL: CIN-DAV, 1991.

Escott, Colin. "The Everly Brothers: Brothers in Arms" (Discography by Neal Umphred). *Goldmine* 19, no. 12 (June 25, 1993): 14–20, 22, 24, 26, 28, 30, 32, 34, 38, 42.

Cadence Records

The Everly Brothers	Cadence	3003	'58	†
	Rhino	211	'85	†
	Rhino	78211	'88	CD†
	Rhino	70211		CS/CD
Songs Our Daddy Taught Us	Cadence	3016	'58	†
	Rhino	212	'85	†
	Rhino	78212	'88	CD†
	Rhino	70212		CS/CD
Best	Cadence	3025	'59	†
The Fabulous Style of the Everly Brothers	Cadence	25040	'60	†
	Rhino	213	'85	†
	Rhino	70213	'88	CS/CD
The Everly Brothers/The Fabulous Style of the Everly Brothers	Ace	932	'90	CD
Folk Songs	Cadence	3059	'62	†
	Rhino	210	'85	†
	Rhino	78210	'88	CD†
15 Everly Hits	Cadence	25062	'63	†

All They Had to Do Was Dream	Rhino	70214	'85	CS/CD
The Best of the Everly Brothers (1957–1960)	Rhino	70173	'87	CS
Cadence Classics: Their 20 Greatest Hits	Rhino	5258	'86	CD
Pure Harmony	Ace	118		LP†
Greatest Recordings	Ace	194	'87	LP/CS
	Ace	903	'87	CD

Warner Brothers Recordings

It's Everly Time	Warner Brothers	1381	'60	†
A Date with the Everly Brothers	Warner Brothers	1395	'60	†
Both Sides of an Evening	Warner Brothers	1418	'61	†
Instant Party	Warner Brothers	1430	'62	†
Golden Hits	Warner Brothers	1471	'62	CS/CD
Christmas with the Everly Brothers	Warner Brothers	1483	'62	
Sing Great Country Hits	Warner Brothers	1513	'63	†
Very Best	Warner Brothers	1554	'64	CS/CD
Rock 'n' Soul	Warner Brothers	1578	'65	†
Gone, Gone, Gone	Warner Brothers	1585	'65	†
Beat 'n' Soul	Warner Brothers	1605	'65	†
In Our Image	Warner Brothers	1620	'65	†
Two Yanks in England	Warner Brothers	1646	'66	†
Hit Sound	Warner Brothers	1676	'67	†
The Everly Brothers Sing	Warner Brothers	1708	'67	†
Roots	Warner Brothers	1752	'68	†
The Everly Brothers Show	Warner Brothers	1858	'70	†
Walk Right Back: The Everly Brothers on Warner Brothers	Warner Bros.	(2)45164	'75/'93	CS/CD

Later Recordings

Stories We Could Tell	RCA	4620	'72	†
	One Way	34509	'97	CD
Pass the Chicken and Listen	RCA	4781	'72	†
	One Way	34508	'97	CD
Home Again	RCA	5401	'85	†
The Reunion Concert (recorded 1983)	Mercury	824479	'84	CD
EB '84	Mercury	822431	'84	LP/CS/CD†
	Razor & Tie	2040	'95	CD
Born Yesterday	Mercury	826142	'85	LP/CS/CD†
Some Hearts	Mercury	823520	'85	LP/CS/CD†
The Mercury Years	Mercury	514905	'93	CS/CD

Compilation Albums

Wake Up, Little Susie	Harmony	11304	'69	†
Christmas with the Everly Brothers	Harmony	11350	'69	†
Chained to a Memory	Harmony	11388	'70	†
Original Greatest Hits	Barnaby	(2)350(E)	'70	†
End of An Era	Barnaby	(2)30260(E)	'71	†
History of the Everly Brothers	Barnaby	(2)15008(E)	'73	†
Greatest Hits	Barnaby	(2)6006(E)	'74	†
Greatest Hits, Vol. 1	Barnaby	4004(E)	'78	†
Greatest Hits, Vol. 2	Barnaby	4005(E)	'78	†
Greatest Hits, Vol. 3	Barnaby	4006(E)	'78	†
Golden Hits (Cathy's Clown)	Pickwick	3030	'71	†
Magical Golden Hits	Candlelite	(2)2505	'76	†

24 Original Classics	Arista	(2)8207	'84	CS/CD†
Living Legends	Pair	(2)1063	'86	CS†
The Fabulous Everly Brothers	Ace	006		CS/CD
Songs Our Daddy Taught Us	Ace	75		CD
In the Studio	Ace	159		LP†
All-Time Greatest Hits	Curb/Warner Bros.	77311	'90	CS/CD
Rare Solo Classics	Curb/Warner Bros.	77472	'91	CS/CD
All I Have to Do Is Dream	Laserlight	418	'94	CD
Wake Up Little Susie	Laserlight	419	'94	CS/CD
Bye Bye Love	Laserlight	420	'94	CS/CD
Heartaches And Harmonies	Rhino	(4)71779	'94	CD
Golden Hits	Hollywood/IMG	439		CS/CD
Don Everly				
Don Everly	Ode	77005	'71	†
Sunset Towers	Ode	77023	'74	†
Brother Juke-Box	Hickory	44003	'77	†
Phil Everly				
Star-Spangled Springer	RCA	0092	'73	†
Phil's Diner	Pye	12104	'74	†
Mystic Line	Pye	12121	'75	†
Living Alone	Elektra	213	'79	†
Edan (with Edan Everly)				
Dead Flowers	Hollywood	61329	'92	CS/CD†

CONNIE FRANCIS

Born Concetta Franconero on December 12, 1938, in Newark, New Jersey.

America's top-selling female recording artist of the late '50s and early '60s, Connie Francis recorded popular up-tempo songs and heartrending ballads during a time dominated by male acts. Rivaled at the time only by Brenda Lee, Francis charted over fifty singles, a record eventually broken by Aretha Franklin. Moving firmly into the pop field in the '60s, Connie Francis proved herself a survivor, eventually returning to touring and recording in the late '80s after years of psychological problems brought on by her rape after a performance in 1974.

Concetta Franconero began accordion lessons at the age of three and sang at local functions as a child. In 1950 she won first place on the national television show *Talent Scouts,* hosted by Arthur Godfrey, who suggested the name change to Connie Francis. From 1950 to 1954 she performed weekly on the NBC-TV variety program *Star Time.* Signed to MGM Records in 1955, Francis recorded ten unsuccessful singles for the label, finally managing a minor hit with "The Majesty of Love" in duet with Marvin Rainwater in late 1957. "Who's Sorry Now," recorded at her father's behest, became her first smash pop hit in 1958. Originally popularized in 1923 and promoted through appearances on Dick Clark's *American Bandstand,* the song was followed by the major pop hit "Stupid Cupid," written by Neil Sedaka and Howard Greenfield. Through 1964 Francis scored hits with standards such as "My Happiness," "Among My Souvenirs," "Mama," and "Together," and softly rocking contemporary songs such as "Everybody's Somebody's Fool" and "My Heart Has a Mind of Its Own" (both top hits written by Greenfield and Jack Keller), "Lipstick on Your Collar," and "Vacation." She also achieved hits with tearful ballads such as "Many Tears Ago," "Breakin' in

CONNIE FRANCIS

a Brand New Broken Heart," "Don't Break the Heart That Loves You," and "Second Hand Love," cowritten by Phil Spector. She appeared in the films *Where the Boys Are* (1960) and *Follow the Boys* (1962), which featured her hit title songs, plus *Looking for Love* (1964) and *When the Boys Meet the Girls* (1965).

Beginning in 1960 Connie Francis recorded albums of Italian, Spanish, Latin, and Jewish favorites that endeared her to both the easy-listening and international audience. Performing at the famed Copacabana nightclub in New York in 1960, Francis turned to the mainstream audience to sustain her career as she faded from the charts after the advent of the Beatles. Francis recorded albums throughout the '60s (including folk and country albums, even an album with Hank Williams Jr.), performed charity work for organizations such as UNICEF and the USO in the late '60s, and toured into the '70s.

Her life would be forever changed when, after a performance at the Westbury Music Fair in New York on November 8, 1974, Connie Francis was raped. Though she endured psychiatric treatment and confinement, a temporarily damaged voice, and the Mafia-style slaying of her brother, she still continued to perform sporadically. In 1981 she made a much-publicized appearance at Westbury. However, in 1983 her father had her committed, against her will, to a psychiatric hospital.

Connie Francis published her memoirs, *Who's Sorry Now,* in 1984, and eventually she regained her health; performing again starting in 1989, she adopted as her theme song the poignant "If I Never Sing Another Song." In 1992 Liberty Records issued Connie Francis's *Tourist in Paradise.*

BIBLIOGRAPHY

Connie Francis. *Who's Sorry Now.* New York: St. Martin's, 1984.

William Ruhlmann. "Connie Francis Sings Everybody's Favorites" (Discography by Neal Umphred). *Goldmine* 19, no. 9 (May 14, 1993): 14–20, 22, 24, 26, 28, 30, 32, 34.

Connie Francis

Who's Sorry Now	MGM	3686	'58	†
Exciting Connie Francis	MGM	3761	'59	†
My Thanks to You	MGM	3776	'59	†
Sings Italian Favorites	MGM	3791	'59	†
Christmas in My Heart	MGM	3792	'59	†
	Polydor	823561	'87	CS/CD
reissued as Connie's Christmas	MGM	4399	'66	†
Sings Rock 'n' Roll Million Sellers	MGM	3794	'59	†
Country and Western Golden Hits	MGM	3795	'60	†
Sings Spanish and Latin American Favorites	MGM	3853	'60	†
Sings Jewish Favorites	MGM	3869	'60	†
Sings More Italian Favorites	MGM	3871	'60	†
Songs to a Swingin' Band	MGM	3893	'61	†
At the Copa	MGM	3913	'61	†
Never on Sunday	MGM	3965	'61	†
Sings Folk Song Favorites	MGM	3969	'61	†
Sings Irish Favorites	MGM	4013	'62	†
Do the Twist	MGM	4022	'62	†
Fun Songs for Children	MGM	4023(M)	'62	†
	MGM	70126(M)		†
Sings Award Winning Motion Picture Hits	MGM	4048	'62	†
Connie Francis Sings Second Hand Love and Other Hits	MGM	4049	'62	†
Country Music, Connie Style	MGM	4079	'62	†
Modern Italian Hits	MGM	4102	'63	†
Follow the Boys (sound track)	MGM	4123	'63	†
Sings German Favorites	MGM	4124	'63	†
Sings Greatest American Waltzes	MGM	4145	'63	†
Mala Femmena (Evil Woman) and Big Hits From Italy	MGM	4161	'63	†
In the Summer of His Years	MGM	4210	'64	†
Looking for Love (sound track)	MGM	4229	'64	†
A New Kind of Connie	MGM	4253	'64	†
For Mama	MGM	4294	'65	†
Sings All Time International Hits	MGM	4298	'65	†
When the Boys Meet the Girls (sound track)	MGM	4334	'66	†
Jealous Heart	MGM	4355	'66	†
Sings Movie Greats of the 60's	MGM	4382	'66	†
Live at the Sahara in Las Vegas	MGM	4411	'67	†
Love, Italian Style	MGM	4448	'67	†
Happiness: Connie Francis On Broadway Today	MGM	4472	'67	†
Grandes Exitos del Cine de los Anos 60's	MGM	4474	'67	†
My Heart Cries for You	MGM	4487	'67	†
Hawaii: Connie	MGM	4522	'68	†
Connie & Clyde	MGM	4573	'68	†
Sings Burt Bacharach/Hal David	MGM	4585	'68	†
The Wedding Cake	MGM	4637	'69	†
Sings the Songs of Les Reed	MGM	4655	'70	†
Sings Greatest Golden Groovy Goodies	MGM	109	'70	†
Connie Francis and the Kids Next Door	MGM	903		†
Spanish and Latin American Favorites	MGM	10014	'71	†
Connie Francis	Metro	519	'65	†

Sings Folk Favorites	Metro	538	'65	†
Sings Songs of Love	Metro	571	'66	†
Incomparable	Metro	603	'67	†
Connie: Italiano	Laurie	8019		†
	Columbia	8098		†
Tourist In Paradise	Liberty	96498	'92	CS/CD†

Connie Francis and Hank Williams Jr.

Sings Great Country Favorites	MGM	4251	'65	†

Anthologies and Compilations

Greatest Hits	MGM	3793	'59	†
More Greatest Hits	MGM	3942	'61	†
Very Best	MGM	4167	'63	†
A Connie Francis Spectacular	MGM	(5)6		†
I'm Me Again: Silver Anniversary Album	MGM	5406	'81	†
Greatest Hits	MGM	5410	'82	†
Greatest Jewish Hits	MGM	5411	'82	†
Greatest Italian Hits	Polygram	5412	'82	†
In Portuguese and Italian	Polydor	827365		†
Very Best	Polydor	827569		CS/CD
Greatest Hits	Polydor	827582		CS
Sings Greatest Italian Hits	Polydor	827584		CS
Rocksides (1957–1964)	Polydor	831698	'88	LP/CS/CD†
Very Best, Vol. II	Polydor	831699	'87	CS/CD
Sings Greatest Latin Hits	Polydor	839924		CD†
De Coleccion	Polydor	527226	'95	CS/CD
The Italian Collection, Vol. 1	Polydor	9556	'97	CD
The Italian Collection, Vol. 2	Polydor	9557	'97	CD
Greatest Hits	Dominion	3346	'94	CS/CD
At Her Best	RCA-Camden	5004		CS
Solid Gold	Pair	1167		CS
Where the Hits Are	Malaco	2003	'91	LP/CS/CD
Kissin', Twistin', Goin' Where the Boys Are	Bear Family	(5)15826	'96	CD

ALAN FREED

Born December 15, 1922, in Johnstown, Pennsylvania; died January 20, 1965, in Palm Springs, California.

One of the most important popularizers of rock 'n' roll during the '50s, Alan Freed was the first disc jockey and concert producer of rock 'n' roll. Often credited with coining the term rock 'n' roll in 1951, ostensibly to avoid the stigma attached to R&B and so-called race music, Freed opened the door to white acceptance of black music, eschewing white cover versions in favor of the R&B originals. A staunch defender of rock 'n' roll and R&B when the music was under attack, Alan Freed began producing rock 'n' roll concerts in 1952. Indulging in the questionable but almost standard practice of taking unsubstantiated songwriting credits and accepting money to play certain records, Freed was ruined by the payola investigation of 1959–60. He was made the scapegoat of the entire scandal, as others, most notably the more established and less daring Dick Clark, escaped virtually unscathed. Dying ignominiously and impoverished in 1965, Alan Freed received a modicum of recognition as a result of the fictionalized 1978 movie *American Hot Wax.*

Alan Freed grew up in Salem, Ohio, performing his first radio work while attending Ohio State University. Following jobs as announcer at WKST and disc jockey at WAKR, he moved to Cleveland's WJW in 1951. Prompted by record shop owner Leo Mintz, he began playing black R&B records on his *Moondog's Rock 'n' Roll Party* show. Played as rock 'n' roll to avoid any racial stigma, the songs proved unexpectedly popular with white youth, and as a consequence, Freed started producing rock 'n' roll concerts. His first, staged in Cleveland in March 1952, was oversold and subsequently canceled, leading to rock 'n' roll's first riot. In September 1954 Freed moved to New York's WINS, where his rock 'n' roll show helped make the station the city's most popular among white audiences. During the mid '50s he began taking partial songwriting credit for songs such as the Moonglows' "Sincerely" and Chuck Berry's "Maybellene." Freed's concert-promotion activities culminated in the establishment of box office records at New York's Paramount Theater in 1957. He also appeared in some of the earliest rock 'n' roll movies, including 1956's *Rock Around the Clock, Don't Knock the Rock,* and *Rock, Rock, Rock,* and 1957's *Mr. Rock 'n' Roll.*

However, Alan Freed's decline began in March 1958, when a stabbing and a number of beatings occurred at one of his concerts in Boston. Rock 'n' roll shows were subsequently banned in several cities and Freed was charged with inciting to riot and unlawful destruction of property, charges that were dismissed seventeen months later. Drawing the ire of Columbia Records' A&R chief, Mitch Miller, Freed quit WINS and switched to New York's WABC, hosting the television show *Dance Party* on WNEW-TV. However, he was fired in November 1959 for refusing "on principle" to sign statements denying his acceptance of bribes for playing records. Experiencing the brunt of the antirock movement, Freed was indicted in 1960 for accepting $30,000 in payola and eventually pleaded guilty in March 1963 to taking $2,700 from two companies. Forced to leave New York, he worked briefly at KDAY in Los Angeles, where he faced charges of income tax evasion. Freed died of uremic poisoning on January 20, 1965, at the age of forty-two, in Palm Springs, California. Some belated recognition of his contributions to rock 'n' roll came with the 1978 release of the Paramount Pictures movie *American Hot Wax,* a fictionalized "week in the life of rock 'n' roll," with Alan Freed as its central character. Freed was inducted into the Rock and Roll Hall of Fame in its inaugural year, 1986.

BIBLIOGRAPHY

Jackson, John A. *Big Beat Heat: Alan Freed and the Early Years of Rock 'n' Roll.* New York: Schirmer Books, 1991.

Rock 'n' Roll Radio (live 1956)	Radiola	1087	'78	CS/CD
Rock 'n' Roll Dance Party, Vol.1	Coral	57063	'56	†
Rock 'n' Roll Dance Party, Vol. 2	Coral	57115	'57	†
Rock & Roll Dance Party: Alan Freed's Rock & Roll Radio	Magnum America	14	'95	CD
TV Record Hop	Coral	57177	'57	†
Rock Around the Block	Coral	57213	'57	†
Alan Freed Presents the King's Henchmen	Coral	57216	'58	†
The Alan Freed Rock 'n' Roll Show	Brunswick	54043	'58	†
Alan Freed's Golden Picks	End	313	'61	†
Alan Freed's Memory Lane	End	314	'62	†
Alan Freed's Memory Lane	End	315	'62	†

BILL HALEY

Born July 6, 1925, in Highland Park, Michigan; died February 9, 1981 in Harlingen, Texas.

Bill Haley and the Comets fused elements of country music, Western swing, and black R&B to produce some of the earliest rock 'n' roll hits. His "Crazy, Man, Crazy" from 1953 was the first rock 'n' roll record to make the pop charts, and "Dim, Dim the Lights (I Want Some Atmosphere)" from 1955 was the first rock 'n' roll song to make the R&B charts. When rereleased as the opening song to the 1955 film *Blackboard Jungle,* "Rock Around the Clock" became an astounding success, eventually selling more than twenty million copies worldwide. In '57, Haley was the first rock musician to tour Great Britain, and he became the first international rock 'n' roll star. He remained popular in Europe as his success abated in the United States. In the later '50s, his band featured outstanding instrumentalists Rudy Pompilli (saxophone) and Fran Beecher (lead guitar). Quickly overshadowed by the rise of Elvis Presley, Bill Haley enjoyed renewed popularity in the United States with the rock 'n' roll revival of the late '60s.

Born in Michigan, Bill Haley moved with his family to Chester, Pennsylvania, and took up guitar before becoming a teenager. He began performing in the early '40s, later manned the Down Homers, then formed the Four Aces of Western Swing, complete with Western outfits, in 1948. The group performed on local radio station WPWA in 1949 and 1950. He subsequently formed the Saddlemen and signed with Essex Records, scoring a major pop hit with "Crazy, Man, Crazy" in 1953. Shedding the Western image, Haley renamed the group Bill Haley and Haley's Comets, later shortened, and signed with Decca in May 1954. "Rock Around the Clock" became a major pop hit in the spring of 1954 and "Dim, Dim the Lights (I Want Some Atmosphere)" became a major pop/major R&B hit at the end of the year.

Featured in the opening of the movie *Blackboard Jungle,* "Rock Around the Clock" became a top pop and smash R&B hit upon rerelease in the spring of 1955. "Burn That Candle" and "See You Later, Alligator" subsequently became near-smash pop and R&B hits, but in the fall of 1955, three members of the group left to form the Jodimars. Replacements included saxophonist Rudy Pompilli and lead guitarist Frank "Fran" Beecher, who had been playing sessions with the group since 1954.

Bill Haley and the Comets appeared in the early rock 'n' roll films *Rock Around the Clock,* performing nine songs, and *Don't Knock the Rock.* Important hits through 1958 included "Rip It Up," the instrumental "Rudy's Rock," and "Skinny Minnie." Overtaken by the rise of more raucous performers such as Elvis Presley and Little Richard, the group switched to Warner Brothers with little success in 1960. Haley began touring and recording for Orfeon Records in Mexico in the early '60s and moved there in 1962.

Bill Haley and the Comets were stars of the rock 'n' roll revival of the late '60s, and they appeared in the Richard Nader concert film *Let the Good Times Roll* in 1973. On February 2, 1976, the band lost a crucial member when Rudy Pompilli died; Bill Haley died of a heart attack in Harlingen, Texas, on February 9, 1981. He was inducted into the Rock and Roll Hall of Fame in 1987.

BIBLIOGRAPHY

Swenson, John. *Bill Haley: the Daddy of Rock and Roll.* New York: Stein and Day, 1983.

Escott, Colin. "Bill Haley: Indisputably the First" (Discography by Neal Umphred). *Goldmine* 17, no. 8 (April 19, 1991): 12–6, 18, 20, 22, 24, 26, 134.

Bill Haley and the Comets

Rock with Bill Haley and the Comets	Essex	202	'54	†
	Somerset	4600	'54	†
	Trans World	202	'56	†
Rock the Joint! the Original Essex Recordings, 1951–1954	Schoolkids'	1529	'95	CD
Shake, Rattle and Roll	Decca (10")	5560	'55	†
Rock Around the Clock	Decca	8225	'56	†
He Digs Rock and Roll	Decca	8315	'56	†
Rock 'n' Roll Stage Show	Decca	8345	'56	†
Rockin' the Oldies	Decca	8569	'57	†
Rockin' Around the World	Decca	8692	'58	†
Rockin' the Joint	Decca	8775	'58	†
Bill Haley's Chicks	Decca	78821	'59	†
Strictly Instrumental	Decca	78964	'59	†
Greatest Hits!	Decca	75027	'68	†
	MCA	161	'85	CS/CD
Golden Hits	Decca	(2)7211	'73	†
	MCA	(2)4010		†
From the Original Master Tapes	MCA	5539	'85	CD
Rockin'	MCA	20015	'73	†
Shake, Rattle and Roll	MCA	20213		†
Bill Haley and the Comets	Vocalion	3696	'63	†
Twisting Knights at the Round Table	Roulette	25174	'62	†
Bill Haley and the Comets	Warner Brothers	1378	'60	†
Bill Haley's Jukebox	Warner Brothers	1391	'60	†
Rock 'n' Roll	Valiant	1831	'70	†
Revival	Warner Brothers	1831	'81	†
Rock Around the Clock King	Guest Star	1454		†
Ten Million Sellers	Guest Star	1474		†
Scrapbook	Kama Sutra	2014	'70	†
The King of Rock and Roll	Alshire	5202	'70	†
Razzle Dazzle	Janus	(2)7003	'71	†
Travelin' Band	Janus	3035	'71	†
Bill Haley and His Comets	Ambassador	98089	'70	†
Rarities	Ambassador	98100		†
The Original Hits '54–'57	Pickwick	3207		†
Bill Haley and the Comets	Pickwick	3256		†
Rock and Roll	GNP Crescendo	2077	'74	LP/CS
Rock Around the Country	GNP Crescendo	2097	'76	LP
Greatest Hits	Piccadilly	3408		†
Rockin' and Rollin'	Accord	7125	'81	†
Mr. Rock 'n' Roll	Accord	7902	'82	†
Live From N.Y.C.	Accord	7960		†
Rock and Roll Giant	Pair	(2)35069		†
Rock Around the Clock	Special Music	4917		CS

BUDDY HOLLY

Born Charles Hardin Holley on September 7, 1936, in Lubbock, Texas; died February 2, 1959, near Mason City, Iowa.

THE CRICKETS

Buddy Holly, lead guitar, vocals; Niki Sullivan, rhythm guitar; Joe Mauldin, standup bass; Jerry Allison (born August 31, 1939, in Hillsboro, Texas), drums. Other members included guitarists Sonny Curtis (born April 9, 1937, in Meadow, Texas), Tommy Allsup and Glen D. Hardin; vocalists Earl Sinks and Jerry Naylor; bassist Waylon Jennings.

BUDDY HOLLY

One of the two great singer-songwriter guitarists of the '50s (the other being Chuck Berry), Buddy Holly was probably the first rock 'n' roll artist to concern himself with virtually every aspect of his music, including arranging and record production. Coming from a country-and-western background, Holly was one of the first white musicians to apply the heavy backbeat of black R&B to country and pop material. With the Crickets, he originated the standard lineup for the rock band (lead and rhythm guitars, bass, and drums) and set the precedent for the self-contained rock band. Recording some of the earliest rockabilly for Decca Records, Holly later utilized the studio techniques of overdubbing and double-tracking under producer Norman Petty. Later employing vocal choirs and a studio orchestra, he became one of the originators of the modern "pop" song within the rock tradition. Probably the first rock 'n' roll legend because of his early accidental death, Buddy Holly's legacy inspired numerous contemporary artists, particularly in Great Britain. His work lives on in the recordings of many artists (Linda Ronstadt in particular), despite a career that lasted just three years.

Buddy Holly took up violin and piano at the age of eleven, soon switching to acoustic guitar. In the seventh grade, he met guitarist Bob Montgomery, with whom he created a popular local performing duo. The two played "western and bop" music on radio station KDAV in Lubbock between 1953 and 1955, recording a number of songs later issued as *Holly in the Hills*. Adding bassist Larry Welborn and guitarist Sonny Curtis, the group opened shows for Bill Haley and Elvis Presley in Lubbock. Holly was soon signed to Decca Records, and three times during 1956 he traveled to Nashville to record under veteran producer Owen Bradley, the second time accompanied by the Three Tunes: Curtis, bassist Don Guess, and drummer Jerry Allison. These recordings, issued in 1958 as *That'll Be the Day,* included an early version of "That'll Be the Day," as well as "Rock Around with Ollie Vee" and "Midnight Shift." However, none of Decca's 1956 singles releases became hits.

Subsequently released by Decca, Buddy Holly started recording at producer Norman Petty's studio in Clovis, New Mexico, in February 1957 with rhythm guitarist Niki Sullivan, bassist Larry Welborn, and Three Tunes drummer Jerry Allison. The session yielded another version of the Holly-Allison collaboration "That'll Be the Day," which found its way to executive Bob Thiele after being rejected by Roulette Records. Thiele released the song on Brunswick Records under the name the Crickets and quickly signed the group. By September, the song had become a smash pop, R&B, and British hit.

In April 1957 the Crickets came together with Sullivan, Allison, and standup bassist Joe B. Mauldin. Norman Petty took over the career of Buddy Holly and the Crickets as manager, producer, sessions leader, and occasional keyboardist, negotiating separate contracts for the Crickets with Brunswick and for Holly with Coral Records. Holly soon scored a smash pop/smash R&B hit with the classic "Peggy Sue" (backed with "Everyday"), while the Crickets had major crossover hits with "Oh, Boy!" (backed with "Not Fade Away") and "Maybe Baby." The Crickets played black theaters such as New York's Apollo and Washington, D.C.'s Howard Theater and their debut album, *The "Chirping" Crickets,* was released at the end of 1957. Buddy Holly and the Crickets soon appeared on television's *Ed Sullivan Show,* but Niki Sullivan left the group in December. Reduced to a trio, Holly was obliged to play both lead and rhythm guitar on tours of the United States, Australia, and England.

Pop-only hits in 1958 included "Think It Over" for the Crickets, and "Rave On" and Bobby Darin's "Early in the Morning" for Buddy Holly. Holly had recorded "Early in the Morning" in New York without the Crickets, but with vocal choir and saxophonist Sam "The Man" Taylor. However, "It's So Easy," "Heartbeat," and "Love's Made a Fool of You," recorded with new guitarist Tommy Allsup, fared poorly. In the fall of 1958, Jerry Allison achieved a minor hit with the frantic "Real Wild Child" as Ivan, backed by Buddy Holly on lead guitar. In September, Holly produced Waylon Jennings's first single, "Jole Blon," with backing by saxophonist King Curtis, who also played on Holly's "Reminiscing." By October, the Crickets had split from Holly, and Holly had left Norman Petty.

Buddy Holly married Maria Elena Santiago in August and moved to New York, where he recorded "True Love Ways," "Raining in My Heart," and Paul Anka's "It Doesn't Matter Anymore" under producer Dick Jacobs, utilizing Jacobs's orchestra. Holly then embarked on a tour of the Midwest with guitarist Allsup, drummer Charlie Bunch, and guitarist-turned-bassist Waylon Jennings. Following a concert at Clear Lake, Iowa, on February 2, 1959, Buddy Holly, then twenty-two, Ritchie Valens ("Donna," "La Bamba"), and J. P. "Big Bopper" Richardson ("Chantilly Lace") died when their chartered plane crashed shortly after takeoff. Jennings had been bumped from the plane and Dion and the Belmonts, also on the tour, had made other travel arrangements.

"It Doesn't Matter Anymore" (backed with "Raining in My Heart") soon became a major pop hit for Buddy Holly. With Holly's death, Sonny Curtis, Joe Mauldin, Jerry Allison, and vocalist Earl Sinks continued as the Crickets, recording for Brunswick and Coral. Curtis, Sullivan, and Allison recruited vocalist Jerry Naylor and switched to Liberty in 1961, staying until 1965. Subsequently reuniting in the early '70s, the Crickets centered around Curtis, Allison, and guitarist Glen D. Hardin, who left in 1973 to join Elvis Presley's band.

Sonny Curtis wrote "Walk Right Back," a near-smash pop hit for the Everly Brothers in 1961, and "I Fought the Law," a near-smash pop hit for the Bobby Fuller Four in 1966. He also wrote the theme song of CBS-TV's *Mary Tyler Moore Show* and cowrote, with Jerry Allison, "More Than I Can Say," a minor hit for Bobby Vee in 1961 and a smash hit for Leo Sayer in 1980. Curtis recorded into the '80s, scoring major country hits with "Love Is All Around" in 1980 and "Good Ol' Girls" in 1981. Bob Montgomery proved successful as a songwriter ("Misty Blue") and independent producer for Johnny Darrell and Bobby Goldsboro. Waylon Jennings struggled as a country-and-western artist through the '70s, finally achieving recognition as an "outlaw" country musician in 1976. Norman Petty died on August 15, 1984, in Lubbock after a long illness. In 1987 Allison, Mauldin, and guitarist-vocalist Gordon Payne recorded *Three Piece,* released on Allison's Rollercoaster label. The album became *T-Shirt* on Epic Records with the addition of the title track, produced by Paul McCartney.

During the '60s Buddy Holly's legacy was kept alive as the Rolling Stones debuted on the American charts with "Not Fade Away," Peter and Gordon hit with "True Love Ways," and the Bobby Fuller Four scored a major hit with Holly's "Love's Made a Fool of You." In the latter half of the '70s, Linda Ronstadt recorded a number of Holly's songs, hitting with "That'll Be the Day" and "It's So Easy." In 1976 Paul McCartney bought the Holly song catalog and initiated the annual Buddy Holly Week celebration (in September) in London. In May 1978, *The Buddy Holly Story*, starring Gary Busey, was released, becoming a surprise film hit and sparking revitalized interest in Holly. Buddy Holly was inducted into the Rock and Roll Hall of Fame in its inaugural year, 1986, and the movie *Peggy Sue Got Married* that same year featured his title song. *Buddy*, a stage musical based on the life and songs of Buddy Holly, debuted in London in October 1989 and toured the United States the following year. In 1996 Decca issued *Not Fade Away (Remembering Buddy Holly)*, which contained cover versions of Holly's songs by the likes of Marty Stuart and Steve Earle, Nanci Griffith, Los Lobos, Joe Ely, and the Tractors.

BIBLIOGRAPHY

Laing, Dave. *Buddy Holly.* New York: Macmillan, 1971.

Peer, Elizabeth, and Ralph Peer II. *Buddy Holly: a Biography in Words, Pictures and Music.* New York: Peer, 1972.

Goldrosen, John. *Buddy Holly: His Life and Music.* Bowling Green, OH: Popular, 1975.

_____. *The Buddy Holly Story.* New York: Quick Fox, 1979.

Flippo, Chet. "The Buddy Holly Story: Friends Say Movie's Not Cricket." *Rolling Stone,* no. 274 (September 21, 1978): 49–51.

Goldrosen, John, and John Beecher. *Remembering Buddy: the Definitive Biography.* New York: Penguin, 1987.

Amburn, Ellis. *Buddy Holly: A Biography.* New York: St. Martin's, 1995.

Lehmer, Larry. *The Day the Music Died: The Last Tour of Buddy Holly, the Big Bopper, and Richie Valens.* New York: Schirmer Books, 1997.

Norman, Philip. *Rave On: The Biography of Buddy Holly.* New York: Simon & Schuster, 1996.

Buddy Holly and Bob Montgomery

Holly in the Hills	Coral	757463	'65	†

Buddy Holly and the Crickets

The "Chirping" Crickets	Brunswick	54038	'57	†
	MCA	31182	'88	CD
	MCA	25170	'88	CS
reissued as Buddy Holly and the Crickets	Coral	57405	'62	†

Buddy Holly

The Nashville Sessions	MCA	3038	'86	†
That'll Be the Day	Decca	8707	'58	†
reissued as The Great Buddy Holly	Vocalion	3811	'67	†
	MCA	31037	'88	CD†
Buddy Holly	Coral	57210	'58	†
	MCA	25239	'89	CS/CD
	Heavy Vinyl	11161	'95	LP
The Buddy Holly Story	Coral	57279	'59	†
The Buddy Holly Story, Vol. 2	Coral	57326	'60	†

Reminiscing	Coral	57426	'63	†
Buddy Holly Showcase	Coral	57450	'64	†
The Best of Buddy Holly	Coral	8	'66	†
Greatest Hits	Coral	57492	'67	†
	MCA	11213	'95	CD
	MCA	11536	'96	CD
Giant	Coral	757504(E)	'69	†
Good Rockin'	Vocalion	73293(E)	'71	†
Buddy Holly: A Rock 'n' Roll Collection	Decca	(2)7207(E)	'72	†
	MCA	(2)4009		†
20 Golden Greats	MCA	3040	'78	†
	MCA	1484		CS/CD
Buddy Holly Complete	MCA	(6)80000	'81	†
reissued as The Complete Buddy Holly	MCA	(6)80000		CS
From the Original Master Tapes	MCA	5540	'85	CD
Words of Love	MCA	20260	'85	†
Best	MCA	20290	'85	CS†
For the First Time Anywhere	MCA	27059	'83	LP/CS†
	MCA	31048	'87	CD†
Legend	MCA	(2)4184	'86	CS
The Buddy Holly Collection	MCA	(2)10883	'93	CS/CD
Buddy Holly	Bella Musica	89919	'90	CD

The Crickets

In the Style with the Crickets	Coral	57320	'61	†
Bobby Vee Meets the Crickets	Liberty	7228	'62	†
Something Old, Something New, Something Blue, Something Else	Liberty	7272	'63	†
California Sun	Liberty	7351	'64	†
The Liberty Years	EMI	95845	'91	CS/CD†
Rockin' 50's Rock and Roll	Barnaby	30268	'71	†
Remnants	Vertigo	1020	'74	†
T-Shirt	Epic	44446	'88	LP/CS/CD†

Sound-Track Album

The Buddy Holly Story	Epic	35412	'78/'87	CS/CD

Original Cast Album

Buddy: The Buddy Holly Story (1989 London original cast)	Relativity/First Night	1046		CS/CD

Tribute Albums

Every Day Is a Holly Day	Emergo	9465	'89	LP/CS/CD†
Not Fade Away (Remembering Buddy Holly)	Decca	11260	'96	CS/CD

WANDA JACKSON

Born October 20, 1937, in Maud, Oklahoma.

Although she managed only one moderate pop hit single with 1960's "Let's Have a Party," Wanda Jackson wrote and recorded some of the wildest and most aggressive female rockabilly of the '50s, including such classics as "Fujiyama Mama" and "Mean Mean Man." Earning the title "Queen of Rockabilly," she started out as a country singer in the mid '50s and returned to country music in the early '60s. Jackson embraced gospel music during the '70s, eventually returning to rock 'n' roll in the '80s with *Rock 'n' Roll Your Blues Away*.

WANDA JACKSON

Wanda Jackson moved to Bakersfield, California, with her family in 1941, returning to Oklahoma City in 1949. She took up piano and guitar in elementary school and had her own radio show on KLPR by the age of thirteen. Heard by honky-tonk artist Hank Thompson in 1954, she was invited to tour with Thompson and signed with Decca Records. She scored a near-smash country hit with "You Can't Have My Love," recorded with Billy Gray, that summer. She toured with Red Foley and appeared on his ABC television show, *Ozark Jubilee* (later known as *Country Music Jubilee* and *Jubilee U.S.A.*), from 1955 to 1960. She toured with Elvis Presley in 1955 and 1956 and he ostensibly convinced her that she could record in the rockabilly style.

Wanda Jackson switched to Capitol Records in 1956 and began recording in Los Angeles with guitarists Buck Owens and Joe Maphis and pianist Merrill Moore under producer Ken Nelson. Her first Capitol single, "I Gotta Know," became a major country hit, but subsequent recordings failed to chart. These included dynamic songs such as "Hot Dog! That Made Him Mad," "Fujiyama Mama," and "Honey Bop," and her own "Cool Love," "Mean Mean Man," and "Rock Your Baby," as well as excellent covers of "Hardheaded Woman" and "Riot in Cell Block Number Nine" through 1961. She toured with Jerry Lee Lewis and Carl Perkins in 1957 and Capitol issued her debut album for the label in 1958. Her classic rockabilly album *Rockin' with Wanda* was released in 1960, the year she achieved her first moderate pop hit with "Let's Have a Party," recorded in 1957 and previously sung by Elvis Presley in his 1956 movie *Loving You*.

Having managed little commercial success in rock 'n' roll, Wanda Jackson returned to country music in 1961 with her own "Right or Wrong," a near-smash country/major pop hit. She followed up with the country smash/major pop hit "In the Middle of a Heartache" and continued to record country material during the '60s. Jackson also wrote "(Let's Stop) Kickin' Our Hearts Around," a near-smash country hit for Buck Owens in 1962. She achieved major country hits on her own throughout the '60s with "The Box It Came In," "Tears Will Be the Chaser for the Wine," "You Don't Have to Drink to Have Fun," "A Woman Lives for Love," and "Fancy Satin Pillows."

Weary from years of touring and suffering from alcohol abuse, Wanda Jackson embraced Christianity in June 1971; she recorded gospel music until the '80s, when she returned to performing rockabilly in Europe. In 1984 she recorded *Rock 'n' Roll Your Blues Away* in Sweden and the album was reissued on Varrick in the United States in 1987. She toured Great Britain and Scandinavia in 1989, and her version of "Let's Have a Party" was featured in the film *Dead Poets Society*. In 1990 she dueted with new country artist Jann Brown on "I Forgot More Than You'll Ever Know." She later recorded two duets with country-rockabilly artist Rosie Flores for Flores's 1995 *Rockabilly Filly* album. Later that year Wanda Jackson resumed touring.

Lovin' Country Style	Decca	4224	'62	†
Wanda Jackson	Capitol	1041	'58	†
Rockin' with Wanda!	Capitol	1384	'60	†
There's a Party Goin' On	Capitol	1511	'61	†
Right or Wrong	Capitol	1596	'61	†
Wonderful Wanda	Capitol	1776	'62	†
Love Me Forever	Capitol	1911	'63	†
Two Sides of Wanda Jackson	Capitol	2030	'64	†
Blues in My Heart	Capitol	2306	'64	†
Sings Country Songs	Capitol	2438	'66	†
Salutes the Country Music Hall of Fame	Capitol	2606	'67	†
Reckless Love Affair	Capitol	2704	'67	†
You'll Always Have My Love	Capitol	2812	'67	†
Best	Capitol	2883	'67	†
Cream of the Crop	Capitol	2976	'69	†
Country!	Capitol	434	'70	†
A Woman Lives to Love	Capitol	554	'70	†
I've Gotta Sing	Capitol	669	'71	†
Praise the Lord	Capitol	11023	'72	†
I Wouldn't Want You Any Other Way	Capitol	11096	'72	†
Country Keepsakes	Capitol	11161	'73	†
Vintage Collections	Capitol Nashville	36185	'95	CS/CD
Please Help Me I'm Falling	Hilltop	6058		†
Leave My Baby	Hilltop	6074		†
We'll Sing in the Sunshine	Hilltop	6116		†
By the Time I Get to Phoenix	Hilltop	6123		†
Tears at the Grand Ole Opry	Hilltop	6184		†
Now I Have Everything	Myrrh	6533	'74	†
Country Gospel	Word	9514	'74	†
Closer to Jesus	Word	9580	'78	†
My Testament	Word	9617	'82	†
Rock 'n' Roll Your Blues Away (recorded in Sweden 1984)	Varrick	025	'87	CS
Rockin' in the Country: the Best of Wanda Jackson	Rhino	70990	'90	CS/CD
Greatest Hits	Curb/Warner	77398	'90	CS/CD
Greatest Hits	Hollywood/IMG	442		CS

ETTA JAMES

Born Jamesetta Hawkins on January 25, 1938, in Los Angeles.

A pioneering R&B star of the '50s who produced a remarkably diverse body of work during five decades, Etta James recorded the R&B classics "Roll with Me, Henry" and "Good Rockin' Daddy" and the soul classic "Tell Mama." Possessing a powerhouse voice that proved remarkably effective on ballads, James influenced white singers such as Janis Joplin. Suffering from heroin addiction and seldom recording between the mid '70s and mid '80s, Etta James reemerged in 1986 with a new round of tours and recordings, publishing her hard-hitting autobiography in 1995.

ETTA JAMES

Born in Los Angeles, Jamesetta Hawkins was singing gospel in the St. Paul Baptist Church at the age of five. She moved to San Francisco in 1950 and formed a singing group with two girlfriends. In 1954 the three auditioned for Johnny Otis and were soon whisked off to Los Angeles to record. At the behest of Otis, the group was dubbed the Peaches and Etta's stage name was devised. They recorded "Roll With Me, Henry," the answer song to Hank Ballard's "Work with Me, Annie," with the Otis band and bass vocalist Richard Berry for Modern Records. Retitled "The Wallflower," the song became a top R&B hit. Within weeks, white artist Georgia Gibbs covered the song for Mercury, resulting in a top pop hit. By year's end, James had scored a smash R&B hit with "Good Rockin' Daddy," but it proved her last for Modern. During the '50s she sang background with the Moonglows on Chuck Berry's "Almost Grown" and "Back in the U.S.A.," and toured with Johnny Otis and Little Richard.

Etta James eventually moved to the Argo subsidiary Chess Records in 1960 with the help of the Moonglows' Harvey Fuqua. She achieved smash R&B hits with the ballads "All I Could Do Was Cry" and "Dearest Darling," and had near-smash R&B hits with "If I Can't Have You" and "Spoonful" in duet with Fuqua, as Etta and Harvey. Smash R&B and moderate pop hits continued through 1963 with the standards "At Last" and "Trust in Me," "Don't Cry Baby," "Something's Got a Hold on Me," "Stop the Wedding," and "Pushover," a major pop hit recorded in Nashville.

Etta James toured and recorded with childhood friend Sugar Pie DeSanto in the mid '60s and the duo managed a moderate R&B hit with "In the Basement" in 1966. The following year Chess sent James to Muscle Shoals, Alabama, to record at the Fame Studio under producer Rick Hall. The resulting album, *Tell Mama,* contained the poignant "I'd Rather Go Blind" and Jimmy Hughes's "Don't Lose Your Good Thing," and yielded two hits, a near-smash R&B/major pop hit with Clarence Carter's classic title song and a near-smash R&B/ moderate pop hit with Otis Redding's "Security." After several more years of modest success and two years without a recording contract, James returned to Chess, managing moderate R&B hits with "I Found a Love" and "All the Way Down," and garnering a Grammy nomination for *Etta James.*

Having finally conquered a long-term heroin addiction, Etta James played the Montreux Jazz Festival in 1977 and opened some shows for the Rolling Stones' 1978 tour. She recorded *Deep in the Night* with producer Jerry Wexler for Warner Brothers in 1978 and *Changes* with producer Allen Toussaint in New Orleans in 1980. In 1986 James recorded two compelling live jazz albums with Eddie "Cleanhead" Vinson and guitarist Shuggie Otis. She later recorded two albums for Island Records before switching to Elektra in 1992. Etta

James was inducted into the Rock and Roll Hall of Fame in 1993, and by 1994 she had moved on to Private Music, where she recorded a Grammy Award-winning album of Billie Holiday songs, as well as two more recent albums. In 1995 Villard Books published her gritty autobiography, *Rage to Survive*.

BIBLIOGRAPHY

James, Etta, and David Ritz. *Rage to Survive*. New York: Villard, 1995.

Early Recordings

Miss Etta James	Crown	5209	'58	†
Best	Crown	5234	'59	†
Twist with Etta James	Crown	5250	'59	†
R&B Queen	Crown	005	'86	†
Etta James Sings	United	7712		†
Best	United	7727		†
Good Rockin' Mama	Ace	33	'81	†
Tuff Lover	Ace	73	'83	†
Good Rockin' Mama/Tuff Lover	Ace	803		CS†
R&B Dynamite	Ace	210	'87	LP/CS/CD
	Flair	86232	'91	CD

Argo/Cadet/Chess Recordings

At Last	Argo	4003	'61	†
	Cadet	4003	'69	†
	Chess	9266	'87	CS/CD
The Second Time Around	Argo	4011	'61	†
	Cadet	4011	'69	†
	Chess	9287	'89	CS/CD
Etta James	Argo	4013	'62	†
	Cadet	4013	'69	†
Etta James Sings for Lovers	Argo	4018	'62	†
	Cadet	4018	'69	†
Top Ten	Argo	4025	'63	†
	Cadet	4025	'69	†
Etta James Rocks the House (recorded in Nashville 1963)	Argo	4032	'64	†
	Cadet	4032	'69	†
	Chess	9184	'88	CS/CD
The Queen of Soul	Argo	4040	'65	†
	Cadet	4040	'69	†
Call My Name	Cadet	4055	'67	†
Tell Mama	Cadet	802	'68	†
	Chess	9269	'88	CS/CD
Etta James Sings Funk	Cadet	832	'70	†
Losers Weepers	Cadet	847	'71	†
Peaches	Chess	(2)60004	'73	†
Etta James	Chess	50042	'73	†
Come a Little Close	Chess	(2)60029	'74	†
	Chess	91509		CS
	MCA	9363	'97	CD
Etta Is Betta Than Evah!	Chess	19003	'75	†

Her Greatest Sides, Vol. 1	Chess	9110	'87	LP/CS
The Sweetest Peaches	Chess	(2)6028	'88	LP/CS
The Sweetest Peaches, Part 1 (1960–1966)	Chess	9280	'88	CD
The Sweetest Peaches, Part 2 (1967–1975)	Chess	9281	'88	CD
The Essential Etta James	Chess	(2)9341	'93	CS/CD
These Foolish Things: The Classic Balladry of Etta James	Chess	9354	'95	CS/CD
Her Best	MCA/Chess	9367	'97	CD
Later Recordings				
Deep in the Night	Warner Brothers	3156	'78	†
	Bullseye Blues	9579	'96	CD
Changes	MCA	3244	'80	†
Etta, Red Hot 'N' Live (recorded 1981)	Intermedia	5014		LP/CS/CD
The Gospel Soul of Etta James	Arrival	864	'89	CS/CD
Seven Year Itch	Island	91018	'88	LP/CS/CD†
	Island	842655	'88	CS/CD
Sticking to My Guns	Island	842926	'90	CS/CD
The Right Time	Elektra	61347	'92	CS/CD
Mystery Lady—Songs of Billie Holiday	Private Music	82114	'94	†
Time After Time	Private Music	82128	'95	CS/CD
Love's Been Rough on Me	Private Music	82140	'97	
Etta James and Eddie "Cleanhead" Vinson				
Blues in the Night, Vol. 1 (The Early Show)	Fantasy	9647	'86	CS/CD
Blues in the Night, Vol. 2 (The Late Show)	Fantasy	9655	'87	CS/CD

LITTLE WILLIE JOHN

Born William John on November 15, 1937, in Cullendale, Arkansas; died May 26, 1968, in Walla Walla, Washington.

One of the most overlooked pioneers of rock 'n' roll and soul, Little Willie John scored more than a dozen pop and major R&B hits between 1955 and 1961 featuring his intense evocative high tenor voice. Influencing a number of black vocalists, including Clyde McPhatter, Sam Cooke, James Brown, and Al Green, John recorded the original and definitive version of "Fever," later covered more successfully by Peggy Lee and the McCoys. A difficult and irascible personality, Little Willie John faded from popularity after 1961's "Take My Love (I Want to Give It All to You)." He died in prison in 1968.

Little Willie John moved with his family to Detroit in 1942, singing in the gospel quartet the United Four with his older sister, Mable. In 1960 Mable John became the first solo female vocalist to record for Motown Records. She scored an R&B smash on Stax Records with "Your Good Thing (Is About to End)" in 1966 and joined Ray Charles's Raeletts in 1968.

William John began performing regularly at Detroit's Book-Cadillac Hotel by the age of eleven and was spotted by Johnny Otis at a Paradise Theater talent contest in 1951. Otis recommended three of the show's acts—Little Willie John, Jackie Wilson, and the Royals—to Syd Nathan of King Records, but only the Royals (who became the Midnighters with the addition of Hank Ballard) were signed to the label. John subsequently toured with R&B bandleader Paul Williams ("The Hucklebuck") and recorded for Prize Records.

Eventually signing with King Records in 1955, Little Willie John recorded under producer Henry Glover and quickly scored a R&B smash with "All Around the World" (also known as "Grits Ain't Groceries"). In 1956 he achieved two two-sided R&B smashes with "Need Your Love So Bad"/"Home at Last" and "Fever"/"Letter from My Darling." "Fever," written by Otis Blackwell and Eddie Cooley, became a top R&B/major pop hit for John, but Peggy Lee had a near-smash pop hit with the song in 1958. John had a major pop/smash R&B hit with "Talk to Me, Talk to Me" in 1958. Other successes for John through 1960 included the major R&B and minor pop hits "You're a Sweetheart," "Leave My Kitten Alone," "Let Them Talk," and "Heartbreak (It's Hurtin' Me)," the pop-only "A Cottage for Sale," and the standard "Sleep," a major crossover hit. Several of Little Willie John's hits were covered by other artists. In 1959 Johnny Preston managed a minor pop hit with "Leave My Kitten Alone"; in 1963 Sunny and the Sunglows had a major pop hit with "Talk to Me"; and in 1969 Little Milton achieved a major R&B hit with "Grits Ain't Groceries."

In 1961 Little Willie John scored major R&B hits with "Walk Slow," the two-sided "(I've Got) Spring Fever"/"Flamingo," and "Take My Love (I Want to Give It All to You)." However, he never achieved another hit, and by 1963 King had dropped him from its roster. In October 1964 John stabbed a man to death in a Seattle club, and in July 1966 he was convicted of manslaughter and sentenced to eight to twenty years in prison. He died at the Washington State Penitentiary in Walla Walla on May 27, 1968, at the age of thirty. The cause was variously reported as a heart attack or pneumonia. James Brown soon recorded the tribute album *Thinking About Little Willie John and A Whole New Thing,* and in 1996 Little Willie John was inducted into the Rock and Roll Hall of Fame.

Fever	King	564	'57	†
Talk to Me	King	596	'58	LP/CS
Mister Little Willie John	King	603	'58	LP/CS/CD
Action	King	691	'60	†
Sure Things	King	739	'61	LP/CS/CD
the Sweet, the Hot, the Teenage Beat	King	767	'61	†
Come On and Join Little Willie John	King	802	'62	†
These Are My Favorite Songs	King	895	'64	†
Little Willie John Sings All Originals	King	949	'66	†
Free at Last	King	1081	'70	†
	BluesWay	6069	'70	†
Little Willie John	Deluxe	1034		†
15 Original Hits	Deluxe	7837		CS/CD

LOUIS JORDAN

Born July 8, 1908, in Brinkley, Arkansas; died February 4, 1975, in Los Angeles, California.

Regarded as the father of R&B—and thus the grandfather of rock 'n' roll—Louis Jordan combined original compositions, humorous performances, and his own dynamic alto saxophone playing propelled by jump blues shuffle rhythms in a small combo context to become one of the first black artists to prove successful with white audiences. Scoring more than fifty major R&B hits in the years 1942–51, including numerous two-sided hits and nearly twenty pop hits, Jordan served as the link between the swing big bands of the '40s and the emerging R&B of the '50s. The prime purveyor of jump blues, he inspired others of the genre such as Wynonie Harris, Roy Milton, and Roy Brown, and early rock 'n' roll artists such as Bill Haley, Chuck Berry, Fats Domino, Bo Diddley, and Ray Charles. Unable to benefit from the rise of rock 'n' roll, Jordan recorded for a variety of labels into the '70s after his long-term tenure with Decca Records ended in 1954.

Louis Jordan learned clarinet as a child, later graduating to alto saxophone. He performed with the Rabbit Foot Minstrels as a teenager and later majored in music at Arkansas Baptist College. He started his professional career with Jimmy Pryor's Imperial Serenaders in 1929, and moved with his family to Philadelphia in 1932. He played with Charlie Gaines and Leroy Smith, among others, and recorded with Louis Armstrong in 1932 and pianist Clarence Williams in 1934. He joined Chick Webb's Orchestra in 1936, performing as occasional soloist and vocalist to primary vocalist Ella Fitzgerald. Jordan recorded with her in 1937 and 1938, leaving Webb in 1938 to he form his own combo in Harlem, initially called the Elks Rendezvous Band. By the end of 1939 he had changed the group's name to the Tympany Five, numbering six to eight members, among whom over the years were pianists "Wild" Bill Davis and Bill Doggett and guitarists Carl Hogan and Bill Jennings.

Signed to Decca Records, Louis Jordan and His Tympany Five began an amazing series of major R&B hits with "Knock Me a Kiss" and "I'm Gonna Leave You on the Outskirts of Town" in 1942. Through 1945 they scored top R&B hits with "What's the Use of Getting Sober," "Ration Blues" (their first pop hit), "G.I. Jive" (a top pop hit), "Mop Mop," and "Caldonia"; and smash R&B hits with "Five Guys Named Moe," "Is You Is or Is You Ain't (Ma' Baby)," "You Can't Get That No More," and "Somebody Done Changed the Lock on My Door." During World War II Jordan frequently recorded for the Armed Forces Radio Service and the V-Disc (V for Victory) Program and appeared in a number of short musical films not unlike today's videos on MTV. He also cameoed in the wartime musical *Follow the Boys* in 1944 and later appeared in the films *Junior Prom* (1946) and *Look Out Sister* (1949).

In the later '40s, Louis Jordan and His Tympany Five scored top R&B hits with "Buzz Me"/"Don't Worry 'Bout That Mule," the classic "Choo Choo Ch-Boogie," "Ain't That Just Like a Woman," "Ain't Nobody Here But Us Chickens" backed by the smash classic "Let the Good Times Roll," "Texas and Pacific," "Jack, You're Dead," "Boogie Woogie Blue Plate," "Run, Joe," "Beans and Cornbread," and "Saturday Night Fish Fry." Jordan also achieved a major pop hit with Bing Crosby on "My Baby Said Yes" in the summer of 1945, and a top R&B and near-smash pop hit with Ella Fitzgerald on "Stone Cold Dead in the Market (He Had It Coming)" in 1946. Other smash R&B hits of the era included "Reconversion Blues," "Beware (Brother Beware)," the oft-covered "Open the Door, Richard," "Barnyard Boogie," "Reet, Petite and Gone," "Don't Burn That Candle at Both Ends," "Pettin' and Pokin'," and "You Broke Your Promise."

In the early '50s Louis Jordan continued to hit with "School Days," the top R&B hit "Blue Light Boogie," "I'll Never Be Free" with Ella Fitzgerald, "Lemonade," and "Tear Drops." He managed his last (smash) hit in the spring of 1951 with "Weak Minded Blues." Jordan formed a short-lived big band in 1951 and offered to run for president in 1952. In 1954, after fifteen years with Decca, he moved to the Los Angeles-based Aladdin Records, subsequently switching to RCA's short-lived X subsidiary for recordings in 1955 and 1956. He also recorded with guitarist Mickey Baker and saxophonist Sam "The Man" Taylor for Mercury in 1956 and 1957.

Despite continued touring, Louis Jordan's popularity faded appreciably with the rise of rock 'n' roll. He recorded in London with the Chris Barber Band in 1962 and recorded for Ray Charles's Tangerine label between 1962 and 1964. In the late '60s he recorded for Pzazz Records, recording for the French Black & Blue label (reissued by Classic Jazz and Evidence) in 1973. He died of a heart attack in Los Angeles on February 4, 1975, at the age of 66.

Louis Jordan was inducted into the Blues Foundation's Hall of Fame in 1983 and into the Rock and Roll Hall of Fame as an Early Influence in 1987. In 1990 the musical *Five Guys Named Moe,* based on his songs, debuted in London, making its way to New York's Broadway in 1992.

BIBLIOGRAPHY

Chilton, John. *Let the Good Times Roll: the Story of Louis Jordan and His Music.* Ann Arbor, MI: University of Michigan Press, 1994.

The Decca Years

Louis Jordan and His Tympany Five 1939–1944	Jazz Archives	158372	'95	CD
In Memoriam (recorded 1940)	MCA	622175	'75	†
Five Guys Named Moe: Original Decca Recordings, Vol. 2	MCA	10503	'92	CS/CD
Louis Jordan and His Tympany Five 1941–1943	Classics	741	'93	CD
Louis Jordan and His Tympany Five 1943–1945	Classics	866	'96	CD
Louis Jordan On Film: Reet, Petite and Gone	Krazy Kat	7414	'83	†
Louis Jordan On Film: Look Out Sister	Krazy Kat	7415	'83	†
Louis Jordan On Film, 1942–1948	Krazy Kat	17		CD
Louis Jordan and His Tympany Five, 1944–1945	Circle	53		CD
Louis Jordan and His Tympany	Circle	97	'88	LP/CS
The Best of Louis Jordan and His Tympany Five	VJC	1037	'92	CD
Louis Jordan and His Tympany Five: Five Guys Named Moe (recorded Hollywood, 1943–1946)	VJC	1037–2		CD
Five Guys Named Moe (live 1948–1949)	Bandstand	1531	'92	CD
Louis Jordan and His Orchestra (recorded 1951)	MCA	8332	'76	†
Best	MCA	(2)24079	'75	†
	MCA	1631	'81	†
Best (1941–1954)	MCA	(2)4079		CS
	MCA	4079		CD
	Decca Jazz	664	'96	CD
Let the Good Times Roll (recorded 1945–1950)	Decca	8551	'58	†
	Coral	59	'70	†
Greatest Hits	Decca	75035(E)	'68	†
	MCA	274(E)	'68	†
Greatest Hits, Vol. 2 (1941–1947)	MCA	1337	'80	†

Later Recordings

One Guy Named Louis: the Complete Aladdin Sessions (recorded 1954)	Capitol Jazz	96804	'92	CD
Rock 'n Roll Call (recorded 1955–1956)	Bluebird	66145	'93	CD
Somebody Up There Digs Me	Mercury	20242	'57	†
	Wing	12126		†
Man, We're Wailin'	Mercury	20331	'58	†
Rock 'n' Roll (Mercury recordings)	Verve	838219	'90	CD
No Moe! Louis Jordan's Greatest Hits (recorded 1956–1957)	Verve	512523	'92	CD
Go Blow Your Horn	Score	4007	'58	†
Louis Jordan and Chris Barber (recorded 1962)	Black Lion	760156	'91	CD
Hallelujah	Tangerine	1503	'64	†
Louis Jordan (recorded 1968–1969)	Pzazz	321		†
I Believe in Music (recorded 1973)	Black and Blue	59059	'74	†
	Classic Jazz	148	'80	†
	Evidence	26006	'92	CD
Great Rhythm & Blues Oldies, Vol.1	Blues Spectrum	101	'72	†
Just Say Moe! Mo' of the Best of Louis Jordan (Aladdin, Mercury, Tangerine, V-Disc and Decca recordings)	Rhino	71144	'92	CD/CS†

B. B. KING

Born Riley B. King on September 16, 1925, near Itta Bena, Mississippi.

B. B. KING

One of the most successful blues artists of the '50s, scoring nearly twenty major R&B hits, including four top hits, B. B. King honed his guitar technique through years of tireless touring. Becoming one of the world's most soulful guitar soloists, King developed a style of playing that featured his trademark arpeggios and "bent" note improvisations, which influenced virtually all subsequent blues guitarists. Perhaps the one blues guitarist who had the greatest impact on white rock guitarists after the '50s—from Eric Clapton and Mike Bloomfield to Johnny Winter and Stevie Ray Vaughan—King ultimately achieved widespread recognition with white audiences with his 1969 tour with the Rolling Stones and the conspicuous success of "The Thrill Is Gone" in 1970. Elevated to the exclusive Nevada casino and supper club circuit by the '70s, he was the first blues singer and guitarist to cross over into extensive mainstream popularity.

B. B. King grew up in Indianola, Mississippi, and sang in local gospel choirs. He acquired his first guitar while in his early teens and with his first group, the Elkhorn Singers, performed in local black clubs. Drafted in 1943, he served in the military for four years and then settled in Memphis, where in 1949 he moved in with his cousin, country blues artist Bukka White, and secured a ten-minute afternoon show on radio station WDIA that ran until 1950. King subsequently formed the Beale Streeters, whose members at various times included Bobby "Blue" Bland and Johnny Ace. King became known as "The Beale Street Blues Boy," later shortened to "B. B."

After initial recordings for the small Nashville-based Bullet label in 1949, B. B. King was signed to the Los Angeles-based Modern/RPM label by Ike Turner. Scoring his first top R&B hit with Lowell Fulson's "Three O'Clock Blues" in 1952, King formed a thirteen-piece band that included a small horn section—a regular feature of his bands throughout his career—and began relentlessly touring the so-called "chitlin" circuit of small black clubs. Through 1954 he scored top R&B hits with "You Know I Love You," "Please Love Me," and "You Upset Me Baby," and smash R&B hits with "Story from My Heart and Soul," "Woke Up This Morning," "My Heart Beats Like a Hammer," and "Whole Lotta Love."

By 1954 B. B. King had graduated to major black venues such as the Howard Theater in Washington, D.C., and the Apollo Theater in Harlem. Smash R&B hits on RPM came out through 1957 with "Every Day I Have the Blues" (his signature song), "Ten Long Years," "Bad Luck" backed with "Sweet Little Angel," and "On My Word of Honor." With the demise of the RPM label, King recorded for Kent Records from 1958 to 1962. R&B hits on Kent included "Please Accept My Love," "Sweet Sixteen," "Got a Right to Love My Baby," "Partin' Time," and "Peace of Mind." "Rock Me Baby" became his first moderate pop hit in 1964, after his departure from Kent.

In 1962 B. B. King signed with ABC Records, recording for both ABC and its subsidiary BluesWay label. Although early albums did not sell particularly well, his *Live at the Regal* album, recorded November 21, 1964, came to be regarded as one of his finest blues recordings. Playing up to 300 engagements a year through the late '70s, King was performing on the rock concert circuit and receiving airplay on underground FM radio by 1966. He scored smash R&B hits with "Don't Answer the Door" in late 1966 and "Paying the Cost to Be the Boss" (also a moderate pop hit) in 1968. By then, King was successfully appearing at Fillmore West and East and receiving praise regarding his playing from white guitarists such as Eric Clapton and Mike Bloomfield. *Lucille* became King's first album chart entry and he was soon introduced to the international white audience with his tour in support of the Rolling Stones in 1969. He became fully established with white audiences worldwide with *Completely Well* and its near-smash crossover hit "The Thrill Is Gone."

Established on the supper club and Nevada casino circuit by the early '70s, B. B. King began recording exclusively for ABC with *Indianola Mississippi Seeds*. In 1971 he recorded *In London* with Peter Green, Alexis Korner, and Ringo Starr. *To Know You Is to Love You* produced major crossover hits with the title song, cowritten by Stevie Wonder, and "I Like to Live the Love." King also enjoyed considerable commercial success in collaboration with old associate Bobby "Blue" Bland on *Together for the First Time: Live.* King recorded for MCA after it had absorbed ABC Records in 1979. That spring he performed thirty shows in the USSR, becoming the first black bluesman to tour that country. B. B. King continued to tour and record for MCA in the '80s and '90s. Noteworthy albums included *There Must Be a Better World Somewhere* and *Live at San Quentin*. In 1985 he appeared in the John Landis film *Into the Night,* achieving a major R&B hit with the title song. Inducted into the Rock and Roll Hall of Fame in 1987, B. B. King scored a minor pop hit in 1989 with "When Love Comes to Town," recorded with the Irish rock band U2.

BIBLIOGRAPHY

King, B.B., and David Ritz. *Blues All Around Me: The Autobiography.* New York: Avon, 1996.

Sawyer, Charles. *The Arrival of B. B. King: the Authorized Biography.* Garden City, NJ: Doubleday, 1980.

Early Recordings

Original Folk Blues, 1949–1950	United	7788		†
Singin' the Blues	Crown	5020(M)	'59	†
	United	7726		†
The Blues	Crown	5063	'59	†
	United	7732		†
Singin' the Blues/The Blues	Flair	86296	'92	CD
	Ace	320		CS/CD
B. B. King Wails	Crown	5115	'59	†
reissued as I Love You So	United	7711		†
	Custom	1049		†
B. B. King Sings Spirituals	Crown	5119	'60	†
	Crown	152	'60	†
	United	7723		†
	Custom	1059		†

The Great B. B. King	Crown	5143	'61	†
	United	7728		†
King of the Blues	Crown	5167	'61	†
	United	7730		†
My Kind of Blues	Crown	5188	'61	†
	United	7724		†
Blues for Me	Crown	5230	'62	†
	United	7708		†
	Custom	1046		†
as More B. B. King	Crown	5230	'62	†
Twist with B. B. King	Crown	5248	'62	†
Easy Listening Blues	Crown	5286	'62	†
	United	7705		†
Blues in My Heart	Crown	5309		†
	Custom	1040		†
as A Heart Full of Blues	United	7703		†
The Soul of B. B. King	Crown	5359	'63	†
	United	7714		†
Swing Low, Sweet Chariot	United	7721	'70	†
Best	Galaxy	8202	'63	†
16 Greatest Hits	Galaxy	8208		†
The Best of B. B. King	Ace	30	'87	LP
The Memphis Masters (recorded 1950–1952)	Ace	50		LP
The Best of B. B. King/the Memphis Masters	Ace	801		CS
King of the Blues Guitar (instrumentals recorded 1960–1961)	Ace	152		LP
Spotlight On Lucille	Ace	187	'87	CD
The Best of B. B. King, Vol. 1 (RPM/Modern recordings)	Ace	198	'87	CS
	Ace	908	'87	CD
The Best of B. B. King, Vol. 2 (RPM/Modern recordings)	Ace	199	'87	LP/CS/CD
My Sweet Little Angel	Ace	300		LP/CD
	Virgin	39103	'93	CD
Heart and Soul	Ace	376		CD
Do the Boogie (Early '50s Classics)	Ace	916		CD
The Fabulous B. B. King	Ace	004		CS/CD
Spotlight on Lucille	Flair	91693	'92	CD†
	Flair	86231		CD
The Best of B. B. King, Vol. 1	Flair	91691	'92	CD†
	Flair	86230		CD
The Fabulous B. B. King	Flair	39653	'94	CD
B. B. King's Early 50s Classics	Flair	39654	'94	CD

Kent Recordings

Rock Me Baby	Kent	512	'63	†
as Rock Me, Baby–14 Great Hits	United	7733	'64	†
Let Me Love You	Kent	513	'65	†
	United	7734		†
B. B. King Live on Stage	Kent	515	'65	†
as Live! B.B. King on Stage	United	7736		†
The Soul of B. B. King	Kent	516	'66	†
	United	7714		†
	Custom	1052		†
Pure Soul	Kent	517	'66	†

The Jungle	Kent	521	'67	†
	United	7742		†
Boss of the Blues	Kent	529	'68	†
	United	7750		†
From the Beginning	Kent	533	'69	†
Underground Blues	Kent	535	'69	†
The Incredible Soul of B. B. King	Kent	539	'70	†
	United	7756		†
Turn On with B. B. King	Kent	548	'71	†
	United	7763		†
Greatest Hits, Vol. 1	Kent	552	'71	†
	United	7766		†
Better Than Ever	Kent	561	'71	†
	United	7771		†
Doing My Thing, Lord	Kent	563	'71	†
Live	Kent	565	'72	†
	United	7772		†
The Original Sweet Sixteen	Kent	568	'72	†
	United	7773		†
B. B. King Anthology	Kent	9011		†

ABC/Bluesway/MCA Recordings

Mr. Blues	ABC	456	'63	†
Live at the Regal	ABC	509	'65	†
	MCA	724	'71	†
	Pickwick	3593	'78	†
	Ace	86	'83	LP†
	MCA	27006		CS
	MCA	31106		CD
	Mobile Fidelity	00548	'91	CD
Confessin' the Blues	ABC	528	'65	†
Blues Is King	BluesWay	6001	'67	†
	ABC	704	'77	†
	MCA	31368	'90	CD
Blues on Top of Blues	BluesWay	6011	'68	†
	ABC	709		†
Lucille	BluesWay	6016	'68	†
	ABC	712	'77	†
	MCA	10518	'92	CS/CD
	Mobile Fidelity	659	'96	CD
Electric B. B.–His Best	BluesWay	6022	'69	†
	ABC	813	'77	†
	MCA	27007		CS/CD
Live and Well	BluesWay	6031	'69	†
	ABC	819		†
	MCA	27008		CS
	MCA	31191	'88	CD
Completely Well	BluesWay	6037	'69	†
	ABC	868	'77	†
	MCA	27009		CS
	MCA	31039	'87	CD
	MCA	11207	'95	CD

Back in the Alley	BluesWay	6050	'73	†
	ABC	878	'77	†
	MCA	27010		CS/CD
Great Moments With B. B. King (BluesWay recordings)	MCA	(2)4124		CS
	MCA	4124		CD
Indianola Mississippi Seeds	ABC	713	'70	†
	MCA	31343	'89	CS/CD
Live at Cook County Jail	ABC	723	'71	†
	MCA	27005		CS
	MCA	31080	'88	CD
In London	ABC	730	'71	†
	MCA	10843	'93	CD
L.A. Midnight	ABC	743	'72	†
Guess Who	ABC	759	'72	†
	MCA	10351	'91	CS/CD
The Best of B. B. King	ABC	767	'73	†
	MCA	27074		CS
	MCA	31040		CD
To Know You Is to Love You	ABC	794	'73	†
	MCA	10414	'91	CS/CD
Friends	ABC	825	'74	†
Lucille Talks Back	ABC	898	'75	†
King Size	ABC	977	'77	†
Midnight Believer	ABC/MCA	1061	'78	†
	MCA	27011		CS/CD
Take It Home	MCA	3151	'79	†
Live "Now Appearing" at Ole Miss	MCA	(2)8016	'80	CS/CD
There Must Be a Better World Somewhere	MCA	5162	'81	†
	MCA	27034	'84	CS/CD
Love Me Tender	MCA	5307	'82	†
	MCA	886		CS/CD
Blues 'n' Jazz	MCA	5413	'83	†
	MCA	27119	'87	CS/CD
Six Silver Strings	MCA	5616	'85	CS/CD
Blues 'n' Jazz/the Electric B. B.	MCA	5881	'87	CD†
The King of the Blues: 1989	MCA	42183	'89	CS/CD
Live at San Quentin	MCA	6455	'90	CS/CD
There Is Always One More Time	MCA	10295	'91	CS/CD
The King of the Blues	MCA	(4)10677	'92	CS/CD
Blues Summit	MCA	10710	'93	CS/CD
B. B. King in London	MCA	10843	'93	CD
Got My Mojo Working	MCA	20541	'94	CS/CD†
How Blue Can You Get?	MCA	11443	'96	CD

Other Recordings

Paying the Cost to Be the Boss	Pickwick	3385	'75	†
Live at the Apollo	GRP	9637	'91	CS/CD
Heart and Soul: A Collection of Blues Ballads	Pointblank/ Virgin	40072	'95	CD
Catfish Blues	Drive	3228	'95	CD
	Allegro	3228	'96	CD†
B. B. King and Friends	Spotlite	15105	'96	CS/CD

B.B. King and Bobby "Blue" Bland

Together for the First Time: Live	Dunhill	(2)50190	'74	†
	MCA	(2)4160	'82	LP/CS
	MCA	4160		CD
Together Again	Impulse	9317	'76	†
	MCA	27012		CS/CD

KING CURTIS

Born Curtis Ousley on February 7, 1934, in Fort Worth, Texas; died August 13, 1971, in New York City.

Generally regarded as the last great tenor saxophone soloist of the staccato, honking style, King Curtis, along with David "Fathead" Newman and Steve Douglas, helped make the saxophone the third most important instrument (behind guitar and piano) in R&B and rock 'n' roll as a sessions player during the late '50s and early '60s. Best known for his exciting and raunchy saxophone solos behind the Coasters (witness "Shoppin' for Clothes"), Curtis was the only saxophonist of the era to become widely known outside the recording studio. By 1971 he had recorded with over 125 artists and become a producer, but shortly after being appointed Aretha Franklin's permanent musical director, King Curtis was stabbed to death in New York City on August 13, 1971.

Curtis Ousley grew up in Fort Worth, Texas, where he obtained his first saxophone at the age of twelve. He played in his high school marching band and formed his first combo while still in high school, performing locally. He toured with Lionel Hampton's Band after graduation and moved to New York in 1952. There he played engagements with a wide variety of groups, including a trio featuring pianist Horace Silver. Curtis replaced Arthur "Red" Prysock in Alan Freed's show band and joined Atlantic/Atco Records as a staff musician in 1958. He first received recognition for his clean, compelling tenor saxophone solos on the Coasters' "Yakety Yak" and subsequently backed virtually all of the Coasters' recordings for Atco.

King Curtis backed dozens of artists over the years, including Sam Cooke, Ray Charles, Bobby Darin, Sam and Dave, the Shirelles, Eric Clapton, the Allman Brothers, Delaney and Bonnie, and Aretha Franklin. He recorded two jazz albums with Wynton Kelly and Nat Adderley in 1960 and scored a top R&B/major pop hit with his Noble Knights (later the Kingpins) in 1962 with the instrumental "Soul Twist" on Enjoy Records. He also toured with Sam Cooke in the early '60s, most notably accompanying the vocalist on his *Feel It! Live at the Harlem Square Club, 1963*. Curtis recorded for Capitol Records, with modest success, in 1963–64.

King Curtis returned to Atlantic Records in 1965, achieving near-smash R&B and moderate pop hits with "Memphis Soul Stew" and "Ode to Billie Joe" on Atco in 1967. He continued to record with the Kingpins on Atco with modest success until his death. Beginning in 1967, Curtis started taking a more active role in the studio, contracting sessions and later producing artists such as Sam Moore (of Sam and Dave), Roberta Flack, Delaney and Bonnie, Donny Hathaway, and Freddie King. In 1971 he was appointed to succeed Donald Towns as Aretha Franklin's permanent musical director. He performed with pianist "Champion" Jack Dupree at the Montreux Jazz Festival in June, but on August 13, 1971, King Curtis was stabbed to death in front of his New York apartment house. He was thirty-seven years old.

King Curtis

Have Tenor Sax, Will Blow	Atco	33–113	'59	†

That Lovin' Feeling	Atco	33–189	'66	†
"Live" at Small's Paradise	Atco	33–198	'66	†
Plays the Great Memphis Hits	Atco	33–211	'67	†
King Size Soul	Atco	33–231	'67	†
Sweet Soul	Atco	33–247	'68	†
Best	Atco	33–266	'68	†
Instant Groove	Atco	33–293	'69	†
Get Ready	Atco	33–338	'70	†
"Live" at the Fillmore West	Atco	33–359	'71	†
Everybody's Talkin'	Atco	33–385	'72	†
New Scene	New Jazz	8237	'60	†
	Fantasy/OJC	198	'85	LP/CD
Azure	Everest	1121	'61	†
Trouble in Mind	Tru-Sound	15001	'62	†
	Fantasy/OBC	512	'88	LP/CS/CD
Old Gold	Tru-Sound	15006	'62	†
It's Party Time	Tru-Sound	15008	'62	†
	Ace	262		LP†
Doing the Dixie Twist	Tru-Sound	15009	'63	†
Old Gold/Doing the Dixie Twist	Ace	614	'95	CD†
Night Train (recorded 1961–1962)	Prestige	24153	'95	CD
Best	Prestige	7709	'68	†
Best–One More Time	Prestige	7775	'70	†
Jazz Groove	Prestige	(2)24033	'73	†
Country Soul	Capitol	1756	'62	†
Soul Serenade	Capitol	2095	'64	†
	Capitol	11798	'78	†
Plays the Hits Made Famous by Sam Cooke	Capitol	2341	'65	†
Best	Capitol	2858	'68	†
	Capitol	11963	'79	†
Best	Capitol Jazz	36504	'96	CD
Sax in Motion	Camden	2242	'63	†
Watermelon Man	Pickwick	3293	'72	†
Soul Time	Up Front	157	'73	†
Soul Twist	Enjoy	2001		†
Soul Twist and Other Golden Classics	Collectables	5119	'89	LP/CS/CD
Golden Classics: Enjoy Records	Collectables	5156		LP/CS/CD
Instant Soul: the Legendary King Curtis	Razor & Tie	2054	'94	CS/CD

King Curtis, Wynton Kelly, and Nat Adderley

Soul Meeting	Prestige	7222	'62	†
	Prestige	7833	'71	†
	Prestige	24033	'94	CD
King Soul	Prestige	7789	'70	†

King Curtis and the Shirelles

Give a Twist Party	Scepter	505	'62	†
Eternally Soul	Scepter	569	'70	†

King Curtis and "Champion" Jack Dupree

Blues at Montreux	Atlantic	1637	'73	†
	Atlantic	81389	'92	CD

THE KINGSTON TRIO

Bob Shane (born February 1, 1934, in Hilo, Hawaii), gtr, bjo, voc; Dave Guard (born November 19, 1934, in Honolulu; died March 22, 1991, in Rollinsford, New Hampshire), gtr, bjo, voc; Nick Reynolds (born July 27, 1933, in San Diego, California), gtr, voc. Guard left in May 1961, to be replaced by John Stewart (born September 5, 1939, in San Diego). Later members included Roger Gambill, George Grove, and Bob Haworth.

The most successful folk group to emerge in the late '50s, the Kingston Trio projected a clean-cut college image that enabled them to avoid the politically suspect stigma attached to folk artists such as Woody Guthrie and the Weavers. Inspiring the formation of other tame all-male acoustic groups such as the Highwaymen and the Brothers Four, the Kingston Trio made folk music commercially viable and opened the way for the early '60s folk movement that introduced Peter, Paul and Mary, Joan Baez, Judy Collins, Bob Dylan, and dozens of others. Disbanding in 1967, the Kingston Trio was resurrected by Bob Shane in the '70s. Second-generation member John Stewart subsequently managed a modest performing and recording career that featured his often poignant and compelling songwriting.

Collegians Bob Shane, Dave Guard, and Nick Reynolds formed the Kingston Trio in San Francisco, California, in 1957. All three played guitar and sang, with Guard and Shane doubling on banjo. Playing local coffeehouses and clubs, most notably the hungry i and the Purple Onion, the Kingston Trio signed with Capitol Records in 1958. Their first and ultimately biggest success came with the top pop hit "Tom Dooley," which also became a near-smash R&B hit. By 1960, they had scored major hits with "Tijuana Jail," "M.T.A.," and "Worried Man." Their early albums sold spectacularly, with their debut album, *The Kingston Trio,* staying on the charts nearly four years, and three of their next four remaining on the charts for more than two years.

Dave Guard left the Kingston Trio in May 1961 to form the Whiskeyhill Singers with Judy Henske. He later moved to Australia, where he hosted a television program, returning to the United States in 1968. He also authored two children's books and recorded *Up and In* in 1989. He died at his home in Rollinsford, New Hampshire, on March 22, 1991, of lymphoma. He was replaced by John Stewart, the founder of the folk group the Cumberland Three. The Kingston Trio enjoyed hits through 1963 with Pete Seeger's "Where Have All the Flowers Gone," Dave Guard's "Scotch and Soda" (only a minor hit, but standard lounge fare today), Hoyt Axton's "Greenback Dollar," and Billy Edd Wheeler's "Reverend Mr. Black." Switching to Decca Records in 1964, they failed to achieve even a minor hit for the label.

In 1972 Bob Shane reconstituted the group with singer-guitarist Roger Gambill and banjoist George Grove, who had a music degree from Wake Forest University. They performed with symphony orchestras and persevered on the college and supper club circuits. All six members of the Kingston Trio—Shane, Reynolds, Guard, Stewart, Gambill, and Grove—reunited for a concert at California's Magic Mountain Amusement Park that yielded a PBS television special hosted by Tom Smothers in 1982. Roger Gambill died in Atlanta, Georgia, on March 20, 1985, at the age of forty-two after suffering a heart attack and stroke. He was replaced by Bob Haworth of the Brothers Four until the late '80s, when Nick Reynolds rejoined the group. In 1993 the Kingston Trio recorded *Live at the Crazy Horse* for the small Silverwolf label.

John Stewart subsequently pursued his own career, recording with Scott Engel, then with Buffy Ford. The Monkees had scored a top hit in 1967 with Stewart's "Daydream Believer," revived as a smash country hit by Anne Murray in 1980. Stewart's recordings for Capitol, including the critically acclaimed *California Bloodlines* (with "July, You're a Woman" and "Lonesome Picker") failed to sell, as did the overlooked *Lonesome Picker Rides Again* (with

"All the Brave Horses" and "Touch of the Sun") for Warner Brothers and *Cannons in the Rain* (with "All Time Woman" and the minor hit "Armstrong") for RCA. John Stewart achieved his biggest success in 1979 with *Bombs Away Dream Babies* on RSO Records. The album featured the smash hit "Gold" and major hit "Midnight Wind," recorded with Stevie Nicks and Lindsey Buckingham of Fleetwood Mac, and the moderate hit "Lost Her in the Sun."

The follow-up to *Bombs Away Dream Babies* sold only modestly for John Stewart, leading him to form his own record company, Homecoming, in the '80s. Albums for the label included *The Trio Years,* rerecordings of songs written for the Kingston Trio, and the poignant *The Last Campaign,* rerecordings of songs composed during and after Bobby Kennedy's 1968 presidential campaign. In 1987 Stewart recorded *Punch the Big Guy* for Cypress with Rosanne Cash, who scored a top country hit with his "Runaway Train" in 1988. In 1992 John Stewart recorded *Bullets in the Hour Glass* for the small but nationally distributed Shanachie label.

Early Recordings

The Kingston Trio	Capitol	996	'58	†
	Capitol	92710	'90	CS/CD
reissued as Tom Dooley	Capitol	16185	'69	†
From the hungry i	Capitol	1107	'59	†
	Capitol	11968		†
Stereo Concert	Capitol	1183	'59	†
At Large	Capitol	1199	'59	†
reissued as Scarlet Ribbons	Capitol	16186		†
Here We Go Again!	Capitol	1258	'59	†
Sold Out	Capitol	1352	'60	†
String Along	Capitol	1407	'60	†
The Last Month of the Year	Capitol	1446	'60	†
	Capitol	93116	'89	CS/CD†
Make Way!	Capitol	1474	'61	†
Goin' Places	Capitol	1564	'61	†

Early Reissues

Tom Dooley/Scarlet Ribbons	Capitol	(2)513		†
the Kingston Trio/From the hungry i	Capitol	96748	'92	CS/CD
At Large/Here We Go Again	Capitol	96749	'92	CS/CD†
Sold Out/String Along	Capitol	96835	'92	CS/CD†
Make Way/Goin' Places	Capitol	96836	'92	CS/CD†

Dave Guard and the Whiskeyhill Singers

Dave Guard and the Whiskeyhill Singers	Capitol	1728	'62	†

Dave Guard

Up and In	Ball Bearing	1989	'89	CS/CD

The Cumberland Three

Folk Scene, U.S.A.	Roulette	25121	'60	†
Civil War Almanac-Vol. 1 (Yankees)	Roulette	25132	'60	†
Civil War Almanac-Vol. 2 (Rebels)	Roulette	25133	'60	†

The Kingston Trio

Close-Up	Capitol	1642	'61	†
College Concert	Capitol	1658	'62	†
Something Special	Capitol	1747	'62	†

New Frontier	Capitol	1809	'62	†
# 16	Capitol	1871	'63	†
Sunny Side!	Capitol	1935	'63	†
Sing a Song with the Kingston Trio	Capitol	2005	'63	†
Time to Think	Capitol	2011	'64	†
Back in Town	Capitol	2081	'64	†
Nick-Bob-John	Decca	74613	'65	†
	Folk Era	5271	'92	CS/CD
Stay Awhile	Decca	74656	'65	†
	Folk Era	5382	'93	CS/CD
Somethin' Else	Decca	74694	'65	†
Children of the Morning	Decca	74758	'66	†
Live at the Crazy Horse	Silverwolf	1001	'93	CD

Anthologies and Compilations

Encores	Capitol	1612(E)	'61	†
Best	Capitol	1705	'62	†
	Capitol	16183		†
Folk Era	Capitol	2180	'64	†
Best, Vol. 2	Capitol	2280	'65	†
	Capitol	16184		†
Best, Vol. 3	Capitol	2614	'66	†
Very Best	Capitol	46624		CD†
The Capitol Years	Capitol	(4)28498	'95	CD
Once Upon a Time	Tetragrammaton	5101	'69	†
Tom Dooley	Pickwick	3260	'71	†
The Kingston Trio	Pickwick	3297	'72	†
Where Have All the Flowers Gone	Pickwick	3323	'72	†
Aspen Gold	DBX	2014	'84	†
Best of the Best	Pro Acoustic	702	'86	CS/CD
Early American Heroes	Pair	(2)1067	'86	CS/CD
Made in the U.S.A.	Pair	1221		CS/CD
American Troubadours	Pair	1240		CD
Rediscover	Folk Era	2001		CS
Hidden Treasures	Folk Era	2036		LP/CS
Stereo Concert Plus!	Folk Era	2037	'87	CS/CD
Treasure Chest	Folk Era	2052		CD
Tune Up	Folk Era	2060	'89	CD
An Evening with the Kingston Trio	Folk Era	2064	'89	CS/CD
Tom Dooley	CSI	40050	'91	CD†
Greatest Hits	Curb/Warner Bros.	77385	'90	CS/CD
Greatest Hits	Special Music	4803		CS/CD
Everybody's Talking	MTA	4134		CS

John Stewart and Scott Engel

I Only Came to Dance With You	Tower	5026	'66	†

John Stewart and Buffy Ford

John Stewart and Buffy Ford	Capitol	2975	'68	†
reissued as Signals Through the Glass	Capitol	2975	'75	†
	Capitol	11988		†
	Capitol	16152		†

John Stewart

California Bloodlines	Capitol	203	'69	†
	Capitol	11987	'79	†
	Capitol	16150		†
Willard	Capitol	540	'70	†
	Capitol	11989	'79	†
	Capitol	16151		†
John Stewart: American Original	Capitol	80091	'93	CS/CD†
The Lonesome Picker Rides Again	Warner Brothers	1948	'71	†
Sunstorm	Warner Brothers	2611	'72	†
Cannons in the Rain	RCA	4827	'73	†
	RCA	3731		†
The Phoenix Concerts	RCA	(2)0265	'74	†
The Phoenix Concerts–Live	One Way	34505	'97	CD
Wingless Angels	RCA	0816	'75	
In Concert	RCA	3513	'80	
Fire in the Wind	Polydor	3027	'77	†
Bombs Away, Dream Babies	RSO	3051	'79	†
	Razor & Tie	2034	'94	CD
Dream Babies Go Hollywood	RSO	3074	'80	†
Blondes	Allegiance	72851	'83	†
Trancas	Affordable Dreams	0001	'84	CS/CD
Centennial	Homecoming	0200	'84	CS
The Last Campaign	Homecoming	0300	'85	LP/CS
	Laserlight	12696	'96	CD
Secret Tapes	Homecoming	0450	'86	CS
The Trio Years	Homecoming	0500	'86	CS
	Laserlight	12697	'96	CD
Secret Tapes II	Homecoming	0650	'88	CS
Neon Beach: Live 1990	Homecoming	0700	'91	CS
Deep in the Noon	Homecoming	0750	'91	CS/CD
An American Folk Anthology	Laserlight	12698	'96	CD
American Journey (The Last Campaign, The Trio Years, An American Folk Song Anthology)	Laserlight	(3)55590	'96	CD
Punch the Big Guy	Cypress	0105	'87	LP/CS/CD†
	Shanachie	8009	'93	LP/CS/CD
Bullets in the Hour Glass	Shanachie	8005	'92	CS/CD
Airdream Believer: A Retrospective	Shanachie	8015	'95	CS/CD
Chilly Winds	Folk Era	14010	'93	CD

BRENDA LEE

Born Brenda Mae Tarpley on December 11, 1944, in Lithonia, Georgia.

Possessing a powerful voice equally adept at mournful ballads and hard-belting rock 'n' roll, Brenda Lee was one of the most popular female vocalists of the late '50s and early '60s, rivaled only by the tamer-sounding Connie Francis. Among Lee's twenty major pop hits were the classics "Sweet Nothins," "I'm Sorry," "That's All You Gotta Do," "I Want to Be Wanted," and "All Alone Am I," plus the Christmas standard "Rockin' Around the Christmas Tree." Scoring her last major pop hit with "Coming on Strong" in 1966, Lee made the transition to country music in the '70s.

BRENDA LEE

Brenda Lee began singing at the age of four, winning an Atlanta television station's children's talent contest at age six. She became a regular on the local radio show *Starmaker's Revue* at seven and performed on the local television show *TV Ranch* from 1951 to 1954. Introduced to country music veteran Red Foley in 1955, she later appeared on his television show *Ozark Jubilee* (later *Country Music Jubilee* and *Jubilee U.S.A.*) and toured with his road show. Signed to Decca Records in 1956, Lee initially recorded rockabilly, scoring her first moderate pop hit in early 1957 with "One Step at a Time," followed by "Dynamite." Debuting in Las Vegas in late 1956, she soon became known as "Little Miss Dynamite" for her powerful voice and diminutive stature.

Brenda Lee scored her first smash pop hit in 1960 with the seductive "Sweet Nothins." That song and the top hit "I'm Sorry" were written by rockabilly artist Ronnie Self. The flip side of "I'm Sorry," the rollicking "That's All You Gotta Do" (written by Jerry Reed), also became a smash hit. Her two 1960 albums became best-sellers as her success continued with the top hit ballad "I Want to Be Wanted," the Christmas classic "Rockin' Around the Christmas Tree," and the smashes "Emotions," "You Can Depend on Me," "Dum Dum" (cowritten by Jackie DeShannon and Eddie Cochran girlfriend Sharon Sheeley), and "Fool # 1." In 1962 Lee began concentrating on nightclub appearances, rather than concerts, and smash hits continued through 1963 with "Break It to Me Gently," "Everybody Loves Me But You" (also written by Ronnie Self), "All Alone Am I," and "Losing You." Subsequent major hits through 1966 included "My Whole World Is Falling Down," "As Usual," "Is It True," "Too Many Rivers," and "Coming on Strong."

For Brenda Lee, the 1969 moderate pop hit "Johnny One Time" marked her reentry into the country field. She seldom performed during the '70s, and by 1973 Decca had been absorbed by MCA Records, for whom, through 1975, she scored country smashes with Kris Kristofferson's "Nobody Wins," "Sunday Sunrise," "Wrong Ideas," "Big Four Poster Bed," "Rock on Baby," and "He's My Rock." She managed country near-smashes with "Tell Me What It's Like," "The Cowgirl and the Dandy," and "Broken Trust" in 1979–80 and helped record *The Winning Hand* with Willie Nelson, Dolly Parton, and Kris Kristofferson in 1983. Her last major country hit came in late 1984 with "Hallelujah, I Love Her So," in duet with George Jones. Reestablished on the Nevada casino circuit in the '80s, Brenda Lee joined Loretta Lynn and Kitty Wells for "Honky Tonk Angels' Medley" from k.d. lang's *Shadowland* album and moved to Warner Brothers Records for *Brenda Lee*.

BIBLIOGRAPHY

VanHecke, Sue. "Brenda Lee: Little Miss Dynamite." *Goldmine* 22, no. 6 (March 15, 1996): 26, 30, 36, 38, 42, 46, 48, 50, 52, 54, 56, 203, 213.

Brenda Lee

Grandma, What Great Songs You Sang	Decca	78873	'59	†
Brenda Lee	Decca	74039	'60	†
This Is . . . Brenda Lee	Decca	74082	'60	†
Emotions	Decca	74104	'61	†
All the Way	Decca	74176	'61	†
Sincerely	Decca	74216	'62	†
That's All, Brenda	Decca	74326	'62	†
All Alone Am I	Decca	74370	'63	†
Let Me Sing	Decca	74439	'63	†
By Request	Decca	74509	'64	†
Merry Christmas from Brenda Lee	Decca	74583	'64	†
	MCA	232		†
	MCA	15021		†
Top Teen Hits	Decca	74626	'65	†
Versatile	Decca	74661	'65	†
Too Many Rivers	Decca	74684		†
Bye Bye, Blues	Decca	74755	'66	†
Ten Golden Years	Decca	74757	'66	†
	MCA	107		†
Coming on Strong	Decca	74825	'66	†
Reflections in Blue	Decca	74941	'67	†
Johnny One Time	Decca	75111	'69	†
Memphis Portrait	Decca	75232	'70	†
Here's Brenda Lee	Vocalion	73795	'67	†
Let It Be Me	Vocalion	73890	'70	†
	Coral	20044	'73	†
Brenda	MCA	305	'73	†
The Brenda Lee Story	MCA	(2)4012	'73	CS
	MCA	4012		CD
New Sunrise	MCA	373	'74	†
Now	MCA	433	'75	†
Sincerely, Brenda Lee	MCA	477	'75	†
The L.A. Sessions	MCA	2233	'76	†
Even Better	MCA	3211	'80	†
Take Me Back	MCA	5143	'80	†
Only When I Laugh	MCA	5278	'81	†
Greatest Country Hits	MCA	5342	'82	†
	MCA	894		CS†
Feels So Right	MCA	5626	'85	†
Anthology Vols. 1 and 2	MCA	(2)10384	'91	CD
	MCA	(2)10405/6	'91	CS†
Brenda Lee	Warner Brothers	26439	'91	CS/CD†
A Brenda Lee Christmas	Warner Brothers	26660	'91	CS/CD
Greatest Hits Live	K-tel	3077	'92	CS/CD

Brenda Lee and Pete Fountain

For the First Time	Decca	74955	'68	†

Brenda Lee, Kris Kristofferson, Willie Nelson, and Dolly Parton

The Winning Hand	Minument	(2)38389	'83	†
	Sony	75067	'95	CS/CD†

JERRY LEIBER AND MIKE STOLLER

Jerry Leiber (born April 25, 1933, in Baltimore, Maryland); Mike Stoller (born March 13, 1933, in New York City).

The single most significant, influential, and popular songwriting-production team of the '50s and early '60s, Jerry Leiber and Mike Stoller became the first independent producers in the history of rock 'n' roll in 1955. Reconstituting the Robins as the Coasters for Atlantic Records, Leiber and Stoller provided them with some of the first songs in rock 'n' roll to incorporate satire and social comment. Rivaled by only Doc Pomus and Mort Shuman as a songwriting-production team, Leiber and Stoller later wrote and produced some of Elvis Presley's finest post–Sun Records recordings. The team was put in charge of the reconstituted Drifters, and the group's smash 1959 hit "There Goes My Baby" melded R&B with the pop tradition through the use of Latin rhythms and quasi-classical strings behind Ben E. King's gospel-style lead vocal. Thereafter, black vocal groups frequently utilized strings in recording, thus heralding the advent of soul music. In 1964 Leiber and Stoller joined George Goldner in the formation of Red Bird Records, where they utilized Brill Building professional songwriting teams such as Jeff Barry/Ellie Greenwich and Carole King/Gerry Goffin to popularize the girl group sound. Thirty years after their heyday, Leiber and Stoller's songs were featured in the successful Broadway production of the musical *Smokey Joe's Cafe* in 1995.

Jerry Leiber met Mike Stoller in Los Angeles in 1949. They soon teamed to write and produce songs for blues artists such as Amos Milburn and Jimmy Witherspoon. Their first R&B hit composition was "Hard Times" by Charles Brown in 1952, followed the next year by the top R&B hit "Hound Dog" by Willie Mae "Big Mama" Thornton. In 1953 Leiber and Stoller formed their own label, Spark Records, for such recordings by the Robins as "Smokey Joe's Cafe" and "Riot in Cell Block # 9."

Signed to the New York-based Atlantic label as independent producers in 1955, Jerry Leiber and Mike Stoller convinced Carl Gardner and Bobby Nunn of the otherwise recalcitrant Robins to form a new group to record on Atlantic's Atco subsidiary. The group was dubbed the Coasters, and between 1955 and 1961 Leiber and Stoller provided them with a series of hit songs that often incorporated wry humor, satire, and sly social commentary. "Searchin'," from 1957, became their first pop smash. Subsequent Coasters hit records of songs by Leiber and Stoller included "Young Blood" (with Doc Pomus), "Yakety Yak," "Charlie Brown," "Along Came Jones," "Poison Ivy," and "Little Egypt."

In 1955 Leiber and Stoller furnished the Cheers with the near-smash "Black Denim Trousers and Motorcycle Boots." Other hit compositions included "The Chicken and the Hawk (Up, Up and Away)" for Joe Turner in 1956, "Lucky Lips" for Ruth Brown in 1957 (her first pop hit), and "Saved" for Lavern Baker in 1961. Elvis Presley scored smash hits with their "Hound Dog" and "Love Me" in 1956, after which the team was contracted to supply songs for Presley's movies. The duo wrote the title songs to *Jailhouse Rock, Loving You,* and *King Creole,* while providing other hit songs such as "Treat Me Nice" and "Don't." Their songs "Kansas City" and "Love Potion #9" became pop hits for Wilbert Harrison and the Clovers, respectively, in 1959.

Following their landmark production of the Drifters' "There Goes My Baby," the team's "Dance with Me" became a major hit for the group in 1959, and they later provided a solo Ben E. King with crossover hits such as "Spanish Harlem" (their most recorded song) and the classic "Stand by Me." Apprentice producer Phil Spector, coauthor with Leiber of "Spanish Harlem," was obviously inspired by the production-arrangement technique of the team, as evidenced by his own hit productions during the first half of the '60s. In 1963 the Drifters scored a near smash hit with the moving "On Broadway," cowritten by Leiber, Stoller, Barry Mann, and Cynthia Weil.

In 1964 Leiber and Stoller formed Red Bird Records with George Goldner and hits on the label included "Chapel of Love," "People Say" and "Iko Iko" by the Dixie Cups, and "Remember (Walkin' in the Sand)," "Leader of the Pack" and "Give Him a Great Big Kiss" by the Shangri-Las. By 1966, weary of their largely administrative duties, Leiber and Stoller had sold out to George Goldner.

Jerry Leiber and Mike Stoller moved to Columbia Records, but productions for the Coasters and others were poorly handled, leading the duo to terminate their agreement with the label. They subsequently retired from the studio, purchasing the Starday/King catalog from Syd Nathan's estate in 1969. In the meantime, several of their songs became hits, including "D.W. Washburn" for the Monkees in 1968 and "Is That All There Is?" for Peggy Lee in 1969.

Selling Starday/King in 1972, Jerry Leiber and Mike Stoller returned to the studio in 1973 to produce albums for Stealers Wheel (including the smash hit "Stuck in the Middle with You"), the Coasters, and T-Bone Walker. They subsequently produced albums for Peggy Lee, Elkie Brooks, and *Procol's Ninth* for Procol Harum. In 1978 the odd set *Other Songs by Leiber and Stoller,* performed by mezzo-soprano Joan Morris, was issued on Nonesuch Records. In 1987 Jerry Leiber and Mike Stoller were inducted into the Rock and Roll Hall of Fame, and four years later Rhino Records released a compilation album of their songs as *There's a Riot Goin' On.* The songs of Leiber and Stoller are the central focus of the Broadway musical *Smokey Joe's Cafe,* which opened in 1995 and, of this writing, is still running.

BIBLIOGRAPHY

Palmer, Robert. *That Was Rock & Roll: the Legendary Leiber and Stoller.* New York: Harcourt Brace, 1978.

Jerry Leiber Beat Band				
Scooby Doo	Kapp	1127	'59	†
Leiber-Stoller Big Band				
Yakety Yak	Atlantic	8047	'61	†
Joan Morris				
Other Songs by Leiber and Stoller	Nonesuch	71346	'78	†
Elvis Presley				
Elvis Sings Leiber and Stoller–Plus Missing Presley Duet	RCA	3026	'91	CS/CD
Jerry Leiber and Mike Stoller				
There's a Riot Goin' On:	Rhino	70593	'91	CS/CD
The Rock and Roll Classics of Leiber and Stoller				
Smokey Joe's Cafe: The Songs of Leiber and Stoller	Atlantic Theatre	(2)82765	'95	CS/CD
('95 original cast album)				

JERRY LEE LEWIS

Born September 29, 1935, in Ferriday, Louisiana.

One of the most outrageous figures of '50s rock 'n' roll, comparable only to Little Richard in his flamboyance, Jerry Lee Lewis was the premier white piano and vocal stylist of the era. Performing frantic, passionate stage shows while projecting an aura of arrogant self-confidence, Jerry Lee Lewis's inimitable piano style, self-taught and virtually unaltered over the course of his career, featured endless glissandos and furious hammering and banging of the instrument, often played with elbows and feet. Recording such rock 'n' roll classics as "Whole Lotta Shakin' Goin' On" and "Great Balls of Fire," Lewis never attained the stature of Elvis Presley or Chuck Berry. Moreover, Lewis suffered a crippling blow to his career through adverse publicity surrounding his marriage to his thirteen year-old cousin, which led to the cancellation of his first British tour in 1958. Eventually reestablished as a country-and-western artist a decade later with hits such as "Another Place Another Time" and "What's Made Milwaukee Famous," Jerry Lee Lewis continued to tour and record into the '90s, despite suffering a series of personal tragedies and health problems.

Jerry Lee Lewis began playing piano at the age of eight, performing in public for the first time at the age of fourteen with a country band at a Natchez Ford dealership in 1949. Playing at area honky-tonks on weekends for four years, he built a solid regional following. In February 1956 Lewis traveled to Memphis to audition for Sun Records, recording a demonstration tape for Jack Clement in the absence of owner Sam Phillips. Returning to Memphis a month later, he discovered that Phillips liked the recordings, which resulted in a record-

Jerry Lee Lewis, 1957

ing contract. His first single, "Crazy Arms," became a moderate country hit. On December 4, 1956, Elvis Presley joined Lewis and Sun stalwarts Carl Perkins and Johnny Cash in an informal session, singing and playing gospel songs. Unknown to them, the performance was recorded. Those recordings by the so-called Million Dollar Quartet were bootlegged for years and available in Europe before their eventual release in the United States in 1990.

In 1957 Jerry Lee Lewis's second single, "Whole Lotta Shakin' Going On," became a smash country-and-western, R&B, and pop hit, bolstered by his appearance on the Steve Allen television show. Supported by backup musicians such as guitarists Hank Garland and Roland Janes and bassist Billy Lee Riley, Lewis quickly scored smash three-way crossover hits with "Great Balls of Fire" and "Breathless" (both written by Otis Blackwell), and the title song to the film *High School Confidential.* He also appeared in the 1957 film *Jamboree.*

In May 1958 Jerry Lee Lewis arrived in England for his first British tour, but it was canceled by the fifth day after the British press revealed, in rather lurid terms, that he was traveling with his thirteen-year-old second cousin-wife, Myra. Back home, he had managed a minor pop hit with "Breakup," but subsequent records were banned by many radio stations. Lewis was unable to score even a moderate hit until 1961 when his version of Ray Charles's "What'd I Say" made all three charts. Despite the fading fortunes of Sun Records, Lewis continued to record for the label until 1963.

Jerry Lee Lewis subsequently switched to the Smash subsidiary of Mercury Records, but commercial success eluded him as he crisscrossed the country playing county fairs, package shows, gymnasiums, and roadhouses. His dynamic stage show was captured live on several albums, including *Live at the Star Club* (recorded in 1964 with the Nashville Teens and eventually released on Rhino in 1992) and *The Greatest Live Show on Earth*. Finally, in 1968, Lewis scored the first of a series of major country-and-western hits with "Another Place Another Time," followed by the classic "What's Made Milwaukee Famous (Made a Loser out of Me)." Subsequent top country-only hits on Smash included "She Still Comes Around (to Love What's Left of Me)," "To Make Love Sweeter for You," "One Has My Name (The Other Has My Heart)" (a top country hit for Jimmy Wakely in 1948), "She Even Woke Me Up to Say Goodbye," and "Once More with Feeling."

In 1970 Jerry Lee Lewis moved to the parent label Mercury for smash country hits such as "There Must Be More to Love Than This," "Touching Home," "Would You Take Another Chance on Me" backed with Kris Kristofferson's "Me and Bobby McGee" (a moderate pop hit), "Sometimes a Memory Ain't Enough," and "He Can't Fill My Shoes." In 1973 he recorded his best-selling album *The Session* in London with guitarists Peter Frampton, Rory Gallagher, and Albert and Alvin Lee. Lewis's late '70s country hits included "Let's Put It Back Together Again" and the classic "Middle Age Crazy."

In 1978 Jerry Lee Lewis switched to Elektra Records, where he scored a major country hit with the autobiographical "Rockin' My Life Away" and a smash country hit (his last) with "Thirty Nine and Holding." His three Elektra albums were later anthologized by Warner Brothers as *Rockin' My Life Away*. In the early '80s, Lewis moved to MCA Records for two albums. Live performances with guitarist James Burton, recorded at the Palomino Club in Los Angeles in 1979–81 and 1985, were released on Tomato Records in the '90s. In 1982 Lewis joined Johnny Cash and Carl Perkins to record *The Survivors* for Columbia Records, and the three later joined Roy Orbison to record *Class of '55* for Columbia in 1986.

During the '80s Jerry Lee Lewis endured declining health, the deaths of wives numbers four and five, and protracted tax disputes with the Internal Revenue Service. He was inducted into the Rock and Roll Hall of Fame in its inaugural year, 1986. The 1989 movie *Great Balls of Fire,* starring Dennis Quaid, portrayed the early years of his career, and the sound-track album included eight newly recorded versions of his classics. In the '90s Lewis opened the nightclub Jerry Lee Lewis' Spot in Memphis, and opened his home to tourists in order to pay off his tax debt. In 1995 Sire Records released Lewis's first full studio album in more than ten years, *Young Blood,* recorded with guitarists James Burton and Al Anderson.

BIBLIOGRAPHY

Cain, Robert J.. *Whole Lotta Shakin' Goin' On.* New York: Dial, 1981.

Palmer, Robert. *Jerry Lee Lewis Rocks!* New York: Delilah, dis. Putnam's, 1981.

Lewis, Myra, with Murray Silver. *Great Balls of Fire: The Uncensored Story of Jerry Lee Lewis.* New York: Morrow, 1982.

Tosches, Nick. *Hellfire: The Jerry Lee Lewis Story.* New York: Delacorte, 1982.

Guterman, Jimmy. *Rockin' My Life Away: Listening to Jerry Lee Lewis.* Nashville, TN: Rutledge Hill, 1991.

Sun Recordings

Jerry Lee Lewis	Sun	1230	'58	†
	Rhino	70656	'89	CS/CD
Jerry Lee's Greatest	Sun	1265	'61	†
	Rhino	70657	'89	CS/CD
Original Golden Hits, Vol. 1	Sun	102	'69	†
Original Golden Hits, Vol. 2	Sun	103	'69	†
Rockin' Rhythm and Blues	Sun	107	'70	†
The Golden Cream of Country	Sun	108	'71	†
A Taste of Country	Sun	114	'71	†
Memphis Rock and Roll	Sun	116		†
Memphis Country	Sun	120	'71	†
Ole Tyme Country Music	Sun	121	'71	†
Monsters	Sun	124	'71	†
Original Golden Hits, Vol. 3	Sun	128	'72	†
20 Original Greats	Sun	1000	'77	†
The Original	Sun	1005	'78	†
Duets	Sun	1011	'78	†
From the Vaults of Sun	Power Pak	247	'74	†
Sun Story, Vol. 5	Sunnyvale	905	'77	†
18 Original Sun Greatest Hits	Rhino	5255	'84	†
Original Sun Greatest Hits	Rhino	70255	'89	CS/CD
Wild One: Rare Tracks from Jerry Lee Lewis (recorded 1957–1963)	Rhino	70899	'89	CS/CD

Jerry Lee Lewis and Johnny Cash

Sunday Down South	Sun	119	'71	†
Sing Hank Williams	Sun	125	'71	†

Jerry Lee Lewis, Carl Perkins, Elvis Presley, and Johnny Cash

The Million Dollar Quartet	RCA	2023	'90	LP/CS/CD

Jerry Lee Lewis

Rockin' with Jerry Lee Lewis	Design	165	'63	†
Live at the Star Club, Hamburg, 1964 (w. Nashville Teens)	Rhino	70268	'92	CS/CD

Smash/Mercury/Wing Recordings

Golden Hits	Smash	67040	'64	†
	Smash	7001	'79	†
The Golden Rock Hits of Jerry Lee Lewis	Smash	826251	'87	LP/CS/CD
The Greatest Live Show on Earth	Smash	67056	'64	†
	Mercury	830528	'87	†
The Return of Rock!	Smash	67063	'65	†
	Wing	16340	'67	†
Country Songs For City Folks	Smash	67131	'70	†
Unlimited	Wing	16406	'68	†
The Legend of Jerry Lee Lewis	Wing	(2)125	'69	†
Live at the International, Las Vegas	Mercury	61278	'70	†
In Loving Memories	Mercury	61318	'71	†
There Must Be More to Love Than This	Mercury	61323	'71	†
Touching Home	Mercury	61343	'71	†
Would You Take Another Chance on Me?	Mercury	61346	'71	†
	Mercury	830399	'87	†
Who's Gonna Play This Old Piano	Mercury	61366	'72	†

Solid Gold Rock 'n' Roll, Vol. 2	Mercury	61372		†
The "Killer" Rocks On	Mercury	637	'72	†
	Mercury	826262	'87	†
The Session	Mercury	(2)803	'73	†
Sometimes a Memory Ain't Enough	Mercury	677	'73	†
Southern Roots	Mercury	690	'74	†
I–40 Country	Mercury	710	'74	†
Boogie Woogie Country Man	Mercury	1030	'75	†
Odd Man In	Mercury	1064	'76	†
Country Class	Mercury	1109	'76	†
Country Memories	Mercury	5004	'77	†
Keeps Rockin'	Mercury	5010	'78	†
Best, Vol. 2	Mercury	5006	'78	†
	Mercury	822789		†
I'm on Fire	Polydor	826139	'85	†
Killer: the Mercury Years, Vol. 1: 1963–1968	Mercury	836935	'89	CS/CD†
Killer: the Mercury Years, Vol. 2: 1969–1972	Mercury	836938	'89	CS/CD†
Killer: the Mercury Years Vol. 3: 1973–1977	Mercury	836941	'89	CS/CD†
Killer Country	Mercury	526542	'95	CS/CD
The Mercury & Smash Recordings	Collectables	5694	'97	CD
Featuring Live & Studio Recordings				

Jerry Lee Lewis and Linda Gail Lewis

Together	Smash	67126	'69	†

Later Recordings

Jerry Lee Lewis	Elektra	184	'79	†
When Two Worlds Collide	Elektra	254	'80	†
Killer Country	Elektra	291	'80	†
My Fingers Do the Talkin'	MCA	5387	'83	†
I Am What I Am	MCA	5478	'84	†
The Complete Palomino Club Club Recordings	Tomato	(2)70385	'91	CD
(recorded 1979–1981, 1985)				
Rockin' My Life Away (recorded at the Palomino Club)	Tomato	70392	'92	CS/CD
Heartbreak	Tomato	70697	'92	CS/CD
Rocket 88 (recorded at the Palomino Club)	Tomato	70698	'92	CS/CD
Live at the Vapors Club (recorded in Memphis, 1990)	Ace	326		CD
Honky Tonk Rock 'n' Roll Piano Man	Ace	332		CD
Pretty Much Country	Ace	348		CD
Great Balls of Fire (music from sound track)	Polydor	839516	'89	CS/CD
Young Blood	Sire	61795	'95	CS/CD

Jerry Lee Lewis, Johnny Cash, and Carl Perkins

The Survivors	Columbia	37961	'82	LP/CS†
	Razor & Tie	2077	'95	CS/CD

Jerry Lee Lewis, Johnny Cash, Roy Orbison, and Carl Perkins

Class of '55	Columbia	830002	'86	LP/CS/CD

Anthologies and Compilations

High Heel Sneakers	Pickwick	3224	'70	†
Roll Over, Beethoven	Pickwick	6110		†
Rural Route # 1	Pickwick	6120		†
Jerry Lee Lewis	Pickwick	2055		†

Drinkin' Wine Spo-Dee O Dee	Pickwick	3344		†
Best of Jerry Lee Lewis	Trip	(2)8501	'74	†
Jerry Lee Lewis	Everest	298		†
I Walk the Line	Accord	7133	'81	†
Milestones (recorded 1956- 1977)	Rhino	(2)1499	'85	†
	Rhino	71499	'89	CS†
All Killer, No Filler: The Anthology	Rhino	(2)71216	'93	CS/CD
Solid Gold	Pair	1132	'86	CS
Great Balls of Fire	Grudge	4513	'89	CS/CD†
Jerry Lee Lewis	Bella Musica	89916	'90	CD†
Best	Curb/Warner Bros.	77446	'91	CS/CD
Greatest Hits	Koch Prasent	399538	'91	CD
Rockin' My Life Away: The Jerry Lee Lewis Collection	Warner Brothers	26689	'91	CS/CD
Great Balls of Fire	CSI	75312	'92	CD
Whole Lotta Shakin'	CSI	75322	'92	CD
At His Best	RCA-Camden	500		CS
You Win Again	Polygram	836689		CS
Greatest Hits Live	Special Music	4811		CD
A Private Party	Live Gold	(2)70007/8		CD
20 Classic Jerry Lee Lewis Hits	Original Sound	888		CS/CD

LITTLE ANTHONY AND THE IMPERIALS

"Little" Anthony Gourdine (born January 8, 1940, in Brooklyn, New York), lead voc; Tracy
Lord, 1st ten; Ernest Wright, 2d ten; Clarence Collins, bar; Gloucester "Nate" Rogers, bs
voc. Sammy Strain (born December 9, 1940) joined in 1964.

One of the few '50s black vocal groups to survive and prosper in the '60s, Little Anthony and the Imperials provided an important link between the doo-wop of the '50s and soul music of the '60s. Achieving their first R&B and pop success in 1958 with the ballad "Tears on My Pillow," the group came back in the mid '60s with a series of smooth crossover hits such as "Goin' Out of My Head" and "Hurt So Bad," written and produced by Teddy Randazzo.

In 1954 "Little" Anthony Gourdine formed a vocal quartet in Brooklyn to perform at local shows. Becoming the Duponts in 1955, the group recorded their first single, "You," for Winley Records. They later recorded for Royal Roost Records and performed at Alan Freed's Easter Show at New York's Paramount Theater in 1957.

Later in 1957 Gourdine formed the Chesters with tenor Tracy Lord, second tenor Ernest Wright, baritone Clarence Collins, and bass singer Gloucester "Nate" Rogers. Initially recording for Apollo Records, the Chesters were signed by Richard Barrett to George Goldner's End label, where they scored a smash pop and R&B hit with "Tears on My Pillow" in 1958 as the Imperials. As Little Anthony and the Imperials, they managed a major R&B hit with "So Much" in 1959 and a major pop and R&B hit with "Shimmy, Shimmy, Ko-Ko-Bop" at year's end.

By late 1961 Anthony Gourdine had left the Imperials to pursue a solo career. Neither he nor the Imperials enjoyed much success, and Gourdine reunited with the Imperials in 1963. Brought to songwriter Teddy Randazzo, the group was signed to DCP Records. Now comprised of Gourdine, Wright, Collins, and first tenor Sammy Strain, the group recorded a series of pop and R&B hits with songs written and produced by Randazzo through 1966. These included "I'm on the Outside (Looking In)," the pop smash "Goin' out of My Head," the pop and R&B smash "Hurt So Bad," and "Take Me Back."

During the late '60s, Little Anthony and the Imperials recorded for Veep and United Artists Records, managing their last major R&B hit with "I'm Falling in Love With You" in 1974 on Avco Records. Sammy Strain joined the O'Jays in 1975, and Little Anthony and the Imperials subsequently disbanded. By 1980 Anthony Gourdine had begun pursuing a career as a lounge entertainer and gospel recording artist. In 1992 Little Anthony (Gourdine) and Imperials members, Ernest Wright, Clarence Collins, and Sammy Strain reunited to play the cabaret and oldies circuit.

The Imperials

We Are Little Anthony and the Imperials	End	303	'59	†
	Collectables	5422		†
Shades of the 40's	End	311	'60	†

Little Anthony and the Imperials

I'm on the Outside (Looking In)	DCP	6801	'64	†
	Veep	16510	'67	†
Goin' out of My Head	DCP	6808	'65	†
	Veep	16511	'67	†
Best	DCP	6809	'66	†
	Veep	16512	'67	†
Payin' Our Dues	Veep	16513	'67	†
Reflections	Veep	16514	'67	†
Movie Grabbers	Veep	16516	'67	†
Best, Vol. 2	Veep	16519	'68	†
Hits	Pickwick	3029	'66	†
	Roulette	25294	'66	†
Forever Yours	Roulette	42007	'69	†
Out of Sight, Out of Mind	United Artists	6720	'69	†
	Liberty	10117	'80	†
Very Best	United Artists	255	'74	†
	United Artists	382	'75	†
Best	Liberty	10133	'81	†
	Liberty	91475		CD†
Best	EMI	38208	'96	CD
Little Anthony and the Imperials	Sunset	5287	'70	†
On a New Street	Avco	11012	'74	†
Best	Rhino	70919	'89	CS/CD
Shimmy, Shimmy Ko-Ko-Bop	Rhino	72158	'95	CS/CD
Best	RCA-Camden	5021		CS/CD
Sing Their Big Hits	Forum Circle	9107		†
For Collectors Only	Collectables	(2)8804		†

Little Anthony

Daylight	Song Bird	3245	'80	†
Little Anthony Sings the Gospel	MCA Special Products	20862	'95	CS/CD

LITTLE RICHARD

Born Richard Penniman December 5, 1932, in Macon, Georgia.

The self-styled "King of Rock 'n' Roll," Little Richard personified the music's wildness and danger, and was probably the first singer to gain widespread popularity on the basis of a frantic, furious presence in recording and performance. Little Richard, along with Chuck

Berry, was one of rock 'n' roll's earliest composers, with his 1956 "Tutti Frutti" one of the first important rock 'n' roll hits (coming shortly after Chuck Berry's "Maybellene"). His boisterous stage act influenced everyone from Jerry Lee Lewis and James Brown to Mick Jagger and Jimi Hendrix. Moreover, his use of outrageous costumes and makeup, a practice later taken up by the likes of David Bowie, Boy George, and Prince, made him perhaps the first androgynous rock star. Little Richard's intensely sexual persona, with its thinly veiled homosexuality, predated the open homosexuality of Bowie, Boy George, and Queen by decades. One of rock 'n' roll's most erratic characters, Little Richard later denounced the music and retreated into Christian fundamentalism, only to return to secular music in the '70s and again in the late '80s.

Little Richard was singing on the streets of Macon by the age of seven. He became the lead singer in a local church choir at the age of fourteen and later joined Dr. Hudson's Medicine Show and Sugarfoot Sam's Minstrel Show. He began performing R&B at Macon's Tick Tock Club and won an Atlanta talent contest in 1951 that led to a recording contract with RCA. His blues-based recordings (which surfaced on Camden Records in 1958 and 1970) failed to sell. He switched to the Houston-based Peacock label for recordings in 1953, again with little success, and worked with the Tempo Toppers in 1953 and 1954.

LITTLE RICHARD, 1957

In 1955, with the encouragement of Lloyd Price, Little Richard sent a demonstration record to Art Rupe of the Los Angeles-based Specialty label that resulted in a new contract. Recording under producer Robert "Bumps" Blackwell at Cosimo Matassa's J & M Studios in New Orleans accompanied by saxophonists Lee Allen and Alvin "Red" Tyler and drummer Earl Palmer, Little Richard's first session yielded the smash R&B and major pop hit classic "Tutti Frutti," quickly covered by Pat Boone. Following the top R&B/smash pop hit "Long Tall Sally" (also covered by Pat Boone) backed with "Slippin' and Slidin'," Little Richard achieved a major crossover hit with "Rip It Up" backed by "Ready Teddy," and an R&B near-smash with "She's Got It" (recorded in Los Angeles). In 1956–57 he appeared in the early rock 'n' roll films *Don't Knock the Rock, The Girl Can't Help It* (with its hit title song), and *Mister Rock 'n' Roll*. The hits continued into 1958 with "Lucille," backed by the unusually soulful "Send Me Some Lovin'," "Jenny, Jenny," "Keep a Knockin' " (recorded in Washington, D.C.), and "Good Golly, Miss Molly."

While touring Australia in October 1957, Little Richard announced his intention to leave rock 'n' roll for the ministry. He subsequently enrolled in Alabama's Oakwood College Seminary to study theology and was ordained a minister of the Seventh Day Adventist Church in 1961. Sessions in New York in 1959 had produced gospel recordings later issued on 20th Century, Goldisc, Crown, Custom, Spin-O-Rama, and Coral. Early '60s sessions for Mercury yielded the gospel album *It's Real*.

Little Richard returned to rock 'n' roll in 1963, touring Europe with the Beatles and the Rolling Stones. He subsequently recorded for Specialty, where he managed a minor crossover hit with "Bama Lama Bama Loo," followed by VeeJay, Modern, Okeh, and Brunswick. During this period Jimi Hendrix was briefly Little Richard's guitar accompanist. Enjoying renewed popularity with the rock 'n' roll revival of the late '60s, Little Richard signed with Reprise Records in 1970 and scored a moderate pop and R&B hit with "Freedom Blues." For *The Second Coming,* he was reunited with Bumps Blackwell, Lee Allen, and Earl Palmer. In 1976 Little Richard returned to ministry, and by 1979 he had recorded *God's Beautiful City* for World Records and had become a full-time evangelist. In October 1985 he was seriously injured in an automobile accident in West Hollywood.

Little Richard was inducted into the Rock and Roll Hall of Fame in its inaugural year, 1986, the year he appeared in the hit comedy movie *Down and Out in Beverly Hills,* which included his first moderate hit in sixteen years, "Great Gosh a' Mighty," and recorded *Lifetime Friend* for Warner Brothers. He dueted with Phillip Bailey on the title song to the 1988 film *Twins* and sang background vocals on the minor U2–B. B. King hit "When Love Comes to Town" in 1989. In 1993 Little Richard performed at Bill Clinton's presidential inaugural.

BIBLIOGRAPHY

White, Charles. *The Life and Times of Little Richard: The Quasar of Rock.* New York: Harmony, 1984; New York: Pocket Books, 1985; New York: Da Capo, 1994.

Specialty Recordings

Here's Little Richard	Specialty	2100	'57	LP/CS
Little Richard, Vol. 2	Specialty	2103	'58	LP/CS
The Fabulous Little Richard	Specialty	2104	'59	LP/CS
His Original Specialty Albums on 3 CDs (reissue of above 3)	Ace	(3)2		CD
His Biggest Hits	Specialty	2111	'63	LP/CS†
Grooviest 17 Original Hits	Specialty	2113	'68	LP/CS
Well, Alright!	Specialty	2136	'70	LP/CS
The Essential Little Richard	Specialty	2154	'89	CS/CD
The Specialty Sessions	Specialty	(5)8508	'90	LP
	Specialty	(3)8508	'90	CD
The Georgia Peach	Specialty	7012	'91	CS/CD
Shag on Down by the Union Hall (recorded 1955–1964)	Specialty	7063	'96	CD
The Specialty Sessions	Ace	(8)1		LP
	Ace	(6)1		CD

Later Recordings

Little Richard	Camden	420	'58	†
reissued as Original	RCA-Camden	420		CS
Every Hour with Little Richard	Camden	2430	'70	†
Greatest Hits/Recorded Live	Modern	1000	'66	†
	United	7775		†

Wild and Frantic Little Richard	Modern	1003	'66	†
	United	7777		†
Right Now	United	7791		†
Little Richard Is Back	VeeJay	1107	'64	†
Explosive	Okeh	14117	'67	†
Greatest Hits Recorded Live	Okeh	14121	'67	†
Greatest Hits Live (recorded 1967)	Epic	40389	'86	CS/CD
Cast a Long Shadow	Epic	30428	'71	†
Forever Yours	Roulette	42007	'68	†
The Rill Thing	Reprise	6406	'70	†
The King of Rock and Roll	Reprise	6462	'71	†
The Second Coming	Reprise	2107	'72	†
Little Richard Live	K-Tel	462	'76	†
Lifetime Friend	Warner Brothers	25529	'86	†

Gospel Recordings

Little Richard Sings Gospel	20th Century	5010		†
Pray Along with Little Richard	Goldisc	4001	'60	†
also issued as Little Richard Sings Freedom Songs	Crown	5362	'63	†
also issued as Little Richard Sings Spirituals	United	7723		†
	Custom	2061		†
Pray Along with Little Richard, Vol. 2	Goldisc	4002	'60	†
Clap Your Hands	Spin-O-Rama	119	'60	†
Coming Home	Coral	757446	'63	†
Little Richard with Sister Tharpe	Guest Star	1429	'63	†
It's Real	Mercury	60656	'61	†
	Lection	839406		LP/CS/CD†
King of the Gospel Singers	Wing	16288	'64	†
God's Beautiful City	World	1001	'79	†
Little Richard Sings the Gospel	MCA	20852	'95	CS/CD†

Little Richard and Jimi Hendrix

Roots of Rock	Archive of Folk and Jazz Music/Everest	296	'74	†
Together	Pickwick	3347		†

Children's Album

Shake It All About	Walt Disney	60849	'94	†

Anthologies and Compilations

Little Richard's Gold	VeeJay	100		†
His Greatest Hits	VeeJay	1124	'64	†
Best	Scepter	18020	'71	†
Little Richard	Buddah	7501	'70	†
Little Richard	Kama Sutra	2023	'70	†
Greatest Hits	Trip	(2)8013	'71	†
Big Hits	GNP Crescendo	9033	'75	LP/CS/CD
Very Best	United Artists	497	'76	†
Tutti Frutti	Accord	7123	'81	†
Compact Command Performance	Motown	9066	'86	CD†
18 Greatest Hits	Rhino	75899	'86	CD
Shut Up!: A Collection of Rare Tracks, 1951–1964	Rhino	70236	'88	CS†
20 Classic Cuts	Ace	195	'87	LP/CS/CD

His Greatest Recordings	Ace	109		LP/CD
Rip It Up	VeeJay/Chameleon	74797	'89	LP/CS/CD†
Little Richard's Grand Slam and Other Greatest Hits	Grudge	4519	'89	CS/CD†
Greatest Songs	Curb/Atlantic	77739	'95	CS/CD
His Best	Dominion	784		CS/CD
Mega-Mix	Dominion	3457	'95	CS/CD
Good Golly Miss Molly	SMS	1	'95	CD
16 Great Hits	Zeta	519		CD†
20 Greatest Hits	Deluxe	7797		CS/CD
His All Time Greats	Special Music	4908		CS

FRANKIE LYMON AND THE TEENAGERS

Frankie Lymon (born September 30, 1942, in New York City; died February 28, 1968, in New York City), lead voc; Herman Santiago (born February 18, 1941, in New York City), 1st ten; Jimmy Merchant (born February 10, 1940, in New York City), 2d ten; Joe Negroni (born September 9, 1940, in New York City; died September 5, 1978), bar; Sherman Garnes (born June 8, 1940, in New York City; died February 26, 1977), bs voc.

As lead vocalist with the Teenagers, Frankie Lymon became the first black teenage singing idol. The group's success inspired the formation of a number of youthful black vocal groups, from the Students in the '50s to the Jackson Five in the '60s. The group's sound influenced young singers such as Ronnie Bennett and Diana Ross, and served as a prototype for both the girl groups and the early Motown groups of the '60s. The group's best-known song, "Why Do Fools Fall in Love," was the subject of perhaps the longest dispute of song ownership, eventually awarded to group members Jimmy Merchant and Herman Santiago in 1992. Frankie Lymon's success was short-lived and by the age of twenty-five he was dead of a heroin overdose.

After forming several short-term vocal groups, two black students from Edward D. Stitt Junior High School in the Washington Heights section of New York City, Jimmy Merchant and Sherman Garnes, recruited neighborhood Puerto Ricans Herman Santiago and Joe Negroni for another group. Ultimately becoming the Premiers, with Santiago as lead singer, the group was joined by Frankie Lymon in 1955. Lymon had grown up harmonizing with his brothers, Lewis and Howie, in the Harlemaire Juniors. The Premiers were discovered by Richard Barrett, talent scout and lead singer of the Valentines, and signed to George Goldner's Gee Records. Under the name the Teenagers Featuring Frankie Lymon, they recorded "Why Do Fools Fall in Love," a song ostensibly written by Merchant and Santiago, released at the beginning of 1956. With Lymon on boyish soprano lead, the song became a top R&B/smash pop hit, as well the first top British hit by an American vocal group. The song was subsequently covered by the Diamonds and Gale Storm, but unlike most songs rerecorded by white artists, the original proved to be the biggest hit.

Sporting a clean-cut, wholesome image and benefiting from dance instructions provided by noted choreographer Cholly Atkins, the group began touring extensively. They soon scored a smash R&B/major pop hit with "I Want You to Be My Girl," followed by the near-smash R&B hits "I Promise to Remember"/"Who Can Explain?" and "The ABC's of Love," all included on their debut album. They also appeared in the 1956 film *Rock, Rock, Rock,* performing "I Am Not a Juvenile Delinquent."

In the meantime, Frankie Lymon's youngest brother, Lewis, formed the Teenchords in 1956. Signed to Richard Robinson's newly formed Fury label, the group became popular on the East Coast, despite achieving no hits. They appeared in the 1957 film *Jamboree* and later recorded for End and Juanita, breaking up in 1958.

In 1957 Frankie Lymon and the Teenagers toured Great Britain, appeared in the film *Mister Rock and Roll,* and scored their last major R&B hit with the ballad "Out in the Cold Again." In the summer of 1957 Lymon scored a pop hit with "Goody Goody," recorded solo in London, and by year's end he had left the group to record solo for Roulette. The Teenagers persevered for a time without Lymon, recording for Roulette, Columbia, and End through 1961. Lymon did not achieve another hit until 1960's remake of "Little Bitty Pretty One." Losing his youthful soprano voice to age, he was unable to make a convincing comeback. After experimenting with narcotics since 1958, Lymon entered a drug rehabilitation program in Manhattan in 1961; nonetheless, in 1964 he was convicted of narcotics possession. The Teenagers briefly reunited with Lymon in 1965, but on February 28, 1968, his body was found in his grandmother's New York residence, the victim of a heroin overdose at the age of twenty-five.

Sherman Garnes died of a heart attack on February 26, 1977, and Joe Negroni died on September 5, 1978, after suffering a cerebral hemorrhage. In the early '80s, surviving members Herman Santiago and Jimmy Merchant reformed the Teenagers with Pearl McKinnon of the Kodaks. In 1981 Diana Ross scored a near-smash pop and R&B hit with "Why Do Fools Fall in Love." Frankie Lymon and the Teenagers were inducted into the Rock and Roll Hall of Fame in 1993.

In 1984 Lymon's widow, Emira, filed for renewal of the copyright to "Why Do Fools Fall in Love," only to discover that it was the property of Morris Levy, who had acquired George Goldner's catalog. Merchant and Santiago pressed their own legal case, and in 1992 a federal court proclaimed them and Lymon the authors, awarding them royalties back to 1969.

The Teenagers

The Teenagers Featuring Frankie Lymon	Gee	701	'57	†
Rock and Roll	Roulette	25036	'58	†
Jerry Blavatt Presents the Teenagers	Roulette	25250	'64	†

Frankie Lymon

Frankie Lymon at the London Palladium	Roulette	25013	'57	†
Rock and Roll with Frankie Lymon	Roulette	25036	'58	†

Frankie Lymon and the Teenagers

Why Do Fools Fall in Love	Accord	7203		†
The Best of Frankie Lymon and the Teenagers	Rhino	70918	'89	CS/CD
Why Do Fools Fall in Love?	Remember	75034	'96	CD
Singing Their Hits	RCA-Camden	5020		CS/CD

Lewis Lymon and the Teenchords

I'm So Happy	Relic	7028	'92	†
Lewis Lymon and the Teen Chords Meet the Kodaks	Collectables	5049		LP/CS/CD

CLYDE MCPHATTER

Born November 15, 1933, in Durham, North Carolina; died June 13, 1972, in New York.

THE DRIFTERS

McPhatter, lead ten; Gerhart Thrasher (born Wetumpka, Alabama), ten; Andrew Thrasher (born Wetumpka, Alabama), bar; Bill Pinckney (born August 15, 1925, in Sumter, South Carolina), bs voc. Later members included lead ten David Baughan (born New York City);

Johnny Moore (born 1934 in Selma, Alabama); Bobby Hendricks (born 1937 in Columbus, Ohio); bar Charlie Hughes; bs voc Tommy Evans.

Along with Ray Charles and Sam Cooke, Clyde McPhatter was one of the most important and influential vocalists of the R&B '50s. He recorded dozens of hits as lead vocalist for Billy Ward's Dominoes, his own Drifters, and as a solo act. His distinctive high tenor voice and gospel phrasing supported by smooth harmonies set the standard for vocalists throughout the '50s and laid the groundwork for the development of soul music in the '60s. Best remembered for the classic "Money Honey" recorded with his Drifters and his solo hits "A Lover's Question" and "Lover Please," McPhatter was relegated to the oldies circuit by the late '60s.

Born to a Baptist preacher father, Clyde McPhatter began singing in his father's choir at the age of five. He later moved to the New York area with his family, turning professional at age fourteen with the gospel group the Mount Lebanon Singers. In 1950 McPhatter met pianist-arranger Billy Ward and joined Ward's Dominoes as lead tenor. Signed to the King Records subsidiary Federal in late 1950, the Dominoes soon scored an R&B smash with "Do Something for Me." Their next hit, the lascivious top R&B hit "Sixty Minute Man," with lead vocals by bass singer Bill Brown, was one of the first R&B vocal-group songs to become a major pop hit. Subsequent R&B hits for the Dominoes included "That's What You're Doing to Me," the top hit "Have Mercy Baby," and "I'd Be Satisfied" with lead vocals by McPhatter.

After training Jackie Wilson as his replacement, Clyde McPhatter left the Dominoes to form the Drifters in May 1953. The lineup stabilized with McPhatter, brothers Gerhart and Andrew "Bubba" Thrasher, and Bill Pinckney. Signed to Atlantic Records by Ahmet Ertegun, the Drifters conducted their first successful recording session in August 1953, producing the top R&B hit and instant classic "Money Honey." Smash R&B hits continued with "Such a Night," "Honey Love" (another major pop hit), "Bip Bam," a stunning harmony version of "White Christmas" (with lead vocals by Pinckney and McPhatter), and "What'cha Gonna Do." In May 1954, McPhatter joined the Air Force and was replaced by David Baughan and later Johnny Moore, who sang lead on the R&B hits "Adorable" and "Ruby Baby" in 1955–56. Frequent personnel changes ensued and the original Drifters broke up in June 1958. Manager George Treadwell, owner of the Drifters' name, drafted all new members for subsequent hit recordings such as "There Goes My Baby" and "Save the Last Dance for Me," which blended pop and gospel musical styles with sophisticated arrangements and orchestrations.

While on leave from the Air Force, Clyde McPhatter recorded "Seven Days" solo, and the single became a smash R&B/moderate pop hit in early 1956. Upon discharge in April 1956, he pursued a solo career on Atlantic Records, scoring a top R&B/major pop hit with "Treasure of Love." Touring with Bill Haley in 1956 and the Fats Domino Caravan in 1957, McPhatter achieved R&B/pop hits with "Without Love (There Is Nothing)," Just to Hold My Hand," "Long, Lonely Nights" (a top R&B hit), "Come What May" and "Since You've Been Gone." His biggest hit, a pop smash/top R&B hit, came in late 1958 with Brook Benton's "A Lover's Question."

Switching to MGM Records in 1959, McPhatter was subjected to inappropriate pop arrangements with the label and subsequently signed with Mercury Records through producer Clyde Otis in 1960. That summer he achieved a major pop/near-smash R&B hit with "Ta Ta," but his next didn't come until early 1962, when he scored a near-smash pop-only hit with Billy Swan's "Lover Please." His remake of "Little Bitty Pretty One" soon became a major pop-only hit, but it proved to be his last. He recorded his last Mercury album in 1968 and later recorded several unsuccessful singles for small labels. McPhatter went to England in 1968 to perform in small clubs and upon his return two years later, Clyde Otis helped him secure a recording contract with Decca Records. However, *Welcome Home* failed to register with the record-buying public. Subsequently relegated to small clubs and the rock 'n' roll revival circuit, McPhatter died in New York of complications arising from heart, liver, and kidney ailments on June 13, 1972, at the age of thirty-eight. He was inducted into the Rock and Roll Fall of Fame in 1987.

Billy Ward and the Dominoes

Billy Ward with Clyde McPhatter	King	548	'58	†
Clyde McPhatter with Billy Ward and His Dominoes	King	559	'58	LP/CS/CD
Billy Ward and the Dominoes Featuring Clyde McPhatter and Jackie Wilson	King	733	'61	LP/CS/CD
Twenty Four Songs	King	952	'66	†
18 Hits	King	5006	'77	†
Sixty Minute Man: The Best of Billy Ward and the Dominoes	Rhino	71509	'93	CD
Meet Billy Ward and His Dominoes	Fat Boy	236	'96	CD

Clyde McPhatter and the Drifters

Clyde McPhatter and the Drifters	Atlantic	8003	'57	†
Rockin' and Driftin'	Atlantic	8022	'58	†
The Greatest Recordings/the Early Years	Atco	33375	'71	CS†
Let the Boogie Woogie Roll: Greatest Hits 1953–1958	Atlantic	(2)81927	'88	CS/CD
The Very Best of the Drifters (includes material from Clyde McPhatter and Ben E. King)	Rhino	71211	'93	CS/CD
Rockin' and Driftin': the Drifters Box	Rhino	(3)72417	'96	CD

Clyde McPhatter

Love Ballads	Atlantic	8024	'58	†
Clyde	Atlantic	8031	'59	†
Best	Atlantic	8077	'63	†
Deep Sea Ball–The Best of Clyde McPhatter	Atlantic	82314	'91	CS/CD
Let's Start Over Again	MGM	3775	'59	†
Greatest Hits	MGM	3866	'60	†
Ta Ta	Mercury	60597	'60	†
Golden Blues Hits	Mercury	60655	'61	†
Lover Please	Mercury	60711	'62	†
Rhythm and Soul	Mercury	60750	'63	†
Greatest Hits	Mercury	60783	'63	†
Songs of the Big City	Mercury	60902	'64	†
Live at the Apollo	Mercury	60915	'64	†
May I Sing for You	Mercury	16224	'65	†
Welcome Home	Decca	75231	'70	†
Greatest Hits	Curb/Warner Bros.	77417	'91	CS/CD

THE MOONGLOWS

Harvey Fuqua (born July 27, 1929, in Louisville, Kentucky), lead bar; Bobby Lester (born Robert Dallas on January 13, 1930, in Louisville; died October 15, 1980), lead ten; Alexander "Pete" Graves (born April 17, 1936, in Cleveland, Ohio), 2d ten; Prentiss Barnes (born April 12, 1925, in Magnolia, Mississippi), bs voc; Billy Johnson (born 1924 in Hartford, Connecticut; died 1987), gtr.

One of the most innovative of the '50s doo-wop vocal groups, the Moonglows were among the first such groups to be recognized as purveyors of rock 'n' roll. Helping to popularize the style of background vocals known as "blow harmony" (open-mouthed rather than hummed harmony), the Moonglows scored two classics with "Sincerely" in 1954 and "Ten

Commandments of Love" in 1958. When the Moonglows disbanded in 1959, co-lead singer Harvey Fuqua formed his own record labels, making the first recordings of the Spinners. He later joined the Motown organization as songwriter and producer. In the '70s Fuqua formed a new group of Moonglows and achieved success as the producer of the New Birth for RCA and Sylvester for Fantasy.

Bobby Lester and Harvey Fuqua started singing together in high school. In 1950 Fuqua moved to Cleveland, where he formed the Crazy Sounds with Prentiss Barnes. The group later added Lester and Pete Graves, coming to the attention of disc jockey Alan Freed through Al "Fats" Thomas. Freed changed the group's name to the Moonglows and recorded one single by the group for his short-lived Champagne label. In 1953 the group signed with Chicago's Chance label, recording five singles. Adding guitarist Billy Johnson, the Moonglows moved to the Chess label in the fall of 1954. Their first single, Fuqua's "Sincerely," with Lester on lead vocals, became a top R&B/major pop hit, but the McGuire Sisters soon covered the song for Coral, scoring a top pop hit. The Moonglows also recorded for the Chess subsidiary Checker as Bobby Lester and the Moonlighters, but achieved no hits. With Lester on lead vocals, the Moonglows' near-smash R&B hits continued through 1956 with Fuqua's "Most of All," "We Go Together" and the up-tempo "See Saw" (a major pop hit), followed by Percy Mayfield's "Please Send Me Someone to Love," with Fuqua on lead vocals. The group appeared in the 1956 film *Rock, Rock, Rock* and toured throughout the '50s.

Bobby Lester dropped out of the Moonglows in 1958, and with Fuqua on lead vocals, the group scored a near-smash R&B/major pop hit with "Ten Commandments of Love" as Harvey and the Moonglows. Fuqua appeared in the 1958 film *Go, Johnny, Go* without the Moonglows, and the group soon broke up. In 1959 Fuqua recruited a Washington, D.C.-based group, the Marquees, for further recordings as the Moonglows. One of the group's co-lead singers was Marvin Gaye. Although none of their recordings proved to be hits, they did perform background vocals on Chuck Berry's 1959 hits "Almost Grown" and "Back in the U.S.A." By 1960 this edition of the Moonglows had disbanded. Fuqua brought Etta James to Chess Records, where the two recorded the smash R&B hit "If I Can't Have You" as Etta and Harvey.

Harvey Fuqua subsequently moved to Detroit, where he met and married Gwen Gordy, Berry's sister. In 1961 Fuqua discovered the Spinners and formed the Harvey and Tri-Phi labels with Gwen Gordy, who had formed her own independent label, Anna, in 1958. On Tri-Phi, the Spinners scored a smash R&B/major pop hit with "That's What Girls Are Made of," with Fuqua on lead vocals and Marvin Gaye on drums. In 1963 Berry Gordy purchased Harvey and Tri-Phi Records, and Fuqua went to work for Motown, bringing with him Marvin Gaye, the Spinners, Johnny Bristol, Shorty Long, and Junior Walker.

Harvey Fuqua produced Marvin Gaye and Tammi Terrell's smash R&B/major pop hits "Ain't No Mountain High Enough" and "Your Precious Love." While at Motown, Fuqua and Johnny Bristol cowrote Gaye and Terrell's near-smash hit "If I Could Build My World Around You," David Ruffin's "My Whole World Ended (the Moment You Left Me)," Edwin Starr's "Twenty-Five Miles," and Junior Walker and the All-Stars' "What Does It Take (to Win Your Love)." Bristol and Fuqua coproduced Stevie Wonder's "Yester-Me, Yester-You, Yesterday," and the original Supremes' final hit, "Someday We'll Be Together," written by Bristol, Fuqua, and Jackie Beavers and originally recorded by Bristol and Beavers.

Meanwhile, Pete Graves had formed a new set of the Moonglows in 1964, but recordings for Lana and other labels proved unsuccessful. In 1971 Bobby Lester briefly formed his own group of the Moonglows. Harvey Fuqua left Motown in 1970, forming yet another set of the Moonglows in 1971 with Lester, Graves, Doc Williams, and Chuck Lewis for one album issued on RCA. Fuqua soon formed his own production company and brought his discovery the New Birth to RCA. The New Birth achieved a smash R&B hit with "I Can Understand" in 1973 and a near-smash R&B hit with "It's Been a Long Time" in 1974 for RCA, and a top

R&B hit with "Dream Merchant" for Buddah in 1975. Bobby Lester revived another group of the Moonglows in the late '70s, touring and recording *One More Time,* but he died of cancer on October 15, 1980. By then Fuqua had formed another production company in San Francisco, producing disco hits for Sylvester on Fantasy Records, including the 1978 R&B smash/major pop hit "Dance (Disco Heat)." Fuqua also produced '80s recordings for Marvin Gaye and continued to write songs and occasionally perform with the Moonglows.

BIBLIOGRAPHY

Propes, Steve. "The Moonglows: the Commandments of Doo-Wop" (Discography by Neal Umphred). *Goldmine* 17, no. 3 (February 8, 1991): 11–13, 32, 36.

The Moonglows

Look, It's the Moonglows	Chess	1430	'59	†
	Chess/MCA	9193	'87	†
The Best of Bobby Lester and the Moonglows	Chess	1471	'62	†
The Moonglows	Chess	701	'76	†
Blue Velvet: The Ultimate Collection	Chess	(2)9345	'93	CD
The Moonglows: Collectors Showcase	Constellation	2	'64	†
The Return of the Moonglows	RCA Victor	4722	'72	†
One More Time	Relic	8001		LP
Moonglows Acapella	Starr Digital	138	'96	CD

The Flamingos and the Moonglows

The Flamingos Meet the Moonglows	VeeJay	1052	'62	
on the Dusty Road of Hits	VeeJay	706	'93	CS

RICK NELSON

Born Eric Nelson on May 8, 1940, in Teaneck, New Jersey; died December 31, 1985, near De Kalb, Texas.

One of the most popular rock 'n' roll artists of the late '50s and early '60s, Rick Nelson was the first artist to benefit from regular television exposure of his songs. Much like the Everly Brothers, he helped make rock 'n' roll more palatable and more popular by effectively combining gentle ballads, a lively rockabilly sound, and pop-style material that appealed to adults as well as their teenage children. Nelson gave early exposure to the songs of Gene Pitney and the Burnette Brothers, and one of rock 'n' roll's most exciting guitarists, James Burton, accompanied him until the late '60s. Although his style lacked the urgency of Elvis Presley or Little Richard, Nelson's recordings showed far more emotional depth than evidenced by teen idols such as Fabian and Frankie Avalon, with whom he was mistakenly lumped. Rick Nelson began exploring country music in 1966 and became one of the pioneers of country-rock with his Stone Canyon Band. Refusing to play Las Vegas and become an oldies act, he was among the first rock artists to record the works of Tim Hardin, Eric Andersen, and Randy Newman. Touring arduously during the '70s and '80s, Rick Nelson returned to his rockabilly sound around 1984, only to die in an airplane crash at the end of 1985.

Born into a show business family, Eric "Ricky" Nelson joined the cast of his parents' *The Adventures of Ozzie and Harriet* radio show in March 1949 at the age of eight. The show moved to television in October 1952, where it ran for a remarkable fourteen years. Ricky studied clarinet, took up drums, and later learned to play the guitar. Signed to Verve Records in 1956—with just several months' experience singing—Ricky scored a smash pop and R&B hit with his first release, a version of Fats Domino's "I'm Walkin'" (fronted by "A Teenager's Romance") after performing the song at the end of the television show on April 10, 1957.

Upon signing a five-year contract with Imperial Records, Ricky Nelson launched his career with the label in October 1957 with the gentle rock smash pop and R&B hit "Be Bop Baby," from his debut album, recorded with guitarist Joe Maphis. He next achieved a pop, R&B and country smash with "Stood Up," backed by Johnny and Dorsey Burnette's "Waitin' in School." By 1958 Nelson had formed his own touring and recording band with James Burton. He scored three-way crossover smash hits with the Burnette brothers' "Believe What You Say," backed by Hank Williams's "My Bucket's Got a Hole in It," and "Poor Little Fool" (written by Eddie Cochran's girlfriend Sharon Sheeley). Nelson costarred in the Howard Hawks-directed classic western *Rio Bravo* with John Wayne and Dean Martin, and continued to have near-smash pop hits with "Lonesome Town"/"I Got a Feeling," "Never Be Anyone Else But You" backed by Dorsey Burnette's "It's Late," and Johnny Burnette's "Just a Little Too Much" backed by "Sweeter Than You." In 1960 he appeared in the comedy film *The Wackiest Ship in the Army* with Jack Lemmon and achieved major pop hits with "I Wanna Be Loved," "Young Emotions," "I'm Not Afraid," and "You Are the Only One."

After the top hit "Travelin' Man," backed by the near-smash "Hello Mary Lou" (written by Gene Pitney), Ricky Nelson shortened his name to Rick on his twenty-first birthday. The hits continued into 1963 with "A Wonder Like You"/"Everlovin'," the smash "Young World," the autobiographical "Teen Age Idol," and "It's Up to You." In 1963 he switched to Decca Records, where his hits included "String Along" and the standards "Fools Rush In," "For You," and "The Very Thought of You."

Eclipsed by the myriad British acts that dominated rock music beginning in 1964, Rick Nelson began exploring country music with 1966's *Bright Lights and Country Music,* managing a minor country hit with "Take a City Bride" in 1967. In 1969 he formed the Stone Canyon Band with pedal steel guitarist Tom Brumley and bassist Randy Meisner (later a founding member of Poco and the Eagles). The group recorded the *In Concert* album, which included "I Shall Be Released," Bob Dylan's "If You Gotta Go, Go Now," and Eric Andersen's "Violets of Dawn," and yielded a moderate pop hit with Dylan's "She Belongs to Me." After recording an entire album of his own songs, *Rick Sings Nelson,* he composed the smash 1972 hit "Garden Party," which related his feelings after being booed for performing contemporary material at an oldies show in October 1971. Nelson and the Stone Canyon Band parted company in 1974.

Touring up to 200 days a year, Rick Nelson produced his *Intakes* album for Epic and conducted recording sessions in Memphis in 1979. He joined Capitol for 1981's *Playing to Win.* In 1984 Nelson starred as a school principal in the television movie *High School USA,* with his mother, Harriet, appearing as his secretary. Around that time he returned to his rockabilly style, touring with James Burton, but on December 31, 1985, he was killed along with six others, including guitarist Bobby Neal, when his plane crashed near De Kalb, Texas.

Several of Rick Nelson's children pursued show business careers. His daughter, Tracy, became an actress and appeared in the television series *Father Dowling Mysteries.* His twin sons, Gunnar and Matthew (born September 20, 1967), began performing in Los Angeles clubs in the mid '80s and recorded their debut album as Nelson for DGC Records in 1990. The best-selling album *After the Rain* yielded four hits, including the top hit "(Can't Live Without Your) Love and Affection" and the smash hit title song.

BIBLIOGRAPHY

Selvin, Joel. *Rick Nelson: Idol for a Generation.* Chicago: Contemporary Books, 1990.

Bashe, Philip. *Teenage Idol, Travelin' Man: The Complete Biography of Rick Nelson.* New York: Hyperion, 1992.

Ricky Nelson

Ricky	Imperial	9048	'57	†
Ricky Nelson	Imperial	9050	'58	†
reissued as Ricky	United Artists	1004	'80	†
Ricky Sings Again	Imperial	9061	'59	†
	Liberty	10134	'81	†
Songs by Ricky	Imperial	9082	'59	†
More Songs By Ricky	Imperial	9122	'60	†
	Imperial	12059		†

Rick Nelson

Rick Is 21	Imperial	12071	'61	†
Album 7 by Rick	Imperial	12082		†
It's Up to You	Imperial	12223	'63	†
A Long Vacation	Imperial	12244	'63	†
Rick Nelson Sings for You	Imperial	12251	'64	†
For Your Sweet Love	Decca	74419	'63	†
Rick Nelson Sings "For You"	Decca	74479	'64	†
	MCA	31363	'90	CD
The Very Thought of You	Decca	74559	'64	†
Spotlight on Rick	Decca	74608	'64	†
Best Always	Decca	74660	'65	†
Love and Kisses	Decca	74678	'65	†
Bright Lights and Country Music	Decca	74779	'66	†
Country Fever	Decca	74827	'67	†
Another Side of Rick	Decca	74944	'67	†
Perspective	Decca	75014	'68	†
In Concert	Decca	75162	'70	†
	MCA	3	'73	†
reissued as In Concert: The Troubadour 1969	MCA	25983	'87	CS/CD
Rick Sings Nelson	Decca	75236	'70	†
	MCA	20		†
Rudy the Fifth	Decca	75297	'71	†
	MCA	37		†
Garden Party	Decca	75391	'72	†
	MCA	62	'74	†
	MCA	31364	'90	CD
Windfall	MCA	383	'74	†
Intakes	Epic	34420	'77	†
Memphis Sessions (recorded late '70s)	Epic	40388	'85	†
Playing to Win	Capitol	12109	'81	†
Live, 1983–1985	Rhino	71114	'89	CS/CD
All My Best (rerecordings of his hits)	Silver Eagle	6163	'88	LP/CS/CD†

Anthologies and Compilations

Rockin' with Ricky (recorded 1957–1962)	Ace	85	'96	CD
Best Sellers	Imperial	9218	'63	†
Million Sellers by Rick Nelson	Imperial	9232	'63	†
Rick Nelson	Sunset	5118	'66	†
I Need You	Sunset	5205	'69	†

Legendary Masters	United Artists	(2)9960	'72	†
	EMI	92771	'90	CS/CD
Very Best	United Artists	330	'75	†
Ricky Nelson Sings Again	Liberty	10134		†
Souvenirs	Liberty	10205		†
Teenage Idol	Liberty	10253		†
Best	EMI America	46588	'87	CS/CD†
Best, Vol. 2	EMI	95219	'91	CS/CD
Rick Nelson Country	MCA	(2)4004	'73	†
The Decca Years	MCA	1517	'82	†
Best (1963–1975)	MCA	10098	'90	CS/CD
Greatest Hits	Rhino	215	'85	†
Greatest Hits	Rhino	215	'85	†
	Rhino	70215		CS†
Greatest Hits	Curb/Warner Bros.	77372	'90	CS/CD
Best	Curb/Warner Bros.	77484	'91	CS/CD
Best of Rick Nelson: Live!	Laserlight	12753	'96	CD
Nelson				
After the Rain	DGC	24290	'90	CS/CD†
Because They Can	DGC	24525	'95	CS/CD

JOHNNY OTIS

Born John Veliotes on December 28, 1921, in Vallejo, California.

A pioneering figure in the development of R&B following the demise of the big bands in the late '40s, Johnny Otis was the most prominent white figure in the history of black R&B. He made an indelible mark as bandleader, sessions musician, club owner, talent scout, record producer, tour leader, and songwriter. He opened one of the first nightclubs exclusively to feature rhythm-and-blues music, the Barrelhouse Club, in Los Angeles in 1948, and organized and led one of the first R&B revues, the prime moving force of R&B, in the early '50s. He also "discovered" a number of great R&B acts for King Records. Largely out of the music business in the '60s, Johnny Otis revived his revue and his nearly dormant career for a stunning performance at the Monterey Jazz Festival in 1970. After involvement with politics and his own nondenominational church during the '70s, Otis reemerged with new recordings in 1982 and resurrected his large-scale revue for tours in the '80s. In the '90s Johnny Otis moved to northern California, where he ran a grocery store in which he performed on weekends.

Raised in a black residential area of West Berkeley, California, Johnny Otis took up drums as a teenager and later learned piano and vibraphone. Making his professional debut in 1939 with the West Oakland House Rockers, Otis left Berkeley in 1941 to tour with various "territory bands." He settled in Los Angeles in 1943, where he joined Harlan Leonard's big band as a drummer and formed his own big band at Club Alabam for engagements and recordings from 1945 to 1947 for Excelsior. The band had a regional hit with "Harlem Nocturne" in 1946, as Otis recorded with Illinois Jacquet, Lester Young, and Charles Brown ("Drifting Blues"). From 1948 into the early '50s, with partner Bardu Ali, he ran the Barrelhouse Club in Watts, California, as perhaps the first nightclub to exclusively feature black R&B performers.

In the early '50s Johnny Otis served as "artists and repertoire" man for King Records, discovering such talents as Esther Phillips, Etta James, Jackie Wilson, Little Willie John, the

Royals (who later became Hank Ballard and the Midnighters), and the Robins (who later became the Coasters). He recorded a series of R&B hits for Savoy in the early '50s as the Johnny Otis Orchestra with the Robins, "Little" Esther Phillips, and Mel Walker, including the top R&B hits "Double Crossing Blues," "Mistrustin' Blues," and "Cupid's Boogie." Otis conducted tours from 1950 to 1954 with the Rhythm and Blues Caravan, believed to be the first large "package" R&B revue to tour nationally. He recorded for Mercury and Peacock in the first half of the '50s and worked as a disc jockey at KFOX beginning in 1954, later hosting a weekly television show from Los Angeles.

Johnny Otis produced the top R&B hits "Hound Dog" for "Big Mama" Thornton in 1953 and the classic "Pledging My Love" for Johnny Ace in 1955. He formed Dig Records in 1955 and recorded for Capitol Records from 1957 to 1959. In 1958 he scored an R&B and pop smash with his own "Willie and the Hand Jive" and appeared in the film *Juke Box Rhythm.* Other hit compositions by Otis included "The Wallflower (Dance with Me, Henry)" for Etta James (1955), "So Fine" for the Fiestas (1959), and "Every Beat of My Heart" for the Pips (1961). Otis recorded for King in the early '60s and seldom toured after the mid '60s. He wrote his autobiography *Listen to the Lambs,* published in 1968, and eventually returned to recording with *Cold Shot.* The album's success led to a contract with Epic Records that produced *Cuttin' Up.*

In 1970 Johnny Otis reassembled a new revue with Joe Turner, Esther Phillips, Roy Milton, Roy Brown, and Eddie "Cleanhead" Vinson for an outstanding Saturday afternoon performance at the Monterey Jazz Festival. Recordings from the show were released in 1971. During the '70s, Johnny Otis became involved in Democratic Party politics as deputy chief of staff for Congressman Mervin Dymally. He formed Blues Spectrum Records in 1974, recording his own band and the likes of Charles Brown, Joe Turner, and Louis Jordan. He was ordained a minister by evangelist Mother Bernice Smith in 1975 and founded the nondenominational Landmark Community Church in Los Angeles in 1978. He also hosted a weekly radio show on KPFK in Los Angeles.

Johnny Otis's son Shuggie (born November 30, 1953, in Los Angeles) debuted in 1965 and was introduced by Al Kooper in 1970 with *Kooper Session.* Shuggie Otis later recorded several albums for Epic Records in the '70s, anthologized on *Shuggie's Boogie* in 1994.

In 1981 Bruce Iglauer of Alligator Records convinced Johnny Otis to record a new album. *The New Johnny Otis Show* was released the following year and Otis soon returned to touring with his new revue, performing at supper clubs and the 1984 Monterey Jazz Festival. In the early '90s Otis moved to Sebastopol, California, where he opened the Johnny Otis Market. He hosted live revue-type music at the market on weekend evenings and live broadcasts of the performances began on KPFA radio from Berkeley, California, in 1994. Johnny Otis was inducted into the Rock and Roll Hall of Fame in 1994. Some of his works as a visual artist were published by Pomegranate Artbooks in 1995.

BIBLIOGRAPHY

Otis, Johnny. *Listen to the Lambs.* New York: Norton, 1968.

―――――. *Upside Your Head: Rhythm and Blues on Central Avenue.* Hanover, NH: Wesleyan University Press, 1993.

Hansen, Terry. "Otisology: the Spirit of Johnny Otis" (Discography by Neal Umphred). *Goldmine* 20, no. 7 (April 1, 1994): 14–20, 22, 24, 26, 28, 32.

Hildebrand, Lee. *Color and Chords: The Art of Johnny Otis.* San Francisco: Pomegranate Artbooks, 1995.

Johnny Otis

The Johnny Otis Show	Savoy	2221	'58	†

The Original Johnny Otis Show (1945–1951)	Savoy Jazz	(2)2230	'78	LP†
	Savoy Jazz	0266	'95	CD
The Original Johnny Otis Show, Vol. 2 (1949–1951)	Savoy Jazz	(2)2252	'78	LP†
Rock and Roll Hit Parade, Vol. 1	Dig	104	'57	†
Creepin' with the Cats: The Legendary Dig Masters	Ace	325		CD
The Johnny Otis Show	Capitol	940	'58	†
The Capitol Years (recorded 1957– 1959)	Capitol	92858	'89	CS/CD†
Cold Shot	Kent	534	'68	†
Snatch and the Poontangs	Kent	557	'70	†
Otisology	Kent	8001	'86	†
Cuttin' Up	Epic	26524	'70	†
Live at Monterey	Epic	30473	'71	†
Back to Jazz	Jazz World	707	'77	†
Great Rhythm & Blues Oldies, Vol. 3	Blues Spectrum	103	'77	†
Great Rhythm & Blues Oldies, Vol. 8	Blues Spectrum	108	'77	†
Great Rhythm & Blues Oldies, Vol. 13	Blues Spectrum	113	'77	†
The New Johnny Otis Show	Alligator	4726	'82	LP/CS/CD
The Spirit of the Black Territory Bands	Arhoolie	384	'92	CS/CD
Shuggie Otis				
Kooper Session: Al Kooper Introduces Shuggie Otis	Columbia	9951	'70	†
Here Comes Shuggie Otis	Epic	26511	'70	†
Freedom Flight	Epic	30752	'71	†
Inspiration Information	Epic	33059	'75	†
Shuggie's Boogie: Shuggie Otis Plays the Blues	Epic/Legacy	57903	'94	CS/CD

LES PAUL

Born Lester Polfuss on June 9, 1916, in Waukesha, Wisconsin.

Although his musical career was highlighted by popular instrumental jazz recordings in the late '40s and a series of pop hits with vocalist-wife Mary Ford in the early '50s, Les Paul achieved his greatest impact as the creator of one of the first commercially successful solid body electric guitars and as the pioneer of studio recording techniques such as echo delay and overdubbing. While the Gibson Les Paul, introduced in 1952, became the favored electric guitar of rock 'n' roll artists from Fran Beecher (with Bill Haley), Scotty Moore (with Elvis Presley), and Link Wray to Jeff Beck, Pete Townshend, and Slash from Guns 'N Roses, Paul's studio techniques became standard practices in the recording industry. He also designed the first eight-track tape recorder and his later innovations included the floating bridge pickup and the electrodynamic pickup.

Lester Polfuss began playing harmonica and experimenting with electronics at the age of nine. By thirteen he had switched to guitar, later joining guitarist Joe Wolverton to perform as Sunny Joe and Rhubarb Red until his late teens. He subsequently moved to Chicago and worked as Rhubarb Red on WJJD in the mornings, and as Les Paul on WIND in the evenings. He built his first guitar pickup in 1934 and began investigating the feasibility of a solid body electric guitar. He formed the Les Paul Trio with Jim Atkins and Ernie Newton in 1936, and they moved to New York in 1938. They joined Fred Waring's Pennsylvanians for three years, playing five nights a week on NBC radio. Around 1941 Paul returned to Chicago, where he designed his first solid body electric guitar, which he dubbed "The Log," and served as musical director for both WJJD and WIND until 1943.

Les Paul moved to Hollywood in 1943 and became acquainted with both Leo Fender and Paul Bigsby. He was drafted into the Armed Forces Radio Service as an entertainer, backing artists such as Dinah Shore and the Andrews Sisters. In July 1944 he played at a Jazz at the Philharmonic performance with trombonist J. J. Johnson, tenor saxophonists Lester Young and Illinois Jacquet, and pianist Nat Cole. In 1945 Paul backed Bing Crosby on his top pop hit "It's Been a Long, Long Time," and built his own sound studio in his garage, where he devised the technique of recording multiple tracks. He backed the Andrews Sisters on their smash 1946 pop hit "Rumors Are Flying," and began his own string of instrumental hits on Capitol Records with "Lover"/"Brazil" in 1948. "Brazil" featured Paul playing six guitars, overdubbed. He continued to score major instrumental hits through 1953 with songs such as "Nola," "Goofus," "Little Rock Getaway," "Josephine," "Whispering," and "Meet Mister Callaghan."

In 1949 Les Paul met and married singer Colleen Summer (born July 7, 1928, in Pasadena, California), who had sung with Gene Autry. She changed her name to Mary Ford and the two began recording a series of pop hits for Capitol that featured Paul's use of multitracking on both guitars and vocals. They scored top pop hits with "How High the Moon" (also a smash R&B hit) in 1951 and "Vaya Con Dios (May God Be with You)" in 1953. From 1951 to 1955 they achieved smash pop hits with "Tennessee Waltz," "Mockingbird Hill" (a smash country hit), "The World Is Waiting for the Sunrise," "Tiger Rag," "Bye Bye Blues," "I'm a Fool to Care," and "Hummingbird." In 1952 Gibson began marketing the Les Paul Gibson solid body electric guitar and Ampex began marketing the first eight-track tape recorder, which Paul had designed several years earlier.

Les Paul and Mary Ford switched to Columbia Records in 1958, with little success. The couple divorced in 1963 and Ford died of diabetes on September 30, 1977. Les Paul withdrew from performing in 1965 to promote Gibson guitars and work on electronics inventions for guitar and recording. He reemerged in 1967 to record *Les Paul Now* and later served as musical director of the ABC television show *Happy Days*. In 1977 and again in 1978 he recorded with guitarist Chet Atkins, but again retired after a heart attack and coronary bypass operation. In 1984 he began performing on Monday nights at Manhattan's Fat Tuesday's nightclub, occasionally accompanied by George Benson, Stephane Grappelli, or Jimmy Page. Les Paul was inducted into the Rock and Roll Hall of Fame as an Early Influence in 1988 and his biography was published in 1993.

BIBLIOGRAPHY

Shaughnessy, Mary Alice. *Les Paul: An American Original.* New York: Morrow, 1993.

The Les Paul Trio

Feed Back: 1944–1945	Circle	67	'86	†
Hawaiian Paradise	Decca (10")	5018	'49	†
Galloping Guitars	Decca (10")	5376	'52	†
Early Les Paul	Capitol	16286	'82	†
The Les Paul Trio (radio transcriptions, 1947)	Glendale	6014	'78	LP
The Guitar Artistry of Les Paul	Columbia		'68	†
Radio Picks	One Way	22085		CD

Les Paul and Mary Ford on 10" Albums

Demand Performance		825		CS
New Sound, Vol. 1	Capitol	226	'50	†
New Sound, Vol. 2	Capitol	286	'51	†
Bye Bye Blues	Capitol	356	'52	†

The Hit Makers	Capitol	416	'53	†
Les and Mary	Capitol	577	'55	†
Les Paul and Mary Ford				
The New Sound	Capitol	226	'55	†
The New Sound, Vol. 2	Capitol	286	'55	†
Bye Bye Blues	Capitol	356	'55	†
The Hit Makers	Capitol	416	'55	†
Les and Mary	Capitol	577	'55	†
Time to Dream	Capitol	802	'57	†
The Hits of Les Paul and Mary Ford	Capitol	1476	'60	†
The World Is Still Waiting for the Sunrise	Capitol	11308	'74	†
The Legend and the Legacy	Capitol	(4)97654	'91	CD
The Best of the Capitol Masters	Capitol	99617	'92	CD
Lover's Luau	Columbia	1276	'59	†
Warm and Wonderful	Columbia	8488	'61	†
Bouquet of Roses	Columbia	8621	'62	†
Swingin' South	Columbia	8728	'63	†
The Fabulous Les Paul & Mary Ford	Harmony	11133	'65	†
	Columbia	11133	'87	CS/CD
16 Most Requested Songs	Columbia	64993	'96	CD
Les Paul and Mary Ford	Pickwick	3122		†
Tiger Rag	Pickwick	3145		†
Greatest Hits!	Pair	1334	'94	CS/CD
Les Paul				
Les Paul Now!	London	44101	'68	†
reissued as The Genius of Les Paul– Multi-Trackin'	London	50016	'79	†
Les Paul and Chet Atkins				
Chester and Lester	RCA	3290	'77	†
Guitar Monsters	RCA	2786	'78	†
Masters of the Guitar Together	Pair	1230	'89	CS/CD

CARL PERKINS

Born April 9, 1932, near Tiptonville, Tennessee; died January 19, 1998, in Jackson Tennessee.

With his smash 1956 hit classic "Blue Suede Shoes," Carl Perkins virtually defined and established rockabilly music in the rock 'n' roll canon and launched Sun Records into national prominence. The song was the first rockabilly record to sell a million copies and one of the first three-way crossover hits, nearly topping the pop, country-and-western, and R&B charts simultaneously. Like Chuck Berry and Buddy Holly (and unlike Elvis Presley), Perkins was one of the first rock 'n' roll artists to write his own songs and play lead guitar. He was also the first rockabilly artist to be booked on national television, but Perkins suffered a major loss of career momentum when he was unable to make the engagement due to a serious automobile accident. His career was revived when the Beatles recorded three of his songs in 1964–65 and he later established himself as a country artist by touring with Johnny Cash for ten years. After leaving Cash in 1976, Carl Perkins toured and recorded with his sons Stan and Greg.

Carl Perkins grew up in Lake County, Tennessee, and obtained his first guitar at the age of six. In 1950 he formed a family band with his older brothers, Jay (rhythm guitar) and

Clayton (standup bass), to play local dances and honky-tonks. Adding drummer W. S. Holland in 1953 and turning professional in 1954, the band signed with Sam Phillips's Memphis-based Flip Records for one single, before switching to Phillips's Sun Records label in 1955. Their second Sun single was "Blue Suede Shoes," which became a smash hit in the country, then pop, then R&B fields in early 1956 and eventually sold two million copies. Booked to appear on the *Ed Sullivan* and *Perry Como* shows, the band was involved in a serious auto accident near Dover, Delaware, enroute to New York on March 22, 1956. Carl was hospitalized for a month (Jay never fully recovered and died in 1958), and as a result Elvis Presley became the first rockabilly artist to appear on network television. Presley's follow-up to his breakthrough hit "Heartbreak Hotel" was a cover version of Perkins's "Blue Suede Shoes," which became a major pop-only hit in April 1956. Carl Perkins managed near-smash country hits later in 1956 with "Boppin' the Blues" and "Dixie Fried," but he did not tour again until 1957 and was unable to reestablish his career's momentum.

On December 4, 1956, a Carl Perkins recording date attended by Sun labelmates Johnny Cash and Jerry Lee Lewis turned into an informal session when Elvis Presley dropped in. Unknown to the four, the session was recorded, and bootleg copies of *The Million Dollar Quartet* circulated for years until RCA finally issued the recordings in 1990.

In 1957 Carl Perkins appeared in the film *Jamboree* and had a major country hit with "Your True Love," yet, in early 1958, he switched from Sun to Columbia Records, where he scored a major country hit with "Pink Pedal Pushers." His career subsequently languished, but in 1964, while on his first British tour with Chuck Berry, he met the Beatles, who soon recorded his songs "Slow Down," "Matchbox," and "Everybody's Trying to Be My Baby." His career was revived, particularly in Europe, and in 1966 he switched to the country label Dollie Records, where he achieved a major country hit with "Country Boy's Dream." He joined Johnny Cash's road show and toured with him from 1965 to 1975. In 1969 he provided Cash with the top country hit "Daddy Sang Bass" and scored a major country hit on his own with "Restless," back on Columbia. Perkins also appeared as a regular on ABC television's *The Johnny Cash Show* from 1969 to 1971.

In 1970 Carl Perkins recorded the sorely overlooked *Boppin' the Blues* with NRBQ. He later recorded an album for Mercury and left Johnny Cash to form a performing band with his sons. In 1976 they conducted recording sessions in Muscle Shoals, Alabama, that eventually surfaced on Accord Records in 1982 and were repackaged by RCA Nashville in 1993. Perkins recorded *Ol' Blue Suede's Back* in 1978 and joined Johnny Cash and Jerry Lee Lewis for the live set *The Survivors,* recorded in West Germany in 1981. Perkins wrote and sang on "Get It" from Paul McCartney's *Tug of War* album and later performed on an HBO cable television special featuring Eric Clapton, George Harrison, Dave Edmunds, and Ringo Starr. In 1986 he recorded *The Class of '55* with Johnny Cash, Jerry Lee Lewis, and Roy Orbison, contributing the autobiographical "Birth of Rock and Roll," which became a moderate country hit.

Inducted into the Rock and Roll Hall of Fame in 1987, Carl Perkins ceased touring in 1991 as he fought the ravages of lung and throat cancer. In 1996 Hyperion Books published Perkins's autobiography (written with David McGee) and Dinosaur Records issued Perkins's final album, both titled *Go Cat Go!* The album contained Perkins's duets with the likes of Paul McCartney, John Fogerty, Paul Simon, and Tom Petty. Carl Perkins died of complications from a series of strokes in Jackson, Tennessee, on January 19, 1998, at the age of sixty-five.

BIBLIOGRAPHY

Perkins, Carl with Ron Rendleman. *Disciple in Blue Suede Shoes.* Grand Rapids, MI: Zondervan, 1978.

_____, and David McGee. *Go, Cat, Go!: The Life and Times of Carl Perkins, the King of Rockabilly.* New York: Hyperion, 1996.

Sun Recordings

Dance Album	Sun	1225	'57	†
reissued as Teen Beat	Sun	1225	'61	†
Original Golden Hits	Sun	111		†
Blue Suede Shoes	Sun	112(E)	'69	†
Best	Trip	(2)8503	'76	†
Matchbox	Pickwick	6103	'77	†
The Sun Story, Vol. 3	Sunnyvale	903	'77	†
Original Sun Greatest Hits (1955–1957)	Rhino	70221	'86	CS
	Rhino	75890	'86	CD
Honky Tonk Gal: Rare and Unissued Sun Masters	Rounder	27	'89	LP/CS/CD

Carl Perkins, Elvis Presley, Johnny Cash, and Jerry Lee Lewis

The Million Dollar Quartet	RCA	2023	'90	LP/CS/CD

Carl Perkins

Whole Lotta Shakin'	Columbia	1234	'58	†
	Sony	1234	'91	CS/CD†
	K-tel	75014	'95	CS/CD
On Top	Columbia	9931	'69	†
Restless: the Columbia Years	Legacy	48896	'92	CS/CD
Country Boy's Dream	Dollie	4001	'66	†
My Kind of Country	Mercury	691	'73	†
The Carl Perkins Show	Suede	6778	'76	†
Live at Austin City Limits	Suede	002	'81	†
Ol' Blue Suede's Back	Jet	35604	'78	†
Presenting Carl Perkins	Accord	7169	'82	†
Boppin' the Blues	Accord	7915	'82	†
Carl Perkins	MCA	39035	'85	†
The Man and the Legend (recorded 1985)	Magnum America	20	'96	CD
Carl Perkins and Sons	RCA Nashville	66216	'93	CS/CD†
Disciple in Blue Suede Shoes	RCA Nashville	66217	'93	CS/CD†
Born to Rock	Universal	76001	'89	LP/CS/CD†
Friends, Family and Legends	Platinum	2431	'92	†
Go Cat Go!	Dinosaur	84508	'96	CS/CD

Carl Perkins and NRBQ

Boppin' the Blues	Columbia	09981	'70/'90	CD

Carl Perkins, Johnny Cash, and Jerry Lee Lewis

The Survivors	Columbia	37961	'82	LP/CS†
	Razor & Tie	2077	'95	CS/CD

Carl Perkins, Jerry Lee Lewis, Roy Orbison, and Johnny Cash

Class of '55	Columbia	830002	'86	LP/CS/CD†
	Mercury Nashville	830002	'94	CS/CD

Anthologies and Compilations

Greatest Hits	Columbia	9833	'69	†
Carl Perkins	Harmony	11385	'70	†
Brown-Eyed Handsome Man	Harmony	31179	'72	†
Greatest Hits	Harmony	31792	'73	†

Jive After Five: The Best of Carl Perkins, 1958–1978	Rhino	70958	'90	CS/CD
Best	Sound	929	'91	CD
Best	Curb/Warner Bros.	77598	'92	CS/CD
Introducing Carl Perkins	Boplicity	8		LP
Twenty Golden Pieces	Bulldog	2034		LP/CS

SAM PHILLIPS

Born January 5, 1923, in Florence, Alabama.

Best remembered as the man who "discovered" and first recorded Elvis Presley, Sam Phillips was instrumental in the development and popularization of rockabilly music. Having previously made the initial recordings of bluesmen such as B. B. King, Howlin' Wolf, and Junior Parker, Phillips switched his attention to white Southern singers after the success and departure of Presley; he signed and recorded the early works of Johnny Cash, Carl Perkins, Roy Orbison, and Jerry Lee Lewis. Independent record companies like Sun pioneered rock 'n' roll and challenged the dominance of established record labels during the '50s. However, Sun Records eventually lost all its major acts to larger labels and its influence was in decline by the end of the '50s.

Sam Phillips was working as a disc jockey at Memphis's WREC when he realized that few facilities existed to record local black performers. In 1950 he opened the Sun recording studio and made early recordings by B. B. King, Howlin' Wolf, and others, leasing them to established independent companies such as Modern/RPM and Chess/Checker. In 1951 Jackie Brenston recorded the top R&B hit "Rocket 88" at Sun Studios for Chess and the song came to be regarded as perhaps the first rock 'n' roll record. Quitting his job as disc jockey and forming the Sun label in 1952, Phillips scored his first R&B hits the next year with Little Junior Parker's "Mystery Train" and Rufus Thomas's "Bear Cat."

In his search for a white singer who sounded black (his actual words were purportedly far less delicate), Sam Phillips found his man in Elvis Presley, who had first come to the Sun studio in July 1953 to make a private recording for his mother. Teamed with guitarist Scotty Moore and standup bassist Bill Black, Presley made his first recordings for Sun, Bill Monroe's "Blue Moon of Kentucky" backed with Arthur "Big Boy" Crudup's "That's All Right (Mama)," in July 1954. With some help from a local disc jockey, "That's All Right (Mama)" became a regional hit. Phillips subsequently recorded Presley's versions of songs written by black writers, backed by country-and-western standards. Country hits for Elvis on Sun in 1955 included "Baby Let's Play House," "I Forgot to Remember to Forget" (a top country hit), and "Mystery Train."

In November 1955 Sam Phillips sold Presley's Sun contract, as well as his master recordings, to RCA-Victor for an unprecedented $35,000. With Presley's departure, Phillips began working with other white Southern singers such as Johnny Cash and Carl Perkins. Perkins soon scored a smash country-and-western, R&B, and pop hit with his own "Blue Suede Shoes" in early 1956, launching rockabilly music into mainstream prominence. Cash achieved his first major pop hit for Sun (after several country hits) with "I Walk the Line" in the fall of 1956, followed by "Ballad of a Teenage Queen," "Guess Things Happen That Way," and "The Ways of a Woman in Love," recorded under arranger-producer Bill Justis.

Issuing the early recordings of Roy Orbison in 1956 (including the minor pop hit "Ooby Dooby"), Sun Records next achieved smash three-way crossover hits in 1957–58 with Jerry Lee Lewis's "Whole Lotta Shakin' Goin' On," "Great Balls of Fire," and "Breathless." In 1957 Phillips formed the subsidiary label Phillips International, and hits on the label included Bill

Justis's instrumental "Raunchy," Carl Mann's "Mona Lisa" and Charlie Rich's "Lonely Weekends." However, by 1958 Johnny Cash, Carl Perkins, and Roy Orbison had left Sun for major established labels, and Jerry Lee Lewis departed in 1963. Sun Records continued to operate in the '60s, but the label failed to produce any more significant hits or discover any important new acts. In 1968 Sam Phillips retired and sold the Sun masters to Nashville's Shelby Singleton. Phillips was inducted into the Rock and Roll Hall of Fame in its inaugural year, 1986.

Sun Records Anthologies

Sun's Gold Hits	Sun	1250	'61	†
Sun Rockabillies, Vol. 1	Sun	1010		†
Sun's Greatest Hits	Rhino	256		†
Sun Records–Blue Flames: A Sun Blues Collection	Rhino	70		CS/CD†
Sun Records–Memphis Ramble: A Sun Country Collection	Rhino	70963		CS/CD†
The Sun Story	Rhino	(2)71103	'86	CS
	Rhino	75884	'87	CD
The Sun Records Collection	Rhino	(3)71780	'94	†
Sun Records Harmonica Classics	Rounder	29	'89	LP/CS/CD
Sun Rockabilly: the Classic Recordings	Rounder	37		LP/CS/CD
Sun's Greatest Hits	RCA	66059	'92	CS/CD

THE PLATTERS

Tony Williams (born April 5, 1928, in Elizabeth, New Jersey; died August 14, 1992, in New York), lead ten; David Lynch (born in 1929 in St. Louis, Missouri; died January 2, 1981, at age 61), 2d ten; Paul Robi (born in 1931 in New Orleans; died February 1, 1989), bar; Herb Reed (born in 1931 in Kansas City, Missouri; bs; Zola Taylor (born in 1934 in Los Angeles), contralto. Later members included Sonny Turner (born in 1939 in Cleveland, Ohio); Nate Nelson (born April 10, 1932, in New York City; died June 1, 1984, in Boston, at age 52); Monroe Powell, and Gene Williams. Mentor-manager-songwriter Buck Ram was born on November 21, 1907, in Chicago and died January 1, 1991, in Las Vegas, at age eighty-three.

Featuring a smooth sophisticated sound and the superb lead tenor voice of Tony Williams, the Platters were among the most successful black vocal group of the '50s. One of the first such groups regularly to ascend the pop charts and enjoy massive popularity with white audiences, the Platters helped launch doo-wop music and influenced generations of vocal groups with their harmonies and arrangements. Masterminded by manager, producer, arranger, and chief songwriter Buck Ram, the Platters were promoted as a popular ballad group, rather than as an R&B group. They scored a series of smash pop and R&B hits between 1955 and 1960, including the classics "Only You," "The Great Pretender," and "The Magic Touch" (all written by Ram). Their recorded success led to appearances on television and the cabaret circuit as well as in rock 'n' roll package shows. The Platters' career went into decline with the 1960 departure of Tony Williams, although a number of groups continued to tour as the Platters into the '90s.

In 1953 in Los Angeles, Tony Williams, David Lynch, Alex Hodge, and Herb Reed formed the Platters and met Buck Ram, a former writer and arranger for the big bands of the '30s and '40s. Becoming their manager in February 1954, Ram added female vocalist Zola Taylor, from Shirley Gunter and the Queens, in May. Paul Robi replaced Alex Hodge in July, and Ram signed the group to the Federal subsidary of Cincinnati's King Records. The group unsuccessfully recorded Ram's "Only You" and other songs for the label, later is-

THE PLATTERS

sued on King and Deluxe. Ram next placed the group with Mercury Records, and in the fall of 1955 they scored a top R&B/smash pop hit with "Only You." The song was quickly covered by the white group the Hilltoppers for Dot, but unlike many recordings originated by black artists, the Platters' version proved to be more successful.

The Platters' recording of Ram's "The Great Pretender" became the first R&B ballad to top the pop as well as R&B charts. Ram's "(You've Got) the Magic Touch" proved a smash pop and R&B hit and the standard "My Prayer" became a top pop and R&B hit in 1956. Although their sound was more akin to that of the Ink Spots and the Mills Brothers than the doo-wop groups of the day, the Platters appeared in several rock 'n' roll movies, including 1956's *Rock Around the Clock* and *The Girl Can't Help It.* Their crossover smashes continued with "You'll Never Never Know" (cowritten by Tony Williams and Paul Robi), "It Isn't Right," "On My Word of Honor," "One in a Million" (cowritten by Williams), "I'm Sorry" backed with "He's Mine," and Ram's "My Dream."

Developing a widely based audience among television viewers, rock 'n' roll fans, and the larger pop audience, the Platters performed at rock 'n' roll shows and supper clubs. In 1958 they scored top pop/smash R&B hits with the classic "Twilight Time" (coauthored by Ram) and the standard "Smoke Gets in Your Eyes," recorded in Paris, France. Subsequent crossover hits included "Enchanted" and the standard "Harbor Lights." The Platters' anthology album *Encore of Golden Hits,* released in early 1960, remained on the charts for more than three years.

In 1961 Tony Williams left the Platters to pursue an inauspicious solo career. He was replaced by Sonny Turner, and the group managed major pop hits with the standards "To Each His Own" and "I'll Never Smile Again." In 1962, Zola Taylor and Paul Robi left the group, to be replaced by Sandra Dawn and Nate Nelson (lead singer of the Flamingos' 1959 crossover hit "I Only Have Eyes for You"), respectively. Switching to Musicor Records, the Platters' last major hits came in 1966–67 with "I Love You 1000 Times" and "With This Ring."

Sonny Turner left the Platters in the early '70s and Nate Nelson left in 1982. Buck Ram maintained the group with lead vocalist Monroe Powell and bass singer Gene Williams through the '80s. During this time former members Paul Robi, Herb Reed, and Tony Williams each toured with their own groups as the Platters. During the '80s, several former members died, including David Lynch (1981), Nate Nelson (1984), and Paul Robi (1989). The Platters were inducted into the Rock and Roll Hall of Fame in 1990. The two principals of the Platters, Buck Ram and Tony Williams, died in 1991 and 1992, respectively.

BIBLIOGRAPHY

Weinger, Harry. "The Platters' Glory Days" (Discography by Neal Umphred). *Goldmine* 18, no. 4 (February 21, 1992): 11–15, 104.

The Platters

The Platters	King	549	'55	†
reissued as Only You	King	651	'59	LP/CS/CD
The Platters	Mercury	20146	'56	†
The Platters–Vol. 2	Mercury	20216	'57	†
The Flying Platters	Mercury	20298	'57	†
Around the World with the Flying Platters	Mercury	60043	'58	†
Remember When	Mercury	60087	'59	†
Reflections	Mercury	60160	'60	†
Life Is Just a Bowl of Cherries	Mercury	60254	'61	†
Encore of Broadway Golden Hits	Mercury	60613	'62	†
Sing for the Lonely	Mercury	60669	'62	†
Moonlight Memories	Mercury	60759	'63	†
Sing All-Time Movie Hits	Mercury	60782	'63	†
Sing Latino	Mercury	60808	'63	†
Christmas with the Platters	Mercury	60841	'63	†
	Mercury	822742	'94	CS/CD
Encore of Golden Hits of the Groups	Mercury	60893	'64	†
10th Anniversary Album	Mercury	60933	'65	†
The New Soul of the Platters	Mercury	60983	'65	†
I Love You 1,000 Times	Musicor	3091	'66	†
Have the Magic Touch	Musicor	3111	'66	†
Going Back To Detroit	Musicor	3125	'67	†
Sweet, Sweet Lovin'	Musicor	3156	'68	†
I Get the Sweetest Feeling	Musicor	3171	'68	†
Singing the Great Hits Our Way	Musicor	3185	'69	†
Greatest Hits, Featuring Paul Robi (recorded 1986)	Jango	775	'87	LP/CS/CD†

Anthologies and Compilations

19 Hits	King	5002	'77	†
19 Original Hits	Deluxe	7835		CS
22 Greats	Deluxe	7862		CS
22 Gold	Deluxe	7884		CS
22 Hits	Deluxe	7895		CS
16 Greatest Hits	Deluxe	7900		CS/CD
Encore of Golden Hits	Mercury	60243	'60	†
	Mercury	826254		†
More Encore of Golden Hits	Mercury	60252	'60	†
	Mercury	8002	'79	†
	Mercury	826246		†
Encores	Wing	16112	'62	†
The Flying Platters	Wing	16226	'63	†
Reflections	Wing	16272	'64	†
10th Anniversary Album	Wing	16346	'66	†

Platterama	Mercury	4050	'82	†
Golden Hits	Mercury	826447	'86	CD†
More Golden Hits	Mercury	830773	'87	CD†
The Magic Touch: An Anthology	Mercury	(2)510314	'91	CS/CD
The Very Best of the Platters	Mercury	510317	'91	CS/CD
New Golden Hits	Musicor	3141	'67	†
Golden Hour	Musicor	3231	'72	†
Golden Hits	Musicor	3251	'73	†
Only You	Music Disc	1002	'69	†
In the Still of the Night	Pickwick	3120	'69	†
Super Hits	Pickwick	3236		†
Only You	Pickwick	(2)2083	'76	†
The Platters	Springboard International	4059	'76	†
Attention	Phillips	6430046	'82	†
Anthology (1955–1967)	Rhino	71495	'85	CS
Red Sails in the Sunset	Allegiance	72913	'88	CD
The Greatest Hits	Bella Musica	89903	'90	CD
Golden Sides of the Platters	Pair	1130		CS
Only Their Best for You	Pair	1239	'91	CS/CD
All the Hits and More	Double Gold	(2)53041	'95	CD
Greatest Hits, Vol. 2	Curb/Atlantic	77825	'95	CS/CD
The Platters	WMO/Qualiton	90303	'96	CD
Pledging My Love	Richmond	2179		CS
With This Ring	Richmond	2184		CS
The Great Pretender	Richmond	2189		CS
Only You	Richmond	2210		CS
Twilight Time	Richmond	2218		CS
You'll Never, Never Know	Polygram	839693		CS
20 Greatest Hits	Fest	4415		CS/CD
Greatest Hits	Special Music	4802		CS/CD
Tony Williams				
A Girl Is a Girl Is a Girl	Mercury	60138	'59	†
Sings His Greatest Hits	Reprise	6006	'61	†
Magic Touch of Tony	Phillips	60051	'62	†

DOC POMUS AND MORT SHUMAN

Doc Pomus (born Jerome Felder on June 27, 1925, in Brooklyn, New York; died March 14, 1991, in New York), Mort Shuman (born November 12, 1936, in Brooklyn, New York; died November 2, 1991, in London, England).

One of the most important rock 'n' roll songwriting teams of the late '50s and early '60s, second only to Jerry Leiber and Mike Stoller, Doc Pomus and Mort Shuman composed more than 500 songs together between 1958 and 1965. With Shuman composing most of the music and Pomus the lyrics, they achieved their greatest success writing for the Drifters ("Save the Last Dance for Me") and Elvis Presley, who recorded more than twenty of their songs. After ending their partnership, Pomus spent more than a decade out of the music business, while Shuman collaborated with others for British acts and produced the highly successful musical revue *Jacques Brel Is Alive and Well and Living in Paris*. In 1995 Forward

Records issued the tribute album *Till the Night Is Gone,* which contained Doc Pomus songs recorded by artists such as Bob Dylan, John Hiatt, Lou Reed, and Los Lobos.

Developing polio as a child and using crutches to walk, Jerome Felder began playing saxophone and singing in Greenwich Village clubs as a teenager, adopting the name Doc Pomus. By the mid '40s he had begun recording blues-based songs for a variety of small labels with little success. In the early '50s he began writing songs, achieving his first success with "Boogie Woogie Country Girl," recorded as the flip side of Big Joe Turner's 1956 R&B smash hit "Corrine Corrina." He also wrote "Lonely Avenue," a smash R&B hit for Ray Charles, and collaborated with Jerry Leiber and Mike Stoller on the Coasters' smash R&B and pop hit "Youngblood." Pomus abandoned singing as an avocation in 1957.

Mort Shuman had studied music at the New York Conservatory and become a passionate devotee of R&B, playing piano behind some of Doc Pomus's recordings. In 1958 he and Pomus formed a songwriting partnership that lasted until 1965. Brought to Hill & Range Publishers by songwriter Otis Blackwell ("All Shook Up," "Don't Be Cruel," and "Great Balls of Fire"), the team took up residence at the famed Brill Building, where other teams such as Neil Sedaka and Howie Greenfield and Gerry Goffin and Carole King toiled for Aldon Music. Pomus and Shuman's earliest hit compositions included three for Fabian, "I'm a Man," "Turn Me Loose," and "Hound Dog Man," Dion and the Belmonts' "A Teenager in Love," the Mystics' "Hushabye," and Jimmy Clanton's "Go, Jimmy, Go."

Between 1959 and 1961 Doc Pomus and Mort Shuman provided the Drifters with a number of songs, including the hits "True Love, True Love," "This Magic Moment," the classic "Save the Last Dance for Me," "I Count the Tears," and "Sweets for My Sweet." Both individually wrote with Phil Spector for Ben E. King after his departure from the Drifters, most notably "Young Boy Blues," by Spector and Pomus. Pomus and Shuman also began supplying songs to Elvis Presley, including "A Mess of Blues," "Surrender," "Little Sister," "(Marie's the Name) His Latest Flame," and "Viva Las Vegas." Also for Elvis, they adapted previously written songs by other writers such as "It's Now or Never" and "Can't Help Falling in Love." Other hit compositions included "Seven-Day Weekend" for Gary "U.S." Bonds, "Can't Get Used to Losing You" for Andy Williams, and "Suspicion" for Terry Stafford (previously recorded by Elvis Presley).

The Pomus-Shuman team went to England in 1964, where Shuman began working with other writers. In 1965 Doc Pomus took a severe fall, requiring hospitalization, and he would remain confined to a wheelchair for the rest of his life. The team separated that year and Pomus subsequently left the music business for more than ten years. Mort Shuman collaborated with others, coauthoring British hits for Billy J. Kramer and the Dakotas ("Little Children," a near-smash American hit), the Hollies, Freddie and the Dreamers, Cilla Black, and the Small Faces. In 1966 he collaborated with producer Jerry Ragavoy for Howard Tate, yielding "Get It While You Can," later recorded by Janis Joplin. Subsequently, Shuman moved to Paris, where he performed occasionally, recorded several albums, and wrote for French recording artist Johnny Hallyday. In 1968 Shuman translated the lyrics of French composer Jacques Brel, later writing, producing, and starring in *Jacques Brel Is Alive and Well and Living in Paris.* Productions of the show were mounted in London and New York, where it ran for seven years. Shuman moved to London in 1986, and in 1988 he wrote the music for the unsuccessful British musical *Budgie,* as well as for several other shows never staged. Mort Shuman underwent a liver operation in the spring of 1991 and died in London at the age of fifty-four on November 2, 1991.

After spending more than a decade as a professional gambler, Doc Pomus returned to music in the late '70s, cowriting with Doctor John (1978's *City Lights* and 1979's *Tango Palace* albums), Willy DeVille (Mink DeVille's 1980 *Le Chat Bleu* album), and B. B. King (1981's *There Must Be a Better World Somewhere*). In 1991 Pomus became the first white person to be awarded the Rhythm and Blues Foundation's Pioneer Award. Later that year, on

March 19, he died of lung cancer at the age of sixty-five in New York. Doc Pomus was inducted into the Rock and Roll Hall of Fame in 1992. In 1995 Forward Records released *Till the Night Is Gone,* which featured recordings of fourteen Doc Pomus songs, many coauthored with Mort Shuman, by artists such as Shawn Colvin, Bob Dylan, Lou Reed, John Hiatt, and Rosanne Cash.

Mort Shuman				
My Death	Reprise	6358	'69	†
Tribute Album				
Till the Night Is Gone: A Tribute to Doc Pomus	Forward	71878	'95	CS/CD

ELVIS PRESLEY

Born January 8, 1935, in East Tupelo, Mississippi; died August 16, 1977, in Memphis, Tennessee.

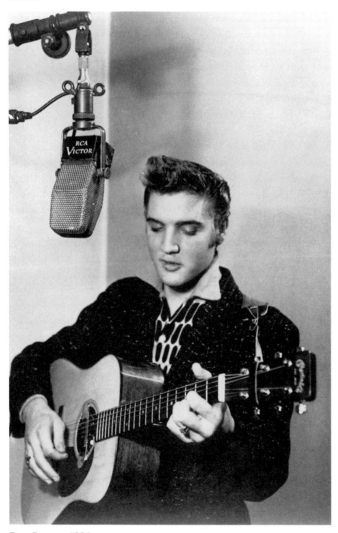

ELVIS PRESLEY, 1956

The biggest single attraction in the history of popular music, Elvis Presley legitimized black R&B music as rock 'n' roll. Some even date the beginning of rock 'n' roll to Presley's first recording session for Sun Records on July 6, 1954. Initially singing in the guttural mumbling style of black R&B artists, he was one of the first white performers of the '50s to exude raw, passionate, sexually charged fervor in performance. As a recording artist, Elvis Presley introduced rock 'n' roll to an entire generation of white teenagers who were unaccustomed to the ardent and intense music of black R&B.

With his move from the small Memphis-based Sun Records label to the major label RCA, Elvis Presley revolutionized the recording industry, scoring a number of hits, including "Heartbreak Hotel," "Hound Dog," "All Shook Up," and "Jailhouse Rock," that topped the pop, country-and-western, and R&B charts simultaneously. Never again would contemporary popular music be dominated by movie stars, crooning male singers, and cabaret entertainers. In identifying a form of music and attendant lifestyle completely distinct from that of his fans' parents, Elvis Presley became the most important symbol of and idol within '50s rock 'n' roll, enhancing its aura of teenage rebellion. However, not all credit for Elvis Presley's unprecedented success can be attributed to the intensity of his '50s performances and recordings. National television appearances and the resulting public controversy did much to spread Presley's fame and notoriety. Also working in his favor was the stunning and compelling guitar playing of Scotty Moore, the vocal accompaniment of the Jordanaires, and the crass yet skillful merchandising of manager "Colonel" Tom Parker.

Although he retained the title "King of Rock 'n' Roll" and remained the music's most widely recognized figure, Elvis Presley's primacy as a rock 'n' roll artist quickly evaporated after his army discharge in 1960. (Presley did record two excellent gospel albums during the '60s, a facet of his career often neglected by biographers.) Elvis began recording inferior material and embarked on a dismal but lucrative career of inane movies (and soundtrack albums) that failed to provide him with the opportunity to test, much less prove, himself as an actor. Never allowed to perform outside the United States and withdrawing from live performances after 1961, his virtual absence led to the emergence of a number of passionless young white male singers cut in his mold such as Frankie Avalon, Fabian, and Bobby Rydell.

With the advent of the rock 'n' roll "revival" of the late '60s, Elvis Presley unexpectedly and unequivocally staged a successful comeback with a December 1968 NBC television special that revealed him to be a passionate, compelling, and unique performer. He also recorded the most consistently engaging material of his later career in Memphis in 1969 and returned to live performance with his celebrated appearance at the International Hotel in Las Vegas, where he quickly established himself as one of the most popular and highly paid cabaret artists in the world. However, by 1973 Elvis Presley had devolved into a "nostalgia" act as his weight increased, health problems developed, and performances became sloppier and more perfunctory.

With Elvis Presley's death in 1977, the cult of personality and exploitation of his recorded legacy began in earnest. His Graceland mansion became the second most visited American home (to the White House) upon opening to the public in 1982, and Presley's image became the third most reproduced in the world (behind Jesus and Mickey Mouse). Elvis Presley's success was virtually unparalleled. By 1995 the total sales figures for his records were estimated to top one billion copies.

Elvis Presley began singing with his parents at the First Assembly of God Church in Tupelo, Mississippi, as a child and later accompanied them to camp meetings and revivals. He obtained his first guitar for his eleventh birthday and moved with his family to Memphis, Tennessee, in September 1948. He sang at a high school variety show in late 1952 and became a truck driver after graduating in June 1953. The next month, in the often told story, he went to the small local Sun Records studio to make a private recording of "My Happiness" for his mother. Noticed by secretary Marion Keisker, Presley was later teamed with guitarist Scotty Moore and standup bassist Bill Black by Sun Records president Sam Phillips. The three rehearsed for several months, returning to the Sun studios on July 6, 1954, to record Bill Monroe's "Blue Moon of Kentucky" and Arthur "Big Boy" Crudup's "That's All Right (Mama)." Local disc jockey Dewey Phillips (no relation to Sam) played the latter song on his radio show and the single became a regional hit. Presley made his professional performing debut at Memphis's Overton Park on August 10, 1954, and was greeted ecstatically by an audience enthralled with his rough, passionate vocals and sexually charged persona.

Elvis Presley, billed as "The Hillbilly Cat," soon began touring the South with Scotty Moore and Bill Black, as his second and third Sun singles became regional hits. In October 1954 they performed on Shreveport's *Louisiana Hayride* radio show (and would continue to do so until December 1956), appearing on the show's television edition the following March. Released in April 1955, "Baby Let's Play House" became a smash country-and-western hit that summer, followed in September by the top country hit "I Forgot to Remember to Forget," backed with Junior Parker's "Mystery Train." Spotted by "Colonel" Tom

Parker, a former carnival barker and erstwhile manager of Eddy Arnold and Hank Snow, Presley signed a new management deal with Parker in November 1955.

Elvis Presley's potent style and raw potential created a bidding war among major record labels. RCA won out with an offer of $35,000, an astoundingly high figure for 1955. In January 1956, backed by guitarists Scotty Moore and Chet Atkins, bassist Bill Black, and drummer D. J. Fontana (who had joined the trio in July 1955), he completed his first recording sessions in Nashville. Presley made his national television debut on the CBS network's *Dorsey Brothers Show* on January 28, 1956, and within weeks his first RCA release, "Heartbreak Hotel," became a top pop and country-and-western and smash R&B hit. On June 5, as "I Want You, I Need You, I Love You" was becoming another three-way crossover smash, Presley appeared on *The Milton Berle Show* to an estimated audience of forty million. Soon, both sides of his first recording with the Jordanaires, "Don't Be Cruel"/"Hound Dog," became top hits in all three fields. Appearing on television's *Ed Sullivan Show* to an estimated audience of fifty-four million on September 9, Elvis was shown only from the waist up.

Elvis Presley's success was phenomenal, and the three-way crossover smashes continued with "Love Me Tender," "Love Me," "Too Much," and "All Shook Up." During 1956 his first movie, *Love Me Tender,* was released, followed in 1957 by *Loving You* and *Jailhouse Rock.* On December 4, 1956, Presley returned to the Memphis Sun studio to join Sun stalwarts Carl Perkins, Jerry Lee Lewis, and Johnny Cash for an informal session of singing and playing gospel songs. Unknown to them, the performance was recorded. Those recordings by the so-called Million Dollar Quartet were bootlegged and available in Europe for years before their eventual release in the United States in 1990. In January 1957 Elvis recorded the four-song gospel E.P. *Peace in the Valley.* The songs were later included on *Elvis' Christmas Album,* which also contained the secular songs "Blue Christmas," "Santa Bring My Baby Back to Me" and "Santa Claus Is Back in Town."

Elvis Presley's three-way crossover smashes continued with "Teddy Bear," "Jailhouse Rock"/"Treat Me Nice," and "Don't"/"I Beg of You." He was allowed a two-month deferment to complete the movie *King Creole,* but on March 24, 1958, he was drafted into the Army. Although he was to record only once during the next two years, the hits did not stop. However, after the three-way crossover smashes "Wear My Ring Around Your Neck" and "Hard Headed Woman," his subsequent crossover smashes were restricted to two fields, pop and R&B. These included "One Night"/"I Got Stung," "(Now and Then There's) a Fool Such as I"/"I Need Your Love Tonight" and "A Big Hunk of Love," the last four his only new recordings during his Army stint.

Discharged on March 5, 1960, Elvis Presley subsequently assembled the so-called "Memphis Mafia" entourage that served to protect and insulate him from the public until July 1976. He began recording far less exuberant and vital material with extra musicians to produce a fuller sound. Nonetheless, "Stuck on You," "It's Now or Never," and "Are You Lonesome Tonight" became smash pop and R&B hits. The ABC-TV television show *Welcome Home, Elvis,* aired May 12, 1960, and featured six minutes of Elvis, for which he was paid $125,000. The show was hosted by Frank Sinatra, a man who had earlier denounced rock 'n' roll as "the most brutal, ugly, desperate, vicious form of expression."

After making his first full album of gospel material, *His Hand in Mine,* in 1960, Elvis Presley appeared at his last public performance for eight years in Honolulu on March 25, 1961. He spent the '60s making a series of lucrative but mindless movies usually staged in exotic locations featuring numerous fleshy but virginal women and only the bare semblance of a plot. He also recorded a few non-sound-track albums as the pop-only smash hits continued with "Surrender," "I Feel So Bad," "(Marie's the Name) His Latest Flame"/"Little Sister," "Can't Help Falling in Love," "Good Luck Charm," and "She's Not You." "Return to Sender" and "(You're the) Devil in Disguise" became his final pop and R&B smashes, with the pop-only major hits "Bossa Nova Baby," "Kissin' Cousins," "Viva Las Vegas," and "Crying in the Chapel" (recorded in 1960) ensuing. Elvis Presley recorded perhaps the finest gospel album of his career, *How Great Thou Art,* for 1967 release. He married Priscilla Beaulieu on May 1, 1967, and his only child, daughter Lisa Marie, was born on February 1, 1968.

In 1968, with the first inkling of a revival of interest in '50s rock 'n' roll, Elvis Presley returned to television for an attempted comeback. Less than a week before the airing of his special, one of his finer latter-day singles, "If I Can Dream," became a near-smash pop hit. The special, televised on NBC on December 3, 1968, featured large-scale production numbers and Presley performing in front of a small audience with old associates Scotty Moore and D. J. Fontana (Bill Black had died on October 21, 1965). The special was one of the five highest-rated shows of the television year and included both "If I Can Dream" and the haunting hit "Memories." It represented, in many ways, the peak of Elvis Presley's career.

Elvis Presley returned to Memphis for the first time in fourteen years to record his next album, *From Elvis in Memphis,* for which he personally chose the songs. Generally regarded as one of his finest latter-day albums, it yielded a smash hit with Mac Davis's socially conscious "In the Ghetto" and included "Power of Love," "Any Day Now," and "Long Black Limousine." Elvis returned to live performance on July 31, 1969, with a monthlong engagement at the International Hotel (later the Hilton) in Las Vegas, backed by a thirty-piece orchestra, chorus, and a five-man combo featuring guitarist James Burton and keyboardist Glen D. Hardin, two of the better instrumentalists in the country. Recordings from the stand comprised the first record of *From Memphis to Vegas / From Vegas to Memphis,* while the second record (later issued as *Elvis Back in Memphis*) was taken from the Memphis sessions. The latter record included "Without Love (There Is Nothing)," "Do You Know Who I Am," and "Stranger in My Own Home." In the meantime, Presley scored a top hit with "Suspicious Minds," a smash hit with Mac Davis's "Don't Cry Daddy," and a major hit with Eddie Rabbit's "Kentucky Rain."

After another monthlong appearance at the International Hotel in February 1970, Elvis Presley began touring selected venues across the United States that would continue until his death in 1977, although he performed infrequently in Las Vegas after 1975. He scored a near-smash country hit with "There Goes My Everything" in 1971 and a smash pop hit with "Burning Love" in 1972. On January 14, 1973, Presley performed at a Honolulu benefit that produced his last major hit album, *Aloha from Hawaii.* Broadcast on NBC-TV and relayed via satellite to forty countries, the special was viewed by an estimated audience of one billion.

At this time Presley's fortunes again began to fade. He and Priscilla divorced on October 11, 1973, and his subsequent live performances became careless and mechanical, as rumors of drug abuse and erratic personal behavior began to circulate. Most of his subsequent successes came in the country field, where he had smash hits with "I've Got a Thing About You," "Help Me," "It's Midnight," "Hurt," "Moody Blue," and "Way Down." His last live performance took place in Indianapolis on June 26, 1977. On August 16, 1977, Elvis Presley died at the age of forty-two in his Graceland mansion in Memphis of heart failure due to prescription drug abuse.

Within three months of Elvis Presley's death, his rendition of "My Way," Frank Sinatra's theme song, became a major pop and smash country hit. The spate of Elvis-related books began the month of his death with *Elvis: What Happened?* by three former members of the Memphis Mafia. In 1981 Albert Goldman's contemptuous biography *Elvis* was published by McGraw-Hill. The Elvis Presley estate opened Graceland to public viewing in 1982, and the mansion became the second most-visited home in America. In 1983, by means of an out-of-court settlement, "Colonel" Tom Parker severed his connection with the estate, which was overseen by Priscilla Presley. Through shrewd merchandising and licensing, Priscilla Presley increased the value of the Presley estate from $5 million to $100 million. In 1992, heir Lisa Marie Presley signed an agreement giving her mother the authority to run the estate for an additional five years (until 1998). "Colonel" Tom Parker died in Las Vegas on January 21, 1997, at the age of eighty-seven of complications from a stroke.

On what would have been Elvis's fiftieth birthday, RCA issued the six-record compilation set of live performances, *A Golden Celebration*. In 1985 Macmillan published *Elvis and Gladys* by Elaine Dundy, and Putnam published Priscilla Presley's *Elvis and Me*. Elvis Presley was inducted into the Rock and Roll Hall of Fame in its inaugural year, 1986. In 1987 the Cinemax cable network broadcast *Elvis '56*, perhaps the most telling of all filmic biographies. In 1988 *Elvis and Me*, based on Priscilla's book, became the top-rated miniseries of the television season and the lavish multimedia production *Elvis: An American Musical* ran in Las Vegas for two months. An Elvis television series ran on ABC television in 1990, and in 1992 RCA released the 5-CD set *The Complete 50's Masters*, arguably the single most important body of work in the history of rock 'n' roll. On the anniversary of Elvis's fifty-eighth birthday the United States Postal Service issued 500 million Elvis stamps, of which an estimated 60 percent were never used. During 1994 longtime Elvis friend Joe Esposito's *Good Rockin' Tonight: Twenty Years on the Road and on the Town with Elvis* was published by Simon & Schuster, and Peter Guralnick's *Last Train to Memphis: The Rise of Elvis Presley* was published by Little, Brown. In 1996 the first ballet based on the music of Elvis Presley, *Blue Suede Shoes*, premiered in Cleveland, and the production made its West Coast debut in San Jose, California, in 1997.

BIBLIOGRAPHY

Hopkins, Jerry. *Elvis: A Biography*. New York: Simon & Schuster, 1971.

_____. *Elvis: The Final Years*. New York: St. Martin's, 1980; New York: Berkley, 1983.

Lichter, Paul. *Elvis in Hollywood*. New York: Simon & Schuster, 1975.

_____. *The Boy Who Dared to Rock: The Definitive Elvis*. Garden City, NY: Dolphin Books, 1978; New York: Gallahad Books, 1982.

Mann, May. *Elvis and the Colonel: From the Intimate Diaries of May Mann*. New York: Drake, 1975.

Barry, Ron. *The Elvis Presley American Discography*. Phillipsburg, NJ: Spectator Service, Maxigraphics, 1976.

Harbinson, William Allen. *The Illustrated Elvis*. New York: Grosset & Dunlap, 1976.

Jones, Peter. *Elvis*. London: Octopus, 1976.

Zmijewsky, Steve. *The Films and Career of Elvis Presley*. Seacaucus, NJ: Citadel, 1976.

Farren, Mick, comp. *Elvis in His Own Words*. New York: Quick Fox, 1977.

West, Red, Sonny West, and Dave Hebler, as told to Steve Dunleavy. *Elvis: What Happened?* New York: Ballantine, 1977.

Roggero, John. *Elvis in Concert*. New York: dis. by Dell, 1979.

Crumbaker, Marge, with Gabe Tucker. *Up and Down with Elvis Presley*. New York: Putnam's, 1981.

Goldman, Albert. *Elvis*. New York: McGraw-Hill, 1981.

Hawkins, Martin, and Colin Escott. *The Illustrated Discography*. London: Omnibus, 1981.

_____. *Elvis Presley*. London: Omnibus, 1987.

Whisler, John A. *Elvis Presley Reference Guide and Discography*. Metuchen, NJ: Scarecrow, 1981.

Worth, Fred L. and Steve D. Tamerius. *All About Elvis*. New York: Bantam, 1981.

_____. *Elvis: His Life from A to Z*. Chicago: Contemporary Books, 1988; New York: Wings Books, 1992.

Carr, Roy. *Elvis Presley: An Illustrated Record*. New York: Harmony, 1982.

Marsh, Dave. *Elvis*. New York: Times Books, 1982; New York: Thunder's Mouth, 1992.

Torgoff, Martin, ed. *The Complete Elvis.* New York: Delilah Books, dis. Putnam's, 1982.

Cotten, Lee. *All Shook Up: Elvis Day-by-Day, 1954–1977.* Ann Arbor, MI: Pierian, 1985.

_____. *The Elvis Catalog.* Garden City, NY: Doubleday, 1987.

_____. "Elvis on Disc." *Pulse!* no. 52 (August 1987): 48, 49, 51, 58, 59.

_____, and Howard A. DeWitt. *Jailhouse Rock: The Bootleg Records of Elvis Presley, 1970–1983.* Ann Arbor, MI: Pierian, 1983.

Tobler, John, and Richard Wootton. *Elvis: The Legend and the Music.* New York: Crescent Books, dis. Crown, 1983.

Sauers, Wendy. *Elvis Presley, A Complete Reference.* Jefferson, NC: McFarland, 1984.

Hammontree, Patsy Guy. *Elvis Presley, A Bio-Bibliography.* Westport, CT: Greenwood, 1985.

Presley, Priscilla, with Sandra Harmon. *Elvis and Me.* New York: Putnam's, 1985.

Vellenga, Dirk. *Elvis and the Colonel.* New York: Delacorte, 1988.

Geller, Larry, and Joel Spector with Patricia Romanowski. *If I Can Dream: Elvis' Own Story.* New York: Simon & Schuster, 1989.

McLafferty, Gerry. *Elvis Presley in Hollywood: Celluloid Sell-Out.* London: Hale, 1989.

Greenwood, Earl, and Kathleen Tracy. *The Boy Who Would Be King: An Intimate Portrait of Elvis Presley.* New York: Dutton, 1990.

Latham, Caroline, and Jeannie Sakol. *"E" Is For Elvis: An A-to-Z Illustrated Guide to the King of Rock and Roll.* New York: New American Library, 1990.

Marcus, Greil. *Dead Elvis: A Chronicle of a Cultural Obsession.* New York: Doubleday, 1991.

Thompson, Charles C., II, and James P. Cale. *The Death of Elvis: What Really Happened.* New York: Delacorte, 1991.

Quain, Kevin, ed. *The Elvis Reader: Texts and Sources on the King of Rock 'n' Roll.* New York: St. Martin's, 1992.

DeWitt, Howard A. *Elvis, the Sun Years: The Story of Elvis Presley in the '50s.* Ann Arbor, MI: Popular Culture, 1993.

Schroer, Andreas. *Private Elvis: The Missing Years, Elvis in Germany.* New York: Morrow, 1993.

Allen, William. *Elvis.* New York: Smithmark, 1994.

Esposito, Joe, and Elena Oumano. *Good Rockin' Tonight: Twenty Years on the Road and on the Town with Elvis.* New York: Simon & Schuster, 1994.

Guralnick, Peter. *Last Train to Memphis: The Rise of Elvis Presley.* Boston: Little, Brown, 1994.

Pierce, Patricia Jobe. *The Ultimate Elvis: Elvis Presley Day by Day.* New York: Simon & Schuster, 1994.

Stanley, David. *The Elvis Encyclopedia.* Los Angeles: General Publishing Group, 1994.

Nash, Alanna. *Elvis Aron Presley: Revelations from the Memphis Mafia.* New York: HarperCollins, 1995.

Gordon, Robert. *The King on the Road: Elvis on Tour, 1954–1977.* New York: St. Martin's, 1996.

Rodman, Gilbert B. *Elvis after Elvis: The Posthumous Career of a Living Legend.* London and New York: Routledge, 1996.

Whitman, Peter O. *The Inner Elvis: A Psychological Biography of Elvis Aron Presley.* New York: Hyperion, 1996.

Moore, Scotty, and James Dickerson. *That's Alright, Elvis: The Untold Story of Elvis's First Guitarist and Manager, Scotty Moore.* New York: Schirmer Books, 1997.

Early Recordings

The Sun Sessions	RCA	1675	'76	†
	RCA	3893		†
The Complete Sun Sessions	RCA	(2)6414	'87	LP†
	RCA	6414	'87	CS/CD
The First Live Recordings (recorded 1955–1956)	Music Works	3601	'84	†

Elvis Presley	RCA	1254	'56	†
	RCA	5198	'84	CS/CD
	RCA	66659	'95	CD
Elvis	RCA	1382	'56	†
	RCA	5199	'84	LP/CS/CD†
	RCA	50283	'94	CS/CD
The Million Dollar Quartet (recorded December 4, 1956)	RCA	2023	'90	LP/CS/CD
Elvis '56	RCA	66856	'96	CS/CD
Elvis '56 Collector's Edition	RCA	66817	'96	CD
Stereo '57	RCA	9589	'89	CS/CD
The Elvis Tapes (interviews recorded in 1957)	Ace	1		CD
Rocker (recorded 1956–1957)	RCA	5182	'84	CS/CD
Elvis' Christmas Album	RCA	1035	'57	†
	RCA	1951	'58	†
	RCA-Camden	2428	'70	CS/CD
	RCA	5486	'85	CS/CD
For LP Fans Only	RCA	1990	'59	CS/CD
A Date with Elvis	RCA	2011	'59/'89	CS/CD
The Complete 50's Masters	RCA	(5)66050	'92	CS/CD
Elvis Is Back	RCA	2231	'60/'88	CD
I Was the One (recorded 1956–1960)	RCA	4678	'83	†

Scotty Moore

The Guitar That Changed the World	Epic	26103	'64	†

Sound Tracks

Loving You	RCA	1515	'57/'88	CS/CD
	RCA	7452	'97	CS/CD
Jailhouse Rock	RCA	7453	'97	CS/CD
King Creole	RCA	1884	'58	†
	RCA	3733		LP/CS/CD
	RCA	7454	'97	CS/CD
G.I. Blues	RCA	2256	'60	†
	RCA	3735		CS/CD
	RCA	7460	'97	CS/CD
Blue Hawaii	RCA	2426	'61	†
	RCA	3683		LP/CS/CD
	RCA	6959	'97	CS/CD
Girls! Girls! Girls!	RCA	2621	'62	†
It Happened at the World's Fair	RCA	2697	'63	†
	RCA	2568	'77	†
Fun in Acapulco	RCA	2756	'63	†
Kissin' Cousins	RCA	2894	'64	†
	RCA	4115	'82	†
Roustabout	RCA	2999	'64	†
Girl Happy	RCA	3338	'65	LP
	RCA	1018		CS
Harum Scarum	RCA	3468	'65	†
	RCA	2558	'77	†
	RCA	3734		†
Frankie and Johnny	RCA	3553	'66	†
	RCA	2559	'77	†

Paradise Hawaiian Style	RCA	3643	'66	†
Spinout	RCA	3702	'66	†
	RCA	2560	'77	†
	RCA	3676	'80	†
	RCA	3684		†
Double Trouble	RCA	3787	'67	†
	RCA	2564	'77	†
Clambake	RCA	3893	'67	†
	RCA	2565	'77	†
Speedway	RCA	3989	'68	†
That's the Way It Is	RCA	4445	'70	†
	RCA	4114		CS
	RCA	54114		CD
	Mobile Fidelity	560	'92	CD
This Is Elvis (selections)	RCA	(2)4031	'81	CS

Sound-Track Compilations

Essential Elvis–The First Movies				
(*Love Me Tender, Jailhouse Rock,* and *Loving You*)	RCA	6738	'88	LP/CS/CD
Harum Scarum/Girl Happy	RCA	66128	'93	CS/CD
Roustabout/Viva Las Vegas	RCA	66129	'93	CS/CD
Girls! Girls! Girls!/Kid Galahad	RCA	66130	'93	CS/CD
It Happened at the World's Fair/ Fun in Acapulco	RCA	66131	'93	CS/CD
Frankie and Johnny/Paradise	RCA	66360	'94	CS/CD
Hawaiian Style Spinout/Double Trouble	RCA	66361	'94	CS/CD
Kissin' Cousins/Clambake/ Stay Away Joe	RCA	66362	'94	CS/CD
Flaming Star/Wild in the Country/Follow That Dream	RCA	66557	'95	CS/CD
Easy Come, Easy Go/Speedway	RCA	66558	'95	CS/CD
Live a Little, Love a Little/ Charro!/	RCA	66559	'95	CS/CD
The Trouble with Girls/Change of Habit				

Gospel Albums

His Hand in Mine	RCA	2328	'60	†
	RCA	1319	'76/'88	CD
	RCA	3935		LP/CS
How Great Thou Art	RCA	3758	'67/'88	LP/CS/CD
He Touched Me	RCA	4690	'72	†
	RCA	1923		CS
	RCA	51923		CD
He Walks Beside Me	RCA	2772	'78	CS
You'll Never Walk Alone	RCA-Camden	2472	'71	CS/CD
Elvis Gospel, 1957–1971	RCA	9586	'89	CS/CD
Amazing Grace: His Greatest Sacred Performances	RCA	(2)66421	'94	CS/CD
Promised Land	RCA	0873		CS/CD

Christmas Albums

Elvis' Christmas Album	RCA	1035	'57	†
	RCA	1951	'58	†
	RCA-Camden	2428	'70	CS/CD
	RCA	5486	'85	CS/CD
Elvis Sings "The Wonderful World of Christmas"	RCA	4579	'71/'88	CD
	RCA	1936	'76	LP/CS
Memories of Christmas	RCA	4395	'87	CS/CD

Blue Christmas	RCA	9800	'89	CS
	RCA	59800		CS/CD
If Every Day Was Christmas	RCA	66482	'94	CS/CD
	RCA	66506	'96	CD

Other RCA Albums 1960–1977

Something for Everybody	RCA	2370	'61	CS/CD
Pot Luck	RCA	2523	'62/'88	CS/CD
The Lost Album (recorded in in Nashville in 1963–1964)	RCA	61024	'91	CS/CD
Elvis for Everyone	RCA	3450	'65/'90	CS/CD†
	RCA	4232	'82	†
	RCA	53450	'95	CS/CD
Elvis (TV Special)	RCA	4088	'68	†
TV Special	RCA	3894		CS
NBC TV Special	RCA	61021	'91	CS/CD
From Elvis in Memphis	RCA	4155	'69	†
	RCA	1456		CS
	RCA	51456		CD
From Memphis to Vegas/From Vegas to Memphis	RCA	(2)6020	'69	†
From Memphis to Vegas	RCA	(2)2656		CS†
The Memphis Record	RCA	6221	'87	CS/CD
(reissue of From Elvis in Memphis and From Vegas to Memphis)				
On Stage (February 1970)	RCA	4362	'70	CS
	RCA	54362		CD
At the International Hotel, Las Vegas	RCA	4428	'70	†
	RCA	3892		CS
	RCA	53892	'92	CD
Back in Memphis	RCA	4429	'70	†
	RCA	61081	'92	CS/CD
Elvis Country	RCA	4460	'71	†
	RCA	3956		†
	RCA Nashville	66405	'94	CD
I'm 10,000 Years Old/Elvis Country	RCA	66279	'93	CS/CD
Love Letters from Elvis	RCA	4530	'71	†
	RCA	54350	'92	CS/CD
Elvis Now	RCA	4671	'72	†
	RCA	54671	'93	CS/CD
Live at Madison Square Garden	RCA	4776	'72	CS
	RCA	54776	'92	CD
Aloha from Hawaii	RCA	(2)6089	'73	†
	RCA	2642		CS
	RCA	52642		CD
The Alternate Aloha	RCA	6985	'88	CS/CD
Elvis	RCA	0283	'73	†
Raised on Rock	RCA	0388	'73	†
	RCA	50388	'94	CS/CD
Good Times	RCA	0475	'74	†
	RCA	50475	'94	CS/CD
Live on Stage in Memphis	RCA	0606	'74	CS
	RCA	50606	'94	CD
Having Fun with Elvis on Stage	RCA	0818	'74	†

Promised Land	RCA	0873	'75	CS/CD
Today	RCA	1039	'75	†
	RCA	51039	'92	CS/CD
From Elvis Presley Boulevard	RCA	1506	'76	CS/CD
Welcome to My World	RCA	2274	'77	CS
	RCA	52274	'92	CD
Moody Blue	RCA	2428	'77	CS/CD
In Concert	RCA	2587	'77	CS
	RCA	52587	'92	CD

Evis's Golden Records

Elvis' Golden Records, Vol. 1	RCA	1707	'58	†
	RCA	5196	'84	CS/CD†
	RCA	67462	'97	CS/CD
Elvis' Golden Records, Vol. 2	RCA	2075	'59	†
50,000,000 Elvis Fans Can't Be Wrong	RCA	5197	'84	CS/CD†
	RCA	67463	'97	CS/CD
Elvis' Golden Records, Vol. 3	RCA	2765	'63	LP/CD†
	RCA	1057		CS†
	RCA	67464	'97	CS/CD
Elvis' Golden Records, Vol. 4	RCA	3921	'68	†
	RCA	1297		CS/CD†
	RCA	67465	'97	CS/CD
Elvis' Golden Records, Vol. 5	RCA	4941	'84	CS/CD†
	RCA	67466	'97	CS/CD

Elvis's Worldwide 50 Gold Award Hits

Elvis' Worldwide 50 Gold Award Hits, Vol. 1	RCA	(4)6401	'70	†
Elvis' Worldwide 50 Gold Award Hits, Vol. 1, Parts 1 and 2	RCA	(2)6401	'88	CD
Elvis' Worldwide 50 Gold Award Hits, Vol. 1, No. 1	RCA	1773		CS
Elvis' Worldwide 50 Gold Award Hits, Vol. 1, No. 2	RCA	1774		CS
Elvis' Worldwide 50 Gold Award Hits, Vol. 1, No. 3	RCA	1775		CS
Elvis' Worldwide 50 Gold Award Hits, Vol. 1, No. 4	RCA	1776		CS
The Other Sides: Worldwide Gold Award Hits, Vol. 2	RCA	(4)6402	'71	†
	RCA	(2)66921	'96	CD

A Legendary Performer

A Legendary Performer, Vol. 1	RCA	0341	'74	CS
A Legendary Performer, Vol. 2	RCA	1349	'76	LP/CS†
A Legendary Performer, Vol. 3	RCA	3082	'78	†
A Legendary Performer, Vol. 4	RCA	4848	'84	CS†

More Anthologies and Compilations

Pure Gold	RCA	0971	'75	†
	RCA	3732		CS
	RCA	53732	'92	CD
Elvis Sings for Children and Grownups, Too	RCA	2901	'78	†
A Canadian Tribute	RCA	7065	'78	†
Our Memories of Elvis	RCA	3279	'79	†
Our Memories of Elvis, Vol. 2	RCA	3448	'79	†
Elvis Aron Presley: 1955–1980	RCA	(8)3699	'80	†

Guitar Man	RCA	3917	'81	†
Greatest Hits, Vol. 1	RCA	2347	'81	†
The Elvis Medley	RCA	4530	'82	†
A Golden Celebration	RCA	(6)5172	'84	CS†
A Valentine Gift for You	RCA	5353	'85	CS/CD
Reconsider Baby (Elvis Sings the Blues)	RCA	5418	'85	CS/CD
Always on My Mind	RCA	5430	'85	CS/CD
Return of the Rocker (recorded 1960–1963)	RCA	5600	'86	LP/CS/CD†
Elvis Country	RCA	6330		CS/CD†
The Number One Hits	RCA	6382	'87	LP/CS/CD
The Top Ten Hits	RCA	6383	'87	CS
	RCA	(2)6383	'87	LP/CD
Elvis in Nashville	RCA	8468	'88	CS/CD†
Heartbreak Hotel, Hound Dog and Other Top Ten Hits	RCA	2079	'90	CS/CD
The Great Performances	RCA	2227	'90	LP/CS/CD
Hits Like Never Before	RCA	2229	'91	CS/CD
Elvis Sings Leiber and Stoller–Plus Missing Presley Duet	RCA	3026	'91	CS/CD
Collectors Gold	RCA	(3)3114	'91	CS/CD
From Nashville to Memphis: the Essential '60s Masters 1	RCA	(5)66160	'93	CS/CD
Heart and Soul	RCA	66532	'94	CS/CD
Command Performances: The Essential '60s Masters 2	RCA	66601	'95	CS/CD
Walk a Mile in My Shoes: The Essential '70s Masters	RCA	(5)66670	'95	CS/CD
A Hundred Years From Now: Essential Elvis, Vol. 4	RCA	66866	'96	CS/CD
Platinum: A Life in Music	RCA	67469	'97	CS/CD
Elvis' Greatest Jukebox Hits	RCA	67565	'97	CS/CD
Elvis Presley Live	Musketeer	9017	'96	CD
Elvis: A Portrait	Musketeer	(2)9517	'96	CD
Symphonic Elvis	Teldec	94573	'96	CS/CD
Elvis	Special Music	(4)4965		CS/CD

Budget Albums

Elvis Sings Flaming Star	RCA-Camden	2304	'69	CS
Let's Be Friends	RCA-Camden	2408	'70	CS
Almost in Love	RCA-Camden	2440	'70	CS
C'mon Everybody	RCA-Camden	2518	'71	CS
I Got Lucky	RCA-Camden	2533	'71	CS
Elvis Sings Hits from His Movies	RCA-Camden	2567	'72	CS
Burning Love and Hits from His Movies, Vol. 2	RCA-Camden	2595		CS/CD
Separate Ways	RCA-Camden	2611	'73	CS
Love Me Tender	RCA-Camden	2650		CS
Double Dynamite	Camden	(2)5001		†
Mahalo	Camden	7064		†
Songs for Children	RCA-Camden	2704		CS/CD
A Legendary Performer, Vol.1	RCA-Camden	2705		CS/CD
A Legendary Performer, Vol. 2	RCA-Camden	2706		CS/CD
Double Dynamite	Pair	1010	'86	CD
Remembering	Pair	1037	'86	CS/CD
Elvis Aron Presley Forever	Pair	1185	'88	CD
Great Performances	Pair	1251		CS/CD
Elvis Country	K-Tel	393		CS

JIMMY REED

Born September 6, 1925, in Dunleith, Mississippi; died August 29, 1976, in Oakland, California.

One of the most influential blues artists of the '50s, Jimmy Reed provided perhaps the first exposure of the blues to the mass white audience with his direct, unsophisticated hit recordings from 1955 to 1961. Recording the classics "Baby What You Want Me to Do" and "Big Boss Man," Reed sang in a mumbled, slurred style that impressed artists as diverse as Slim Harpo, Elvis Presley, and Mick Jagger. Perhaps the most popular blues artist of the '50s, Jimmy Reed outsold virtually every practitioner of the blues during the decade, except for B. B. King.

Born on a plantation in Mississippi, Jimmy Reed grew up with Eddie Taylor, who later became a semiprofessional musician and taught Reed the fundamentals of guitar and harmonica as a youth. Moving to Chicago in 1943, Reed served in the Navy from 1944 to 1945. Following his discharge, he married and moved to Gary, Indiana, reuniting with Taylor in 1949 in a musical partnership the lasted through the '60s. Frequently playing Chicago area clubs, Reed first recorded for the Chance label in 1953 and subsequently failed an audition with Chess Records. He soon signed with the newly formed Chicago-based VeeJay label, for whom he recorded until 1965. Playing simple guitar and harmonica accompanied by guitarist Taylor, Reed scored his first R&B hit (a smash) in 1955 with "You Don't Have to Go." Subsequent R&B smashes included "Ain't That Lovin' You Baby", "You've Got Me Dizzy," and "Little Rain," and by 1958 Reed was established as Chicago's biggest-drawing blues act.

Jimmy Reed scored his biggest success with 1957's "Honest I Do, " a smash R&B and moderate pop hit, followed by the R&B smash "I'm Gonna Get My Baby." Developing severe problems with unreliability and alcoholism, he was nonetheless consistently on both charts in the early '60s, beginning with the classic "Baby What You Want Me to Do." Scoring his last R&B and pop crossovers with "Big Boss Man" and "Bright Lights Big City" in 1961, Reed's *At Carnegie Hall* album was actually a studio re-creation of his live concert.

Jimmy Reed toured Great Britain in 1963, and with the demise of VeeJay Records in 1966, recorded with little success for Exodus and the BluesWay subsidary of ABC in the latter half of the '60s. He toured Europe with the American Folk Blues Festival in 1968 and recorded for a variety of labels in the '70s . Afflicted with epilepsy since 1957, Reed toured until the mid '70s , despite the condition and his chronic alcoholism. On August 29, 1976, he died of respiratory failure after an epileptic seizure in Oakland, California, at the age of fifty. Jimmy Reed was inducted into the Blues Foundation's Hall of Fame in 1980 and the Rock and Roll Hall of Fame in 1991.

Jimmy Reed

I'm Jimmy Reed	VeeJay	1004	'58	†
Rockin' with Reed	VeeJay	1008	'59	†
Found Love	VeeJay	1022	'60	†
Now Appearing	VeeJay	1025	'60	†
Jimmy Reed a Carnegie Hall	VeeJay	(2)1035	'61	†
Just Jimmy Reed	VeeJay	1050	'62	†
T'Ain't No Big Thing	VeeJay	1067	'63	†
The Best of the Blues	VeeJay	1072	'63	†
The Twelve String Guitar Blues	VeeJay	1073	'64	†
Jimmy Reed at Soul City	VeeJay	1095	'64	†
The Legend, the Man	VeeJay	8501	'65	†
Jimmy Reed at Carnegie Hall	Exodus	(2)307		†
Just Jimmy Reed	Exodus	310		†

Sings the Best of the Blues	Exodus	311		†
The New Jimmy Reed Album	BluesWay	6004	'67	†
Soulin'	BluesWay	6009	'67	†
Big Boss Man	BluesWay	6013	'68	†
Down in Virginia	BluesWay	6024	'69	†
Jimmy Reed at Carnegie Hall	BluesWay	(2)6073	'73	†
Let the Bossman Speak	Blue On Blues	10001	'71	†

Jimmy Reed and Johnny Winter

Live at Liberty Hall Houston Texas 1972	New Rose	5113	'93	CD

Anthologies and Compilations

The Best of Jimmy Reed	VeeJay	1039	'61	†
Jimmy Reed at Carnegie Hall/ The Best of Jimmy Reed	Mobile Fidelity	00566	'92	CD
More of the Best of Jimmy Reed	VeeJay	1080	'64	†
Time to Dance	Ace	1023	'63	†
Best	Exodus	308		†
Somethin' Else	Sunset	5218	'68	†
Very Best	Buddah	4003	'69	†
Jimmy Reed	Archive of Folk and Jazz Music/Everest	234	'69	†
Wailin' the Blues	Tradition	2069	'69	†
Soul Greats	Up Front	101		†
The Soulful Sound of Jimmy Reed	Up Front	108	'70	†
Best	Up Front	125		†
History of	Trip	(2)8012	'72	†
I Ain't from Chicago	BluesWay	6054	'73	†
The Ultimate Jimmy Reed	BluesWay	6067	'73	†
The Best of Jimmy Reed	GNP Crescendo	(2)10006	'74	LP/CS
	GNP Crescendo	0006		CD
Cold Chills	Antilles	7007	'76	†
Greatest Hits	Hollywood/IMG	445		CS
The Classic Recordings	Tomato	(3)71660	'95	CD

NEIL SEDAKA

Born March 13, 1939, in Brooklyn, New York.

Coming from a doo-wop background, yet classically trained, Neil Sedaka composed more than 1,000 tunes, including a dozen major pop hits he recorded between 1959 and 1963 that were coauthored with Howard Greenfield, his lyricist until 1972. Toiling at New York's famed Brill Building under Don Kirshner, the team achieved their first success as the writers of Connie Francis's "Stupid Cupid." Sedaka's own hits included "Oh! Carol," written for fellow songwriter Carole King, and "Breaking Up Is Hard to Do," perhaps his finest song. Sedaka ceased performing and recording after his popularity faded with the advent of the British Invasion, yet he continued to write songs. In the early '70s Sedaka successfully attempted a comeback, first in Great Britain and then in the United States. Signing with Elton John's Rocket label, he scored top pop hits with "Laughter in the Rain" and "Bad Blood." Although his careful mixture of early and recent material worked well on television and the cabaret circuit, Neil Sedaka has not had a major hit since 1980's "Should've Never Let You Go," recorded with his daughter Dara.

Extensively trained in the classics on piano from the age of nine, Neil Sedaka wrote his first song with sixteen-year-old Brooklyn buddy Howard "Howie" Greenfield when he was thirteen. Sedaka joined the high school vocal group the Tokens with Hank Medress in 1955, recording two Sedaka-Greenfield songs. Medress later realigned the group in the '60s, scoring a top hit with "The Lion Sleeps Tonight." In 1957 Sedaka won a piano scholarship to the famed Juilliard School of Music, where he studied for two years.

In 1958, through songwriters Doc Pomus and Mort Shuman, Sedaka and Greenfield were signed as professional songwriters to Al Nevins and Don Kirshner's Aldon Publishing Company, housed in New York's Brill Building, where Carole King, Gerry Goffin, Barry Mann, and Cynthia Weil worked. Sedaka and Greenfield's first songwriting success came in the summer of 1958 when Connie Francis had a major hit with their "Stupid Cupid." They later provided her with "Where the Boys Are," and Greenfield also coauthored her hits "Everybody's Somebody's Fool," "My Heart Has a Mind of Its Own," and "Breakin' in a Brand New Heart," as well as the Shirelles' "Foolish Little Girl."

Neil Sedaka signed his own recording contract with RCA-Victor Records and soon achieved a major pop and R&B hit with "The Diary" at the end of 1958. In 1959 he toured Great Britain for the first time and played piano on Bobby Darin's smash pop and R&B hit "Dream Lover." Over the next four years, he regularly scored major pop hits with Greenfield collaborations such as "Oh! Carol," written for Carole King, "Stairway to Heaven," and "Calendar Girl" (both near-smash hits), the classic "Breaking Up Is Hard to Do" (a top hit), and "Next Door to an Angel," all of which became major R&B hits. "Little Devil" and "Happy Birthday, Sweet Sixteen," one of their most enduring compositions, were near-smash pop-only hits, and Sedaka achieved his last moderate hits for more than ten years with "Alice in Wonderland," "Let's Go Steady Again," and "Bad Girl" in 1963. In early 1962 the Everly Brothers scored a near-smash pop hit with "Crying in the Rain," cowritten by Howie Greenfield and Carole King.

In 1966, after three years of relative failure, Neil Sedaka ceased recording and live performances to concentrate on his songwriting with Greenfield. In 1969–70 their songs "Working on a Groovy Thing" and "Puppet Man" became major pop hits for the Fifth Dimension. Buoyed by the 1971 success of Carole King's *Tapestry*, Sedaka attempted a comeback on mentor Don Kirshner's Kirshner label with *Emergence*, which he regarded as his best album. The 1971 album failed to sell in the United States, but he nonetheless encountered success in Great Britain, returning to live performance at London's Royal Albert Hall. In 1972 Sedaka moved to London, where he teamed with new lyricist Phil Cody, effectively ending his partnership with Greenfield, who died in Los Angeles on March 4, 1986, at the age of forty-nine.

Neil Sedaka produced his second Kirshner album, *Solitaire*, recording it and the British-only album *The Tra-La Days Are Over* with a group called Hot Legs, which later became 10 cc. He subsequently recorded two more British albums, and in 1974 he was signed by Elton John's newly formed Rocket label. Sedaka's first Rocket album, *Sedaka's Back*, was a compilation of songs from his three British albums and produced three American pop hits, the top hit "Laughter in the Rain," written with Phil Cody, and the major hits "The Immigrant" (dedicated to John Lennon) and "That's When the Music Takes Me." In 1975 the Captain and Tenille scored a top hit with Neil Sedaka and Howie Greenfield's "Love Will Keep Us Together," and the Carpenters achieved a major hit with Sedaka and Phil Cody's "Solitaire." Sedaka's *The Hungry Years* yielded a top hit with "Bad Blood," recorded with Elton John and cowritten with Cody, and a near-smash with an engaging, slowed-down version of "Breaking Up Is Hard to Do." Sedaka subsequently scored a major hit with "Love in the Shadows" and a moderate hit with "Steppin' Out" on Rocket. He appeared in his first American television special on NBC in 1976.

Neil Sedaka switched to Elektra Records in 1977 and managed his last (major) hit in 1980 with "Should've Never Let You Go," recorded with his daughter Dara. *My Friend* was a collection of recordings he made between 1974 and 1980. In 1982 Putnam published Sedaka's autobiography *Laughter in the Rain*. In the mid '90s, Neil Sedaka enjoyed European success with recordings of his own lyrics put to the classical melodies of Chopin, Tchaikovsky, and Rachmaninoff, among others.

BIBLIOGRAPHY

Sedaka, Neil. *Laughter in the Rain: My Own Story.* New York: Putnam's, 1982.

Neil Sedaka

Neil Sedaka	RCA-Victor	2035	'59	†
Circulate	RCA-Victor	2317	'60	†
Little Devil and His Other Hits	RCA-Victor	2421	'61	†
Italiano	RCA	10140	'64	†
Live in Australia	RCA	1540	'76	†
Emergence	Kirshner	111	'71	†
	RCA	1789	'76	†
Solitaire	Kirshner	117	'72	†
	RCA	1790	'76	†
Sedaka's Back	MCA/Rocket	463	'74	†
	Rocket	3046	'75	†
The Hungry Years	Rocket	2157	'75	†
Steppin' Out	Rocket	2195	'76	†
	Rocket	3049	'78	†
A Song	Elektra	102	'77	†
All You Need Is Music	Elektra	161	'78	†
In the Pocket	Elektra	259	'80	†
Now	Elektra	348	'81	†
Superbird	Intermedia	5015		LP/CS
Come See About Me	MCA	5466	'84	†
Tuneweaver	Varese Sarabande	5549	'95	CD

Anthologies and Compilations

Sings His Greatest Hits	RCA-Victor	2627	'62	†
	RCA	0928	'75	†
	RCA	3465		CS
	RCA	53465	'92	CD
Oh! Carol and Other Hits	RCA	0879	'75	†
	RCA	2088	'90	CS
Pure Gold	RCA	1314	'76	†
'50s and '60s	RCA	2254	'77	†
Many Sides	RCA	2524	'78	†
All Time Greatest Hits	RCA	6876	'88	CS/CD
All Time Greatest Hits, Vol. 2	RCA	2406	'91	CS/CD
Let's Go Steady Again	RCA-Camden	1151	'75	†
Stupid Cupid	RCA-Camden	1147	'76	†
Oh! Carol and Other Big Hits	RCA-Camden	2701		CS/CD
Breaking Up Is Hard to Do–The Original Hits	Pickwick	7006	'76	†

Greatest Hits	Rocket	2297	'77	†
My Friend (recorded 1974–1980)	Polydor	(2)831235	'86	LP/CS/CD†
	Polydor	831235		CS
Singer, Songwriter, Melody Maker	Accord	7152	'81	†
Neil Sedaka's Diary	Pair	1283	'91	CS/CD†
Greatest Hits Live	K-Tel	3083	'92	CS/CD
Laughter in the Rain: The Best of Neil Sedaka	Varese Sarabande	5539	'94	CS/CD

BIG JOE TURNER

Born May 18, 1911, in Kansas City, Missouri; died November 24, 1985, in Inglewood, California.

Providing an essential link between the blues and rock 'n' roll, Big Joe Turner is best remembered for his classic 1954 hit "Shake, Rattle and Roll," one of the pioneering songs of rock 'n' roll. Although Turner enjoyed his greatest recorded success with Atlantic Records between 1951 and 1956, rock 'n' roll was actually his second (or third) successful musical career. He started out as an important member of the burgeoning Kansas City jazz scene and helped popularize boogie woogie in the late '30s with pianist Pete Johnson. He also pursued an influential career as one of the most potent blues shouters of the '40s. He was one of the few jazz and blues singers of his generation to become popular with the teenage rock 'n' roll audience. After spending the '60s in relative obscurity, Big Joe Turner returned to jazz and blues, singing on the Pablo label with the likes of Count Basie and Jimmy Witherspoon.

Big Joe Turner began singing in Kansas City clubs in his early teens and formed a musical partnership with boogie woogie pianist Pete Johnson near the end of the '20s. Touring with regional bands led by Bennie Moten and Count Basie, among others, Turner first went to New York in 1936, returning in 1938 with Pete Johnson to perform on Benny Goodman's *Camel Caravan* CBS radio show and the legendary Spirituals to Swing concerts at Carnegie Hall, the first concert series to promote black music to white audiences.

Big Joe Turner soon took up a four-year residence at the exclusive Cafe Society Uptown and Downtown clubs in New York with Johnson, often joined by Albert Ammons and Meade Lux Lewis. The three pianists became known as the Boogie Woogie Boys, and Turner's debut recording of "Roll 'Em Pete" with Johnson launched the boogie woogie craze. Usually accompanied by Johnson, Turner recorded for National Records from 1938 to 1940, producing the classic "Cherry Red" in 1939. He then recorded for Decca from 1940 to 1944, usually backed by Johnson, but occasionally accompanied by Willie "The Lion" Smith, Art Tatum, or Freddie Slack. In 1941 Turner traveled to Hollywood to appear in Duke Ellington's *Jump for Joy* revue.

Subsequently based largely on the West Coast, Big Joe Turner continued to record with Johnson after World War II, first for National (1945–47), where he scored a smash rhythm-and-blues hit with "My Gal's a Jockey." His National recordings were later issued on Savoy. Through 1950, Turner recorded for labels such as Aladdin, RPM, Downbeat/Swingtime, MGM, Freedom, and Imperial (in New Orleans). In 1949, for National, he recorded "Battles of the Blues" with rival Wynonie Harris, scoring his second R&B hit in 1950 with "Still in the Dark" on Freedom. The Aladdin and Imperial recordings were later issued on EMI, and the Swingtime recordings on Arhoolie.

After ending his partnership with Pete Johnson, Big Joe Turner signed with Atlantic Records in 1951, initiating a series of smash R&B hits with the ballad "Chains of Love," a moderate pop hit covered by Pat Boone in 1956. "Chill Is On" and the ballad "Sweet Six-teen" (later associated with B. B. King) became smash R&B hits, as did "Honey Hush" (also a major pop hit), recorded in New Orleans, and "TV Mama," recorded in Chicago with gui-tarist Elmore James. The classic "Shake, Rattle and Roll" became a top R&B and major pop hit in the spring of 1954, and the song was later covered by Bill Haley and Elvis Presley.

Big Joe Turner continued to score R&B smashes through 1956 with "Well All Right," "Flip, Flop and Fly," "Hide and Seek," the two-sided "Morning, Noon and Night"/"The Chicken and the Hawk (Up, Up and Away)," "Corrine Corrina" (a moderate pop hit), and "Lipstick, Powder and Paint." In 1956 Turner once again teamed with Pete Johnson for the classic *Boss of the Blues* album. Turner appeared in the 1956 film *Shake, Rattle and Roll* and toured with the rock 'n' roll package shows of Red Prysock and Alan Freed in 1956 and 1957, respectively. Turner managed two more major pop-only hits with "Love Roller Coaster" and "(I'm Gonna) Jump For Joy." He appeared at the Monterey Jazz Festival in 1958 and then toured Europe for the first time. He left the Atlantic label in 1961.

In the '60s, Big Joe Turner moved to Los Angeles, where he occasionally recorded for Kent and Coral while continuing to tour Europe and America regularly. He performed at the Monterey Jazz Festival in 1964 and toured Europe with the American Folk Blues Festi-val in 1966. Recording for the BluesWay label in 1967, Turner worked with the Johnny Otis Show in the late '60s, appearing with his show at the Monterey Jazz Festival in 1970. In 1971 Turner recorded for the French Black & Blue label, later issued on Evidence Records, and subsequently returned to his jazz and blues style for two albums with Count Basie on Pablo Records. He appeared with Basie in the 1974 documentary film on Kansas City jazz, *The Last of the Blue Devils.*

Big Joe Turner recorded albums for Pablo throughout the '70s, accompanied by Pee Wee Crayton, trumpeters Dizzy Gillespie and Roy Eldridge, and alto saxophonist Eddie "Cleanhead" Vinson, among others. By the early '80s, Turner was suffering from diabetes and arthritis, walking on crutches and having to perform sitting down. He recorded with Roomful of Blues in 1983 and Knocky Parker and the Houserockers in 1984, recording his final album with Jimmy Witherspoon in 1985. He died of a heart attack in Inglewood, Cali-fornia, on November 24, 1995, at the age of seventy-four. Big Joe Turner was inducted into the Blues Foundation's Hall of Fame in 1983 and the Rock and Roll Hall of Fame in 1987.

Early Recordings

1938–1941	L'Art Vocal	10	'92	CD
Kansas City Jazz	Decca	8044	'53	†
I've Been to Kansas City, Vol. 1 (recorded 1940–1941)	Decca Jazz	42351	'90	CS/CD†
Early Big Joe (recorded 1940–1944)	MCA	1325		†
Every Day in the Week (recorded early to mid '50s)	Decca Jazz	621	'93	CD
Joe Turner and the Blues	Savoy	14012	'58	†
Careless Love	Savoy	14106	'63	†
Blues'll Make You Happy	Savoy Jazz	406	'85	†
Have No Fear, Big Joe Is Here (recorded 1945–1947)	Savoy Jazz	(2)2223		†
	Savoy Jazz	0265	'95	CD
Jumpin' the Blues (recorded 1948 with Pete Johnson Orchestra)	Arhoolie	2004	'62/'81	CS
Tell Me Pretty Baby (recorded with Pete Johnson Orchestra 1947–1949)	Arhoolie	333	'92	CD
Steppin' Out (recorded late '40s)	Ace	243	'88	†
Joe Turner and Pete Johnson	EmArcy	36014	'55	†
Jumpin' with Joe–The Complete Aladdin and Imperial Recordings (recorded late '40s– early '50s)	EMI	99293	'93	CD

Atlantic Recordings

Boss of the Blues (recorded with Pete Johnson 1956)	Atlantic	1234	'56	†
	Atlantic	8812	'76	†
	Rhino	8812		CS/CD
Kansas City Jazz	Atlantic	1235	'56	†
Joe Turner	Atlantic	8005	'57	†
Rockin' the Blues	Atlantic	8023	'58	†
Big Joe Is Here	Atlantic	8033	'59	†
Big Joe Rides Again	Atlantic	1332	'59	†
	Rhino	90668	'88	CS/CD
Best	Atlantic	8081	'63	†
Memorial Album: The Rhythm and Blues Years	Rhino	81663	'86	CS/CD
Greatest Hits	Rhino	81752	'87	CS/CD

Big Joe Turner and T-Bone Walker

Bosses of the Blues, Vol. 1 (recorded 1969)	Bluebird	8311	'89	CD

Big Joe Turner and Count Basie

Flip, Flop and Fly (recorded 1972 with Count Basie Orchestra)	Pablo	937	'75/'89	CS/CD
The Bosses (recorded 1973)	Pablo	709	'75	†
	Fantasy/OJC	821	'94	CD

Pablo/Fantasy Records

Trumpet Kings Meet Joe Turner	Pablo	717	'75	†
(recorded 1974 with Dizzy Gillespie, Roy Eldridge, and others)	Fantasy/OJC	497	'90	LP/CS/CD
Everyday I Have the Blues (recorded 1975 with Pee Wee Crayton)	Pablo	818	'76	†
	Fantasy/OJC	634	'91	LP/CS/CD
Nobody in Mind (recorded 1976)	Pablo	760	'76	†
	Fantasy/OJC	729	'92	CD
In the Evening (recorded 1976)	Pablo	776	'76	LP/CS
	Fantasy/OJC	852	'95	CD
Life Ain't Easy (recorded 1976)	Pablo	883	'83	†
	Fantasy/OJC	809		CD
Things That I Used to Do (recorded 1977)	Pablo	800	'77	†
	Fantasy/OJC	862	'96	CD
Midnight Special	Pablo	844		CD
Stormy Monday (recorded 1974, 1975, 1977, 1978)	Pablo	943	'91	CD
Have No Fear, Joe Turner Is Here	Pablo	863	'82	†
The Best of "Big" Joe Turner	Pablo	404	'82	CS/CD
Kansas City Here I Come	Pablo	904	'82	†
	Fantasy/OJC	743	'92	CD

Big Joe Turner and a Roomful of Blues

Blues Train	Muse	5293	'83	LP/CS/CD

Big Joe Turner and Jimmy Witherspoon

Patcha, Patcha, All Night Long (recorded 1985)	Pablo	913	'86	LP/CD
	Fantasy/OJC	887	'96	CD

Other Recordings

Turns on the Blues	Kent	542		†
	United	7759		†
Still the Boss of the Blues	United	7790		†
Singing the Blues	BluesWay	6006	'67	†
	Mobile Fidelity	00780	'90	CD†

Roll 'Em	BluesWay	6060	'73	†
Texas Style (recorded 1971)	Evidence	26013	'71/'92	CD
Great R&B Oldies	Blues Spectrum	104	'81	†
Joe Turner (recorded 1984 with Knocky Parker and the Houserockers)	Southland	0013		LP
Rock This Joint	Intermedia	5008	'84	LP/CS
The Very Best of Joe Turner–Live	Intermedia	5026		CS/CD
The Blues Boss–Live	Intermedia	5030		LP/CS
Everyday I Have the Blues	Intermedia	5036		LP/CS
Roll Me Baby	Intermedia	5043		LP/CS
Big, Bad and Blue: The Big Joe Turner Anthology	Rhino	(4)71550	'93	CD†
Shake, Rattle and Roll	Tomato	71666	'94	CD

RITCHIE VALENS

Born Richard Valenzuela on May 13, 1941, in Pacoima, California; died February 3, 1959, near Clear Lake, Iowa.

RICHIE VALENS

In an all-too-brief career, Ritchie Valens was the first Chicano rock 'n' roll star, scoring his best remembered hit, "La Bamba," just barely a month before his untimely death with Buddy Holly and the Big Bopper on February 3, 1959. Ultimately followed by other Chicano acts such as Chan Romero (author of "Hippy Hippy Shake"), Chris Montez, and Cannibal and the Headhunters, Ritchie Valens attracted a new audience with the 1987 movie and sound track *La Bamba*, featuring musical performances of his songs by Los Lobos.

Of Mexican-American and Native-American descent, Richard Valenzuela grew up in poverty in Pacoima, California. He took up acoustic guitar at age nine and manufactured his first electric guitar at eleven. While attending Pacoima Junior High School, he joined the mixed-race band the Silhouettes and quickly became the group's frontman. In the spring of 1958, he auditioned for Bob Keene, owner of the Hollywood-based label Del-Fi Records. Keene signed him to the label, shortening his name to Ritchie Valens, and his first recording session yielded "Come On, Let's Go," a major R&B and moderate pop hit. In August he made his first U.S. tour with Eddie Cochran and appeared on Dick Clark's *American Bandstand*. He returned to Los Angeles to record his own ballad "Donna" and a rocked-up version of the traditional Mexican folk song "La Bamba," later performing at his old junior high school and filming a segment for the film *Go, Johnny, Go.*

In November "Donna" became a smash pop and R&B hit, quickly followed by the major flip-side pop hit "La Bamba." He again appeared on *American Bandstand* and subsequently joined "The Winter Dance Party" tour of Buddy Holly, J. P. "The Big Bopper" Richardson, and Dion and the Belmonts. Following a concert at Clear Lake, Iowa, on February 2, 1959, Ritchie Valens, then seventeen, Buddy Holly, and the Big Bopper died when their chartered plane crashed shortly after takeoff. Released posthumously in April, Ritchie Valens's debut album contained "Come On, Let's Go," "Donna," and "La Bamba," plus "That's My Little Suzie," a minor pop hit. Within a year, Del-Fi had assembled two more albums of his recordings.

Ritchie Valens's recordings were reissued by Rhino, beginning in the early '80s. In 1987, at the behest of the Valenzuela family, the Chicano rock band Los Lobos recorded eight songs, including versions of Valens's his first three hits, for the film musical of his life, *La Bamba,* starring Lou Diamond Phillips. Los Lobos scored a top pop hit with "La Bamba" and a major pop hit with "Come On, Let's Go." Unreleased tapes by Ritchie Valens discovered in 1990 were issued by Ace Records as *The Lost Tapes.*

BIBLIOGRAPHY

Mendheim, Beverly. *Ritchie Valens: The First Latino Rocker.* Tempe, AZ: Bilingual Press, 1987.

Lehmer, Larry. *The Day the Music Died: The Last Tour of Buddy Holly, the Big Bopper, and Ritchie Valens.* New York: Schirmer Books, 1997.

Ritchie Valens	Del-Fi	1201	'59	†
	Rhino	70231	'87	†
Ritchie	Del-Fi	1206	'59	†
	Rhino	70232	'87	†
Ritchie Valens/Ritchie In Concert at Pacoima Jr. High	Ace	953		CD
	Del-Fi	1214	'60	†
	Del-Fi	71214		CD
	Rhino	70233	'87	†
His Greatest Hits	Del-Fi	1225	'63	†
His Greatest Hits, Vol. 2	Del-Fi	1247	'64	†
Rockin' All Night: The Very Best of Ritchie Valens	Del-Fi	9001	'95	CD
The Original Ritchie Valens	Guest Star	1469	'63	†
The Original La Bamba	Guest Star	1484	'63	†
Ritchie Valens	MGM	117(E)	'70	†
The History of Ritchie Valens	Rhino	(3)2798	'81	†
Best (1958–1959)	Rhino	200	'81	†
	Rhino	70178	'86	CS/CD
The Ritchie Valens Story	Rhino	71414	'93	CS/CD
	Del-Fi	71011		CD
La Bamba '87 (various artists)	Original Sound	8887		CS/CD
The Lost Tapes	Ace	317	'92	CD
	Del-Fi	9009		CD
Best	Ace	387		CD

GENE VINCENT

Born Vincent Eugene Craddock on February 11, 1935, in Norfolk, Virginia; died October 12, 1971 in Newhall, California.

One of the most engaging, if tragic, figures in the history of rock 'n' roll, Gene Vincent personified the wild, lusty, lower-class side of the music as a touring artist. Scoring one of the earliest smash rockabilly hits with the classic "Be-Bop-a-Lula" in 1956, Vincent recorded some of the most exciting, libidinous rockabilly of the era, propelled by the outstanding lead guitar work of Cliff Gallup. However, lacking the charisma of Presley and the clean-cut good looks of rising stars such as Buddy Holly and Ricky Nelson, Vincent was discounted as a major artist in the United States by 1958. Withdrawing to England, he was seriously injured in the car crash that killed Eddie Cochran in 1960. Becoming immensely popular in Great Britain, Vincent unsuccessfully attempted an American comeback in the late '60s.

Quitting high school in 1951 to join the Navy, Gene Vincent suffered severe injuries to his left leg in a motorcycle crash while serving that left him permanently disabled. While convalescing after his discharge in May 1955, he took up singing, and by March 1956 he was sitting in with the house band at Norfolk's WCMS radio. He was noticed by local disc jockey "Sheriff" Tex Davis, who arranged for Vincent to record a demonstration tape with a backing group, subsequently dubbed the Blue Caps. Davis forwarded the tape, which included "Be-Bop-a-Lula," to Ken Nelson of Capitol Records, which was seeking an answer to RCA's Elvis Presley.

Gene Vincent signed with Capitol and he and the Blue Caps (lead guitarist Cliff Gallup, rhythm guitarist Willie Williams, standup bassist Jack Neal, and drummer Dickie Harrell) traveled to Nashville in May 1956, where they recorded four songs. "Be-Bop-a-Lula" became a near-smash pop, country and R&B hit, but the flip side, "Woman Love," was banned by some radio stations as too risqué. Touring extensively, the group returned to Nashville in June to complete recordings for their first album, which included "Who Slapped John" and the neglected rockabilly classic "Blue Jean Bop." By September Paul Peek had replaced Willie Williams, and the group soon appeared in the film *The Girl Can't Help It* with Little Richard, Eddie Cochran, and Fats Domino. Scoring a minor hit with "Race with the Devil," the group recorded their second album in October, but Gallup left in December, to be replaced by lead guitarist Johnny Meeks. Vincent was rehospitalized in early 1957 and later that year the group achieved major pop and near-smash R&B hits with "Lotta Lovin'" and "Dance to the Bop." By June the band included only one original member, Dickie Harrell. In early 1958 Vincent and the band appeared in the film *Hot Rod Gang,* performing four songs.

Plagued by reports of hotel wrecking and involvement with underage females, Gene Vincent began receiving limited airplay. His unruly and ribald stage act and rowdy lower-class image were attracting less attention than the boy-next-door types. Vincent began drinking heavily, and by the end of 1958 he had abandoned the Blue Caps. At the end of 1959, he moved to Great Britain where he toured regularly, adopting black leather stage attire, becoming one of the country's biggest-drawing attractions. In early 1960 he scored major British hits with "Wild Cat" and "My Heart" and toured the country with Eddie Cochran. However, on the night of April 16, 1960, he was badly injured in a car crash that killed Cochran. Vincent subsequently managed major British hits with "Pistol Packin' Mama" and "She She Little Sheila," but his physical and psychological state deteriorated through neglect and alcohol and drug abuse. His Capitol contract expired in 1963, and in 1964 he recorded a British-only album for Columbia Records.

Gene Vincent returned to America in 1966 and enjoyed some renewed popularity with the rock 'n' roll revival of the late '60s. However, his attempts at a comeback on Dandelion and Kama Sutra Records fared dismally. Gene Vincent died in obscurity of cardiac failure attributed to a bleeding ulcer on October 13, 1971, in Newhall, California, at the age of thirty-six. He was inducted into the Rock and Roll Hall of Fame in 1998. In 1993 Jeff Beck recorded *Crazy Legs,* an entire album of Vincent's songs.

BIBLIOGRAPHY

Hagarty, Britt. *The Day the World Turned Blue.* Vancouver, British Columbia: Talonbooks, 1983.

Gene Vincent and His Blue Caps

Blue Jean Bop	Capitol	764	'56	†
Gene Vincent and His Blue Caps	Capitol	811	'57	†
Gene Vincent Rocks and the Blue Caps Roll	Capitol	970	'58	†
Hot Rod Gang (sound track)	Capitol (EP)	985	'58	†
A Gene Vincent Record Date	Capitol	1059	'58	†
Sounds Like Gene Vincent	Capitol	1207	'59	†
The Bop That Just Won't Stop	Capitol	11286	'74	†
Gene Vincent	Capitol	94704	'90	CS/CD
Gene Vincent and His Blue Caps	Curb/Warner Bros.	77623	'93	CS/CD
The Screaming End: The Best of Gene Vincent and His Blue Caps	Razor & Tie	2123	'97	CD

Gene Vincent

Crazy Times	Capitol	1342	'60	†
Gene Vincent's Greatest	Capitol	380(E)	'69	†
	Capitol	16208		†
	Capitol	91151		CD†
I'm Back and I'm Proud	Dandelion	102	'69	†
Gene Vincent—If You Could See Me Now	Kama Sutra	2019	'70	†
The Day the World Turned Blue	Kama Sutra	2027	'71	†
Forever	Rolling Rock	022	'82	†
Rockabilly Fever	Intermedia	5074		LP/CS
Ain't That Too Much	Sundazed	12004	'93	CD
Bird Doggin'	Fat Boy	228	'95	CD

Jeff Beck and the Big Town Playboys

Crazy Legs	Epic	53562	'93	CS/CD

DINAH WASHINGTON

Born Ruth Jones in Tuscaloosa, Alabama, on August 29, 1924; died in Detroit, Michigan, on December 14, 1963.

One of the most evocative and versatile female vocalists of the '40s and '50s, equally adept at jazz, blues, R&B, and pop ballads, Dinah Washington scored over thirty R&B hits between 1948 and 1955. With her penetrating voice, impeccable phrasing, and uncommonly clear diction, she was one of the strongest influences on the female vocalists of R&B and soul, particularly through her distillation of gospel and jazz voicings. However, Washington seldom managed to cross over to the white popular audience and thus failed to benefit from the rise of rock 'n' roll. She eventually broke through with the 1959 classic "What a Diff'rence a Day Makes" and two popular duets with Brook Benton.

DINAH WASHINGTON

Ruth Jones moved with her family to Chicago as an infant and began singing in the choir at St. Luke's Baptist church as a child. She subsequently took up piano and eventually became the choir's director. After winning an amateur contest at the Regal Theater at the age of fifteen, she appeared in local night clubs but returned to gospel music as pianist and lead singer for the Sallie Martin's Singers in 1940 and 1941. Working clubs again beginning in 1941, she was heard by bandleader Lionel Hampton at the Garrick Club in 1943. Quickly hired, she took the name Dinah Washington and recorded jazz aficionado Leonard Feather's "Evil Gal Blues" and "Salty Papa Blues" with Hampton's Septet in late 1943. She sang with Hampton's band until 1946.

In 1945, Dinah Washington made her first solo recordings for Apollo (reissued on Delmark) in Los Angeles, subsequently signing with Mercury Records in 1946. Through the mid '50s, she recorded with the orchestras of Cootie Williams, Teddy Stewart, Jimmy Cobb, and Hal Mooney, among others. She scored her first near-smash R&B hit with Fats Waller's "Ain't Misbehavin'" in the spring of 1948. Through the end of the decade, she achieved major R&B hits with "West Side Baby," "Am I Asking Too Much" (her first top hit), "You Satisfy," "Baby Get Lost" (another top hit) backed by "Long John Blues," and "Good Daddy Blues."

While recording jazz with the likes of Clifford Brown, Clark Terry, Maynard Ferguson, and Wynton Kelly for Mercury and EmArcy, Dinah Washington scored smash R&B hits on Mercury through 1954 with "I Only Know," "It Isn't Fair," "Time Out for Tears," "Trouble in Mind" backed with "New Blowtop Blues," "TV Is the Thing (This Year)," and "Teach Me Tonight." Successful covers included "It's Too Soon to Know," "I Want to Be Loved," "I'll Never Be Free," "Cold Cold Heart," "Wheel of Fortune," and "I Don't Hurt Anymore." However, only two of her R&B hits, "I Want to Be Loved" and "Teach Me Tonight," made the pop charts.

Dinah Washington achieved several major R&B hits in 1955–56 and again in 1958. She also recorded albums of material associated with Fats Waller and Bessie Smith in the late '50s. She performed at the Newport Jazz Festival in 1958 and appeared in the resulting film, *Jazz On a Summer's Day*. In 1959 she broke through into the pop market with the standards "What a Diff'rence a Day Makes," a smash R&B and near-smash pop hit, and "Unforgettable," a major R&B and pop hit. She soon recorded with labelmate Brook Benton, scoring top R&B and smash pop hits with "Baby (You've Got What It Takes)" and "A Rockin' Good Way (to Mess Around and Fall in Love)." Subsequently recording primarily ballads, she had a top R&B and major pop hit with "This Bitter Earth" in 1960 and a R&B smash and major pop hit with the standard "September in the Rain" in 1961. She then switched to Roulette Records, but managed only a few minor pop-only hits. She died at the age of thirty-nine in Detroit on December 4, 1963, of an overdose of alcohol and drugs. Dinah Washington was inducted into the Rock and Roll Hall of Fame in 1993.

BIBLIOGRAPHY

Haskins, James. *Queen of the Blues: A Biography of Dinah Washington.* New York: Morrow, 1987.

Early Recordings

Mellow Mama (recorded 1945)	Delmark	451	'92	LP/CS/CD
A Slick Chick (on the Mellow Side) (recorded 1943–1954)	EmArcy	(2)814184	'81	†
After Hours with Miss D	EmArcy (10")	26032	'54	†
	EmArcy	36028	'55	†
Dinah Jams	EmArcy	36000	'54	†
	EmArcy	1013		†
Dinah Jams (recorded 1954)	EmArcy	814639		CD
For Those in Love	EmArcy	36011	'55	†
	EmArcy	514073	'92	CD
Dinah	EmArcy	36065	'56	†
	EmArcy	1038		†
	EmArcy	842139	'91	CS/CD
In the Land of Hi-Fi	EmArcy	36073	'56	†
	EmArcy	826453	'86	CD
The Swingin' Miss D	EmArcy	36104	'56	†
Sings Fats Waller	EmArcy	36119	'57	†
reissued as The Fats Waller Songbook	Verve	818930		CD
Sings Bessie Smith	EmArcy	36130	'58	†
reissued as The Bessie Smith Songbook	EmArcy	826663	'86	CD
Newport '58	EmArcy	36141	'58	†
The Jazz Side of Miss D (recorded 1954–1958)	EmArcy	401		†
	Jazz World	(2)312	'95	CD

Mercury Recordings

Dinah Washington Songs	Mercury (10")	25060	'50	†
Dynamic Dinah	Mercury (10")	25138	'51	†
Blazing Ballads	Mercury (10")	25140	'51	†
Music for a First Love	Mercury	20119	'57	†
Music for Late Hours	Mercury	20120	'57	†
The Best in Blues	Mercury	20247	'57	†
The Queen	Mercury	60111	'59	†
What a Diff'rence a Day Makes	Mercury	60158	'59	†
	Mercury	8006		†
	Mercury	818815		CS/CD
	Ultradisc	1698	'97	CD
Newport '58	Mercury	60200	'59	†
Sings Fats Waller	Mercury	60202	'59	†
Unforgettable	Mercury	60232	'60	†
	Mercury	510602	'91	CS/CD
I Concentrate on You	Mercury	60604	'61	†

For Lonely Lovers	Mercury	60614	'61	†
September in the Rain	Mercury	60638	'61	†
Tears and Laughter	Mercury	60661	'62	†
I Wanna Be Loved (with Quincy Jones Orchestra)	Mercury	60729	'62	†
The Good Old Days	Mercury	60829	'63	†

Mercury Anthologies and Compilations

The Complete Dinah Washington on Mercury, Vol. 1 (1946–1949)	Mercury	(3)832444	'87/'94	CD
The Complete Dinah Washington on Mercury, Vol. 2 (1950–1952)	Mercury	(3)832448	'87/'94	CD
The Complete Dinah Washington on Mercury, Vol. 3 (1952–1954)	Mercury	(3)834675	'88	CD
The Complete Dinah Washington on Mercury, Vol. 4 (1954–1956)	Mercury	(3)834683	'88	CD
The Complete Dinah Washington on Mercury, Vol. 5 (1956–1958)	Mercury	(3)838952	'89	CD
The Complete Dinah Washington on Mercury, Vol. 6 (1958–1960)	Mercury	(3)838956	'89	CD
The Complete Dinah Washington on Mercury, Vol. 7 (1961)	Mercury	(3)838960	'89	CD
This Is My Story, Volume 1	Mercury	60788	'63	†
reissued as Golden Hits	Mercury	60788	'85	†
Golden Hits, Vol. 1	Mercury	822867	'85	CS
This Is My Story, Vol. 2	Mercury	60789	'63	†
The Queen and Quincy (with Quincy Jones)	Mercury	60928	'65	†
Dinah Discovered	Mercury	61119	'67	†
Dinah Washington	Mercury	830700	'87	CS/CD
Sings the Blues	Mercury	832573	'87	CD

Brook Benton and Dinah Washington

The Two of Us	Mercury	60244	'60	†
	Mercury	526467	'85	CD

Roulette Recordings

Dinah '62	Roulette	25170	'62	†
In Love	Roulette	25180	'62	†
	Roulette Jazz	97273	'91	CD
Drinking Again	Roulette	25183	'62	†
Back to the Blues	Roulette	25189	'62	†
Dinah '63	Roulette	25220	'63	†
	Blue Note	94576	'90	CD
In Tribute	Roulette	25244	'63	†
Stranger On Earth	Roulette	25253	'64	†
Dinah Washington	Roulette	25269	'64	†
Best	Roulette	25289	'65	†
The Best of Dinah Washington: The Roulette Years	Roulette Jazz	99114	'93	CS/CD

Other Recordings

The Great Songs	Verve	512905	'92	CS/CD
Jazz 'Round Midnight	Verve	514363	'93	CS/CD
The Dinah Washington Story	Verve	514841	'93	CD
Verve Jazz Masters 19: Dinah Washington	Verve	518200	'94	CD
Verve Jazz Masters 40: Dinah Washington Sings Standards	Verve	522055	'94	CD
Teach Me Tonight (recorded at the Newport Jazz Festival)	Jazz Hour	73565	'95	CD
All of Me (recorded August1954–December 1961)	Jazz Time	8122	'96	CD
How to Do It	Pearl	7818	'97	CD
The Classic Dinah	Pair	1138		CS
Golden Classics	Collectables	5200		LP/CS/CD

MUDDY WATERS

Born McKinley Morganfield on April 4, 1915, in Rolling Fork, Mississippi; died April 30, 1983, in Westmont, Illinois.

MUDDY WATERS

One of the few black blues artists to gain widespread recognition and admiration from white audiences, Muddy Waters was instrumental in establishing the sound and style of Chicago blues that influenced generations of black blues musicians. His first release on Chess Records, "Rollin' Stone," was later adopted as the name of both the heavily R&B-influenced English group and the underground rock music-oriented publication. Fully established as an R&B performer and recording artist by 1952 with his powerful and intricate vocal style and distinctive, hard-driving bottleneck guitar playing, Muddy Waters's early '50s band was one of the first electric blues bands in the world. During the '50s and '60s, virtually every practitioner of the Chicago style of blues played in his band, including Otis Spann, Buddy Guy, Little Walter Jacobs, and James Cotton, making Waters's band the proving ground for young blues musicians. Along with Willie Dixon, Muddy Waters was one of the premier composers of classic and enduring blues songs, including "I Got My Mojo Working" and "Baby Please Don't Go."

At an early age Muddy Waters moved to Clarksdale, Mississippi, where he grew up on the Stovall plantation. He began playing harmonica as a child, switching to guitar at age seventeen. Strongly influenced by blues guitarists Son House and Robert Johnson, Waters developed a distinctive style of acoustic guitar playing using a bottleneck that produced a remarkable biting, stinging sound. Becoming one of the area's best known and most popular blues performers through engagements at picnics, dances, and small clubs, he was sought out by folklorist Alan Lomax, who first recorded Waters during the summers of 1941 and 1942. These classic recordings stand as a monument to the artistry of Muddy Waters and alone represent a major accomplishment in a career that lasted forty years.

In May 1943 Muddy Waters permanently left Mississippi for Chicago, where he played in local clubs and obtained his first electric guitar in 1945. Around 1946 he made his first commercial recordings for Columbia Records, but they were not released until years later, on the Testament label. Signing with Aristocrat Records (which became Chess Records in 1949), Waters recorded the blues classics "(I Feel Like) Going Home" and "I Can't Be Satisfied" in early 1948 and the pairing became Aristocrat's biggest selling single. He began playing larger clubs and scored a local hit with "Rollin' Stone," his first release on Chess.

Around 1950 Muddy Waters began recording with harmonica players Little Walter Jacobs and Walter Horton. Waters soon scored the near-smash national R&B hits "Louisiana Blues" with Jacobs and "Long Distance Call" with Horton in 1951. Forming his own band with Jacobs and second guitarist Jimmy Rogers, Waters hit with "Honey Bee," "Still a Fool" and "She Moves Me," near-smash R&B hits. Augmented by pianist Otis Spann, this legendary blues band, the prototype of all subsequent Chicago blues bands, defined the style of modern electric blues. Jacobs left the band in 1952 and later recordings featured Horton or Jacobs sitting in. Smash R&B hits for Waters through 1954 included "Mad Love" and the Willie Dixon-composed classics "I'm Your Hoochie Coochie Man," "Just Make Love to Me" (perhaps better known as "I Just Want to Make Love to You") and "I'm Ready." "Manish Boy" (a reworking of Bo Diddley's "I'm a Man"), "Trouble No More," "Forty Days and Forty Nights," and "Don't Go No Further" extended Waters's smash R&B hits into 1956. Subsequent recordings included "Just to Be with You" and his own "Got My Mojo Working." Jimmy Rogers left the band around 1956, but Otis Spann stayed on until his death in 1968.

In 1955 Muddy Waters brought Chuck Berry to Chess Records, where he was quickly signed. However, by 1956 Waters was becoming overshadowed by the rise of rock 'n' roll as practiced by Berry, Bill Haley, Elvis Presley, and others. Waters's last R&B hit came in 1958 with "Close to You," recorded with harmonica player James Cotton, bassist Willie Dixon, and Otis Spann. In 1958 Waters and Spann toured Europe for the first time and Chess issued Waters's debut album as *The Best of Muddy Waters,* which contained most of his best remembered recordings made between 1948 and 1954.

Muddy Waters was able to maintain some of his popularity in conjunction with the folk movement of the late '50s and early '60s and was introduced to the jazz audience through his appearance at the 1960 Newport Jazz Festival with Otis Spann and James Cotton. Backed by Buddy Guy, Waters played acoustic guitar on *Folk Singer,* which included "Feel Like Going Home" and the Sonny Boy Williamson classic "Good Morning, Little School Girl." Waters toured Europe with the American Folk Blues Festival in 1963 and appeared at the Newport Folk Festival in 1964, 1967, and 1969. He also performed at the Monterey Jazz Festival in 1966 and 1968. Late '60s albums included couplings with Bo Diddley and Little Walter, and Bo Diddley and Howlin' Wolf. The Chess subsidiary Cadet also issued two deplorable attempts to capitalize on "psychedelic" music for Waters, *Electric Mud* and *After the Rain.*

Touring steadily, Muddy Waters and Otis Spann recorded *Fathers and Sons* with white blues musicians such as Mike Bloomfield and Paul Butterfield in 1969. By this time, Waters was receiving the praise of a number of British and American artists strongly influenced by his work, including Bloomfield, Eric Clapton, and Mick Jagger. However, when Leonard Chess died in October 1969, the Chess organization was bought out and Waters no longer received the kind of personal treatment to which he had become accustomed. A variety of albums were issued on Chess through 1975, including *The London Muddy Waters Sessions,* recorded with Steve Winwood and Rory Gallagher.

In 1976 Muddy Waters moved to Blue Sky Records. He again received sympathetic treatment from his record label, with Johnny Winter producing. Waters toured and recorded *Hard Again* with Winter and James Cotton, and *I'm Ready,* featuring Winter and old associates Walter Horton and Jimmy Rogers. Waters toured the country in 1978, concluding the year as the opening act for Eric Clapton in Europe. *Live* was a compilation of recordings made during the 1977 and 1978 tours. Waters's final Blue Sky album was issued in 1981. On April 30, 1983, Muddy Waters died in the Chicago suburb of Westmont of a heart attack at the age of sixty-eight. His popularity remains undiminished, as Chess reissued many of his recordings beginning in 1987, the year he was inducted into the Rock and Roll Hall of Fame.

BIBLIOGRAPHY

Rooney, Jim. *Bossmen: Bill Monroe and Muddy Waters.* New York: Dial, 1971; New York: Da Capo, 1991.

Obrecht, Jas. "Muddy Waters: Bluesman, 1915–1983." *Guitar Player* 17, no. 8 (August 1983): 48, 52–54, 57, 67–70.

Muddy Waters

Down at Stovall's Plantation (recorded 1941–1942)	Testament	2210	'69	†
The Complete Plantation Recordings/ the Historic 1941–1942 Library of Congress Field Recordings	Chess	9344	'93	CS/CD
Chicago Blues: In the Beginning	Testament	2207		†
His Best, 1947 to 1955	MCA/Chess	9370	'97	CD
Best (recorded 1948–1954)	Chess	1427	'58	†
	Chess	9255	'87	CS
	Chess	31268	'87	CD
reissued as Sail On	Chess	1539	'69	†
More Real Folk Blues (recorded 1948–1952)	Chess	1511	'67	†
	Chess	9278	'88	CS/CD
Trouble No More: Singles (1955–1959)	Chess	9291	'89	LP/CS/CD
Sings Big Bill Broonzy (recorded 1959–1960)	Chess	1444	'61	†
	Chess	9197	'87	CS†
At Newport 1960	Chess	1449	'61	†
	Chess	9198	'86	LP/CS
	Chess	31269	'86	CD
Folk Singer	Chess	1483	'64	†
	Chess	9261	'87	LP/CS
	Mobile Fidelity	593	'93	CD
	Mobile Fidelity	201	'94	LP
Folk Singer/Sings Big Bill Broonzy 1949–1964)	Chess	5907		CD
The Real Folk Blues (recorded 1949–1964)	Chess	1501	'66	†
	Chess	9274	'88	LP/CS/CD
Muddy, Brass and the Blues	Chess	1507	'66	†
	Chess	9286	'89	CS/CD
They Call Me Muddy Waters	Chess	1553	'71	†
	Chess	9299		CS/CD
AKA McKinley Morganfield	Chess	(2)60006	'71	†
Live at Mr. Kelly's	Chess	50012	'71	†
	Chess	9338	'92	CS/CD
London Muddy Waters Sessions	Chess	60013	'72	†
	Chess	9298	'89	CS/CD
Can't Get No Grindin'	Chess	50023	'73	†
	Chess	9319	'90	LP/CS/CD
"Unk" in Funk	Chess	60031	'74	†
	Chess	91513		CS/CD
At Woodstock	Chess	60035	'75	†
reissued as The Muddy Waters Woodstock Album	Chess	9359	'95	CS/CD
Muddy Waters	Chess	(2)203	'77	†
Rolling Stone	Chess	9101		LP/CS/CD
Rare and Unissued	Chess	9180		LP/CS/CD
The Chess Box	Chess	(6)80002	'89	CS
	Chess	(3)80002	'89	CD
One More Mile: Chess Collectibles, Vol. 1 (recorded 1948–1972)	Chess	(2)9348	'94	CS/CD

Muddy Waters, Bo Diddley, and Little Walter

Super Blues	Checker	3008	'67	†
	Chess	9168		CS/CD

Muddy Waters, Howlin' Wolf, and Bo Diddley

| The Super Super Blues Band | Checker | 3010 | '68 | † |
| | Chess | 9169 | | CS |

Muddy Waters, Otis Spann, and Others

Fathers and Sons	Chess	(2)127	'69	†
	Chess	(2)50033		†
	Chess	(2)92522	'89	LP/CS
	Chess	92522	'89	CD

Muddy Waters and Otis Spann

| Collaboration | Tomato | 71661 | '95 | CD |

Muddy Waters and Howlin' Wolf

| London Revisited | Chess | 60026 | '74 | † |

Muddy Waters and Memphis Slim

| Chicago Blues Master, Vol. 1 | Capitol | 29375 | '95 | CD |

Muddy Waters

Electric Mud	Cadet	314	'68	†
	MCA	9364	'97	CD
After the Rain	Cadet	320	'69	†
Goin' Home Live in Paris 1970	New Rose	5099	'93	CD
Mud in Your Ear	Muse	5008	'73	LP/CS
	Muse	6004		CD
Live in Switzerland 1976	Landscape	908	'91	CD†
Muddy Waters Chicago Blues Band: Live in Switzerland 1976, Vol. 2	Landscape	921	'93	CD†
Unreleased in the West (Live 1976)	Moon/FTC	8507	'92	CD
Unreleased in the West, Vol. 2	Moon/FTC	75112	'92	CD
Hard Again	Blue Sky	34449	'77	CS/CD
I'm Ready	Blue Sky	34928	'78	CS/CD
Muddy "Mississippi" Waters Live	Blue Sky	35712	'79	CS/CD
King Bee	Blue Sky	37064	'81	CS/CD
Blue Skys	Epic Associated/ Legacy	46172	'92	CS/CD
Muddy Waters	Bella Musica	89930	'90	CD†
Mean Mistreater	CSI	75112	'92	CD
Goodbye Newport Blues	Magnum America	15	'95	CD
Blues Straight Ahead	Drive	3212	'95	CD
Baby Please Don't Go	Iris	305	'95	CD
Baby Please Don't Go	Vogue	670410		CD†
Live at Newport (with B.B. King and Big Mama Thornton)	Intermedia	5022		LP/CS
Sweet Home Chicago	Intermedia	5071		LP/CS
The Warsaw Sessions	Kicking Mule	79		LP
The Warsaw Sessions, Vol. 2	Kicking Mule	80		LP

Paul Rodgers and Others

| A Tribute to Muddy Waters | Victory | 480013 | '93 | CS/CD |

The Muddy Waters Tribute Band

| You're Gonna Miss Me (When I'm Dead and Gone) | Telarc | 33335 | '96 | CS |
| | Telarc | 83335 | '96 | CD |

HANK WILLIAMS

Born Hiram Williams on September 17, 1923, in Mount Olive, Alabama; died January 1, 1953, in Oak Hill, West Virginia.

HANK WILLIAMS

One of the most important country-and-western artists of all times, Hank Williams was the most influential country artist in the development of rock 'n' roll. He was instrumental in the ascent of country music in the early '50s, propelling an essentially regional music into the public mainstream. Williams was also one of the first county artists consistently to cross over into pop, and covers of his songs by mainstream artists such as Tony Bennett, Rosemary Clooney, and Jo Stafford demonstrated that a "minority" music could transcend its confines and appeal to the widespread pop audience. Writing virtually all of his own songs, Williams's success as a singer-songwriter can be seen as the beginning of the end for the dominance of popular music by Tin Pan Alley, with its separation of songwriter and performer, with the record company's artist-and-repertoire representative as the controlling link. Moreover, his deeply emotional and direct style of songwriting articulated the everyday concerns of his listeners and influenced generations of country songwriters as well as aspiring rock 'n' roll performer-songwriters. Williams was the most popular honky-tonk artist of his time and his band lineup of guitar, fiddle, and standup bass preserved the string band tradition of early country music while promoting innovations such as steel guitar and electric guitar. Much like Jimmie Rodgers, Williams's sound included a strong element of black blues, an influence later reflected by rockabilly artists. Indeed, his up-tempo songs such as "Rootie Tootie," "Honky Tonkin'" and "Hey, Good Lookin'," with their regular guitar breaks, served as blueprints for early rockabilly. Although his influence was obscured by the proliferation of musical styles in the '50s and '60s, he reemerged as an inspiration to the evolution of country-rock in the late '60s and "New Country" in the '80s and '90s.

Largely raised by his mother, Hiram "Hank" Williams obtained his first guitar at the age of eight. At eleven he began frequenting Saturday night dances, learning guitar from a local black man, Rufe Payne, known as Tee-Tot. In July 1937 Hank's mother moved to Montgomery, Alabama, where she opened a boarding house. Her son soon won a local talent contest and began performing twice a week on radio station WSFA as "The Singing Kid." Also in 1937 he formed the first version of his band, the Drifting Cowboys, playing rough-and-tumble venues in Alabama with his mother serving as manager. He worked in a Mobile shipyard from 1942 to 1944, subsequently returning to the honky tonk circuit with mainstay Don Helms on steel guitar. In December 1944, Williams married Audrey Sheppard, who subsequently joined his troupe, despite limited talent. In September 1946, the Williamses traveled to Nashville, where Fred Rose signed Hank to a songwriting contract with the newly formed Acuff-Rose publishing company. Williams made his first recordings for the Sterling label in December and signed with MGM Records the following spring with the help of Rose, who became his mentor, manager, collaborator, and record producer.

Recording with the likes of fiddler Chubby Wise, steel guitarist Jerry Byrd, lead guitarist Zeke Turner, and pianist Owen Bradley into 1949, Hank Williams's first MGM release, "Move It on Over," became a smash country hit in the summer of 1947. During 1948 he scored a major country hit with the classic "Honky Tonkin'" and a near-smash country hit with "I'm a Long Gone Daddy," while recording "Rootie Tootie" and the gospel-inspired "I Saw the Light." He joined the cast of the *Louisiana Hayride* radio show on KWKH in Shreveport, Louisiana, in the summer of 1948 and became the featured artist on the show's package tours. In 1949 Williams recorded "Lovesick Blues," originally recorded by Emmett Miller in 1925, and the song became a top country hit, remaining on the charts for nearly a year and penetrating the pop charts several months after its release. Invited to perform at the *Grand Ole Opry,* Williams debuted on June 11, 1949, and his performance of the song inspired an unprecedented six encores and launched him into national prominence.

A prolific songwriter, Hank Williams poured out country hits throughout his lifetime. He scored eight major country hits in 1949, including "Wedding Bells," "Mind Your Own Business," and "My Bucket's' Got a Hole in It." However, neither "There'll Be No Teardrops Tonight" nor "I'm So Lonesome I Could Cry," arguably his most affecting song, became hits. In July 1949 Williams formed the most enduring group of the Drifting Cowboys for touring and recording. The members included steel guitarist Don Helms and fiddler Jerry Rivers. Williams recorded with his wife, Audrey, and in Nashville's thinly veiled secret, recorded as Luke the Drifter, producing melodramatic monologues such as "Pictures from Life's Other Side," "Too Many Parties (and Too Many Pals)," and "Men with Broken Hearts." His son, Randall Hank Williams, was born in Shreveport on May 26, 1949.

A marvelous showman whose magnetic stage presence was undeniable, Hank Williams was also a heavy drinker. Coupled with the use of painkillers to ease the pain of a congenital spinal defect that had been made worse when he was thrown from a horse at the age of seventeen, Williams's alcoholism often caused his performances to suffer. Williams was also known for playing with guns, destroying hotel rooms, and literally throwing money away. His life with Audrey was in a state of constant conflict, as she attempted to run his career.

In 1950 Hank Williams achieved three top country hits with "Long Gone Lonesome Blues," "Why Don't You Love Me," and "Moanin' the Blues," as well as five other major country hits. The hits continued in 1951 with the top country and major pop hits "Cold, Cold Heart" and "Hey Good Lookin'" (backed by "My Heart Would Know"), plus five other major country hits, including the smashes "I Can't Help It (If I'm Still in Love with You)" and "Baby, We're Really in Love." That year four pop artists covered "Cold, Cold Heart," with Tony Bennett achieving a top pop hit. "Hey, Good Lookin'" became a near-smash pop hit for Frankie Laine and Jo Stafford late in the year. Additionally, Williams achieved perhaps the biggest success of his touring career in the summer of 1951 on the Hadacol Caravan, performing with the likes of Bob Hope, Jack Benny, Carmen Miranda, Minnie Pearl, and the orchestras of Tony Martin and Dick Haymes.

In 1952 Hank Williams scored country smashes with "Honky Tonk Blues," "Half as Much," and "Setting the Woods on Fire." "Jambalaya (On the Bayou)" became a top country and major pop hit, and "You Win Again" became a major country hit. During the year, Rosemary Clooney achieved a top pop hit with "Half as Much," Jo Stafford had a near-smash pop hit with "Jambalaya (On the Bayou)," and Frankie Laine and Stafford managed a major pop hit with "Tonight We're Setting the Woods on Fire."

But also by 1952 Hank Williams's life had become an awkward, miserable debacle. Hank and Audrey Williams divorced on May 29, 1952, and, on August 11, 1952, he was fired from the *Grand Ole Opry* due to his unreliability and drunkenness. The Drifting Cowboys joined Ray Price and Hank rejoined the *Louisiana Hayride,* but was reduced to playing small clubs with pickup bands. He married Billie Jean Jones on October 18, 1952, repeating their wedding vows twice on stage in New Orleans the next day. At year's end he had a top country hit with "I'll Never Get out of This World Alive."

Booked to play a New Year's Day engagement in Canton, Ohio, with Hawkshaw Hawkins and Homer and Jethro, Hank Williams had hired a cab driver to drive his Cadillac. A Tennessee state trooper pulled the car over for speeding near Rutledge, observing to Carr that the man in the back seat appeared dead. Nonetheless, Carr drove on, eventually stopping in Oak Hill, West Virginia, where he did find Williams dead in the back seat. Death was attributed to a severe heart attack. During 1953 Williams had posthumous country hits with the two-sided top hit "Your Cheatin' Heart"/"Kaw-Liga" and the smashes "I Won't Be Home No More" and "Weary Blues from Waitin'," an overdubbed demonstration record.

Many of Hank Williams's recordings were issued on albums in the ensuing years and reissued in 1960. Beginning in 1965 his albums were released with overdubbed strings and voices (including three sets of *Hank Williams and Strings*), and many of his albums were again issued in 1968 with overdubs and electronically-produced stereo. Essentially a singles artist, Williams's hits have been issued on a number of enduring compilation albums. In 1985 Polydor began releasing carefully edited compilations of virtually all of his original recordings made between 1946 and 1952. Early recordings with only voice and guitar were issued by the Country Music Foundation in the late '80s. Hank Williams was inducted into the Rock and Roll Hall of Fame as an Early Influence in 1987.

Over the years the songs of Hank Williams have been recorded by country-and-western, R&B, rock 'n' roll, and pop artists. "Your Cheatin' Heart" has been recorded by more than 300 artists. Ray Charles scored major pop hits with "Your Cheatin' Heart" and "Take These Chains from My Heart" in 1962–63, and B. J. Thomas achieved a near-smash pop hit with "I'm So Lonesome I Could Cry" in 1966. Country-rock acts from the late '60s on featured his material, as did "New Country" artists of the '80s and '90s. Among the most intriguing tribute records are Waylon Jennings's "Are You Sure Hank Done It This Way," Moe Bandy's "Hank Williams, You Wrote My Life," and Kris Kristofferson's "If You Don't Like Hank Williams." In 1995 The The issued the Hank Williams tribute album *Hanky Panky.*

Hank Williams's son began performing as Hank Williams, Junior, at the age of eight. He joined the *Grand Ole Opry* in 1962 and made his first recordings at the age of thirteen. He scored his first hit, a country smash, with a version of his father's "Long Gone Lonesome Blues" in 1964. He also performed the vocals for the film biography of his father, *Your Cheatin' Heart,* starring George Hamilton, and scored his second country smash hit in 1966 with the ironic recitation, "Standing in the Shadows." Hank Jr. recorded with Connie Francis, recorded voice-overs to his dead father's songs, and completed some of his father's unfinished songs, achieving a smash country hit with "Cajun Baby" in 1969. He eventually broke away from his father's legacy in the mid '70s with the album *Hank Williams Jr. and Friends,* ultimately establishing himself as one of country music's most popular artists in the late '70s with hits like "Family Tradition" and "Whiskey Bent and Hell Bound." In 1996 Curb/Atlantic released *Men with Broken Hearts,* credited to Hank Williams Sr., Hank Williams Jr., and Hank Williams III.

In 1985 Catherine Yvonne Stone began legal attempts to win her share of the Hank Williams fortune. Born to Nashville secretary Bobbie Jett on January 6, 1953, in Montgomery, Alabama, Stone was adopted and raised by Williams's mother, Lilly Stone. When the mother died, the girl was placed in a foster home and subsequently adopted by the Deuprees of Mobile, Alabama, in 1956. In 1967 an Alabama circuit judge ruled that Stone had no rights to the estate, since she had been adopted, and documents signed by Hank Williams and Bobbie Jett were sealed. Bobbie Jett died in 1974, before Stone learned that she was her mother. Although Stone's paternity was never disputed, her claims against the estate were bitterly opposed by the Acuff-Rose publishing house and Hank Williams Jr. Stone was ruled to be Hank Williams's illegitimate daughter in 1987, and in 1989 the Alabama Supreme Court ruled that she had been defrauded in the '60s. In 1993, Cathy Stone, who performed and recorded as Jett Williams, agreed to an out-of-court settlement.

BIBLIOGRAPHY

Williams, Roger M. *Sing a Sad Song: The Life of Hank Williams.* Garden City, NY: Doubleday, 1970; Urbana: University of Illinois Press, 1981.

Caress, Jay. *Hank Williams: Country Music's Tragic King.* New York: Stein and Day, 1979.

Flippo, Chet. *Your Cheatin' Heart: A Biography of Hank Williams.* New York: Simon & Schuster, 1981; Garden City, NY: Doubleday, 1985.

Koon, George William. *Hank Williams: A Bio-Bibliography.* Westport, CT: Greenwood, 1983.

Williams, Jett. *Ain't Nothin' as Sweet as My Baby: The Story of Hank Williams' Lost Daughter.* New York: Harcourt Brace, 1990.

Escott, Colin. "Hank Williams: Long Gone Lonesome Blues (Discography by Neal Umphred). *Goldmine* 17, no. 12 (June 14, 1991): 8–16, 18, 20.

_____. *Hank Williams: The Biography.* Boston: Little, Brown, 1994.

Early Albums (10″)

Hank Williams Sings	MGM	107	'52	†
Moanin' the Blues	MGM	168	'52	†
Memorial Album	MGM	202	'53	†
Hank Williams as Luke the Drifter	MGM	203	'53	†
Honky Tonkin'	MGM	242	'54	†
I Saw the Light	MGM	243	'54	†
Ramblin' Man	MGM	291	'54	†

MGM/Metro Recordings

Ramblin' Man	MGM	3219	'55	†
Memorial Album	MGM	3272	'55	†
Moanin' the Blues	MGM	3330	'56	†
I Saw the Light	MGM	3331	'56	†
	Mercury Nashville	811900	'93	CS/CD
Honky Tonkin' 36 of Hank Williams' Greatest Hits	MGM	3412	'57	†
	MGM	(3)2	'57	†
36 More of Hank Williams' Greatest Hits	MGM	(3)4	'58	†

Sing Me a Blue Song	MGM	3560	'58	†
The Immortal Hank Williams	MGM	3605	'58	†
reissued as First, Last and Always, Hank Williams	MGM	3928	'61	†
The Unforgettable Hank Williams	MGM	3733	'59	†
The Lonesome Sound of Hank Williams	MGM	3803	'60	†
Wait for the Light to Shine	MGM	3850	'60	†
Greatest Hits	MGM	3918	'61	†
	Mercury Nashville	823291		CS
Hank Williams Lives Again	MGM	3923	'61	†
Sing Me a Blue Song	MGM	3924	'61	†
Wanderin' Around	MGM	3925	'61	†
I'm Blue Inside	MGM	3926	'61	†
The Spirit of Hank Williams	MGM	3955	'61	†
On Stage! Hank Williams Recorded Live	MGM	3999	'62	†
Greatest Hits, Vol. 2	MGM	4040	'62	†
14 More Greatest Hits, Vol. 2	MGM	4040	'62	†
On Stage, Vol. 2	MGM	4109	'63	†
14 More Greatest Hits, Vol. 3	MGM	4140	'63	†
Very Best	MGM	4168	'63	†
Very Best, Vol. 2	MGM	4227	'64	†
Lost Highway (and Other Folk Ballads)	MGM	4254	'64	†
The Hank Williams Story	MGM	(4)4267	'65	†
Kaw-Liga and Other Humorous Songs	MGM	4300	'65	†
The Legend Lives Anew (Hank Williams with Strings)	MGM	4377	'66	†
More Hank Williams and Strings	MGM	4429	'66	†
I Won't Be Home No More	MGM	4481	'67	†
Hank Williams and Strings, Vol. 3	MGM	4529	'68	†
In the Beginning	MGM	4576(E)	'68	†
The Essential Hank Williams	MGM	4651(E)	'69	†
Life to Legend	MGM	4680(E)	'70	†
24 of Hank Williams' Greatest Hits	MGM	(2)4755(E)	'70	†
reissued as 24 Greatest Hits	Mercury	823293	'93	CS/CD
24 Karat Hank Williams	MGM	(2)240(E)	'70	†
Archetypes	MGM	4954(E)	'74	†
A Home in Heaven	MGM	4991(E)	'76	†
On Stage Recorded Live	MGM	1042(E)	'76	†
Live at the *Grand Ole Opry*	MGM	5019(E)	'76	†
24 Greatest Hits, Vol. 2	MGM	25041(E)	'77	†
reissued as 24 Greatest Hits, Volume II	Mercury	823294	'93	CS/CD
Hank Williams	Metro	509	'65	†
Mr. and Mrs. Hank Williams (with Audrey)	Metro	547	'66	†
The Immortal Hank Williams	Metro	602	'66	†

Luke the Drifter

Luke the Drifter	MGM	3927	'55	†
reissued as Beyond the Sunset	MGM	4109	'63	†
	MGM	4138	'63	†
	Mercury Nashville	831574	'87	CS/CD †
Movin' On–Luke the Drifter	MGM	4380	'66	†

Hank Williams and Hank Williams Jr.

Hank Williams, Sr., and Hank Williams, Jr.	MGM	4276	'65	†

Hank Williams, Sr., and Hank Williams, Jr., Again	MGM	4378	'66	†
The Legend of Hank Williams in Song and Story	MGM	4865(E)	'73	†
Insights into Hank Williams in Story and Song	MGM	(2)4976(E)	'74	†
The Best of Hank and Hank Back to Back: Like Father, Like Son	Curb/Warner Bros.	77552	'92	CS/CD
	K-Tel	3049	'92	CS/CD

Later Releases

40 Greatest Hits	Mercury Nashville	(2)821233	'84	CS/CD
Rare Takes and Radio Cuts	Polydor	823695	'84	†
Hank Williams on the Air	Polydor	827531	'85	†
I Ain't Got Nothin' But Time, December 1946–August 1947	Polydor	825548	'85	†
Lovesick Blues, August 1947–December 1948	Polydor	825552	'85	†
Lost Highway, December 1948–March 1949	Polydor	825554	'86	†
I'm So Lonesome I Could Cry, March 1949–August 1949	Polydor	825557	'86	†
Long Gone Lonesome Blues, August 1949–December 1950	Polydor	831633	'87	†
Hey Good Lookin', December 1950–July 1951	Polydor	831634	'87	†
Let's Turn Back the Years, July 1951–June 1952	Polydor	833749	'87	†
I Won't Be Home No More, June 1952–September 1952	Polydor	833752	'87	†
The Original Singles Collection	Mercury	(3)847194	'90	CS/CD
Health and Happiness Shows	Mercury Nashville	517862	'93	CS/CD
The Hits, Vol. 1	Mercury Nashville	522338	'94	CS/CD
The Hits, Vol. 2	Mercury Nashville	528237	'95	CS/CD
The Collectors' Edition	Mercury Nashville	(8)527419	'95	CD†
Low Down Blues	Mercury Nashville	532737	'96	CS/CD
Lonesome Blues	Polygram Special Products	843769		CS/CD
Hank Williams and the Drifting Cowboys On Radio	Golden Country	2207	'82	†
Just Me and My Guitar	Country Music Foundation	006	'85	CS
The First Recordings	Country Music Foundation	007	'86	CS
Rare Demos: First to Last	Country Music Foundation	067	'90	CS/CD
I Saw the Light	Special Music	5032	'94	CS/CD
The Legend Lives Anew	Rebound	520332	'95	CS/CD
The Legendary Hank Williams, Sr.	RCA-Camden	5008		CS
Grand Ole Country Classics	Pair	1165		CS

Hank Williams Sr./Hank Williams Jr./Hank Williams III

Men with Broken Hearts	Curb/Atlantic	77868	'96	CS/CD

JACKIE WILSON

Born June 9, 1934, in Detroit; died January 21, 1984, in Mount Holly, New Jersey.

Jackie Wilson launched his solo career in 1957 with songs cowritten by Berry Gordy Jr., later the founder of the Motown empire. Wilson became one of the first R&B vocalists to enjoy success in the early rock 'n' roll era and came to be regarded as one of the first great soul singers. A masterful live performer and stupendous dancer (Michael Jackson later incorporated many of his stage moves), Wilson sang both rockers and ballads passionately with his astonishingly wide-ranging, fervent voice. He scored a dozen smash R&B and major pop hits between 1958 and 1961, including "Lonely Teardrops," "I'll Be Satisfied," "Night," and "Doggin' Around," but was eclipsed by the emergence of the soul music of Atlantic, Stax, and Motown Records in the '60s. Although he managed a smash pop and top R&B hit with the classic "(Your Love Keeps Lifting Me) Higher and Higher" in 1967, he was later relegated to the oldies circuit. In one of rock 'n' roll's greatest tragedies, he suffered a massive heart attack on stage on September 29, 1975, and eventually died on January 21, 1984.

A Golden Gloves boxing champion in Detroit at the age of sixteen, Jackie Wilson was "discovered" by Johnny Otis at a talent show in 1951. He sang with the Thrillers, an R&B quartet, and recorded for Dizzy Gillespie's Dee Gee label, eventually replacing Clyde McPhatter in Billy Ward's Dominoes in 1953. The group's first release with Wilson, "You Can't Keep a Good Man Down," became a near-smash R&B hit and was soon followed by the R&B smash "Rags to Riches." Wilson was lead singer on the Dominoes first pop hit, "St. Therese of the Roses" in 1956, but opted for a solo career in late 1957, to be replaced by Eugene Mumford.

Signing with Brunswick Records, Jackie Wilson recorded in New York and soon achieved a minor pop hit with "Reet Petite," cowritten by Berry Gordy, Jr. Gordy also cowrote Wilson's major pop and R&B smash hits "To Be Loved," "That's Why," and "I'll Be Satisfied," and his top R&B and smash pop hit classic "Lonely Teardrops." Wilson also appeared in the 1959 film *Go, Johnny, Go,* singing "You'd Better Know It."

Performing engagements at major Los Angeles, Las Vegas, and New York nightclubs and recording a variety of material, including bland pop material and classical adaptations such as "Night," "Alone at Last" and "My Empty Arms," Jackie Wilson suffered through intrusive arrangements and critical neglect in the early '60s. Nonetheless, he scored four two-sided crossover hits in 1960–61 with "Night"/"Doggin' Around," "(You Were Made for) All My Love"/"A Woman, a Lover, a Friend," "Alone at Last"/"Am I the Man," and "My Empty Arms"/The Tear of the Year." "Night" was a pop smash, while "Alone at Last" and "My Empty Arms" were near-smash pop hits. "Doggin' Around" and "A Woman, a Lover, a Friend" were top R&B hits. Later in 1961 Wilson achieved major pop and R&B hits with "Please Tell Me Why" and "I'm Comin' Back to You," followed by the moderate pop hits "Years from Now" and "The Greatest Hurt." He subsequently formed a songwriting partnership with Alonzo Tucker that yielded a top R&B and smash pop hit with "Baby Workout" in 1963. Later major R&B and moderate pop hits included "Shake a Hand" (with Linda Hopkins) and "Shake! Shake! Shake!"

Although he continued to score hits over the next three years, Jackie Wilson didn't achieve another major pop and smash R&B hit until he began recording in Chicago with producer Carl Davis. Under Davis, Wilson staged a dramatic comeback with "Whispers (Gettin' Louder)," the classic "(Your Love Keeps Lifting Me) Higher and Higher," a top R&B and smash pop hit, and "I Get the Sweetest Feeling." He recorded with Count Basie in 1968 and managed his last near-smash R&B and moderate pop hit with late 1970's "This Love Is Real" He was subsequently relegated to the oldies revival circuit, despite continued R&B hits into 1975. On the night of September 29, 1975, while performing at the Latin Casino near Cherry Hill, New Jersey, Wilson was stricken with a massive heart attack that left him in a coma. He remained hospitalized until his eventual death on January 21, 1984, at the age of forty-nine. Jackie Wilson was inducted into the Rock and Roll Hall of Fame in 1987.

BIBLIOGRAPHY

Pruter, Robert. "Jackie Wilson: The Most Tragic Figure in Rhythm 'N' Blues" (Discography by Robert Pruter and Michael Sweeney). *Goldmine* 17, no. 22 (November 1, 1991): 10–16, 18, 20.

Billy Ward and the Dominoes

14 Hits (1951–1965)	King	5005	'77	†
14 Original Greatest Hits	Deluxe	7838		CS
21 Hits	King	5008	'77	†
21 Original Greatest Hits	Deluxe	7841		CS
Featuring Clyde McPhatter and Jackie Wilson	King	733	'60	LP/CS/CD
Billy Ward and the Dominoes	Decca	8621	'56	†
Sixty Minute Men: The Best of Billy Ward and the Dominoes	Rhino	71509	'93	CD
Meet Billy Ward and His Dominoes	Fat Boy	236	'96	CD

The Dominoes

Have Mercy Baby	Charly	44		CD†

Jackie Wilson and the Dominoes

14 Hits	King	5007	'77	†

Jackie Wilson

14 Hits	Deluxe	7840		CS
He's So Fine	Brunswick	54042	'58	†
Lonely Teardrops	Brunswick	54045	'59	†
So Much	Brunswick	754050	'60	†
Sings the Blues	Brunswick	754055	'60	†
My Golden Favorites	Brunswick	754058	'60	†
A Woman, a Lover, a Friend	Brunswick	754059	'60	†
You Ain't Heard Nothin' Yet	Brunswick	754100	'61	†
By Special Request	Brunswick	754101	'61	†
Body and Soul	Brunswick	754105	'62	†
Sings the World's Greatest Melodies	Brunswick	754106	'62	†
At the Copa	Brunswick	754108	'62	†
Baby Workout	Brunswick	754110	'63	†
Merry Christmas	Brunswick	754112	'63	†
My Golden Favorites, Vol. 2	Brunswick	754115	'64	†
Somethin' Else	Brunswick	754117	'64	†
Soul Time	Brunswick	754118	'65	†
Spotlight on Jackie Wilson	Brunswick	754119	'65	†
Soul Galore	Brunswick	754120	'66	†
Whispers	Brunswick	754122	'67	†
Higher and Higher	Brunswick	754130	'67	†
	Rhino	71850	'95	CS/CD
I Get the Sweetest Feeling	Brunswick	754138	'68	†
Greatest Hits	Brunswick	754140	'69	†
Do Your Thing	Brunswick	754154	'69	†
It's All a Part of Love	Brunswick	754158	'70	†
This Love Is Real	Brunswick	754167	'73	†
You Got Me Walking	Brunswick	754172	'71	†
Greatest Hits	Brunswick	754185	'72	†
Beautiful Day	Brunswick	754189	'73	†
Nowstalgia	Brunswick	754199	'74	†
Very Best	Ace	913	'87	CD
Nobody But You	Brunswick	754212	'77	†
The Jackie Wilson Story	Epic	(2)38623	'83	LP/CD†
The Jackie Wilson Story, Vol. 2	Epic	39408	'85	†
The Soul Years	Kent	027		†

Higher and Higher	Kent	901	'86	†
Reet Petite	Ace	125	'85	†
	Ace	902	'86	CD
Through the Years: A Collection of Rare Album Tracks and Single Sides	Rhino	70230	'87	†
Merry Christmas from Jackie Wilson	Rhino	70574	'91	CS/CD
Mr. Excitement	Rhino	(3)70775	'92	CS/CD
Very Best	Rhino	71559	'93	CS/CD
Jackie Wilson and Linda Hopkins				
Shake a Hand	Brunswick	754113	'63	†
Jackie Wilson and Count Basie				
Manufacturers of Soul	Brunswick	754134	'68	†

LINK WRAY

Born May 2, 1935 (although some claim 1930), in Dunn, North Carolina.

One of the most influential rock 'n' roll guitar instrumentalists of the '50s, Link Wray pioneered the use of tremolo, distortion, and feedback with his classic 1958 single "Rumble." Forming perhaps the very first power trio with his brothers in the '50s, Wray produced a raw, violent, ominous sound unlike anything heard to date. Often basing his instrumentals on chordal themes, Wray has been called both "the grandfather of the power chord" and "the father of heavy metal." Although his popularity was short-lived, his style influenced not only British guitarists such as Pete Townshend, Jeff Beck, and Jimmy Page, but latter-day practitioners of heavy metal, punk, and grunge as well.

Part Shawnee Indian, Link Wray's family moved to Arizona, where he took up guitar at the age of eight, forming a country band with his brothers Vernon (rhythm guitar, piano) and Doug (drums) in the late '40s. While serving a four-year stint in the Army, Link contracted tuberculosis in Korea, necessitating the removal of a lung and a period of convalescence. Resettling near Washington, D.C., Link, advised to limit his singing, concentrated on guitar and formed a new trio with brother Doug and bassist Shorty Horton, with brother Vernon switching to producer-manager and occasional accompanist. Initially recording as Luck Wray for Starday Records in 1956, Link Wray met local disc jockey Milt Grant and backed Fats Domino and Rick Nelson on Grant's television show. The two devised "Rumble," and upon release on Cadence Records, the instrumental became a major pop and R&B hit in 1958, despite being banned from airplay in several locales, including New York City and Boston.

The group soon switched to Epic Records, where they scored a major pop hit with "Rawhide" and recorded their first album. By 1963 they had moved to Swan Records, achieving a minor pop hit with "Jack the Ripper" and recording a second album. Much of the Swan material, regarded as some of the group's finest, was reissued on Ace as *Early Recordings*. By 1966 Link had withdrawn to a family farm in Accokeek, Maryland, where he set up a recording studio, called the Three Track Shack, in a converted chicken coop. Playing the occasional local engagement, Wray recorded at Three Track for years, and the product was eventually released to high acclaim but poor sales on Polydor as *Link Wray*. Polydor subsequently issued two more Link Wray albums, including *Be What You Want,* recorded with David Bromberg and Jerry Garcia. In 1972 Wray produced the British pub rock band Eggs Over Easy's *Good 'n' Cheap* album.

In the first half of the '70s Link Wray recorded for Great Britain's Virgin label. He linked up with rockabilly revivalist Robert Gordon in the late '70s , recording two albums with him. Wray recorded for Visa at the end of the '70s and several British labels in the '80s. He moved to Denmark in the early '80s. In the '90s, Link Wray recorded in Denmark and his songs were featured in the films *Desperado, Pulp Fiction,* and *Independence Day.* In 1997 he conducted his first American tour in twenty years.

Link Wray and His Wraymen

Link Wray and the Wraymen	Epic	3661	'60	†
Walkin' with Link	Epic/Legacy	47904	'92	CD
Jack the Ripper	Swan	510	'63	†
Early Recordings	Ace	6	'78	†

Link Wray

Great Guitar Hits	Vermillion	1924		†
Sings and Plays Guitar	Vermillion	1925		†
Yesterday and Today	Record Factory	1929	'70	†
Link Wray	Polydor	244064	'71	†
Be What You Want	Polydor	5047	'73	†
The Link Wray Rumble	Polydor	6025	'74	†
Bullshot	Visa	7009	'79	†
Live at the Paradiso (recorded 1979)	Visa	7010	'80	†

Reissues of British Recordings

Live in '85/Growling Guitar (recorded mid–late '60s)	Chiswick	972		CD
Apache/Wild Side of the City Lights	Ace	931		CD

Anthologies and Compilations

There's Good Rockin' Tonight	Union Pacific	002	'73	†
Guitar Preacher: The Polydor Years	Polydor	7717	'95	CD
Good Rockin' Tonight	Ace	69	'85	†
Rumble Man	Ace	266	'89	†
The Original Rumble Plus 22	Ace	924		CD
Growling Guitar	Big Beat	65	'87	LP
Rumble! The Best of Link Wray	Rhino	71222	'93	CD

Vernon Wray (with Link Wray)

Waste	Vermillion	1972		†

Link Wray with Robert Gordon

Robert Gordon with Link Wray	Private Stock	2030	'77	†
	One Way	34493	'97	CD
Fresh Fish Special	Private Stock	7008	'78	†
Red Hot 1977–1981	Razor & Tie	2061	'95	CD

BIBLIOGRAPHY

DISCOGRAPHIES, RECORD CHARTS, AND RECORD GUIDES

Albert, George, and Frank Hoffman, comp. *The Cash Box Country Singles Charts, 1958–1982.* Metuchen, NJ: Scarecrow, 1984.

————. *The Cash Box Album Charts, 1955–1974.* Metuchen, NJ: Scarecrow, 1988.

Berry, Peter E. *. . . And the Hits Just Keep on Comin'.* Syracuse, NY: Syracuse University Press, 1977.

Bridgerman, Chuck. *Record Collector's Fact Book: Handbook of Rock & Roll, Rhythm & Blues, and Rockabilly Originals and Reproductions.* Vol. 1. 45 RPM 1952–1965. Westminster, MD: Dis; Cockeysville, MD: distributed by Liberty, 1982.

Bronson, Fred. *The Billboard Book of Number One Hits.* New York: Billboard Publications, 1988.

————, and Adam White. *The Billboard Book of Number One Rhythm and Blues Hits.* New York: Billboard Books, 1993.

Brooks, Elston. *I've Heard These Songs Before: The Weekly Top Ten Tunes for the Past Fifty Years.* New York: Morrow Quill Paperbacks, 1981.

Clayson, Alan. *The Best of Rock: The Essential CD Guide.* San Francisco: Collins, 1993.

DeCurtis, Anthony, and James Henke. *The Rolling Stone Album Guide.* New York: Random House, 1992.

Docks, L. R. *1915–1965 American Premium Record Guide.* Florence, AL: Books Americana, 1980, 1982.

Edwards, John W. *Rock 'n' Roll Through 1969: Discographies of All Performers Who Hit the Charts, Beginning in 1955.* Jefferson, NC: McFarland, 1992.

Edwards, Joseph. *Top 10's and Trivia of Rock & Roll and Rhythm & Blues, 1950–1973.* St. Louis: Blueberry Hill, 1974.

Emerson, Lucy. *The Gold Record.* New York: Fountain, 1978.

Erlewine, Michael, Vladimir Bogdanov, Chris Woodstra, and Stephen Thomas Erlewine, eds. *All Music Guide: The Experts' Guide to the Best CDs, Albums & Tapes.* San Francisco: Miller Freeman, 1992, 1994, 1997.

————. *All Music Guide to Country.* San Francisco: Miller Freeman, 1997.

Erlewine, Michael, Vladimir Bogdanov, and Chris Woodstra. *All Music Guide to Rock: The Best CDs, Albums and Tapes: Rock, Pop, Soul, Rhythm and Blues and Rap.* San Francisco: Miller Freeman, 1995.

Erlewine, Michael, Chris Woodstra, Vladimir Bogdanov, and Cub Koda. *All Music Guide to the Blues: The Experts' Guide to the Best Blues Recordings.* San Francisco: Miller Freeman, 1996.

Felton, Gary S. *The Record Collector's International Directory.* New York: Crown, 1980.

Gambaccini, Paul, comp. *Rock Critics Choice: The Top 200 Albums.* New York: Quick Fox, 1978.

————. *The Top 100 Rock 'n' Roll Albums of All Time.* New York: Harmony, 1987.

Gillett, Charlie, and Stephen Nugent, eds. *Rock Almanac: Top Twenty Singles, 1955–73, and Top Twenty Albums, 1964–73.* New York: Doubleday, 1976.

————. *Rock Almanac: Top Twenty American and British Singles and Albums of the 50's, 60's and 70's.* Garden City, NY: Anchor, 1978.

Goldstein, Stewart, and Alan Jacobson. *Oldies But Goodies: The Rock 'n' Roll Years.* New York: Mason/Charter, 1977.

Gonzalez, Fernando L. *Disco-File: The Discographical Catalog of American Rock and Roll and Rhythm and Blues Vocal Harmony Groups.* Flushing, NY: Gonzalez, 1977.

Guterman, Jimmy, and Owen O'Donnell. *The Worst Rock and Roll Records of All Time: A Fan's Guide to the Stuff You Love to Hate.* Secaucus, NJ: Carol, 1991.

Heggeness, Fred. *Goldmine Country & Western Record & CD Price Guide.* Iola, WI: Krause, 1996.

Helander, Brock. *The Rock Who's Who: A Biographical Dictionary and Critical Discography Including Rhythm-and-Blues, Soul, Rockabilly, Folk, Country, Easy Listening, Punk, and New Wave.* New York: Schirmer Books, 1982.

————. *The Rock Who's Who.* 2d ed. New York: Schirmer Books, 1996.

Hill, Randall C. *The Official Price Guide to Collectible Rock Records.* Orlando, FL: House of Collectibles, 1980.

Hounsome, Terry, and Tim Chambre. *Rock Record.* New York: Facts on File, 1981.

Hounsome, Terry. *New Rock Record.* New York: Facts on File, 1983.

————. *Rock Record: A Collectors' Directory of Rock Albums and Musicians.* New York: Facts on File, 1987.

The Illustrated Book of Rock Records: A Book of Lists. New York: Delilah, dis. Putnam, 1982.

Jasper, Tony, comp. *The Top Twenty Book: The Official British Record Charts, 1955–1982.* Poole, Dorset: Blandford, 1983.

Leadbitter, Mike, and Neil Slaven. *Blues Records: 1943–1966.* New York: Oak, 1968.

————. *Blues Records: 1943–1970.* London: Record Information Services, 1987.

Leibowitz, Alan. *The Record Collector's Handbook.* New York: Everest House, 1980.

Marsh, Dave. *The Heart of Rock & Soul: The 1001 Greatest Singles Ever Made.* New York: Plume, 1989.

Marsh, Dave, and John Swenson, eds. *The Rolling Stone Record Guide.* New York: Random House, 1979.

————. *The New Rolling Stone Record Guide.* New York: Random House/Rolling Stone Press, 1983.

McAleer, Dave. *The All Music Book of Hit Singles.* San Francisco: Miller Freeman; dis. Publishers Group West, Emeryville, CA, 1994.

Miron, Charles. *Rock Gold: All the Hit Charts from 1955 to 1976.* New York: Drake, 1977.

Murrels, Joseph, comp. *The Book of Golden Discs.* London: Barrie and Jenkins, 1974, 1978.

————. *Million Selling Records from the 1900s to the 1980s: An Illustrated Directory.* New York: Arco, 1985.

Music Master, The 45 RPM Record Directory: 35 Years of Recorded Music 1947 to 1982. Allison Park, PA: Record-Rama, 1983.

Naha, Ed, comp. *Lillian Roxon's Rock Encyclopedia.* New York: Grosset and Dunlap, 1978.

The Official Price Guide to Records. Orlando, FL: House of Collectibles, 1983.

Osborne, Jerry. *Record Album Price Guide.* Phoenix, AZ: O'Sullivan Woodside, 1977.

————. *Record Albums, 1948–1978.* Phoenix, AZ: O'Sullivan Woodside, 1978.

————. *Popular & Rock Records, 1948–1978.* Phoenix, AZ: dis. O'Sullivan Woodside, 1978.

————. *Popular & Rock Price Guide For 45's: The Little Record with the Big Hole.* 2d ed. Phoenix, AZ: O'Sullivan Woodside, 1981.

————. *Rock, Rock & Roll 45's.* 3d ed. Phoenix, AZ: O'Sullivan Woodside, 1983.

————. *A Guide to Record Collecting.* Phoenix, AZ: O'Sullivan Woodside, 1979.

————. *Blues, Rhythm & Blues, Soul.* Phoenix, AZ: O'Sullivan Woodside, 1980.

Propes, Steve. *Those Oldies But Goodies: A Guide to 50's Record Collecting.* New York: Macmillan, 1973.

————. *Golden Goodies: A Guide to 50's and 60's Popular Rock and Roll Record Collecting.* Radnor, PA: Chilton, 1975.

Pruter, Robert, ed. *The Blackwell Guide to Soul Recordings.* Cambridge, MA: Blackwell, 1993.

Rees, Dafydd, and Luke Crampton. *DK Encyclopedia of Rock Stars.* New York: DK, 1996.

Rees, Tony. *Rare Rock: A Collector's Guide.* Poole, Dorset: Blandford; New York: dis. Sterling, 1985.

Rohde, H. Kandy. *The Gold of Rock and Roll: 1955–1967*. New York: Arbor House, 1970.

Rolling Stone. *The Rolling Stone Album Guide*. New York: Random House, 1992.

Rosen, Craig. *The Billboard Book of Number One Albums: The Inside Story Behind Pop Music's Blockbuster Records*. New York: Billboard, 1996.

Roxon, Lillian. *Rock Encyclopedia*. New York: Grosset and Dunlap, 1969.

Scott, Frank, and Al Ennis. *The Roots & Rhythm Guide to Rock*. Pennington, NJ: A Cappella Books, 1993.

Shapiro, Bill. *The CD Rock & Roll Library: 30 Years of Rock & Roll on Compact Disc*. Kansas City, MO: Andrews and McMeel, 1988.

Strong, M. C. *The Great Rock Discography*. Edinburgh: Canongate, 1995.

Tee, Ralph. *The Best of Soul: The Essential CD Guide*. San Francisco: Collins, 1993.

Tudor, Dean. *Popular Music, An Annotated Guide to Recordings*. Littleton, CO: Libraries Unlimited, 1983.

————, and Nancy Tudor. *Contemporary Popular Music*. Littleton, CO: Libraries Unlimited, 1979.

————. *Grass Roots Music*. Littleton, CO: Libraries Unlimited, 1979.

————. *Black Music*. Littleton, CO: Libraries Unlimited, 1979.

Umphred, Neal. *Goldmine's Price Guide to Collectible Record Albums 1949–1989*. Iola, WI: Krause, 1991.

————. *Goldmine's Rock 'n' Roll 45 RPM Record Price Guide*. Iola, WI: Krause, 1992, 1994.

Whitburn, Joel. *The Billboard Book of Top 40 Hits, 1955 to Present*. New York: Billboard Publications , 1983.

————. *The Billboard Book of Top 40 Hits*. 6th ed. New York: Billboard Books, 1996.

————. *Billboard Top 1000 Singles, 1955–1987*. Milwaukee, WI: Hal Leonard, 1988.

————. *Billboard Top 1000 Singles, 1955–1990*. Milwaukee, WI: Hal Leonard , 1991.

————. *The Billboard Book of Top 40 Albums*. New York: Billboard Publications, 1987. 3d ed. New York: Billboard Books, 1995.

Whitburn, Joel. Record Research Collection (includes Pop Memories 1890–1954; Top Pop: Singles 1955–1993; Top Albums 1955–1992; Top R & B Singles 1942–1988; Top Country Singles 1944–1993; Top Adult Contemporary 1961–1993; Pop Memories 1890–1954; Pop Annual 1955–1994 ; plus yearly supplements entitled Music Yearbook). Menomenee Falls, WI: Record Research, 1988, 1992, 1993, 1994, 1995.

ALMANACS

Bego, Mark. *The Rock & Roll Almanac*. New York: Macmillan, 1996.

Best, Kenneth. *Eight Days a Week: An Illustrated Record of Rock 'n' Roll*. San Francisco: Pomegranate Artbooks, 1992.

Laufenberg, Frank. *Rock and Pop Day by Day: Birthdays, Deaths, Hits and Fact*. Ed. Hugh Gregory. London: Blandford, 1992.

Marchbank, Pearce, and Miles. *The Illustrated Rock Almanac*. New York: Paddington, 1977.

Tobler, John. *This Day in Rock: Day by Day Record of Rock's Biggest News Stories*. New York: Carroll & Graf, 1993.

ENCYCLOPEDIAS, DICTIONARIES, AND GENERAL REFERENCE

Aquila, Richard. *That Old Time Rock & Roll: A Chronicle of an Era 1954–1963*. New York: Schirmer Books, 1989.

Bane, Michael. *The Outlaws: Who's Who in Rock*. New York: Facts on File, 1981.

————. *White Boy Singin' the Blues*. New York: Penguin, 1982.

Belz, Carl. *The Story of Rock*. New York: Oxford University Press, 1969, 1972; New York: Harper Colophon, 1973.

Benson, Dennis C. *The Rock Generation*. Nashville: Abingdon, 1976.

Berry, Jason, Jonathan Foose, and Tad Jones. *Up from the Cradle of Jazz: New Orleans Music Since World War II.* Athens: University of Georgia Press, 1986.

Betrock, Alan. *Girl Groups: The Story of a Sound.* New York: Delilah, dis. Putnam, 1982.

Boeckman, Charles. *And the Beat Goes On: A Survey of Pop Music in America.* Washington, D.C.: Robert B. Luce, 1972.

Broven, John. *Walking to New Orleans: Rhythm and Blues in New Orleans.* Gretna, LA: Pelican, 1988.

Brown, Len, and Gary Friederich. *Encyclopedia of Rock and Roll.* New York: Tower, 1970.

Bufwack, Mary A., and Robert K. Oermann. *Finding Her Voice: The Saga of Women in Country Music.* New York: Crown, 1993.

Busnar, Gene. *It's Rock 'n' Roll* New York: Wanderer, dis. Simon & Schuster, 1979.

———. *The Superstars of Rock: Their Lives and Their Music.* New York: Messner, 1980.

Chapple, Steve, and Reebee Garofalo. *Rock 'n' Roll Is Here to Pay: The History and Politics of the Music Industry.* Chicago: Nelson-Hall, 1977.

Clarke, Donald, ed. *The Penguin Encyclopedia of Popular Music.* London: Viking; New York: Viking Penguin, 1989.

———. *The Rise and Fall of Popular Music.* New York: St. Martin's, 1996.

Clifford, Mike. *The Harmony Illustrated Encyclopedia of Rock.* 5th ed. New York: Harmony, 1986. 6th ed., 1988.

Cohn, Nik. *Rock from the Beginning.* New York: Stein and Day, 1969.

Cooper, B. Lee. *Rockabilly: A Bibliographic Resource Guide.* Metuchen, NJ: Scarecrow, 1990.

Cotten, Lee. *Shake, Rattle and Roll: The Golden Age of American Rock 'n' Roll.* Ann Arbor, MI: Pierian, 1989.

Crenshaw, Marshall. *Hollywood Rock.* New York: HarperPerennial, 1994.

Curtis, James M. *Rock Eras: Interpretations of Music & Society, 1954–1984.* Bowling Green, OH: Bowling Green State University Popular Press, 1987.

Dalton, David, and Lenny Kaye. *Rock 100.* New York: Grosset & Dunlap, 1977.

David, Andrew. *Rock Stars: People at the Top of the Charts.* Northbrook, IL: Domus, 1979; New York: Exeter, 1979.

Dawson, Jim, and Steve Propes. *What Was the First Rock 'n' Roll Record?* Boston: Faber and Faber, 1992.

Deffa, Chip. *Blue Rhythms: Six Lives in Rhythm and Blues.* Urbana: University of Illinois Press, 1996.

Dellar, Fred, Alan Cackett, and Roy Thompson. *The Harmony Illustrated Encyclopedia of Country Music.* New York: Harmony, 1987.

Denisoff, R. Serge. *Solid Gold: The Record Industry, Its Friends and Enemies.* New Brunswick, NJ: Transaction, 1975.

———. *Solid Gold: The Popular Record Industry.* New Brunswick, NJ: Transaction, 1975.

———. *Tarnished Gold: The Record Industry Revisited.* New Brunswick, NJ: Transaction, 1986.

———, and William D. Romanowski. *Risky Businss: Rock in Film.* New Brunswick, NJ: Transaction, 1991.

Dickerson, James. *Goin' Back to Memphis: A Century of Blues, Rock 'n' Roll, and Glorious Soul.* New York: Schirmer Books, 1996.

Ehrenstein, David, and Bill Reed. *Rock on Film.* New York: Delilah, dis. Putnam's, 1982.

Elson, Howard. *Early Rockers.* London: Proteus, 1982.

Escott, Colin. *Good Rockin' Tonight: Sun Records and the Birth of Rock 'n' Roll.* New York: St. Martin's, 1991.

———. *Tattooed on Their Tongues: A Journey Through the Backrooms of American Music.* New York: Schirmer Books, 1996.

_____, and Martin Hawkins. *Catalyst: The Story of Sun Records.* London: Aquarius, 1975.

_____. *Sun Records: The Brief History of the Legendary Recording Label.* New York: Quick Fox, 1980.

Field, James J. *American Popular Music, 1950–1975.* Philadelphia: Musical Americana, 1976.

Frame, Peter. *Rock Family Trees.* New York: Quick Fox, 1980.

_____. *Rock Family Trees 2.* New York: Quick Fox, 1983.

Fredericks, Vic, ed. *Who's Who in Rock 'n Roll.* New York: Frederick Fell, 1968.

Gabree, John. *The World of Rock.* New York: Fawcett, 1968.

Gaines, Steve. *Who's Who in Rock 'n Roll.* New York: Popular Library, 1975.

Garofalo, Reebee. *Rockin' Out: Popular Music in the USA.* Needham Heights, MA: Allyn & Bacon, 1997.

George, Nelson. *The Death of Rhythm & Blues.* New York: Pantheon, 1988.

Gillett, Charlie. *The Sound of the City: The Rise of Rock 'n' Roll.* New York: Outerbridge & Dienstfry; dis. Dutton, 1970; London: Souvenir, 1971, 1983; New York: Dell, 1972.

_____. *The Sound of the City: The Rise of Rock and Roll.* New York: Pantheon, 1983, 1984.

_____. *Making Tracks: The Story of Atlantic Records.* New York: Outerbridge and Lazard, 1973.

_____. *Making Tracks: Atlantic Records and the Growth of a Multi-Billion-Dollar Industry.* New York: Dutton, 1974.

_____, ed. *Rock File.* London: New English Library, 1972.

Green, Douglas B. *Country Roots: The Origins of Country Music.* New York: Hawthorn, 1976.

Gregory, Hugh. *Soul Music A–Z.* London: Blandford; New York: dis. Sterling, 1991.

_____. *1000 Great Guitarists.* San Francisco: GPI, 1994.

Gribin, Anthony Joel, and Matthew M. Schiff. *Doo-Wop: The Forgotten Third of Rock 'n Roll.* Iola, WI: Krause, 1992.

Groia, Philip. *They All Sang on the Street Corner: New York City's Rhythm and Blues Vocal Groups of the 1950's.* Setauket, NY: Edmond, 1974.

_____. *They All Sang on the Corner: A Second Look at New York City's Rhythm and Blues Vocal Groups.* West Hempstead, NY: P. Dee, 1983.

Gross, Michael, and Maxim Jakubowski, eds. *The Rock Yearbook, 1981.* New York: Virgin, 1980.

Grossman, Loyd. *A Social History of Rock Music: From the Greasers to Glitter Rock.* New York: McKay, 1976.

Guitar Player. Rock Guitarists. Saratoga, CA: Guitar Player Productions, 1974.

_____. *Rock Guitarists.* Vol. 2. Saratoga, CA: Guitar Player Productions, 1977.

Guralnick, Peter. *Feel Like Going Home: Portraits in Blues and Rock n' Roll.* New York: Outerbridge and Dienstfrey, 1971.

_____. *Lost Highway: Journeys and Arrivals of American Musicians.* Boston: Godine, 1979.

_____. *Sweet Soul Music: Rhythm and Blues and the Southern Dream of Freedom.* New York: Harper & Row, 1986.

Haislop, Neil, Ted Lathrop, and Harry Sumrall. *Giants of Country Music.* New York: Billboard Books, 1995.

Haralambos, Michael. *Right On: From Blues to Soul in Black America.* London: Eddison, 1974; New York: Drake, 1975; New York: Da Capo, 1979.

Hardy, Phil, and Dave Laing, eds. *The Encyclopedia of Rock.* Vol. 1: *The Age of Rock 'n' Roll.* St. Albans: Aquarius, 1976.

_____. *The Encyclopedia of Rock: 1955–1975.* St. Albans: Panther, 1977.

_____. *Encyclopedia of Rock.* New York: Schirmer Books, 1988.

_____. *The Faber Companion to 20th-Century Popular Music.* London and Boston: Faber & Faber, 1990.

Heatley, Michael. *The Ultimate Encyclopedia of Rock: The World's Most Comprehensive Illustrated Rock Reference.* New York: HarperPerennial, 1993.

Helander, Brock. *The Rock Who's Who: A Biographical Dictionary and Critical Discography Including Rhythm-and-Blues, Soul, Rockabilly, Folk, Country, Easy Listening, Punk, and New Wave.* New York: Schirmer Books, 1982.

_____. *The Rock Who's Who.* 2d ed. New York: Schirmer Books, 1996.

Herzhaft, Gerard. *Encyclopedia of the Blues.* Fayetteville: University of Arkansas Press, 1992.

Hildebrand, Lee. *Stars of Soul and Rhythm & Blues.* New York: Billboard Books, 1994.

Hoare, Ian, ed. *The Soul Book.* New York: Dell, 1976.

Hopkins, Jerry. *The Rock Story.* New York: New American Library, 1970.

Jacobs, Philip. *Rock 'n' Roll Heaven.* New York: Gallery, 1990.

Jahn, Mike. *Rock: From Elvis to the Rolling Stones.* New York: Quadrangle/New York Times Book Company, 1973.

Jancik, Wayne. *The Billboard Book of One-Hit Wonders.* New York: Billboard Books, 1990.

_____, and Ted Lathrop. *Cult Rockers.* New York: Simon & Schuster, 1995.

Jasper, Tony. *Understanding Pop.* London: S.C.M., 1972.

Jenkinson, Philip, and Alan Warner. *Celluloid Rock: Twenty Years of Movie Rock.* London: Lorrimer, 1974.

Kienzle, Rich. *Great Guitarists: The Most Influential Players in Blues, Country Music, Jazz and Rock.* New York: Facts on File, 1985.

Knapp, Ron. *American Legends of Rock.* Springfield, NJ: Enslow, 1996.

Laing, Dave. *The Electric Muse: The Story of Folk into Rock.* London: Metheun, 1975.

Landau, Jon. *It's Too Late to Stop Now: A Rock 'n' Roll Journal.* San Francisco: Straight Arrow, 1972.

Larkin, Colin, ed. *The Guinness Encyclopedia of Popular Music.* 6 vols. New York: Stockton, 1996.

Larkin, Rochelle. *Soul Music.* New York: Lancer, 1970.

Lazell, Barry, ed. *Rock Movers and Shakers.* New York: Billboard Publications, 1989.

Logan, Nick, and Bob Woffinden. *The Illustrated New Musical Express Encyclopedia of Rock.* London and New York: Hamlyn, 1977.

_____, comp. *The Illustrated Encyclopedia of Rock.* New York: Harmony, 1977.

_____. *The Harmony Illustrated Encyclopedia of Rock.* New York: Harmony, 1982.

Lydon, Michael. *Rock Folk: Portraits From the Rock 'n' Roll Pantheon.* New York: Dial, 1971.

_____. *Boogie Lightnin'.* New York: Dial, 1974.

Macken, Bob, Peter Fornatale, and Bill Ayres. *The Rock Music Source Book.* Garden City, NY: Anchor, 1980.

Marcus, Greil. *Rock and Roll Will Stand.* Boston: Beacon, 1969.

_____. *Mystery Train: Images of America in Rock 'n' Roll Music.* New York: Dutton, 1975, 1990.

Marsh, Dave, and Kevin Stein. *The Book of Rock Lists.* Garden City, NY: Dell: A Dell/ Rolling Stone Press Book, 1981.

_____, and James Bernard. *The New Book of Rock Lists.* New York: Simon & Schuster, 1994.

May, Chris. *Rock 'n' Roll.* London: Socion, n.d.

_____, and Tim Phillips. *British Beat.* London: Socion, n.d.

McNutt, Randy. *We Wanna Boogie: An Illustrated History of the American Rockabilly Movement.* Hamilton, OH: HHP, 1988.

Melhuish, Martin. *Heart of Gold: 30 Years of Canadian Pop Music.* Toronto: CBC, 1983.

Meltzer, Richard. *The Aesthetics of Rock.* New York: Something Else, 1970.

Miller, Jim, ed. *Rolling Stone Illustrated History of Rock & Roll.* New York: Rolling Stone Press, 1976, 1980.

Morrison, Craig. *Go Cat Go!: Rockabilly Music and Its Makers*. Urbana: University of Illinois Press, 1996.

Naha, Ed, comp. *Lillian Roxon's Rock Encyclopedia*. New York: Grosset and Dunlap, 1978.

Nite, Norm N. *Rock On: The Illustrated Encyclopedia of Rock 'n' Roll: The Solid Gold Years*. New York: Thomas Y. Crowell, 1974.

_____. *Rock On: The Illustrated Encyclopedia of Rock n' Roll*. 3 vols. New York: Harper & Row, 1982.

_____. *Rock On Almanac: The First Four Decades of Rock 'n' Roll: A Chronology*. New York: Harper & Row, 1989; Harper Collins, 1991; New York: HarperPerennial, 1992.

O'Brien, Lucy. *She Bop: The Definitive History of Women in Rock, Pop and Soul*. New York: Penguin, 1996.

Ochs, Michael. *Rock Archives: A Photographic Journey Through the First Two Decades of Rock & Roll*. Garden City, NY: Doubleday, 1984.

O'Donnell, Jim. *The Rock Book*. New York: Pinnacle, 1975.

Palmer, Robert. *Deep Blues*. New York: Viking, 1981; New York: Penguin, 1982.

_____. *Rock & Roll: An Unruly History*. New York: Harmony, 1995.

Palmer, Tony. *All You Need Is Love: The Story of Popular Music*. New York: Grossman, 1976.

Paraire, Philippe. *50 Years of Rock Music*. New York: Chambers, 1992.

Pareles, Jon, and Patricia Romanowski, eds. *The Rolling Stone Encyclopedia of Rock & Roll*. New York: Rolling Stone Press/Summit Books, 1983; New York: Simon & Schuster, 1983.

Pascall, Jeremy. *The Illustrated History of Rock Music*. New York: Galahad, 1978.

_____, and Rob Burt. *The Stars and Superstars of Black Music*. Secaucus, NJ: Chartwell, 1977.

Passman, Arnold. *The Dee Jays*. New York: Macmillan, 1971.

Petrie, Gavin, ed. *Black Music*. London: Hamlyn, 1974.

_____. *Rock Life*. London and New York: Hamlyn, 1974.

Phoebus. *The Stars and Superstars of Rock*. London: Phoebus / Octopus Books, 1974.

_____. *Country Music*. London: Phoebus, 1976.

_____. *The Stars and Superstars of Black Music*. London: Phoebus, 1977.

Pollock, Bruce. *In Their Own Words*. New York: Macmillan, 1975.

_____. *When Rock Was Young: A Nostalgic Review of the Top 40 Era*. New York: Holt, Rinehart, 1981.

_____. *Hipper Than Our Kids: A Rock & Roll Journal of the Baby Boom Generation*. New York: Schirmer Books, 1993.

Pruter, Robert. *Chicago Soul*. Urbana: University of Illinois Press, 1991.

Redd, Lawrence N. *Rock Is Rhythm and Blues: The Impact of Mass Media*. East Lansing, MI: University of Michigan Press, 1974.

Rivelli, Pauline, and Robert Levin, eds. *The Rock Giants*. New York: World, 1970.

_____, eds. *The Black Giants*. New York: World, 1970.

Robinson, Richard, ed. *Rock Revolution*. New York: Popular Library, 1976.

_____, and Andy Zwerling. *The Rock Scene*. New York: Popular Library, 1971.

Rolling Stone. *The Rolling Stone Interviews*. New York: Paperback Library, 1971.

_____. *The Rolling Stone Interviews*. Vol. 2. New York: Paperback Library, 1973.

_____. *The Rolling Stone Interviews: Talking with the Legends of Rock & Roll, 1967–1980*. New York: St. Martin's / Rolling Stone Press, 1981.

Romanowski, Patricia, and Holly George-Warren, eds. *The New Rolling Stone Encyclopedia of Rock & Roll*. New York: Fireside, 1995.

Roxon, Lillian. *Rock Encyclopedia*. New York: Grosset and Dunlap, 1969.

Sandahl, Linda J. *Rock Films: A Viewer's Guide to Three Decades of Musicals, Concerts, Documentaries and Soundtracks, 1955–1986*. Poole, Dorset: Blandford, 1987.

Santelli, Robert. *The Big Book of Blues: A Biographical Encyclopedia*. New York: Penguin, 1993.

Schafer, William J. *Rock Music: Where It's Been, What It Means, Where It's Going*. Minneapolis: Augsburg, 1972.

Schicke, Charles A. *Revolution In Sound: A Biography of the Recording Industry*. Boston: Little, Brown, 1974.

Scoppa, Bud. *The Rock People*. New York: Scholastic, 1973.

Shapiro, Nat, and Bruce Pollock. *Popular Music, 1920–1979: A Revised Cumulation*. Detroit: Gale, 1985.

Shaw, Arnold. *The Rock Revolution* . New York: Crowell-Collier, 1969.

————. *The World of Soul: Black America's Contribution to the Pop Music Scene*. New York: Cowles, 1970.

————. *The Rockin' 50's: The Decade That Transformed the Pop Music Scene*. New York: Hawthorn, 1974.

————. *Honkers and Shouters: The Golden Years of Rhythm and Blues*. New York: Macmillan, 1978.

————. *Dictionary of American Pop / Rock*. New York: Schirmer Books, 1982.

————. *Black Popular Music in America*. New York: Schirmer Books, 1986; Macmillan, 1990.

Smith, Wes. *The Pied Pipers of Rock 'n' Roll: Radio Deejays of the 50s and 60s*. Marietta, GA: Longstreet, 1989.

Spitz, Robert Stephen (Bob). *The Making of Superstars: Artists and Executives of the Rock Music Business*. Garden City, NY: Anchor, 1978.

Stambler, Irwin. *Encyclopedia of Popular Music*. New York: St. Martin's, 1965.

————. *Guitar Years: Pop Music from Country and Western to Hard Rock*. Garden City, NY: Doubleday, 1970.

————. *Encyclopedia of Pop, Rock, and Soul*. New York: St. Martin's, 1975, 1989.

————, and Grelun Landon. *Encyclopedia of Folk, Country, and Western Music*. New York: St. Martin's, 1969, 1983.

Stuessy, Joe. *Rock & Roll: Its History and Stylistic Development*. Englewood Cliffs, NJ: Prentice Hall, 1990.

Sumrall, Harry. *Pioneers of Rock and Roll: 100 Artists Who Changed the Face of Rock*. New York: Billboard Books, 1994.

Szatmary, David P. *A Time to Rock: A Social History of Rock 'n' Roll*. New York: Schirmer Books, 1996.

Tee, Ralph. *Soul Music: Who's Who*. Rocklin, CA: Prima, 1992.

Tobler, John. *Guitar Heroes*. New York: St. Martin's, 1978.

————. *30 Years of Rock*. New York: Exeter, dis. Bookthrift, 1985.

Tobler, John, and Stuart Grundy. *The Guitar Greats*. New York: St. Martin's, 1984.

Tobler, John, ed. *Who's Who in Rock & Roll*. New York: Crescent, 1991.

Tosches, Nick. *Unsung Heroes of Rock 'n' Roll*. New York: Scribner's, 1984.

Van Der Horst, Brian. *Rock Music*. New York: Watts, 1973.

Vinson, Lee. *Encyclopedia of Rock*. New York: Drake, 1976.

Ward, Ed, Geoffrey Stokes, and Ken Tucker. *Rock of Ages: The Rolling Stone History of Rock and Roll*. New York: Rolling Stone Press: Summit Books, 1986.

Warner, Jay. *Billboard Book of American Singing Groups: A History, 1940–1990*. New York: Billboard Books, 1992.

Wexler, Jerry, and David Ritz. *Rhythm and the Blues: A Life in American Music*. New York: Knopf, 1993.

White, Timothy. *Rock Stars*. New York: Stewart, Tabori, 1984.

————. *Rock Lives: Profiles and Interviews*. New York: Henry Holt, 1989.

Wood, Graham. *An A–Z of Rock and Roll.* London: Studio Vista, 1971.

York, William, ed. *Who's Who in Rock Music.* Seattle: Atomic, 1978; New York: Scribner, 1982.

Yorke, Ritchie. *The History of Rock 'n' Roll.* London: Eyre Methuen, 1976; Toronto: Methuen/Two Continents, 1976.

INDEX